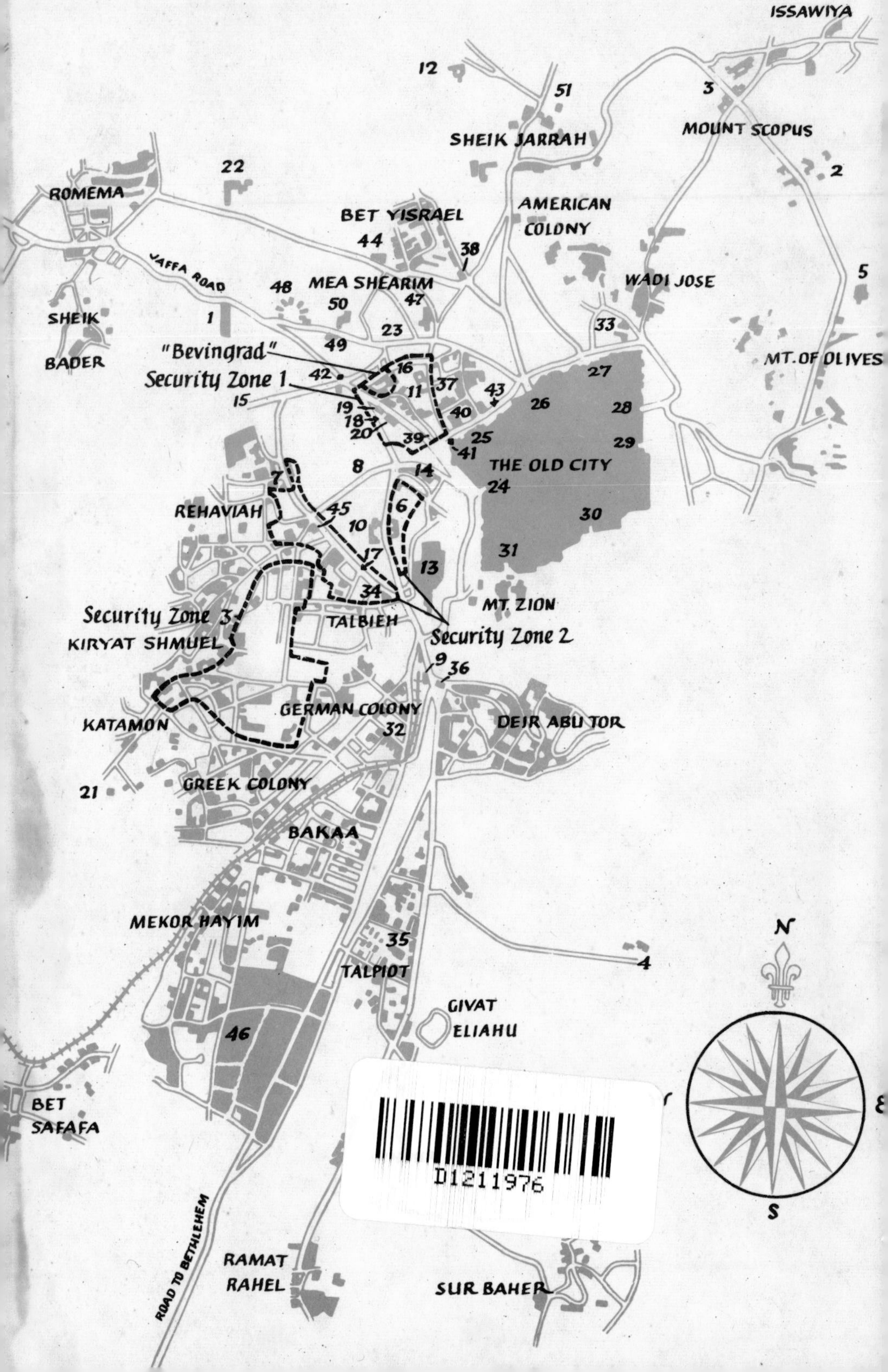

ISSAWIYA
12
51
3
MOUNT SCOPUS
SHEIK JARRAH
22
2
ROMEMA
AMERICAN COLONY
BET YISRAEL
44
38
JAFFA ROAD
48
MEA SHEARIM
WADI JOSE
5
50
47
SHEIK BADER
1
23
33
"Bevingrad"
49
16
MT. OF OLIVES
Security Zone 1
42
27
11
37
43
15
19
18
20
40
26
28
39
25
41
29
THE OLD CITY
8
14
7
24
6
REHAVIAH
45
10
30
17
31
13
34
MT. ZION
Security Zone 3
TALBIEH
Security Zone 2
KIRYAT SHMUEL
9
36
GERMAN COLONY
KATAMON
32
DEIR ABU TOR
21
GREEK COLONY
BAKAA
MEKOR HAYIM
N
35
4
TALPIOT
GIVAT ELIAHU
46
BET SAFAFA
S
ROAD TO BETHLEHEM
RAMAT RAHEL
SUR BAHER

THE
FAITHFUL
CITY

THE SIEGE OF JERUSALEM, 1948

⎍⎍⎍⎍⎍⎍⎍⎍⎍⎍⎍⎍⎍⎍⎍⎍⎍⎍⎍

by

DOV JOSEPH

SIMON AND SCHUSTER

NEW YORK / 1960

—

PUBLISHED IN ISRAEL

by

SCHOCKEN PUBLISHING HOUSE Ltd., TEL-AVIV

DEDICATION

*To our daughter, Leila,
and her comrades*

And I will restore thy judges as at first,
And thy counsellors as at the beginning;
Afterward thou shalt be called
The city of righteousness,
The faithful city.

ISAIAH 1:26

CONTENTS

Chief Rabbi Herzog addressing a welcome to Dr. Chaim Weizmann

The Military Governor's Council: Dr. Joseph is sitting in the center in a dark suit

Bevingrad entrance to Russian compound, showing a Russian church in the rear

Arabs burning automobile in presence of British policeman

Top right: Religious Jews training in the Israeli army

Bottom right: Builders of Jerusalem's fortifications

Below: Children filling sacks with sand to build fortifications during the siege

Arabs looting and burning a commercial center

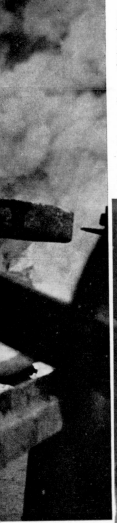

Herbert Meyerowitz — photo prisma

Palestine Post explosion

Count Bernadotte and Dr. Joseph, accompanied by United Nations officials, in the courtyard of the Jewish Agency

I

THE HOLY CITY

⊓⊔⊓⊔⊓⊔⊓⊔⊓⊔⊓⊔

BORN HALFWAY AROUND the world from Jerusalem, in Canada, I was nineteen before I first saw the Holy City. Three years later, in 1921, I left Montreal and settled in Jerusalem, where I practiced law and raised a family. More than a quarter of a century later I found myself in charge of the destinies of Jerusalem during the weeks it was besieged and the months it fought desperately to survive. So the city of Jerusalem occupies many different levels in my emotions and my memories, like the layers an archaeologist uncovers when he digs into the stone and the rubble on which the ancient capital of Judaism has been built.

Deepest of the layers for me is the mingling of legend, fable and fact which has kept Jerusalem through two thousand years the chief symbol of his religion for every Jewish child. My father died when I was four, and I was brought up by my grandfather in Montreal. He had emigrated with his family from Eastern Europe to escape the rising wave of pogroms and persecution in Czarist Russia at the end of the last century. He was a devout Jew, to whom tradition, precept and observance of the moral and ritual codes of Judaism all centered around the Holy City and its Temple.

My mother used to sing me to sleep with a song which ran: "You, my child, will open for me the gates of Jerusalem." From the days when I first learned to talk, I can remember another song of hers about how Mother Zion sat in a small ruined chamber of the Temple crooning her baby to sleep with the dream of the return of her people. In time I brought my mother to Jerusalem, where she lived the last decades of her life, and she is buried there.

As we grew up in Montreal, we learned that the Temple had been destroyed first by Nebuchadnezzar, and that the Jews had returned to build a more splendid Temple than the first. We were told that when this, too, was doomed in the time of the Romans, all the patriarchs went up to heaven to the Holy One and begged him to spare Jerusalem. He relented, we knew, to the extent of promising the patriarchs that His Divine Presence, which hovered constantly over the Temple, would go forth into exile with His people. How we wept at the story of the Divine Presence, called the Shechina, a mighty angel with white wings as wide as the world, standing poised over the Temple as the Romans burned it, then over its walls, then over Jerusalem, until with an eternity of reluctance it went forth into exile with Israel!

Wherever a Jew may go, he takes with him these old memories of Jerusalem. In time we learned that the earthly Jerusalem was only the material embodiment of the real Jerusalem, the spiritual Jerusalem, the celestial city which dwelt in heaven. Bits and pieces of the oldest story in the world seeped into our consciousness as we grew up, from the discourses of old rabbis, from songs and commentaries on the Bible texts.

We knew that when the Jews had the Temple no one was allowed, on pain of death, to enter the Holy of Holies, its inmost chamber, except the High Priest, and even he only after prayers and ablutions on the Day of Atonement. When the Romans destroyed it, in the year 70 of this era, they plowed the ground to make the destruction complete, so that no man knows now just where the Holy of Holies was. This was not just a story for children. When Sir Moses Montefiore, the distinguished English Jew, visited Jerusalem in 1839, he had himself carried in a sedan chair so that his feet might not accidentally step on the spot where the Holy of Holies had been.

After two thousand years of exile, this tradition has acquired a life of its own, independent of buildings or monuments or specific streets of Jerusalem. The Jerusalem to which Jews have wished to return since the Diaspora began in the ancient city, the true heartland of Zion in the Judaean hills. For hundreds of years, our holidays have featured the greeting "Next year in Jerusalem." A patch on one wall of every orthodox Jewish house has been left unattended for the sake of Jerusalem. The bridegroom at a Jewish wedding feast still crushes a glass under his right foot to show his grief at the destruction of the Temple. The climax of the most important prayer recited thrice daily by religious Jews is: "And to Jerusalem Thy city shalt Thou return in mercy, as Thou hast promised."

For Jews, it has always been the one Holy City, the focal point of our religion, our traditions and our history.

The first time I saw Jerusalem was in 1918, when I volunteered as a soldier in the Jewish Legion of the British Army in the campaign to take Palestine from the Turks. I was already a Zionist by conviction, having been a delegate to a Canadian Zionist convention when I was barely nine and the founder of Canadian Young Judaea, a Dominion-wide organization of Zionist youth. I had been in charge of recruiting in Montreal and was determined to take part myself in the liberation of the Holy Land. This was when I resolved to settle there, and to help accept the challenge to create the national home for the Jewish people which had been made explicit the year before in the Balfour Declaration. In 1921, when I had finished my law studies at McGill University and Laval University in Montreal, I came to Palestine. I have lived in Jerusalem ever since.

There were then, and there are now, three Jerusalems. The first is the Old City, an irregular quadrilateral surrounded by a massive wall over two miles long. Inside the wall are the Holy Places of three religions. The Mosque of Omar, built around the rock on which, legend has it, Abraham was prepared to sacrifice his son Isaac, is a Moslem shrine. The Church of the Holy Sepulcher is on the site called Golgotha or Calvary, the burial place of Christ. The Via Dolorosa is also here. The Wailing Wall, part of which dates from the time of Solomon's Temple, has been for generations the goal of pilgrimages by Jews to mourn the destruction of the Temple. In the dead of night, the Shechina or Divine Presence was believed to appear as a white dove, cooing in sorrow with the mourners, and the drops of dew which cover the stones in the morning were said by legend to be the tears wept by the wall itself in sympathy with Israel.

West of the ancient wall which encircles this Old City, there had grown the core of a new Jerusalem. This was, until about 1927, a narrow strip extending from the Jaffa Gate into the Mamillah Road and up the Jaffa Road as far as the Mahaneh Yehuda

quarter, with offshoots southward to where the present Jewish
Agency buildings stand and northward to the Jewish religious
quarters clustering around Meah Shearim and extending to the
Lutheran Schneller's orphanage. Away to the south stood the railway station and the adjoining German Templars' Colony, where
the British officials of the Palestine administration made their
homes.

In what was known as the Jaffa Road area were the offices of
those institutions which the Jewish people were developing to
organize and protect their interests in the city and in all of Palestine. There too were the principal shops and restaurants of the
city, its cinema, its business offices, and the government district
offices. The central headquarters of the British administration
which governed the country under a League of Nations mandate
were far away in the Augusta Victoria Institute on the Mount of
Olives.

East and north of the Old City there were Jewish areas too, especially the Hebrew University on Mount Scopus next to the
Mount of Olives. South of the Old City, on the road to Bethlehem, the British built in 1930 a massive Government House for
their High Commissioner, who was the effective ruler over all
of Palestine and Transjordan. Later, the Rockefeller Foundation
built its fabulous archaeological museum outside Herod's Gate,
and the clockwise sweep of land from north through east and south
to southwest of the Old City included a few Jewish quarters mixed
with rather more Arab districts all the way beyond the King
David, Jerusalem's largest hotel, and the Y.M.C.A. Building with
its tower which overlooks the entire city.

The third Jerusalem lay outside this ring around the Old City
and consisted chiefly of suburbs which grew up during the thirty
years of British rule under the mandate. Most of these were Jewish,
built by families like my own which had moved to Palestine, or
financed by Jews abroad for their co-religionists. But some were
Arab villages, where the fruit and vegetables were grown which fed
the city, and others were colonies of Americans, Germans, Greeks,
Armenians, Frenchmen, Russians, literally dozens of communities
which had been pulled to Jerusalem by religious or missionary motives. Only old residents can remember the full range of these
little colonies. One family of Christians whom I knew and liked
lived in the Deir Abu Tor Christian Arab quarter in daily expectation of the Second Coming of Christ. They framed a motto over

the doorway, "Perhaps Today," and when they went out for a pic-
nic on the Mount of Olives they always took along an extra cup
and plate.

These three Jerusalems made up what was aptly called "a mosaic
of distinct communities, each living in proud dissociation from its
fellows." Each had its "notables," or leading members, who contrived somehow, in endless wrangles under British direction, what
little government the city had. At least until 1929 and for periods
after that year, the city lived in troubled peace, in some prosperity
and considerable squalor, and in its ancient rituals, under the clear
and heavy sunlight of Judaea. Jerusalem is a city built of rose-
colored limestone, and the sun and the stone combine to give it a
very special kind of light in which the mountains and the sky seem
to run into each other. Perhaps this added to the historical associations which always attracted deeply religious people of many faiths
to the city. It is certainly a reason why men who have settled there
strike roots which go down far and hold them fast.

So it was with me. The private practice of law was hard and
complicated but interesting. I was married in Jerusalem, to Goldie
Hoffman, whom I had known in Montreal where we grew up together and who came to Palestine as ardent a Zionist as I. This was
the city in which we raised our children, and in which we gave our
hearts to the struggle for the establishment of a national home in
Palestine and eventually of the state of Israel. The second goal replaced the first only gradually in our minds, mainly as a result of
our growing realization that the British would never allow an independent national home for the Jews within the British Commonwealth. This was a bitter conclusion for us, who had been brought
up and educated in Canada, to accept, but as it grew clearer, our
determination to stay grew stronger. It was in 1929, after serious
riots in which the British did nothing to control Arab mobs attacking Jews, that we decided to build our own home in Rehaviah, one
of the residential districts lying just beyond the Jewish Agency
Building in what were then the outskirts of new Jerusalem. We
still live in this house, and all the years of living there have added
their weight to what the city means to us.

It was in March 1936 that David Ben Gurion, then chairman of
the Jewish Agency for Palestine and later Israel's first Prime Minister, asked me to join him and Moshe Shertok (later Sharett) in the

Political Department of the Jewish Agency, as its honorary legal adviser. The Jewish Agency for Palestine was the executive arm of the World Zionist Organization, through which Jews all over the world were working for Jewish settlement in Palestine. One month later, in April, the Arab riots started which were to continue sporadically for three years until the outbreak of World War II. In fact, I was Shertok's associate in the Political Department, but unlike him I had always lived in Jerusalem, where the High Commissioner was, and the Grand Mufti, the religious head of Palestine's Moslems, and most of the riots. From now on I attended only to the most important matters in my private law practice and threw myself into full-time Zionist activity.

For the next twelve years, the Political Department of the Jewish Agency functioned as a government within a government. Under the terms of the mandate, it was empowered to represent the Jews in developing the Jewish national home in Palestine. So the High Commissioner turned to us, as he did to the Vaad Leumi, (or National Council of Palestine Jews), or to the religious communities, or to the Grand Mufti or to Arab organizations, on matters which concerned each of us. The Jews themselves looked to us, naturally, to represent them with the British mandatory power. Even the ultra-orthodox Jews who were not Zionists turned to us on matters of security or immigration which required action by the High Commissioner's office.

These were the tragic years of Hitler's consolidation of power over Germany, so there was much to be done and frighteningly little time in which to do it. Our growing anger at the obstacles with which the British slowed our work was matched by a growing fear of the Nazi threat to the Jews all over Europe. I attended the Zionist Congress at Geneva in August 1939, at which it was decided that even the British White Paper of that year, which violated the mandate by setting rigid limits to Jewish immigration into Palestine and to the purchase of land for Jewish settlement, should not deter us from all-out aid to any anti-Hitler war effort. So the Jewish Agency Executive asked me to fly back to Jerusalem to take full charge of its Political Department until the others could return, and to alert our people to the imminence of war and the need to organize to fight it.

As soon as I arrived, I sought an interview with General Michael G. H. Barker, who was then commanding all British military forces in Palestine. He was a typical British officer—tall, lanky, dour, curt but not unkindly. I believe he was one of the few British generals who had risen from the ranks. He was clearly amused, if not a little scornful, at my offer to put at his disposal the Jewish manpower and womanpower of Palestine in the event of war. He pointed to a large war map of the Middle East which covered one wall of his office.

"Take a look at this map, Dr. Joseph," he said, not without sarcasm. "To the immediate north of Palestine, you see Lebanon and Syria. These are under French control and so we need lose no sleep over our northern borders. There is Transjordan on our east, where we are not without authority ourselves and have a pretty good British-trained force at our disposal, the Arab Legion. Beyond that is Iraq, where British influence is no negligible factor. To the south we have Egypt, which, as you know, is controlled by Britain. That leaves the Mediterranean coast line. I admit that Italy is uncommitted, but there is a great, big sea in between. I have not heard," he added with a smile, "that the Jewish Agency possesses much of a navy, and we British are not without ships, you know. What would we need your soldiers for?"

General Barker was very pleased with the strategic picture he had drawn. Within months, Vichy France held control of Syria and Lebanon. Italy had joined the war on the Axis side. A little later the revolt of Raschid Ali, a pro-Axis leader, removed Iraq from any helpful role in British strategy. By 1941, the Egyptian Minister of Defense had handed over his confidential British documents to the Italians, the King was a British prisoner in his palace, and Egypt was defenseless before Rommel's army. In Transjordan the British-officered Arab Legion had mutinied. The former Grand Mufti of Jerusalem was Hitler's guest in Berlin, broadcasting anti-British propaganda to the Middle East and recruiting Moslem fascists in Yugoslavia to help the Nazis.

So the unconditional offer of the Jewish Agency to raise manpower for the Allied war effort was later accepted by the British, grudgingly but of necessity. I was put in charge of recruiting Jews for the British Army; our enlistments totaled thirty thousand. Jewish Palestinian units were rushed to El Alamein to help hold the line against Rommel. Someday it will be possible to publish complete details of the plan worked out by us with British authorities to organize the Jews of Palestine for a last-ditch battle in case the Nazi troops broke through in Egypt, to cover the withdrawal of British forces to India. The whole of Jewish Palestine was mobi-

lized on the Allied side. Our scouts led the advance into Syria. We
dropped parachutists into Central Europe to help organize resistance. We geared our factories and farms to help supply Allied
armies in the Middle East. For example, all the land mines used
against Rommel came from Jewish factories in Palestine. So did
parachutes and tents and mechanical small parts, small naval
craft and precision instruments.

What was our reward when the war ended? A Labor government
of Great Britain, which was heavily pledged to our support, decided for reasons deeply obscured in the politics of oil and of empire to back the Arabs against us. Its Foreign Minister, Ernest
Bevin, carried out this policy in a spirit of bitter anti-Semitism. It
was executed in Jerusalem by men among whom many were tired,
disillusioned, of small stature, vengeful. Those Jews who had survived Nazi extermination were pouring out of concentration camps
all over Europe, but the British refused to let them come to
Palestine. They turned back ships in the Mediterranean and
hunted down illegal refugees on the beaches. The Jews replied with
what weapons they had; on June 18, 1946, Hagana—the underground Jewish defense forces of Palestine—blew up eight bridges
on the frontiers and cut off communication with neighboring
Arab countries. June 29, 1946, was "Black Saturday." On that day
the British decided to break the Jewish will to resist. They arrested
2,600 young men and leaders in the Jewish population, confiscating
all the hidden arms and ammunition they could find, and interned
them as prisoners in concentration camps at Rafa on the Egyptian
frontier, at Athlit and at Latrun. Among those detained at Latrun
were four members of the Jewish Agency Executive, including myself. We were held there for four and a half months.

This was the true climax of an old, unhappy story. For the
next year and a half, the chief events were to take place outside
Jerusalem and outside Palestine. The issue had become one for the
whole world, and so it moved to the United Nations. But I cannot
help feeling that after Black Saturday each of the contending
parties knew that the issue had been truly joined, that now only
its own strength and determination counted, and that the promises of others would prove worthless in measure as they were not
backed up by the kind of strength which shows itself in deeds.
For me, the true test now was whether the energy of Jews who

shared all the many layers of my commitment to Jerusalem could be harnessed in an effective struggle to control our own destiny. The legend and its spiritual basis and the memories were all bright and shining, but could they win and make a nation?

The British faced the same problem in their own terms. When General Allenby captured Jerusalem from the Turks in 1917, he entered the city on foot, out of respect for its sacred character. The Balfour Declaration had made its fair and generous promise of a homeland for the Jews. Individual British soldiers and administrators had tried from time to time to operate their mandate with the farsighted wisdom which could undoubtedly have led Arabs and Jews to live in peace together. The new Labor government of Britain was committed in its program to internationalism, to an orderly liquidation of colonialism, and to some retribution to the Jews for what they had suffered from the Nazis. Yet these fair intentions and the honorable traditions out of which they grew were now to be tested against the tough realities of empire.

The tough realities won. Their victory had been foreshadowed from the first take-over by the British of this part of the old Ottoman Empire. The traditional imperial technique of "divide and rule" had played some part, undoubtedly, in the original decision to support a Jewish homeland in Palestine. But it also led to fumbling support of an Arab nationalism which was not an expression of the wrongs and grievances of the Arab masses but, instead, the jockeying for power of Arab chieftains who had little in common except their dislike of Western domination. And the old game of empire was difficult to play in the old way in a generation when Britain's need for oil and its profits and for a Middle Eastern anchor to its imperial lifeline both gave the Arabs what amounted virtually to a veto power over British diplomacy in their area.

So for eighteen years the mandate had been steadily whittled down in operation. As early as May 1922 the British had unilaterally removed Transjordan from the mandated area of Palestine and set it up as a vassal emirate, subsidized and with an army trained and officered by Britishers, to protect the flank of the Suez Canal. The following years were punctuated by outbreaks, investigations and commissions to solve the problems caused by the divide-and-rule policy. One of the most searching of these was the Peel Commission, in 1936, which suggested partition of Palestine into two states, one Arab and one Jewish; its recommendation was ignored by Whitehall. Instead, the notorious 1939 White Paper appeased the Arabs to the point of restricting all Jewish immigration, after five years, to what the Arabs would allow, and holding land sales down to some 4 per cent of the mandated territory. After the war, when hundreds of thousands of Jews were eager to move from refugee camps to Palestine, the old dilemma had been sharpened, and Ernest Bevin, backed by large sections of British colonial and military thinking as well as by the United States Department of State and the international oil companies, came down flatly on the Arab side.

From June 1946, deeds outweighed intentions. Both sides were being tested by events. President Truman's support of the immediate admission of 100,000 Jews to Palestine helped us. The rising temper of the British public against the terrorism of dissident Jewish organizations—and there was real terrorism in Palestine—hurt us. A widespread sense of Christian guilt over the fate of six million Jews in Europe, and the feeling that at least the survivors should be given a fair chance, worked in our favor. And against us was the accident that British foreign policy was in the hands of Ernest Bevin, a man who combined a profound ignorance of Jewish and Arab problems with obstinacy and a cordial and sincere dislike of Jews. He once said that having read the Bible and the Koran he knew all that one had to know about the Arab-Jewish question. He publicized his determination that the one country the survivors of the Nazi holocaust penned up in the concentration camps of Europe would not be allowed to enter was Palestine. His ruthlessness and his ignorance took on dimensions which actually moved public opinion in our favor in many countries of the world.

His problems were not eased by the report of the Anglo-American Committee of Inquiry in 1946. This was a body he had set up, but its recommendations were for the immediate admission of 100,000 Jews and abolition of restrictions on the sale of land—in effect, an annulment of the 1939 White Paper. The British refused to accept its proposals, enforcing the ban on immigration with even greater vigor. The Jews answered that this was an act of aggression against the Jewish people, and the Zionist Congress in December 1946 demanded the re-establishment of Palestine as a Jewish commonwealth. Ever since Black Saturday in June, both we Jews who lived in Palestine and the endless succession of British regiments who were sent out to support the disintegrating mandate knew in our hearts that some big change must come. We were learning again the old truth that a house divided against itself cannot endure. The British came to realize—not for the first time nor the last in the history of their empire—that you can do almost anything with bayonets except sit on them. Acts of resistance, terror or repression followed each other in quicker and quicker tempo. In despair and anger, Bevin announced in the House of Commons that the Palestine problem would be submitted for solution to the United Nations. He apparently expected that the United Nations, impressed by their difficulties, would alter the terms of the mandate so as to free Britain from the burden of the Jewish-national-home policy.

Fortunately for us, the United Nations was still young. It had not as yet been quite paralyzed by the interplay of power politics. It was still hopeful of avoiding the fate of the old League of Nations. It was fired by the need to make some just reparation for the unparalleled tragedy that had befallen the whole of the Jewish people through the breakdown of international morality and the inability or unwillingness of organized mankind to act in time to prevent the tragedy. So, as by a small candle burning in the murk of international politics, the way was lit for as impartial and just a decision upon Palestine as was possible in the world of international politics.

At the request of the British government, the U.N. appointed a United Nations Special Committee on Palestine, which came to be known as UNSCOP, to investigate matters in Palestine and the position of Jewish refugees in Europe, and to make recommendations. On August 31, 1947, the committee published its report. It recommended that the British mandate be terminated; that the independence of Palestine be achieved as soon as possible; that Palestine be partitioned into sovereign Arab and Jewish states, both to be democratic in character and to safeguard the rights and interests of the minorities; that there be an economic union between the two states to provide for customs, currency, transport and joint economic development; that the city of Jerusalem form a demilitarized and neutralized *corpus separatum* with an international trusteeship and a governor under the U.N., and that these should come into being by September 1, 1949; that during the transitional period the British should carry on the administration under the control of the U.N. and should admit 150,000 Jewish immigrants and abolish the land transfer regulations; that the two new states ensure protection of the Holy Places and freedom of conscience, language and education. The Arab state was to include western Galilee, Samaria and Judaea (excluding the city of Jerusalem), and a coastal strip from Ashdod to Rafa on the Egyptian frontier. The Jewish state was to include eastern Galilee, the Plain of Esdraelon, the coastal plain (apart from the aforesaid Arab strip) and the whole of the Beersheba subdistrict, which included all of the Negev.

There was a minority report supported by two of the ten members of the committee which favored a federation of Jewish and Arab states, with a federal authority controlling national defense, foreign relations, immigration and other services.

Both reports were referred to a Palestine Ad Hoc Committee of the U.N., headed by Dr. Herbert Evatt, the Australian Foreign Minister. He proposed that the majority and minority reports be considered by two separate subcommittees, thus preventing interminable wrangling and enabling those members favoring the resolution to work out a comprehensive plan for submission to the Assembly. He also exercised his authority as chairman resolutely to rule out of order every proposal designed to impede the committee's progress. Dr. Evatt thus won the eternal gratitude of Jews by his skill and his determination to force the issue, unsabotaged in his committee, to a vote in the United Nations Assembly. An ugly and tangled problem had at long last been taken from the hands of men haunted by their past mistakes and powerless to bend an old imperial formula to the needs of a modern world. The proposed partition was far from what we wanted, but many tens of thousands of Jews in Europe, Asia and Africa were looking for a home, and we were prepared to take what was offered.

I was a member of the Political Committee of the World Zionist Organization, and in this capacity I went to the United States in September 1947 to take part in the last-minute efforts to secure a favorable vote on partition in the United Nations Assembly. Our plane was quarantined on arrival, on the curious grounds that cholera had broken out in Egypt. It was hard to believe that the difference between Egypt and Palestine was not known to the United States health authorities, but the attendants at our detention quarters on Staten Island were afraid to enter our rooms and pushed our food in to us on wheeled trays. After four days, during which we gave each other lectures on the meaning of Succoth, geography triumphed and we were released to go to Lake Success.

And so I was suddenly face to face with the possible fulfillment of a lifetime's aspirations. They were not the ordinary aspirations of one's daily routine, but the hopes which lie at the root of our spiritual beings. Such hopes stem from the ancestral bloodstream of people; they are of the stuff of one's dreaming and waking moments; they are that part of life by which man lives if his soul is not to perish.

The resolution to be voted upon on November 29, 1947, was the majority proposal of the Palestine Committee. It would need a two-thirds majority vote for acceptance. The canvass of votes had meant a long, sustained, nerve-racking and uncertain political struggle. The representatives of all member nations of the U.N. had been approached, the situation had been explained to their home governments, and in many instances no firm commitment could be obtained in favor of the proposal nor could we know whether they would oppose it or abstain from voting. Symptomatic of the uncertainty, and of some of the methods employed to win the decision, was the case of a woman representative of one of the smaller nations. She had been assiduously courted by the strikingly handsome representative of one of the Arab states and by his romantic persuasion won over to vote against the measure in the U.N. Political Committee, although we of the Jewish Agency had been assured of her country's support by well-informed circles at her home capital. Urgent measures were taken to make the facts known to the lady's Foreign Ministry, and a new delegate—a man this time—was appointed to represent his country in the Assembly. He voted for the partition proposal.

At the very last moment, just as the voting was about to begin, the delegate for the Lebanon rose to outline what he said was a new proposal, a plan for a federation of Arab and Jewish areas, which ought to be considered before the final vote was taken. For a moment it looked as though the political trickery and finesse of the Arabs would snatch the possibility of a favorable decision from our grasp; our poll had shown that such a contingency did exist. The situation was saved by the American representative, Herschel V. Johnson, who rose to urge that the Lebanon proposal was identical with the minority report earlier put forward to the U.N. Political Committee. It had been rejected there because it afforded no basis for a suitable compromise and needed no further consideration. He pressed the Assembly to proceed with the vote.

There was a tense moment in which we Jewish observers held

our breath as the President, Dr. Oswaldo Aranha of Brazil, leaned over for a whispered consultation with Trygve Lie, the U.N. Secretary General. He then sat up and ruled that he accepted the United States' contention and that the vote would be taken immediately.

In alphabetical order, the senior representative of each nation was called on to state his position. With taut nerves, we counted the tally in our minds. The actual voting took three minutes; it seemed to me to stretch the length of the Jewish exile. At last it became clear that the resolution would pass. I burst into tears and said to a lady sitting next to me, who was a complete stranger, "We've got it! We've got it! We've won!"

Pandemonium broke loose in the hall the moment that President Aranha declared the result of the voting: thirty-three for, thirteen against and ten abstentions. Applause rolled round the walls. Men embraced each other sobbing with joy; women were almost hysterical with gladness. The face of the British delegate was grim and set, and the Arab representatives sat white with a fury which was to express itself, in a few short hours, in a wave of disorder, murder and sabotage throughout Palestine. But for the brief spell, it was our moment. The President knocked good-humoredly for order with his gavel, but the hubbub continued to mount. The meeting was adjourned; the delegates streamed into the lobby; the galleries emptied and the Jewish observers who were present were left to savor the sweet fulfillment of that moment of destiny.

"When the Lord brought about the redemption of Zion," exulted the Psalmist, "we were like those that dream. Our mouths were filled with laughter and our tongues with a joyful shout." There is no way in which men can express the utterly overflowing gladness of the heart. The whole of one's being becomes a prayer. It is true we embraced each other; we clapped one another on the shoulders or, according to our individual temperaments, murmured or shouted. the conventional words of congratulations. But how could we express the meaning of our deep involvement in the climax of the final struggle to end some seventy generations of Jewish homelessness and exile? How give full vent to the joy of redemption that once again we would be free to live in an independent Jewish state? Was a trace of the Divine Presence that had gone into exile with Israel to be found lingering in those halls, which would always retain for us an element of sanctity? Is that why we were reluctant to leave? We stood there in excited knots, amid the flat untidiness and the sense of frustrating incompleteness that always haunts an empty hall after a great meeting.

Finally my wife and I made our way from Lake Success back to New York City and the offices of the Jewish Agency at 16 East Sixty-sixth Street. There we found a hastily arranged celebration of Zionist leaders, at which Shertok and a few others made short speeches. We went out into the streets, the feeling of history being made still strong in us, but we found a normal city going about its business. Evidently few of the two and a half million Jews in New York had already heard the good news that after two thousand years the Jewish people were to be accepted again into the family of nations. Even in restaurants where Jewish men of letters could be found, there was little excitement. The indifference weighed us down. If only we could have been in Jerusalem at that moment!

In Palestine, we learned later, it was entirely different. Joy billowed up and poured over the whole Jewish population like a great flood. Because of the difference in time, the news came to Jerusalem after midnight, but the people had not been sleeping. The streets were filled with singing and dancing; even British soldiers, remembering Old Testament readings, were moved by the sanctity of the moment and joined in the celebration. The synagogues were packed to the doors. Rams' horns were sounded. A friend later told me that it was like the moment of creation described in the Book of Job, when all the sons of morning shouted together. Even the most agnostic confessed that at that moment they felt the hand of God was upon them. Just as the twenty-ninth of November was passing into a new day, so was the blackness of exile turning into a bright future heralded by the mighty panoply of color of the purple dawn of the mountains surrounding the city of Jerusalem.

Early that Sunday morning, Ben Gurion spoke to the people. He said this act of historic justice would partially atone for the wrongs done to the Jews over the past 1,800 years, and he thanked all those who had helped to create a new Jewish state. But he told the Jewish people to face the facts.

"The U.N. decision," he asserted, "imposes a heavy responsibility upon the Jewish population in Palestine and the entire Jewish people. It is, in fact, a challenge to all the scattered communities of Israel to bring forth the great strength, spiritual and material, necessary for the building of the Jewish state, for the absorption of large numbers of immigrants from Europe, the Orient and elsewhere, for the development of our wasteland and the creation of an independent Jewish society which will express the great ideals of the prophets of Israel: human brotherhood, social justice and peace among the nations. First let us remember our brethren pining in camps far from the homeland, in inimical diasporas in Yemen, Iraq and other Middle Eastern countries. We shall not rest till we bring them here to live and work with us. Today we have become a free people."

That same morning, the Jewish Agency issued a brief message to the Yishuv, the Jewish population of Palestine: "The main theme behind the spontaneous celebrations we are witnessing today is the Yishuv's desire to seek peace and its determination to achieve fruitful co-operation with the Arabs. We hope that the Arab masses will not allow themselves to be misled into any acts of violence. The Jewish people are also called upon to keep from being provoked into any irresponsible deeds."

What was the rejoicing all about, and what were the reasons for the sober second thoughts which filled our minds as we looked to the future? The partition plan which had been passed was far from what we had hoped for, but unfortunately it was still more than we could count on getting without fighting for it.

In brief, the U.N. resolution provided that:

The British mandate in Palestine was to be terminated and all British armed forces were to leave the country as soon as possible, but, in any event, not later than August 1, 1948.

The British authorities were to arrange to evacuate an area within the territory allocated to the Jewish state, including a seaport and hinterland adequate to provide facilities for a substantial immigration. This was to be done as early as possible, but not later than February 1, 1948.

An independent Arab state and an independent Jewish state as well as an international trusteeship regime for the city of Jerusalem and its environs were to come into existence two months after the complete evacuation of the British armed forces, but not later than by October 1, 1948.

A United Nations commission to implement the Assembly's resolution was to be set up, consisting of representatives of five member states.

The administration of Palestine was to be gradually turned over to this commission by the mandatory power as it withdrew its armed forces. The mandatory power was to co-ordinate its plans for withdrawal with the plans of the commission to take over and administer the areas evacuated. The British mandatory power was required to refrain from taking any action to prevent, obstruct or delay implementation of the resolution.

The commission was to fix the frontiers of the Jewish and Arab states and the Jerusalem international area in accordance with the provisions of the resolution. The area of the Jewish state was estimated to be 5,500 square miles (including the Negev desert area) and that of the Arab state 4,500 square miles. The Jewish state would have a population of some 558,000 Jews and 40,500 non-Jews, the Arab state 804,000 Arabs and 10,000 Jews. There would be about 100,000 Jews and a similar number of Arabs in the Jerusalem area enclave.

The commission, in consultation with respective Jewish and Arab public bodies and political parties, was to establish a provisional Council of Government in each of the states by April 1, 1948. These councils were to function under the general supervision of the commission.

These provisional Councils of Government were, during the transitional period, to have full authority in their areas, including control of immigration and regulation of land transfer.

The provisional councils were to enlist an armed militia from residents in their respective areas to maintain order and prevent frontier clashes.

Elections to a constituent assembly were to be held in both of the states within two months of the British evacuation of the areas.

Arabs and Jews living in Jerusalem were to be free to opt for citizenship in the Arab or Jewish state.

The commission was to draft an undertaking which was to be entered into by both provisional councils with regard to economic union and transit facilities.

Provision was made for access to and care of the Holy Places and for the protection of religious and minority rights.

As regards the city of Jerusalem, the resolution provided that it be placed under an international trusteeship system by means of a trusteeship agreement which would designate the United Nations as the administering authority in respect of the city. The trusteeship was to appoint a governor who was to be neither an Arab nor a

Jew nor a citizen of the Arab or Jewish state. The governor would
be assisted by suitable legislative, executive and judicial organs.
The protection of the Holy Places, buildings and sites was to be entrusted to a special police force, the members to be neither Jews nor
Arabs.

These provisions would thus have placed the administration of
the city of Jerusalem in the hands of a single individual with exceedingly wide powers. It would deprive the inhabitants of the
city, both Jews and Arabs, of the same measure of independent rule
by their own governments as was given to Jews and Arabs in the
areas to be included in the two states that were to be set up.

Finally, the United Nations Assembly moved at once to give effect to its resolution by setting up the commission to implement it.
It consisted of representatives of five small states: Bolivia, Czechoslovakia, Denmark, Panama and the Philippines. Dr. Carl Lisicky,
of Czechoslovakia, was appointed chairman. At almost the same
time, the Trusteeship Council of the United Nations appointed
representatives of Australia, China, France, Mexico, the United
States and Great Britain to work out plans for the administration
of Jerusalem. Trygve Lie expressed the hope that the commission
would reach Palestine by December 15.

Neither of these plans worked. Both were doomed to failure by
the opposition of the Arabs, the sabotage of Great Britain and the
determination of the United States Department of State to take
back from President Truman control over American policy in the
Middle East.

The Jews themselves had not accepted the resolution with unqualified satisfaction. In particular, the proposal that Jewish Jerusalem, with its 100,000 Jews and its numerous Jewish public bodies
and learned institutions, should be detached from the Jewish state
evoked resentment. There was equal regret over the exclusion of
western Galilee, an area particularly suitable for Jewish agricultural
settlement and the absorption of newcomers. Grave doubts were
further expressed as to the practicability of the proposed economic
union, which would involve heavy financial sacrifices for the Jewish
commonwealth. In spite of all these misgivings, the partition settlement was accepted by the bulk of the Jewish community as offering
the only practicable way out from the untenable White Paper
regime which for over nine years had played havoc with Jewish immigration and reconstruction.

The Arabs' attitude was, however, crystal-clear. They would have no truck with the partition proposals. They claimed full independence for a Palestine in which Jews would be a permanent minority. The Arab representatives told the United Nations that the Arabs would drench the soil of Palestine with the last drop of their blood in resisting the partition plan. The Arab League, created by the British Foreign Office in 1943 in the hope that it would prove a convenient instrument through which British power might be exercised and perpetuated in the Middle East, exploited the situation. It had become a Frankenstein monster, a central force in speeding the elimination of British and Western influence from the Middle East. It called for self-determination in Palestine by the majority of its inhabitants, which meant by the Arabs. It insisted that the whole of Palestine should be an Arab country. It ignored completely the solemnly undertaken and internationally guaranteed promises to the Jewish people in Palestine.

The third party to the dispute, the British government, seemed determined to confuse the world as to its ultimate intentions. Its basic aim, to maintain a British position in the Middle East by reliance on the Arabs against the Jews, had suffered a serious setback. There is some reason to believe that many Britishers in important positions had by now had so much trouble with both Jews and Arabs that they wished a plague on both our houses and welcomed the surrender of the mandate. But others had not given up the game, and they were quick to announce publicly that Britain could not accept responsibility for partition nor participate in implementing it. This was a clear signal to Arab politicians that they could expect British support for intransigent opposition to the plan.

The United States position had been crucial, since it had been certain to influence the attitude of most of the South American members of the Assembly. President Truman's support of free immigration of 100,000 Jews into Palestine had already been a decisive factor in forcing the issue before the United Nations, and the United States had cast its vote for partition. But this was far from the end of the story, and the State Department, like the British, was still confident that the Arabs could be appeased, the Jews silenced and the old order of things re-established.

Most surprising of all, in view of what was to happen later, was the Soviet Union's decision to support partition. Semyon Tsarapkin, the U.S.S.R. delegate, told the United Nations that the Jews could not be denied the right to create their own state. Whatever the motives of the U.S.S.R., the agreement of the U.S. and the

U.S.S.R. on a major political proposal (for the first time since the U.N. was established) was hailed at that time as a favorable omen for peace and co-operation in the world.

In the light of present-day Russian policy in the Middle East, it is interesting to note that the Russians in particular took umbrage at the Arab attitude to the resolution. *Izvestia* attacked it as a breach of the United Nations decision, describing the Arabs as anti-Communist reactionaries aiming to establish fascist dictatorship in the Middle East. Another Russian journal, *Trud,* wrote that "the day will come when the Arabs will be compelled to respect the decision of the United Nations concerning Palestine."

Only the Jews and the Arabs were to hold firmly to their positions during the crucial period that now began. The Big Powers continued to change their minds and their instructions to their delegates as the cold war, the problems of empire and the precarious balance of diplomatic power dictated. It is sometimes hard for Jews not to forget that the years 1947 and 1948, which were so decisive for us, also included the Truman Doctrine, the Marshall Plan, the dissolution of Nationalist China and the Communist takeover of Czechoslovakia. Having partitioned Palestine on paper, the United Nations turned to other problems, and our debate moved back literally within hours to the land where the issue had been joined in the first place. I flew back as quickly as I could to Jerusalem, the Holy City whose future was at stake, the city which was home to 100,000 Jews like myself whose devotion would now be tested.

II

THE WINTER WAR

 Ⴢ

T HE FIRST SHOTS were fired in Jerusalem on Sunday, November
30, at an ambulance on its way to the Hadassah Hospital on
Mount Scopus. Three Arabs stationed near Lod (formerly Lydda)
Airfield killed five Jews in a bus bound from Natanya to Jerusalem.
Another bus traveling from Hadera to Jerusalem was attacked
with hand grenades. In Tel Aviv's Carmel Market, on the border
between the Jewish city and what was Arab Jaffa, murder was done.
In Haifa, shots were fired at Jews passing through the Arab quarter,
and in the south of the country stoning of buses started.

The next day brought a slight rise in the number, tempo and
gravity of the attacks. Shooting, stoning and window smashing
went on sporadically throughout the country. Attacks were made
on the Polish and Swedish consulates, and the Czechoslovak consulate was threatened; these countries had supported the partition
proposal. Arabs began to leave their homes in Jewish quarters to
live with their own people, and Jews in Arab quarters did the same.
In Jerusalem the first large-scale encounter between Arabs and
Jews took place. An Arab mob poured out of the Jaffa Gate bran-
dishing sticks and shouting against the Jews. They went along the
Mamillah Road up Princess Mary Avenue, a Jewish shopping
thoroughfare. This illegal demonstration was headed by an armored car manned by British police. The Arabs encountered a wall
of Hagana men at the top of the street, whereupon they halted
their advance and took to looting the shops while the police looked

on. They dispersed only when two Hagana officers fired over their heads.

There were attacks on Jews throughout the city. Buses, ambulances and a funeral convoy were fired on, an autobus was blown up by a land mine, bombs were thrown into cafés, killing and wounding, the central prison was broken open and two Arab gangleaders freed, pedestrians were stabbed and sniped at, several buildings were blown up, Molotov cocktails were thrown into shops, a synagogue was set on fire.

These were only rumblings of the real storm that was brewing. The Arab Higher Committee, which had been set up in 1936 to represent Palestinian Arabs vis-à-vis the British administration, had been in continuous executive session, and it proclaimed a three-day strike throughout the country to begin on Tuesday, December 2. It enforced the closing of all Arab shops, schools and places of business and sent great crowds into the streets and the mosques of Jerusalem and other cities, where agitators and religious leaders were ready to incite them.

The British, with their inimitable *sang-froid*, put their telescope up to their blind eye and assured the world that the situation was not serious. But the first day of the strike showed that the situation was much uglier than it had been in previous riots and disturbances between Arabs and Jews. The British police and military authorities allowed the mobs to get out of hand. That Tuesday morning saw two crowds of several hundred Arabs, armed with sticks, stones and some firearms, advance from the Jaffa and Damascus gates of the Old City into the now largely Jewish sections of the New City. They smashed windows, looted shops, attacked any Jews they caught. When Jewish organized defense units went into action, they were quickly disarmed by the British police; some of the confiscated arms were later found on killed and captured Arab rioters. When the mobs were eventually dispersed, sixteen Hagana men were held by the British for being in illegal possession of arms and a further search for weapons was made in Jewish quarters by police and soldiers.

The British eventually imposed a nineteen-hour curfew in the Arab quarters of the capital. But the Jews could not rely on this— for many Arabs broke curfew with no perceptible consequences— and the Mishmar Ha'am, the uniformed guard force organized by the Jews to deal with such situations, patrolled the border areas between Jewish and Arab zones. Convoys had to be established

from the outlying suburbs of Jerusalem and Jewish villages to the
center of the city. Jews no longer found it safe to attend sessions of
the law courts in Jerusalem; municipal and government employees
had to stay away from work to avoid attacks by their Arab colleagues.

Hagana, the Jewish defense organization, began by exercising a
maximum of restraint. Their orders were to prevent any attempt to
frustrate by force the U.N. decision, to repel any attack upon the
Yishuv, and not to molest peaceful Arabs. They still hoped that the
British authorities would take measures to stop the rioting, and
that some kind of agreement would be reached with the Arabs. A
hard practical reason for self-restraint was the British policy of confiscating weapons, a policy consistently carried out with zeal against
Jews but not against the Arabs. But the rioting spread across the
country and grew worse. By December 4, the Arabs in the Old City
were breaking curfew with impunity and attacking synagogues.
The next day, the Jewish Agency and the Vaad Leumi, the national
council representing all the Yishuv or Palestine Jews, issued an
order calling up all men and women between seventeen and
twenty-five for national service, and the Hagana began to take over
general responsibility for defense against attacks. The second week's
toll was seventy-one Arabs killed, seventy-four Jews, and nine British.

Behind the Arab rioters there emerged the first outlines of an
organized Arab plan to nullify the United Nations decision. The
secretary of the Arab League, which tried to co-ordinate the Arabs
outside Palestine in active opposition to the U.N. partition resolution, announced that a technical committee was at work on tactical
plans. He predicted a long struggle and called initially for volunteers to a people's army rather than for direct intervention by
armies of the Arab states. But by December 8 the Premier of Iraq,
Salah Jabr, had committed his country to armed intervention. The
end of the month saw an Egyptian brigadier general, Mohammed
Saleh Harb Pasha, inspecting Arab volunteers in Syria and calling
for a volunteer movement in Egypt. The Lebanese Minister of Defense announced that he had been present himself at an attack on
Jews at Huleh in the north of Palestine and that his ministry had
set up a special committee to raise funds, enlist volunteers and obtain arms for the struggle in Palestine. Much of the initial violence
in Jerusalem was organized directly by the ex-Grand Mufti in the
hope of provoking the Jews to countermeasures which would make

effective propaganda in neighboring countries where he needed
help. The Near East Broadcasting Company's programs from Cyprus, controlled by the British Foreign Office, blanketed the Arab
world with the ex-Grand Mufti's material.

There were some instances of Arabs making peace with their
Jewish neighbors. In Herzliya on December 10, Arab and Jewish
mukhtars met and agreed to keep out any strangers trying to use
their settlements as bases for hostile actions. The headmen of
Fejja village at a peace parley the next day asked two Jewish
friends to convey to the people of Petah Tikva their desire for cooperation and friendly relations. The two parties met on the
Petah Tikva-Lydda highway, and the Arabs showed the Jews the
local guards who had been posted along the road to prevent attacks upon Jewish traffic. Agitators would be kept out of the village,
the headmen promised.

On December 18, the Jews of Holon and the Arabs of the neighborhood entered into a peace agreement. A similar agreement
was reached a week later by Jews and Arabs of the Emek Hefer
area and by Magdiel and the Abu Kishk Arabs. In an exchange of
letters between Mayor Yisrael Rokach of Tel Aviv and Mayor
Youssef Haikal of Jaffa, both agreed to call upon their residents to
maintain peace and quiet. In the first week of January, the Hagana
distributed a leaflet in Arabic all over Palestine describing the
harm being done to Arabs themselves by the rioting. "We can have
peace in this country if we drive the warmongers and inciters
away," the pamphlet said. "Peace to those who desire peace." It
was signed "Hagana." But the Arab Higher Committee refused to
issue such a call to peace in Palestine, while in the neighboring
Arab countries the populace was being incited against the Jews.

This was the unhappy situation I found when I returned to Jerusalem from Lake Success in the first week of December. I wrote
my wife, who had to remain in the United States for a few weeks
longer: "Everyone here is on duty and very busy. The situation
promises to improve in the immediate future, but only temporarily.
Our people feel confident they can handle any situation. All are intensely engaged in strengthening our position. Road travel between
Tel Aviv and Haifa is normal. The Tel Aviv-Jerusalem route is
still convoyed and unsafe. Jerusalem is tense, with everyone on
guard and on constant lookout for trouble."

Next to defense, the biggest problem which faced us was how to
take over authority from the British in our part of Palestine. Here

the British were adamant in refusing any co-operation at all. At Lake Success, they succeeded in completely hamstringing the Implementation Commission which had been appointed by the United Nations. They were brutally specific: they would allow no militia to be set up by the U.N.; they would permit no provisional governments until the end of the mandate; they would not allow the commission even to come to Palestine until May 1. When we officially requested the commission to secure details of British plans for evacuation, the commission was told that these plans could not be disclosed either to the Jews or the Arabs. If the British hope was to sabotage the U.N. resolution, to produce complete chaos and to encourage the Arabs to push the Jews into the sea so that the imperial position could be recovered, this was exactly the course of action best designed to achieve those goals.

This was no surprise to us. As early as October 1947, Ben Gurion had had a discussion with Sir Alan Cunningham, who was to be the last of the British High Commissioners. "If troubles begin," Sir Alan had told him, "I fear that we shall not be able to help you; we shall not be able to defend you." Ben Gurion could only reply frankly that if he had to choose between the present policy of the British and their leaving the country, he would prefer the latter. Reporting to the Jewish Agency Executive, he told us that we would have to improvise both a defense force and an economic and governmental machinery by ourselves if we were to avert complete collapse.

The next day, October 13, Mrs. Golda Meyerson (later Meir) discussed with the High Commissioner a series of questions ranging from warehouses and communications to the water supply for Jerusalem. She suggested that he name liaison officers to be in touch with the Jewish Agency. His reply was: "We shall not be able to hand over to you services in one part of the country. We shall not be able to set up a state for you." Two months later, when Arab disorders had started, she saw him again to ask for a less anti-Jewish policy on the part of the police and to inquire why the Jews should be penalized because the Arabs would not agree to set up their provisional government under the U.N. plan. All she got was the same dusty answer.

So we were under no illusions about the policy which was going to win for the British evacuation the name "Operation Chaos." But we ourselves were far from ready. Under the mandate, Jewish organizations in Jerusalem had been amorphous, well-meaning but often ineffective, wastefully overlapping. Besides the Jewish

Agency and the Vaad Leumi, there was a community council for
Jerusalem called the Vaad Hakehilla. This body rarely held elections, took no vital part in the life of the community and busied
itself chiefly with supervising the relations of Jewish religious sects
and burial societies. In December, it set up an emergency committee called the Vaadat Hamatzav to cope with the emergency situation which developed almost immediately in the supply of food
and kerosene. But this group had no money and almost no moral
authority. So the Jewish Agency stepped in with another committee,
the Vaad Leumi joined forces with it, and a new body was formed
called the Vaadat Hamosadot Le-Inyanai Yerushalayim, or Committee of the National Institutions for Matters Pertaining to Jerusalem. The name was quickly shortened to the Jerusalem Emergency
Committee. I was asked to head this body with Golda Meyerson,
and since she was soon detailed to other work, I was left in charge.

At once we were swamped with demands and complaints, chiefly
from sections of the community like the ultra-orthodox Jews, that
they were not represented. Protracted haggling and bargaining
over representation on any new public body was an established
tradition in Jerusalem. We tried not to waste our time on these de-
sires of old "notables" of the community for prestige and position,
but they acted as a constant drag on us until at the eleventh hour I
was finally given unlimited powers to prepare Jerusalem for siege.

Our situation was serious enough. We were isolated in the heart
of an Arab area with only a few Jewish settlements in the neighborhood, which were themselves sorely beset. We produced very
little of our food and other requirements. Our communications by
road or rail passed through Arab territory. Our population was
scattered throughout the city. We had no industry worth talking
about. What trade there was depended in a measure on the Arab
population of Jerusalem and its hinterland and to a lesser extent
on neighboring Arab countries. A considerable part of our population were supported by charity or tourism or were employed in
government offices or national institutions. The British authorities
took no steps to care for the needs of the Jewish population, and a
situation rapidly developed where we were satisfied if they did
nothing overt to harm our interests.

Jerusalem was the most isolated of all the large Jewish settlements in Palestine. Thirty miles of the road which joined it to Tel

Aviv passed through Arab territory where the monotony of enmity was not broken by a single Jewish village. The eight miles nearest to Jerusalem did have Jewish colonies from Maaleh Hahamisha eastward. But the heights in these parts were dotted with hostile Arab villages, while Kastel, site of an ancient Roman fortress and by its natural position the dominant strong point commanding the whole approach to the capital, was in Arab hands and strongly held by them. The Arab villages nestling in the highest hills about Jerusalem were quite secure from Jewish attack by virtue of their position and the vigilance of the British in checking all Jewish transport on the road for arms. The villagers had time and enough to devote themselves to attacks on Jewish transport without having to worry about safeguarding their rear or flanks. There were additional factors. While most of the Arabs of Palestine were at first not particularly enthusiastic about the struggle against the Jews, the clans in the vicinity of Jerusalem were fanatical supporters of the family of Haj Amin el Husseini, the former Grand Mufti of Jerusalem. The Jewish population of Jerusalem itself was dispersed into noncontiguous suburbs; the need to protect them and the Jewish colonies in the vicinity of the capital absorbed fighting forces which might otherwise have been able to take decisive action to clear the heights and free the road to Tel Aviv, always assuming that such an operation could go forward without embroiling the Jews with the British forces.

The Jewish quarter of the Old City was completely surrounded by areas heavily populated by Arabs. This was also true of much of new Jerusalem and its suburbs. To the west of the city, the Jewish suburbs of Bet Hakerem and Bait Vegan were separated from the rest of the city by the Arab suburbs of Sheikh Bader, Lifta, Romema and the Arab lands west of Rehaviah. To the north, the Hebrew University and the Hadassah Hospital were cut off from the Jewish center by Wadi el Joz, Sheikh Jarrah and the American colony. To the east, Talpiot was separated from the center by Bakaa and the Greek and German colonies. The outer Jewish suburb of Mekor Hayim faced the Arab village of Bet Safafa between the village and the center of Jerusalem.

The entire city of Jerusalem is undulating land, interspersed by valleys and by isolated spurs and ridges, some of which are 150 feet higher than the low points of the city. To make the problem of defense still harder, the British had enclosed what amounted to one third of new Jerusalem in security zones surrounded by barbed wire. These zones were closed to Jews except for a few autobuses a day, while armed Arabs were allowed to pass through them freely. Whatever the policy of the High Commissioner was, this was the practice followed by officers in charge of the zones. Moreover, the zones cut up some of the Jewish areas into separated parts and made collective defense hopelessly difficult. Most of the British offices were in Arab or mixed quarters where we could give no protection to Jewish officials who had to work there. The law courts, for example, were in the Russian Compound, where Jewish lawyers could go, from December on, only at peril of their lives. Yet the British Chief Justice and his associate judges ruled formally that lack of public security was no excuse for adjournment of a case on the failure of a lawyer to run the gantlet of Arab street mobs.

This was the city we had to defend. It was lived in, in the spring of 1948, by 99,300 Jews, 33,700 Moslems and 31,300 Christians. We constituted nearly one sixth of all the Jews in Palestine. In addition to these problems set us by geography, our freedom of action was further circumscribed by the diplomatic and strategic consequences of the city's designation as an international city, and most of all by the heavy concentration of British forces in Jerusalem. Their retention of strategic strong points, their strengthening of the Arabs by an official policy of specious "neutrality," and the direct, if unofficial, military help given by many British police and soldiers to the Arabs, all combined to make our situation tougher. To save us, we looked first of all to the Hagana, which had been training the whole of the Jewish population since the 1930s for just such an emergency as we now faced.

A large proportion of the men and women in Hagana had served in the British Army in World War II. Many had taken staff and training courses in British military schools. Other Hagana officers were men with experience in the ranks of Continental and other armies, some of those with the special contribution to make of experience in ghetto fighting and in partisan warfare. Among the best officers we had, finally, were men with further training in the kibbutzim, or co-operative settlements. The late Orde Wingate, famous as a British general in the war against the Japanese, became the best-loved foreigner in Palestine in the 1930s when he organized and trained young Jews from the kibbutzim to defend themselves against the Arabs in the *me'o'ra'ot*—the Hebrew equivalent of the Irish "troubles"—in 1937 and 1938. His code name was *"hayedid"* —"the friend."

The quality of human material was to prove decisive in all ranks. Because of immigration restrictions, Jews who managed to get to Palestine tended to be dedicated persons with highly developed feelings of patriotism and great self-reliance. This became especially important in the early stages of the war, when Jews nearly always found themselves fighting in very small units. The volunteers who came in 1948 brought key personnel like pilots, men who could improvise the manufacture of munitions and experts in the use of armor and artillery. Finally, a detailed knowledge of the country had been acquired by all younger members of Hagana as part of their training from school on.

The command and striking forces of the Hagana in the winter of 1948 were four Palmach brigades, consisting of 2,100 fighters and 1,000 reserves. These men did the hardest fighting of the war and lost the best of their members. Field troops were known as Chish; these numbered some 1,800 enlisted men, with 10,000 reserves. There were 32,000 men in the Mishmar Ha'am, or Home Guard, whose job it was to help defend their immediate localities, in villages, towns or cities. We also had the youth battalions who were in training as replacements for the Palmach troops but were immediately available for auxiliary services; their numbers were now augmented by young men crowding the sixty enlistment offices opened throughout the country.

At the beginning of the war, the Jews had some fifteen thousand weapons: rifles of all makes and ages, some light machine guns, a few medium machine guns, a handful of 3-inch mortars. We had hand grenades, explosives and Sten guns, mostly the product of our own secret arsenals. When the ports were open, after the British left, we could finally acquire the armament needed to make this a real army.

For Hagana was illegal and underground until the end of the mandate. From 1946, when an ultimate showdown was seen as inevitable by both Jews and British, our efforts to build its strength had been matched by British searches for arms and arrests of Hagana leaders. We had contrived training centers in Jerusalem—at the Teachers' Seminary in Bet Hakerem and at the Hebrew University—and in a few more distant settlements, one at the Dead Sea and one in the group of Jewish villages around Kfar Etzion. Shooting ranges had been set up close to the city. Training in grenade throwing and mortar firing was carried on in the kibbutzim, which had controlled their own affairs for years and which the British seldom came near and the Arabs feared to enter. The boys and girls in these settlements had an uncanny knowledge of the countryside, a tradition of living dangerously, a good deal of experience in illegal operations like the landing of refugees along the beaches, and the strong mixture of self-reliance and teamwork which has always been a central feature of kibbutz life.

The Hagana intelligence network was made up of taxi drivers and government officials, newspapermen and waitresses and policemen. During the early months of the struggle, intelligence was essential to protect illegal arms from confiscation. They had to be buried so as to defeat discovery with mine detectors and other scientific equipment. This enormously complicated the business of defense. Obviously, arms that are well hidden are hard to get at in an emergency. In order to hold down losses, caches had to be numerous and small. These problems were worst of all in Jerusalem, where British troops searched Jews coming in and out of each Jewish quarter. At vital points on highways, they established check posts to search Jewish convoys for arms. Hiding places, known as "slicks," were built into many vehicles, and the technique of hiding arms became an art and almost a national pastime.

Mobile "slicks" were a large part of the answer. This often meant the use of carefully selected girls and women who could carry weapons past the check posts, for the behavior of the British toward women was, with very few exceptions, correct. Thus trucks on the convoys would carry two or several hitchhikers who were carefully trained, tough Palmach veterans, of whom at least one would be a girl who had a Sten gun and possibly hand grenades concealed on her person. Similarly a taxi or bus traveling the road would have its complement of women, one or two of whom would be carrying arms. These girls were not just passive gun carriers. In the event of attack they fought as competently and as bravely as the men.

The desk on which this book is written contains a "slick" in which vital documents were hidden at critical moments. The tea table in our lounge has another, and it was often a matter of some grim humor for my wife and myself to entertain a British official who did not know that information he desperately wanted was a few inches from where he sat.

Before organized fighting began, these Hagana forces took over the job of patrolling the streets of Jerusalem, setting up posts throughout the city with telephone lines to headquarters, trying to protect Jewish life and property. Most of the men continued their jobs in working hours, and when their absence was essential their comrades did their work without extra pay. It was dangerous work. On December 4 two girls were arrested for carrying arms and sentenced to three years' imprisonment, while four men received five-year sentences for discharging firearms. One non-Jew, to his credit, wrote a letter to the *Palestine Post:*

As a spectator on the side-lines and a countryman of neither side, may I, through the courtesy of your columns, express my tremendous admiration of the fortitude, courage and restraint of the members of the Hagana under provocation as galling as it is criminal, with little or no help from those quarters from which it could have been expected in view of repeated official statements on the subject of law and order?

I can never hope to witness again, anywhere else in the world, a better discipline, a greater courage or a more admirable spirit than that which has been displayed by the Jewish people as a whole ever since Partition was approved by the U.N.

To these official forces of the Jewish community must be added two organizations which were even deeper underground. The Irgun Zvai Leumi—National Military Organization—sometimes called by its Hebrew initials, "Etzel," consisted of 5,000 members by the winter of 1948, while the Lohmei Herut Yisrael—Israel Freedom Fighters—called "Lehi" or the Stern Gang, numbered 1,000. These were both terrorist organizations, born out of terror and pogroms and British police rule in Palestine and fanatically committed to the use of terror to win freedom. Their lack of training and professional skill in fighting often proved disastrous, and before the fighting was over their tactics had cost the Jewish community dearly. They were expected to merge with Hagana when it became the official armed force of Israel, but in fact they remained a constant worry and anxiety to Hagana commanders until the war was over.

Their acts of reprisal against British personnel and unoffending Arabs dismayed most of the Jews of Palestine. On balance, they cost us much more by their provocation than they added to our military strength. Yet their dedication to their own programs was formidable, and their deception and subterfuge fantastic: the Stern Gang succeeded at different times in planting a man inside the Jewish Agency and another in the High Commissioner's office. Although the Etzel was connected with a political movement, with its leaders openly in the Herut party, the Stern Gang was made up of non-partisan misguided patriots. They were dagger men who believed in "the holy lie" and "the holy murder." There was intense horror in the Jewish community against their acts, combined with respect for their motives and often for their members as human beings. Our own efforts to uncover and control them, like those of the British, foundered on the most contemptible word in the Hebrew language, which is *mosser*, the word for informer.

The first four months of fighting, up to the end of March, saw the Jews chiefly on the defensive. The Arabs dominated the hill country and the main roads; besides cutting communications between Jewish settlements and looting, they seemed chiefly interested in disorganizing life, keeping Jewish nerves on edge, killing enough people to dishearten us and force us to abandon our efforts to establish a nation in our part of the country. With their enormous superiority in numbers, the leaders of the Arab world were clearly confident that once the British had left they could take over Palestine without a major military campaign.

Losses were not light on either side, and they grew steadily. On December 15 the British government gave the figures of casualties for the fortnight since December 1 as 190 killed, 174 seriously wounded, 361 slightly wounded; of these, 80 Jews killed and 50 seriously wounded. In the next week there were 37 Jews killed. In the fourth week of December casualties were reported as 66 killed. By January 10 official figures showed 769 Jews, 1,069 Arabs and 123 British killed. According to British official statements, these figures rose in every succeeding month. In February they reported 495 killed and 1,180 wounded, of whom 200 killed and 579 wounded were Jews.

On the Arab side, the fighting was done by armed bands of widely differing size. The smaller ones were organized by local Arab chieftains or leaders, some of them co-operating haphazardly in an ineffectual country-wide body known as the Arab National Guard. The larger ones were set up by military commanders financed by Arab governments outside Palestine. Fawzi el Kawkji was typical of these, an Arab guerrilla leader who had figured in the 1936-39 riots in Palestine and who now headed a large contingent of Syrians in the hills of Samaria. All the bands were very loosely grouped in a shaky organization under the Arab League.

They had some real advantages. As initiators of most of the actions, they could name their own tactics. They were in the center of a great semicircle of contiguous Arab states, the borders of which were open to unimpeded infiltration into Palestine. Most of the hill and mountain country was in their hands. They had, at the outset of the fighting, a marked superiority in numbers and in weapons. It was a tradition among the Arabs that every adult should possess some kind of lethal weapon. They knew the country intimately, and most of them learned the use of weapons from early youth. The physique of the Palestinian Arab was on the whole good; he lived a hardy life in the open air which prepared him for military service. Many of the Arabs knew some of the Jewish villages well, having worked there as laborers.

Most important of all, they had at all times the passive, and sometimes the active, help of the British. No effort was made to check their movements across the frontiers. Arab desertions, with weapons, from the police force were not checked; the border police, which was 95 per cent Arab, was dissolved and allowed to join the armed bands with full equipment. Some of the deserters were British; on March 10, a British spokesman stated that 233 British soldiers and police had deserted since January 1. Nearly all of these men are believed to have joined the Arab gangs. Fulfillment of existing contracts to supply arms to the Arab states from Britain itself meant a steady and continuing supply of weapons.

They had disadvantages too. Family and clan feuds made even local co-operation difficult and a unified high command impossible. Local Arabs were often on bad terms with volunteers from across the borders; there were ugly memories of the unofficial levies and the confiscation of livestock which similar volunteer bands had brought in the riots of 1936-39. Most of the Arabs who fought privately owned their own weapons. They were good individual fighters, but had had little training as soldiers. Their officers in the higher ranks were often political adventurers rather than military men, and they had practically no lower echelons of noncommissioned officers.

In addition, the mind of the Arab fighter was not entirely on the business in hand. In many cases he had been induced to join the ranks by promises of pillage and loot, and often he endangered oper-

ations by taking advantage of any opportunities for such diversions.
To all this must be added the lack of initiative engendered in the
Arab by the semifeudal system under which he lived, and his il-
literacy and lack of education. The owners of orange groves were
not delighted to lose their labor force at harvest time, and the
ordinary fellaheen wanted to get their crops in the ground.

On the Jewish side, the initial effort was inevitably to safeguard
the lives of Jews, to speed the process of delimitation of Jewish and
Arab areas, and to open up communications between Jewish quarters. Inside Jerusalem, this meant a long series of short, sharp
engagements, punctuated by riots and explosions, while we tried to
prepare the city for the decisive ordeal which was clearly ahead.

The riot on Tuesday, December 2, which has already been mentioned, showed us how little help we could expect from the British,
who were still claiming responsibility for law and order. By nightfall that day the Commercial Center, a small compound of Jewish
warehouses and stores just outside the Jaffa Gate to the Old City,
had been looted and burned. Forty shops were destroyed. The police had not stopped the rioters, but they had arrested sixteen Hagana men on arms charges. When Mrs. Meyerson saw the Chief Secretary, the High Commissioner's top official, on the same day on
behalf of the Jewish Agency, she showed him photographs of the
police officer responsible for the area watching with folded arms
the Arab looting. The Chief Secretary remarked to her that the
pictures seemed to prove that the police had done nothing, and he
promised to make an inquiry. There the matter ended.

That same evening, our commanders were assembled and told
that in the future they should not hesitate to open fire in similar
situations. We also began attacking buildings serving as centers of
armed Arabs. Orders were not to take the initiative, not to waste ammunition, and not to fire when this might lead to discovery of
arms by the British. Both sides were fighting on a hit-and-run basis.
We blew up a flour mill in Bet Safafa which was a center of Arab
fighting, and a soda-water factory near the entrance to Romema,
and the Supreme Moslem Council headquarters near the American
Colony.

One of their centers which troubled us most was at Sheikh Jarrah,
where the Arabs were in position to fire on the road to Mount Scopus and the Hadassah Hospital. We had to move doctors and
patients in armor-plated buses, and movement of students and faculty to the Hebrew University became impossible. The university

closed its doors on Mount Scopus on December 31; they have not yet been reopened. On January 13, we carried out Operation Jebussi, an attempt to reopen the Mount Scopus road. Hagana forces captured both Sheikh Jarrah and the Police Training School. Then the British intervened and we surrendered both points to the British on their promise not to permit armed Arabs into the area. The promise was not kept. Sheikh Jarrah was turned over to the Arabs forty-eight hours after we withdrew.

Similar actions took place at this time against the Arab villages of Bet Safafa and Sur Baher, where constant Arab sniping was directed at the Jews of the Mekor Hayim quarter and Talpiot. My elder daughter, a Hagana soldier, fought in the trenches facing Bet Safafa. The struggle here was relentless day after day and night after night, with constant sniping and intermittent sorties to blow up buildings or throw grenades at each other. Early in January a special conference of Jewish Agency leaders, Hagana commanders and experts on Arab affairs had produced a change in our tactics. Henceforth we would take sharp retributive action in every zone where we were subject to attack. We still would not take the initiative against any area which did not serve as a base or training center, and we would choose fewer and heavier punitive actions rather than minor reprisals. Most significant of all, we decided that in the event of action by the British the Hagana in future would not hesitate to open fire.

This new policy made possible slow but gradual consolidation of the scattered Jewish quarters of new Jerusalem and restricted Arab freedom to launch attacks. One of our chief goals was to eliminate a hotbed of armed Arabs in Katamon, a well-to-do residential quarter from which almost constant sniping was directed at Rehaviah and at Kiryat Shmuel. So, on January 5, the Hagana blew up one of the Arab headquarters there, the Semiramis Hotel, during a torrential thunderstorm in the middle of the night. It was a terrific explosion which blew out windows in the entire area. A party of Royal Engineers joined in the rescue work; at least eleven people were killed and four were missing. By the end of the month, we had blown up another center of snipers in Katamon, the Shahin House, but we did not succeed in dislodging the Arabs from all of Katamon until the British evacuation.

Another outlying quarter in which there was bitter large-scale fighting throughout the struggle was Yemin Moshe. This quarter, situated to the east of the New City, facing Mount Zion and close

to the Jaffa Gate, was regarded by the Arabs as a possible springboard for an attempt to breach the Old City gates. They consequently kept it under constant attack and made extraordinary efforts
to capture and wipe it out.

The first large-scale attack was launched by the Arabs on
February 10. Attacking from the Commercial Center to the north,
a force of about 150 Arabs, steel-helmeted and in uniform, attacked
the quarter for six hours. They were the best guerrilla fighters in
the neighborhood; the action had been planned to offset a fall in
Arab morale resulting from a number of local military developments, especially the blowing up by the Stern Gang of an Arab
building near the Jaffa Gate the day before. Covering fire was provided for the attackers. One of them tried to carry in explosives, but
a Hagana sharpshooter picked him off, detonating the dynamite
and killing five Arabs, wounding nine others. This was one engagement in which British troops fulfilled their duty by joining in the
action against the attackers. Sixteen Arabs were killed and fifty-nine
wounded, including Sheikh Yassin Abu Bakri, then Arab commander in the Old City.

Engagements like this were less important during the early months
of 1948 than a series of explosions which literally rocked the city
and which were clearly designed to shock the Jewish population and
break its morale. The first of these, on February 1, completely
wrecked the building on Hassolel Street of the *Palestine Post,* an
English-language paper of moderate Zionist views and a determined opponent of terrorism. The explosion was caused by an
army-type car filled with dynamite which had been parked next to
the building. Surrounding buildings caught fire, the streets were
covered by a sea of broken glass. The newspaper managed to publish, in abridged and stencil form. The Arabs denied responsibility
for this action to foreign correspondents, and although no conclusive evidence could be produced it was widely believed even by
non-Jews that British policemen had done the job.

There was no question of British responsibility for the next
major outrage. A squad of British soldiers, carrying out a search
for arms in the Bet Israel quarter on February 13, arrested four
young Hagana men and marched them not to the nearby police
station but to a purely Arab neighborhood outside the Damascus
Gate. There the sergeant major in charge released them, unarmed,
in the middle of a mob of rioting Arabs. They were murdered in
cold blood; their bodies were found an hour later.

The Jewish community was shocked at this act, but also deeply angered. British authorities recognized their responsibility, and the commanding general ordered a full and immediate investigation. But the principal consequence of the atrocity was an immediate order by Hagana in Jerusalem to its members "from now on to resist with arms any attempt by British forces to search for weapons or to make arrests, unless those forces are accompanied by Jewish police."

Ten days later, on February 22, at ten minutes past six on a Sunday morning, three trucks loaded with dynamite exploded on Ben Yehuda Street in the center of new Jerusalem. Six-story buildings crumbled, others caught fire, the street looked as if it had been heavily bombed from the air. It took more than twenty-four hours to complete rescue work; fifty-two dead were found and 123 persons were wounded.

This explosion produced almost mass hysteria against the British. The Arabs were quick to deny any connection with the crime. A handbill appeared in the streets a few days later signed by British fascists declaring that they were responsible, but Sir Oswald Mosley was reported to have disclaimed this. David Rees Williams, Parliamentary Under-Secretary for Colonial Affairs, announced immediately in the House of Commons, "Since the Government does not believe the allegations that British troops were involved, there is no question of an inquiry at this time."

On behalf of the Jewish Agency, I appointed a commission of inquiry of three leading lawyers, one of whom is today the president of Israel's Supreme Court. After a thorough and public investigation, they reported that the crime had clearly been committed by Britishers. The convoy of trucks had been seen by many witnesses to be British, operated by British personnel. Whose orders were being followed could not be discovered, and it was possible that the trucks were among the many vehicles being reported "missing" at that time by British authorities, and their drivers among the more than two hundred deserters who had already joined the Arab forces.

Evidence has since come to light in John Phillips' recently published book *Odd World*. The author, a *Life* photo-reporter who was with the Arab Legion in May 1948, writes about a British soldier he met at Abdullah el Tel's headquarters in the Old City, presumably a deserter. The soldier told Phillips, "I pulled Ben Yehuda," and complained that the Mufti had "refused to pay me the five hundred pounds he had promised."

While the organized Jewish forces were trying to clear the debris and help the victims, Etzel and Stern Gang gunmen went out looking for any Britishers they could find; they killed ten and wounded twenty. More important was an immediate decision that Hagana members would no longer conceal their arms. The Jewish Agency met the same day and on my proposal decided to demand of the High Commissioner that Britishers should no longer enter Jewish parts of the city. By nightfall, British troops had been withdrawn to the security zones and the northern outskirts. They never appeared again in Jewish parts of Jerusalem, other than the main thoroughfares, except by permission of Hagana officers.

Another wholesale murder took place on March 11 when an automobile of the United States Consulate General, flying the American flag, drove into the carefully guarded courtyard of the Jewish Agency and the Vaad Leumi. Since the guard on duty recognized the car and its Christian Arab driver and knew it to be of the American consulate, he did not search it. The driver, named Anton Daoud, managed to slip out of the premises and was next heard of in Venezuela. Soon after he parked the car in front of one of the buildings there was a terrific explosion which tore down part of the building, killed thirteen persons, including the veteran Zionist leader Dr. Leib J. Yaffe, one of the founders of the Keren Hayesod (Palestine Foundation Fund), and wounded one hundred others. The U.S. consulate expressed their deep regret at the occurrence, and the consul who delivered their letter added that he knew the driver personally and found it difficult to believe that a man of his rather limited intelligence could have planned all the details. We could only agree that there was undoubtedly a directing hand behind such acts.

By the end of March even the Arabs must have begun to wonder if the Jews could be shocked, intimidated and demoralized into abandoning our plan to accept partition and make it work. The Jewish settlements had held their own. Not a single Jewish village had been abandoned. Hagana's call-up of men and women had now enrolled 21,000 young people between the ages of seventeen and twenty-five. We were learning to manufacture simple weapons for ourselves, and, more important, arms were on their way from Czechoslovakia. A Jewish air force now had thirty light planes for scouting duty and the supplying of isolated points. A United Nations report listed the total casualties in Palestine from December 1 to April 3 at 6,187. One third of them were dead. More Arabs had been killed, according to these figures, than Jews, and there had been 430 British casualties. Nevertheless when, at the end of March, the Security Council called for a truce, the Arabs ignored the appeal while the Jews announced they were ready to agree.

What the Arabs did not know, or appreciate, was our real weakness in Jerusalem. As early as February, serious shortages of meat, fish, milk, eggs, fresh vegetables and fruit had become common. Electricity was erratic and kerosene in very short supply. By the third week of March, a food convoy failed completely, for the first time, to get through to the city. Jerusalem was now truly besieged. By the end of the month it was fair to say that only two weeks' supply of emergency foodstuffs stood between Jerusalem and starvation.

As early as January, I had a survey made of the food supply situation in the city and a table drawn up by nutrition experts of Jewish Jerusalem's weekly needs item by item. The report I received showed that stocks of food in the city were very low and that any break in the supply line could cause real hunger in a very short time. The basic reason, of course, was that the mounting hostilities had cut us off from the Arab countryside which had traditionally produced and sold much of the food eaten in Jerusalem. As head of the Jerusalem Emergency Committee, I knew that this threat required us to build up reserves of foodstuffs. But neither the committee nor I had enough authority to overcome the inevitable inertia, the factional and personal rivalries and the outright opposition which we encountered.

One of the chief difficulties, for example, lay in the attitude of the tradesmen. They refused in these early months of the year to lay in stocks for two or three weeks unless they were given an assurance in advance that they could sell at whatever prices they wished in the event of a scarcity. They feared price control, and they demanded that the authorities finance the laying in of supplies. No solution to this problem had been found by either the Jewish Agency or the Vaad Leumi, to which it was referred. But even if financing had been available there were no warehouses organized to supply the scattered Jewish districts of the city. New local stores would have to be established, new guard systems for the warehouses and transport between them, and a system of rationing and price control, unpopular as these might be.

We could count on the railroad even less than on the highway to

Tel Aviv. There were daily sabotage and looting, and nightly attacks by armed Arab bands. In one instance, they stole five freight cars of canned milk destined for the British Army. No one was arrested. The loot was attractive. It involved little risk. Sometimes Arabs took leisurely hours to transfer goods from a derailed train into their trucks. Our pleading with the British authorities to let us provide escorts on the trains was completely unavailing. During the 1936-39 disorders, the Arabs had tried the same game and it was stopped quickly by the employment of a few hundred Jewish supernumerary police. But now the British refused to do this; their own energies were too completely concentrated on their sea blockade of our coast, the hunting down of immigrants who managed to slip through the blockade, and interference with our efforts to defend ourselves and establish an economic base for the new state envisaged by the United Nations.

The situation with the road to Tel Aviv, which was our lifeline, was no better. At first there were occasional spasmodic efforts to clear the road by British military action for a few days at a time. But these soon petered out. The British authorities refused to drive the armed bands out of the hills which controlled the road, to convoy and protect traffic themselves, or to allow us to arm our convoys. It took several months before they gave up confiscating the arms of Hagana convoys and before they allowed the Jewish supernumerary police, who were paid by us, to use their eighteen armored cars to patrol the roads.

So by the end of March it was clear that the problem would be solved by Jews or not at all. I was in Tel Aviv on April 10 for a meeting of the Zionist General Council and to attend personally to some supply and convoy problems. My journey from Jerusalem had been full of portent of the new trials ahead. We traveled in an armored bus which was fired on by Arabs. At one point, the bus and the convoy stopped and through the peepholes I could watch our armed escort climbing the hillside to drive off an Arab band which was attacking us.

At ten o'clock that night I attended a meeting of the Jewish Agency Executive over which Ben Gurion was presiding. He outlined the security situation and expressed the fear that Jerusalem was likely to be completely cut off from the rest of the country. It might be for weeks and it might be for months. He was aware of what my committee had done to prepare stocks for the city. But the position was still unsatisfactory. In consequence, Ben Gurion continued, Jerusalem was in a state bordering on hunger. The last food convoy, not a large one, had taken ten days to reach Jerusalem. The Arabs had concentrated their forces around the city. We had succeeded by dint of a great effort in freeing the road, but food was not brought in. There seemed to be no prospect of getting food, as there was no one person responsible for dealing with the problem. There were no trucks, no drivers. He doubted whether Jerusalem had enough food for a fortnight. He was afraid that our struggle to open the road would have been in vain if matters were not put right. We must get the food by force if there was no other way, and there must be someone responsible for this. The frame of mind of people in Jerusalem gave him cause for concern. Jerusalem was not an easy city from the point of view of the composition of its population. The spirit of the people was of prime political significance. If we did not see to it that Jerusalem got a large-sized convoy of food within a couple of days, our military effort would have been wasted.

I intervened here to explain the difficulties. Truck owners would not risk their trucks going to Jerusalem unless they were insured against damage or destruction of their vehicles. Wholesalers would not supply food if they were not guaranteed against loss by enemy action or price control. There was a shortage of vehicles since Tel Aviv had been cut off by the British from Haifa and the north as a punitive measure for certain terrorist acts, and many Tel Aviv trucks could not return from Haifa.

Ben Gurion continued: Could we make an *ad hoc* arrangement so that it would be possible to confiscate, to expropriate, to enlist vehicles and men, to give guarantees that vehicles lost would be paid for, to do everything necessary to get the convoys to Jerusalem? We had to make two decisions at once. First, we had to find a man to carry the responsibility with full power to make decisions. Second, we must appropriate 100,000 Palestine pounds (in 1948 the value of a Palestine pound was $4.02)—Jerusalem was worth that amount to us—and an appropriation without a cent in cash would not do. This man must have authority to enter into financial obligations, to requisition vehicles and to enlist drivers.

It was thereupon decided that I be given full powers to procure the necessary supplies for Jerusalem and to get them there. Power to requisition, furnish guarantees and give undertakings would be in my terms of reference. If truck drivers had to be conscripted with their vehicles by Hagana, this too would be included in my authority. Ben Gurion then asked, Would I be prepared to assume this responsibility? I answered in the affirmative. "At once?" asked Ben Gurion. "At once," I answered, and we both understood the words literally.

The task was placed squarely on my shoulders. I had full and unlimited powers. Others could and would advise me and had been doing so already. But the burden of decision was now mine alone, and on those decisions might well depend the issue as to whether Jerusalem would be part of the Jewish state that was to come into being in one month's time. The Eternal City of my people, founded by King David nearly three thousand years ago, was in peril. Twice it had been destroyed, once in the days of Nebuchadnezzar two and a half millenniums ago, and again by the Roman general Titus in the year 70. Its people had been driven forth under the bloody spur of the Roman conquerors. For nearly two millenniums it had languished, while they were in exile praying for its welfare in an anguish of longing. Now, after two generations of backbreaking toil and courageous effort, it was being won back again. Jerusalem was once more in danger and I was called to the duty of trying to assure its safety and welfare.

For years I had not been a formally religious Jew who prayed three times a day with his face turned toward the ruined wall where the ancient Temple stood. The modern world had claimed me for its own. Nevertheless, I had lived most of my life in Jerusalem and had devoted most of my waking energies and a large part of my dreams to the restoration of the nationhood of my people. I think that for many of my generation these activities took up and sublimated the spiritual demands which other Jews had for so many centuries satisfied by prayer. But at that moment I felt the wings of Providence fluttering over me and my whole being became a prayer that I should succeed in my task.

It was nearly midnight, but committees were still in session. I went to the offices of the Sherut Haklali, of Tel Aviv, an emergency volunteer group made up of older Hagana members not liable for active service. I asked for a room and sat down to work with several of their ranking members. I sent at once for the top officials of the Jewish Agency's transport department and for certain Hagana men.

The first thing was to make a quick survey of all food supplies in stock in Tel Aviv, with lists of wholesalers and their supplies. The transport men were given the job of assembling one hundred trucks, using Hagana men if necessary to requisition them. I drew up a preliminary list of supplies we needed in Jerusalem, and details were worked out of how to get them. If we could receive the consent of owners, well and good; if not, we would requisition them, dividing the burden fairly among the wholesalers. It was two o'clock in the morning before we had mapped out the first job and assigned everyone to his share of it.

Jewish legend tells us that when our patriarch Jacob was about to cross the brook Jabbok, with the dark angel with whom he had just struggled behind him and his brother Esau waiting for him with murder in his heart on the farther bank, he still did not neglect to ferry the small and imponderable things over the stream. And such imponderables counted in our discussions that evening.

"What about cigarettes, Dr. Joseph?" asked one of the committee, just as we began to breathe a sigh of relief that the long list approached completion.

"Cigarettes? It's food we need. It would be criminal to waste three valuable tons of load on cigarettes."

"You say that because you are a nonsmoker, Dr. Joseph," he demurred stoutly.

I realized that I was in a dilemma and that, no matter how right I might be on logical grounds, I was hardly in a position to judge. I did not smoke, but most Jerusalemites did. So I called in five smokers from the next room and put the question to them very bluntly.

"Are we entitled to use up convoy space and risk the lives of men just to send cigarettes to Jerusalem?"

The answer was unanimous. "Send some cigarettes!"

I was very surprised at the verdict of this impromptu jury, but the cigarettes were included. Only later during the siege, when I saw even respectable residents of Jerusalem scanning the sidewalks and gutters for cigarette butts, did I feel convinced that a right decision had been made.

The next few days my time was taken up with forming a working committee in Tel Aviv of loyal men who were deeply concerned for the fate of Jerusalem. This committee would draw against the Jewish Agency in purchasing supplies and in taking over trucks in which to convoy them. None of the negotiations turned out to be quick or easy. One large wholesaler, I remember, was willing to recognize the priority of Jerusalem's need for his supplies, but he wanted some security for the six thousand Palestine pounds involved. This was a large sum in those days. I needed the supplies badly and at once. He wanted either cash or a promissory note by

the Jewish Agency. I explained that I could not furnish such a note
quickly. He looked obstinate.

"All right," I said, "I'll tell you what I'll do. I'll give you my personal note, and if we both live through the war I'll pay you."

The effect was extraordinary. I thought he was going to have a
fit as he started to protest in a purple rage. At last I got the drift of
what he was trying to say. Who wanted notes? My personal word
was good enough. Who asked for notes? Who said he was not as
good a Zionist as anyone else, anywhere in the country? Jerusalem was as much his as it was anybody else's.

In most instances, we got what we needed without having to use
too much pressure. But it all took time and patience, and time was
one commodity we could neither buy nor requisition.

I waited until news came that our first convoy had reached Jerusalem safely. But when I wanted to go myself, to push the Jerusalem end of my new job, I was told that the road had been cut
again and that Hagana would not allow any vehicles to pass until a
new operation had been successful against the Arab villages which
blocked the route. But I had to be back in Jerusalem, and the fact
that the road was cut only made this more urgent. Special arrangements were therefore put in hand to get me there. In the same fix
were Yitzhak Ben Zvi, the president of Vaad Leumi and later to be
the second President of Israel, and the late Rabbi Meir Bar-Ilan,
leader of the religious Zionists throughout the world. We were
taken in a Piper Cub plane to the Dead Sea. Such a load in a small
aircraft was neither comfortable nor very secure. We touched down
on a small improvised airstrip near the potash works on the northern shore. There we were to join a convoy which traveled without
interference by the Arabs because the British were interested in the
potash getting to Jerusalem smoothly, to be transported thence by
rail to Haifa for shipment on to England.

By the time we arrived, that day's convoy had already set out, and
we were lodged overnight in the workers' camp. The men were
eager to hear our story of developments in Tel Aviv, and we were
moved by the account of their experience, isolated as they were in
an Arab environment. They had sweated and toiled for years to get
the potash works going and they were determined to keep it in
operation and to defend it to the last.

The next morning we were accommodated in a light armored car
belonging to the company, cooped up very uncomfortably with
some workers who also had business in Jerusalem. Our escort was

a guard of British police who were friendly with the potash workers —so the latter told us. This gave us a feeling of security. The rest of the convoy consisted of a number of trucks loaded with potash and the vehicle carrying the British escort.

We rode along smoothly enough until, some seven miles from Jerusalem, the convoy stopped with a jerk. Presently we heard someone knocking on the rear door of our armored car. We looked through the peephole and saw that it was a British policeman. We opened up. He told us that an Arab gang had set up a roadblock and established a strong point beside the highway. The officer in charge of the convoy was at that moment negotiating with the leaders of the gang to allow the vehicles to pass. He warned us that if the Arabs found out that there were Jewish leaders in the convoy it would be impossible to get through without a battle. We were heavily outnumbered. He therefore warned us that no matter how long we had to wait we should keep out of sight. We were not to risk detection by even getting near the peephole.

It was a bad moment. We could not go forward nor could we reverse, for the Arabs had selected the spot for their block with great skill and the road was too narrow to reverse the convoy. Our lives depended on the British guard and their good will and good faith. We had plenty of solid reasons to suspect both. Relations between us and the British were very strained and every British policeman was thoroughly acquainted with the anti-Jewish policies of his authorities.

The wait was only a half hour, but to us, self-imprisoned and apprehensive in the overcrowded, stifling armored car, it seemed like an eternity. At last the convoy moved on and we reached Jerusalem without further incident.

JERUSALEM - Old City

1 Wailing Wall
2 Church of the Holy Sepulchre
3 Zion Gate
4 Dung Gate
5 Jaffa Gate
6 New Gate
7 Damascus Gate
8 Herod's Gate
9 St. Stephen's Gate
10 Golden Gate
11 Church of the Cross
12 Hurva Synagogue
13 Yochanan Ben Zakkai Syn.
14 Nissan Beck Synagogue
15 Stambuli Synagogue
16 Street of the Jews
17 Matzot Factory
18 Via Dolorosa
19 Batei Mahse
20 Misgav Ledah Hospital
21 Bethel St.
22 David's Tower
23 Gethsemane
24 David St.
25 Citadel
26 Police Barracks
27 Kahana Position
28 Karliner Synagogue
29 Chabad St.

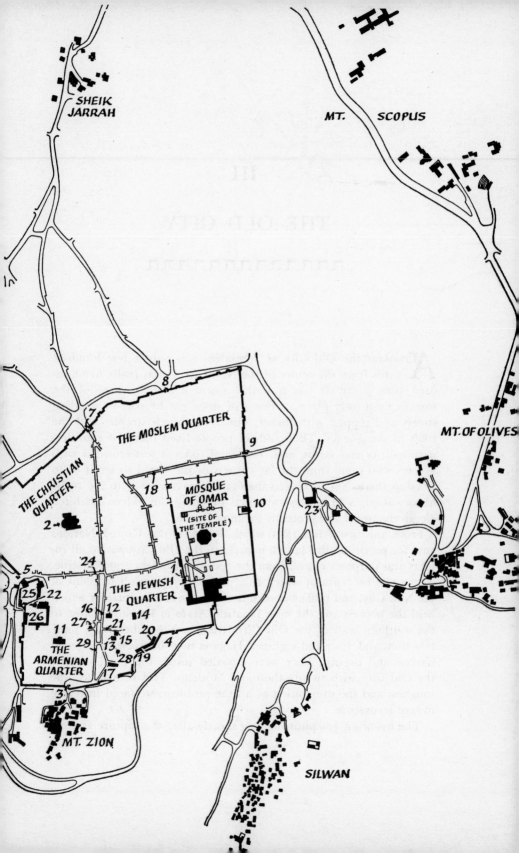

SHEIK
JARRAH

MT. SCOPUS

MT. OF OLIVES

8

7

THE MOSLEM QUARTER

9

THE CHRISTIAN
QUARTER

18

MOSQUE
OF OMAR

(SITE OF
THE TEMPLE)

10

2

23

24

1

5

THE JEWISH
QUARTER

25 22

16 12 14

26

27 21

11   20

29   15

13   4

28 19

17

3

MT. ZION

SILWAN

THE
ARMENIAN
QUARTER

III

THE OLD CITY

ⅠⅬⅬⅬⅬⅬⅬⅬⅬⅬⅬⅬⅬⅬⅬⅬⅬⅬⅬⅬ

ALTHOUGH the Old City of Jerusalem was only a few hundred yards from the center of the New City, it was really five hundred years away. It was a walled town, a citadel, some of the world's most holy places, a forest of stone cut by narrow winding streets and topped with domes, minarets, church steeples and the roofs of synagogues. Thousands of people lived there, of countless nationalities and faiths, and in normal times it was crowded with visitors who came from the far corners of the world to see it or to worship there. Yet its chief inhabitant always seemed to me to be history itself, a brooding awareness of being the oldest inhabited city in the world and probably the most famous.

From the first Arab riots which followed the United Nations vote for partition, the Jewish quarter in the Old City was to all intents and purposes cut off from the rest of Jerusalem and Palestine. There was no point at which it adjoined any Jewish-held point of the New City, and traffic between them had to cross a corridor which held the poorest and the most fanatical Arabs of Palestine. Close to the southern wall of the Old City lived, in November 1947, some two thousand Jews and eighteen Hagana men between the ages of sixteen and twenty. They were crowded inside the small area of the Old City with twenty thousand Moslems. This constituted the toughest and the unhappiest of all the problems we faced in trying to save Jerusalem.

The historian Josephus, writing shortly after the capture and destruction of Jerusalem in the year 70 of this era, gave a brief history of the Old City of Jerusalem up to his time:

It had been taken five times before, though this was the second time of its desolation; for Shishak, the king of Egypt, and after him Antiochus and after him Pompey, and after them Sosius and Herod took the city, but still preserved it. But before all these, the king of Babylonia conquered it, and made it desolate, one thousand four hundred and sixty-eight years and six months after it was built.

And from King David, who was the first of the Jews who reigned therein, to the destruction under Titus, were one thousand one hundred and seventy-nine years . . . yet hath not its great antiquity, nor its vast riches, nor the diffusion of its nation over the habitable earth, nor the greatness of the veneration paid to it on a religious account, been sufficient to preserve it from being destroyed. And thus ended the siege of Jerusalem.

The Romans razed the walls. Part of the western wall of the Temple that Herod rebuilt was left standing and still stands to this day. Following a revolt under Bar Kochba, some sixty years after the destruction by Titus, the Emperor Hadrian gave orders that what was left of the Jewish city be completely obliterated and plowed over as a symbolic act signifying the end of the city for all time.

Yet as the generations passed, life, and some Jews, returned. They clustered around the ruins of the Temple. They had no political ambitions. They were content to live in the direst poverty and in the most perilous conditions, if only they could kiss the last sacred stones that remained of the Temple of their former glory. Centuries of history rolled over them. The heathen Romans went and Christian Roman emperors succeeded them, men whom a fanatical early Church convinced that the presence of Jews on the holiest site of Christianity was an abomination. The plight of the Jews in Jerusalem went from bad to worse. In almost every generation Jews paid with their lives for their religious beliefs. But they clung to their hopeless lives of grinding poverty beneath the shadow of the Wall, awaiting the coming of the Messiah who would redeem them and restore the Temple. Then they, the remnant that survived, would be right there to enter into their kingdom.

The Byzantine Christian emperors faded away before the rising power of Islam, which succeeded to the rule of Jerusalem. The Jews who still remained enjoyed a greater toleration for a while and their numbers increased, although they were inferior in the eyes of the law. The dynastic struggles of the Moslem world undermined their position as each new conqueror massacred and pillaged, and the more fanatical sects again wrote their fury in the blood of the Jews of Jerusalem. At the end of the eleventh century Jerusalem was conquered by the Crusaders, who massacred all the Jews and Moslems they found in the city, and the thread of Jewish settlement in it was broken for a time. But when the Crusaders' rule ended the Jews again made their way into the city. The great Jewish traveler of the Middle Ages, Benjamin of Tudela, visited the city about the year 1170 and found some Jews living there. With the city's conquest by Saladin, the Jews again settled in Jerusalem. Since then Jews have always lived there. In the thirteenth century the Jewish population increased considerably by large immigration from England and France. The chain of conquests continued and the situation of the Jews changed from conqueror to conqueror.

In 1260 the Tartars captured and destroyed the city and the Jews had to flee for their lives. Seven years later the famous Jewish scholar and philosopher Nachmanides came from Spain to settle in Jerusalem. He built a synagogue and was joined by some of the Jews who had fled.

So the narrative went on. The Jews clung desperately to Jerusalem, and gradually, as the centuries passed, they concentrated in a series of courtyards not far from the Wailing Wall and in the shadow of the Temple area. Each expulsion in the greater world brought more homecomers who felt that if the world outside held only the promise of wandering, exile and death, they might just as well seek what precarious safety life held within the precincts of the ancient Temple. The Old City of Jerusalem gradually developed a collection of Jewish communities from all parts of the globe: from Spain and the lands of North Africa, from Persia, along the road from Samarkand, from Bokhara, from Kurdistan, from Yemen and other Arab lands. They came from Greece and Turkey and Germany and Italy, and from the countries of Central and Eastern Europe. Many spoke a kind of derivative language of old Castilian, called Ladino, a heritage of the days of the glory of Spanish Jewry. Others spoke Judaeo-German or Yiddish, some spoke Aramaic or Persian, while Arabic was the language of those from Arab lands. In two things they were united: their reverence for the law as interpreted by the rabbis and their prayers in the holy tongue of Hebrew for the restoration, by a miraculous act of God, of the Temple around whose ruin all their orisons were concentrated.

In the middle of the nineteenth century some elements of modernity crept in and a few of the more daring Jews went outside the walls and established houses and suburbs in what is today new Jerusalem. They were helped by Sir Moses Montefiore of England and by the estate of Judah Turo, the American patriot. By November 1947 Jerusalem, within the walled city, was almost exclusively a spiritual center. The drift away from the narrow confines of the Old City had gone on steadily until there remained for the most part the ultra-orthodox to whom life anywhere but in the shadow of the Temple ruins was inconceivable. The constant attacks by Arabs since the 1929 riots and the general insecurity of life in an area largely dominated by Arabs had forced the exit of many who would otherwise have stayed.

For some of those Old City Jews the political struggle in the days of the mandate had possessed no meaning. They were removed from the secular strife and ambitions of the powers on this earth. It was all one to them whether Arab or Christian, Turk or Briton, ruled. There was only one king they recognized, the King of Kings, and only one dominion which interested them, that of the Messiah whom God would send in His own good time. If anything, the pretensions of Jews to rule in the Holy Land irritated them most, for they thought that Jews should not impatiently forestall what God alone would bring about only when He saw fit. These were only a minority of the Old City community, but their point of view expressed the feeling of many Old City Jews toward the new Jews of Palestine and, later, of Israel. They could not understand the hatless and beardless youths and the carefree girls with their short pants and short sleeves who took the holy language of prayer and turned it into the profane speech of the market place and the workshop. As things turned out, this had some effect on the morale of these young people when they came to defend the inhabitants against Arab attacks. Many of them felt that they were fighting for people who did not share the sense of urgency in the struggle for the restoration of Jewish nationhood.

The Jews who inhabited the Jewish quarter had almost no productive life there. There were numerous cabalists, dreamers and others who lived like the sparrows on the rooftops and took no thought of material things. Sometimes they sent out emissaries to solicit donations from Jews abroad. This system, which financed the necessities of life for most of these Jews, was called *haluka,* which means what it literally was, a handout.

Later, the development of the New City outside the walls and the efforts of farsighted philanthropists like Sir Moses Montefiore to establish small industries and other forms of viable economic life for the Old City Jews brought some change. A few began to work for their living, doing handicrafts, working in trades in the New City and engaging in retail business. With the advent of the Zionists the trend away from *haluka* began to influence the ways of the younger generation. But the events of November 1947 found a great proportion of the Jews of the quarter still living in great poverty, on charity. Many spent their whole time in the study of the Law or in associations for the purpose of praying and reciting the Psalms.

The streets of the quarter were narrow and crooked and some of them very steep. Many were vaulted over so that the sunlight rarely penetrated. Sanitary conditions were primitive. The houses consisted of low, square, domed rooms built around open courts. One could walk for several hundred meters on the roofs without having to touch the ground. The windows were heavily latticed and protected by iron screens. Shops were closed by massive wooden doors and iron bars.

The main buildings in the Jewish quarter were synagogues and Yeshivoth—institutions for rabbinical study. Some of the twenty-seven synagogues in the quarter were rich in historical associations. The Yohanan ben Zakkai Synagogue was supposed to have been built on the spot where the famous rabbi of that name prayed before going to see Vespasian, later Roman Emperor, at the time of his siege of Jerusalem. Two other synagogues nearby were the Stambuli and the Hurva Rabbi Yehuda Hechasid, the most sacred place of worship of the Ashkenazi Jews. Here, for example, were preserved the colors of the Jewish Legion, in which I and several Israeli leaders of today served when we first came to Palestine in 1918. This was the place where Sir Herbert Samuel, the First High Commissioner of Palestine (now Viscount Samuel), worshiped. Another important synagogue was the one called Nissan Bak, with interesting engravings on its walls, including a lion of Judah mourning the downfall of Israel.

This, then, was the area which we were determined to keep, if we could, for the new Jewish state. The whole quarter covered an area of something less than 450 by 325 yards, the equivalent of about fifteen American football fields. Located in the southern part

of the Old City and on the slope of Mount Zion, one of its boundaries was the wall between Zion Gate and the Dung Gate. The Moslem quarter lay directly to its north, and during the 1936-39 riots
the British had built concrete walls across many of the passages
which connected the two. An iron gate had been set up at the northern end of the Street of the Jews. On the east, empty lots separated
the quarter from the Mosque of Omar and the Wailing Wall,
which was about 160 yards from the nearest Jewish courtyard. Once
Jews had lived next to the Wall, but they had gradually been forced
to move farther away by the Arab disturbances. On the west, the
Jewish quarter was bounded by the Armenian quarter of the Old
City.

Disorders in the Old City began with an Arab demonstration on
December 1, accompanied by the stoning of Jewish homes and firing
at Jewish buses. The next day three Jews were shot through a break
in the concrete wall separating the Arab and Jewish quarters. On
December 8 two Jews were stabbed to death and an attempt was
made to break into a synagogue, and three days later Arabs set fire
to a Jewish house and tried to mob the quarter. Sniping by now had
become regular. Shops were forced to close, schools did not open,
sanitary services stopped functioning. The Arab attacks were designed to drive the Jews out of the Old City and physically to destroy the Jewish quarter.

After one night of violence and terror, the Armenian and Christian communities, which had lived in friendship with the Jews,
broke off contact with them. This cut the Jews off from their chief
intermediaries with the Arab venders of vegetables. Food could now
reach them only by convoy through Arab districts. The British supplied guards for the evacuation of Arabs from their homes in the
Jewish quarter and for those Jews who wished to move into the
New City. Those Jews who left said they did so because their livelihood was outside the Old City and they did not wish to eat the
bread of charity.

The technique of the Arab attacks on the Jewish quarter, in fact
the technique of fighting in the Old City in general, had not
changed much since the days of the Romans. The revolver and the
submachine gun replaced the bow and arrow, and the mortar the
ballista. The struggle remained one of fighting from house to house,
from window to window and from roof to roof. Each battle, of the

hundreds fought by day and by night during the six months the siege of the Old City lasted, was identical in principle and resembled the battles which had taken place throughout the centuries in such Eastern cities.

The Hagana command now made its preparations for the defense of the quarter. It was divided into two main sections; one comprised all the part eastward of the Street of the Jews and the other all the area sloping upward to the west of it.

The enemy consisted of members of Arab gangs. They took control of the Armenian quarter and used their mosques for military purposes. Later they were helped by the Arab Legion, which seized positions on Mount Zion and sniped over Zion Gate. British secret-service men could be seen moving about among the Arabs. Ten British policemen were stationed permanently in an Arab mill just opposite our Kahana position.

In general the Armenians remained neutral. They did, however, provide a number of spies for the Arabs. They walked about the Jewish quarter photographing our positions. The Assyrians, who lived mostly in the Armenian quarter, maintained strict neutrality.

The immediate Hagana problem was to increase its force inside the Old City from eighteen to at least 120 men. By private arrangement with a few British guards, two buses and three taxis entered the Jewish quarter on December 10 and their passengers quickly scattered to their positions. This was the only substantial reinforcement that was to arrive. The occasional bribing of another British guard or the introduction of personnel disguised as teachers or religious functionaries added only a handful more. The total number of armed defenders never exceeded 150 and eventually, by the attrition of war, fell far below that figure. The Arabs, of course, entered the Old City at their will without being searched.

Hagana arms were mainly revolvers, Sten guns and hand grenades. There were one 2-inch mortar with very few shells, one Lewis machine gun, about a dozen rifles, some explosives, wireless equipment and medical supplies. The Hadassah Medical Organization maintained a medical unit inside the quarter throughout the siege.

Some ammunition had been hidden in the Old City in advance. One of the chief caches, which included ten tommy guns, was a "slick" held by the Etzel, who obstinately refused to reveal its whereabouts to the defenders. This dissident organization at first refused to take orders from the Hagana commanders. They could not be utilized rationally. They often left positions that we thought were standing firm, without informing us beforehand. We were thus exposed unnecessarily to the danger of enemy infiltration. The conduct of all the members of the dissident organizations in the Old City highlighted the profound difference which exists between the organization of acts of terrorism and the steady, trained action required to defend or carry out the planned operations of a nation at war.

There were cases of British officers who behaved with strict correctness in the Old City, but these were eclipsed by the conduct of their fellow officers and N.C.O.s. The worst offenders seemed to be younger officers, especially second lieutenants. One famous British regiment, at the beginning of April, set a record of infamous conduct when a young lieutenant who had a particular hatred of Jews demanded the surrender of men who, he claimed, had fired at his positions. He was shown that the Jews could not possibly have fired, and that in fact they did not do so. His soldiers nevertheless began a search for arms. They murdered a Jew at prayer in his home, killed his daughter, robbed his home, butchered an insane woman and beat whomever they could lay their hands on. They brought their wounded to be treated by a Jewish doctor even while they were shelling the quarter; the doctor did his duty by the wounded.

A Hagana commander described the situation in the Old City when he spoke at the "Vocal Newspaper" of the Palestine Journalists' Association in Tel Aviv on January 24. "Little by little the Jews in the Old City are becoming accustomed to living under the Arab blockade and to the constant attacks," he said. "The enemy's intention has been to get them to the point where they would evacuate, but the people will not abandon the city." In one case a mother of ten children, who was cut off from her home, asked for a police escort to return and instead was offered an escort to bring her children out of the Old City. She refused.

We never solved the problem of supplying the Old City. At the end of December the Arabs set up roadblocks, manned by armed men, to stop all Jewish traffic into the Jewish quarter. The British authorities were responsible for these roadblocks, since their police stood by as the Arabs enforced their control of entry. It took the most agonizing negotiations to arrange for a British convoy to escort our trucks past these roadblocks. This was no military matter, but a straightforward political act: the British wanted the Jews out of the Old City and were prepared, if necessary, to starve them into leaving.

The distance the convoys had to travel was only a few hundred yards, and an operation would normally take from twenty to thirty minutes. The trucks, already loaded, were inspected by British police and Army. Three armored cars and a strong escort would convoy them to the Zion Gate, which was the gate the Arabs insisted be used for such convoys. The police inspector would unlock the gate from the inside and send a patrol to remove the bars the Arabs had set up outside. Then the trucks would back to the gate one by one and be unloaded very rapidly by some forty Jewish porters, who carried the goods another 150 yards to some of the houses where they were stored.

In the first five days of January, not an ounce of food entered the Old City. There was an acute shortage of kerosene for cooking and no milk whatsoever for the children. An official of the Jewish Agency who was inside the Old City reported that while the inhabitants of the Jewish quarter were not starving, they were completely isolated and contact had to be re-established. Jewish dead in the Old City had been unburied for five days. On the fifth of the month the matter was twice raised with the authorities. The government was asked to see that convoys went through at all costs, or they would have to be sent through under Jewish armed escort. The regular answer received from the British was that the matter was "delicate."

It was while these negotiations were going on that the Etzel decided to plant a bomb at the Arab National Guard outpost at the Jaffa Gate entrance to the Old City, which was blocking food convoys to the Jewish quarter. It killed fourteen Arabs and wounded forty others. While retreating, three of the Jews were shot dead by police and soldiers. This happened on January 7, which was the day the British had finally promised that a convoy would go through. Naturally, it did not pass that day. Negotiations continued without result. Finally our spokesman announced, "If you hear a loud explosion from the direction of the Old City, you can take it that we have blown a hole in the wall." It would have been no mean undertaking to make a hole in the Old City wall, which was some four yards thick at the top and about ten yards thick at ground level. But the announcement, made without histrionics, in cold, level terms, had its effect. The British promised to see to it that convoys passed through.

By the end of January it was arranged for three convoys a week to enter the Old City by the Zion Gate route. The British area commander, Brigadier C. P. Jones, told Major Chaim Herzog of Hagana, who negotiated the arrangement, that no persons could be convoyed, for fear that Hagana men might be sent in. He added his personal view that Hagana should be withdrawn entirely in order to reduce tension. Major Herzog, a former member of the English bar who is now chief of intelligence of the Israeli Army, pointed out that this would result in a general massacre, which would have taken place weeks before if Hagana had not been there to protect the residents.

The British tried for months to get Hagana out of the Old City. Their arms searches were more rigorous here than anywhere else. They arrested young men on the street, searched them, and released them only in the New City with no chance of re-entering the Jewish quarter. In such circumstances we had no scruples about smuggling in Hagana men and arms by every possible means. Sometimes weapons were disassembled and packed in with the food, but this was a risky business, involving the cancellation of a convoy when it was detected.

There was a real lack of co-ordination on the British side. For humanitarian reasons, their food-licensing authority allocated certain supplies of flour, rice and sugar to the Jewish residents of the Old City, but their Army refused to allow sufficient trucks through the gates to transport them. By February, fairly large quantities of these commodities had accumulated in the new-Jerusalem offices of the Vaad Leumi, to be consumed eventually by other Jews.

The British hope was that scarcity of food and able-bodied men would force Jewish evacuation. When a Jewish police sergeant reported to his British inspector that the Jews had no food in the Old City, the latter said, "Why don't they leave? I can get them all out safely in one day." He was told that, although short of food, the Jews had a good defense. "Do you think so?" was the reply. "It will end in a massacre." British policy was made crystal-clear in the middle of April when the High Commissioner invited Chief Rabbi Yitzhak Herzog to see him and insisted that the Jews leave the Old City. Rabbi Herzog replied that we could not do so, as we were trustees guarding the heritage of all past generations of Jews. This was a sacred trust.

We kept up pressure on the authorities to open a route to the Old City, since by refusing genuine residents permission to return to the Old City the authorities had separated wives from their husbands and mothers from their children. On January 25 we authorized Ben Zvi to try to secure from H. H. Pollock, the British District Commissioner, permission for teachers and kindergarten personnel to go in. At a press conference on February 1, I gave the lie to British public declarations that Jews were permitted to enter the Old City. I noted that Rabbi Yitzhak Ornstein, who was in charge of arrangements at the Wailing Wall, had been trying for weeks to return to the Old City and had not yet received permission. "We shall not forego the right of every Jew to have access to this place, holy to the entire Jewish people, and to pray there," I said. "It is the duty of the government, which still rules the country, to assure to the Jews access to the Old City and the Wailing Wall."

The pressure had some effect. Rabbi Ornstein was permitted to enter the Old City, together with ten other inhabitants who had been cut off from their families, with the convoy which went through the gate on February 16. On its return journey the convoy brought out the first products of the handicrafts workshops recently established by my committee. In the next convoy a Jewish social worker was allowed to enter. At the beginning of March an official British spokesman claimed that ninety persons had been taken into the Old City since February 6 and a total of 140 since the disorders began.

Considering our difficulties, it is not surprising that the Old City inhabitants frequently felt that they were being abandoned to their fate, a feeling which naturally lowered morale. Nor was it unreasonable for some Jewish leaders to conclude that the British had sinister designs as regards the Old City. Even the non-Zionist Jews, the Agudat Israel, realized this. Early in January, when the High Commissioner told them he was prepared to negotiate for peace in the Old City on condition that the Hagana men were withdrawn, they rejected the proposal, saying they had learned better from our experience in the 1929 Arab riots, when such conduct on our part, in reliance on similar British assurances, had resulted in the massacre of the Jews in Hebron.

But the inhabitants themselves grew more and more dejected. Those who had supplies of food began to sell them at exorbitant prices. Certain elements, mainly of the "Neturei Karta," the most extreme sect of ultra-orthodox Jews, started demonstrations, shouting that "the Hagana has eaten our food." It was an ugly period.

At this time (on January 4) I arranged for Major Colin Gluckman (later Gillon), formerly of South Africa and now Solicitor General of Israel, to go into the Old City to make a survey of the situation and to reassure the inhabitants. As a result of his report we were able to take some measures to ease the position of the civilians.

Although the Jerusalem Emergency Committee was not responsible for the military strategy of the defense of Jerusalem, the question of the possible evacuation of the Old City was discussed. There was never any question of giving up our claim to this part of Jerusalem. But there was no shadow of doubt that holding on to it enormously complicated our problems. From a military point of view, the Old City represented a dead loss of energy, supplies and men. From a supply point of view, it presented an insoluble problem. But I myself never considered evacuation. Even if we had attributed evacuation to the British failure to maintain order and to grant us access, it would have meant a heavy blow to Jewish morale and a great encouragement to the Arabs. The Old City meant too much to the Jews for us to evacuate it unless driven out by force of arms.

There was no organization inside the Old City through which we could work. Basically, nothing had changed in the political life of these Old City Jews for hundreds of years. Such public authority as existed was exercised nominally by a loose, badly run, irregular communal council which represented Jews who had come here from all over the world on the basis of the country or sometimes the city of their origin. People lived and worshiped in these separate clans, and their leaders were quarrelsome "notables" who used the council almost solely for acrimonious debate over questions of personal or clan prestige. The headman, or *mukhtar*, of the Jewish quarter was a real-estate broker named A. Mordechai Weingarten. The British administrators leaned heavily on him in all matters affecting the Old City. A native of Jerusalem, he was of medium height, round-faced, with beady eyes and a small, rounded brown beard, a man who managed to look obsequious and vain at the same time.

When the siege began, Mishmar Ha'am, the people's guard which did such yeoman work in new Jerusalem, consisted in the Old City of exactly one man. With schools and shops closed, children ran wild in the streets. Telephone communication with the New City was slow and jammed until January, when it broke down completely, leaving only the Hagana radio link, which was not available for civilian use. There were no jobs, no money and, worst of all, almost no food supplies.

This was the situation in which my committee had to work. I was convinced at once that we could work only through Hagana. This was to prove extremely difficult, since Hagana was not officially there. Our only alternative was to allow Weingarten to control the distribution of food and other essential supplies, which would have given him control over the morale of the population. So, in February, we smuggled in a new Hagana commander, Avraham Halperin, in the guise of a medical orderly, to deal with both military and civil affairs. He was an excellent man for the job and in my opinion might possibly have changed the fate of the Old City if he could have stayed. A teacher by profession, he had been in charge of religious services for Hagana for a long time. He was a tall, ascetic-looking man, with a blond beard and blue eyes. He knew the Old City intimately; he could find his way through most of the Jewish quarter beneath ground, through cellars or over the roofs. He also had real ability as an organizer, and the power of quick decision. He was a courageous and truly religious man and thus acceptable to the inhabitants as well as the fighters.

He found a demoralized population, which had already fallen to 1,700 in number, and a Hagana company whose spirits and morale were fairly good. He decided wisely to concentrate first on the civilians. His first step was to organize a series of meetings to explain the situation to the inhabitants. This led at once to an expansion of the one-man Mishmar Ha'am; he obtained fourteen recruits at first, with part-time help from others, and was able to organize a civil guard in three regular watches to check Arab infiltration, to keep the streets clean and to control the prices of commodities against profiteering. These men wore armbands and black berets designating their organization and were recognized as legitimate by the British.

The distribution of food was now reorganized. The grocery, vegetable and general stores were reopened. Such supplies as the British would allow through were purchased in bulk in new Jerusalem and then distributed to the storekeepers according to the number of their registered customers. Ration cards were prepared and distributed as a check on fair shares for all. All flour and other vital commodities in the shops were confiscated and distributed equally all round at official prices.

The supply of bread· was also assured by an order to break into three abandoned and locked Arab bakeries. These were put in order, bakers were found and mobilized, and henceforth bread was distributed free to those in need. This was an important step. It restored confidence in the Hagana and it helped to lessen the feeling of siege. As soon as the British learned that bread was being distributed free they attempted to discover where it was coming from, but their inquiries and searches did not reveal the secret.

Halperin took energetic measures to see that citizens were kept informed as to what was going on. Wall newspapers were prepared in typescript with information mainly compiled from the Kol Hamagen, or Voice of the Defender, radio station, which broadcast regularly from new Jerusalem. An employment office was set up where able-bodied persons could get jobs for pay on public works of all kinds.

When the siege began there were only two nurses in the quarter, but a medical team was soon sent in by Hadassah. It included a surgeon, and this team continued to operate right through the siege. A dental team joined them later. A social-welfare department was set up for those too old or sick to take care of themselves. A special worker was allocated to deal with them; they received a dole from the Jewish Community Council, and blankets and bedding were provided where needed. Perhaps for the first time in the history of the Old City, beggars practically disappeared from the streets.

Energetic steps were also taken to deal with the problem of idle children wandering about aimlessly in the streets and alleys of the quarter. They got in the way of the defenders and occasionally made their way into the Arab quarter, and a number were injured by mines and bullets. They were now sent to school, and Hagana detailed teachers to give them regular lessons. Those who were too old for schooling were put to work and also had to attend compulsory vocational training classes. In the schools, clubs were established to occupy the children creatively during their leisure hours.

But the older children were trained as runners and messengers in the Hagana, and they distinguished themselves by great courage during the bursts of fighting. They knew every devious route in the quarter and how to make contact in the most impossible situations. Among the finest of these young heroic messengers was a group of twelve known to be young delinquents. Other children acted as agents in obtaining arms from British soldiers. They would play around in the vicinity of the British and ask them to show them their arms. Sometimes the children would take a few bullets out and ask the soldiers how much they wanted for them; sometimes they just filched a magazine or two without asking. What they obtained went into Hagana stores. This was an unpleasant business and there were great searchings of heart among the Hagana as to whether it should be encouraged. It was felt on balance that in view of the attitude of the British and the desperate shortage of all equipment, any measures were justified in the life-and-death struggle to defend the Old City.

The Hagana company in the Old City did not escape Halperin's eagle eye. As soon as he found that the measures to care for the civilian population were well in train, he began a general tightening up of discipline and training. He explained his ideas at a meeting he had with them. The Hagana must remain in the Old City in order to serve as a bridgehead for the future. Their stay might well be very protracted. The district must be divided into a series of blocks completely autonomous militarily, so that if one fell to a sudden attack it would not involve the fall of the others. Nevertheless, communication had to be maintained between them, by tunneling through cellars, or over roofs, or by other means, some of which he explained. Secondary and support positions had, therefore, to be established and further mining of the area undertaken. The Jewish area had to be pushed out toward the enemy in lieu of any forward observation facilities, and to this end the no man's land should be encroached upon gradually.

The practical steps taken with the Hagana were drastic. Hitherto defenders had got up in the morning more or less when they liked, and although they had defended their positions against attack with tigerish ferocity and determination they had done so at the expense of their last nervous resources. Between actions and spells of duty, they had sat around smoking, talking, arguing, listening to the radio, playing gramophone records over and over again or games of chess, dominoes or checkers.

Now the girl defenders, who had been dispensed with by Halperin's predecessor, were mobilized again, and these helped both to alleviate the shortage of manpower and to give a sense of greater solidity to the positions. Communications between the various posts were improved, and the defenses as a whole were woven together into an integrated and coherent framework. Orders of the day were now issued regularly. There were set conferences of post commanders. Every day half the defenders at a time—those who were not on duty—were paraded formally. Steady and intensive training was introduced in the use of whatever small arms and weapons the defenders possessed, so that each man should become thoroughly expert in the use of arms. Hitherto this had not been done, through fear of taking weapons out of the "slick" or hiding place because of the danger of British searches and confiscations. Small battle groups of five or six men were organized and leadership within each group was developed and encouraged in the absence of enough trained N.C.O.s. Since there were not enough personal weapons to go around, each defender was armed at least with one hand grenade.

Military police were organized from the units held in reserve, and they supervised the movements of all the defenders. Cleanliness of weapons was insisted upon; they were inspected daily in all the posts. Personal cleanliness was strictly enforced. The work on fortifications, communications, connections between posts, breastworks and other defenses was energetically undertaken and speeded up, with the enlistment of civilian workers. Arab sniping was met with sharp retaliation, which sometimes meant the driving of Arabs from their houses and the pushing forward of the post.

The best training and organization in the world would have been of little avail without weapons. There is a view that the defenders of the Old City were just as well equipped with arms as those in the New City and that the constant cry for more from the Old City was somewhat excessive. It is true that a certain stockpiling had taken place inside the Jewish quarter, but the area was much smaller and the searches by the British more frequent and more thorough and, since they followed within moments any Jewish reaction to Arab attack, generally more successful than in the New City.

The defenders, therefore, fraternized with the British N.C.O.s, invited them for drinks and talks and persuaded them to sell ammunition, explosives and the like. The first big buy had been at the end of January, when two British engineers offered us a quantity of explosives, equipment for mining, grenades, and rifle and Sten gun ammunition. They asked for one thousand Palestine pounds. There was not a penny in the Hagana chest, but five hundred pounds were borrowed from one of the charitable funds and five hundred from a local merchant.

Submachine guns and ammunition were also obtained from the Arabs themselves through Armenian intermediaries. One consignment was found to be of British and of Hagana manufacture; it was part of a transport of arms which had been sent by the Jews to the relief of the Etzion bloc and had been captured by Arabs when the convoy was destroyed at Nebi Daniel.

All of this was accomplished, somehow, without the British being able to discover who was at the head of Hagana in the quarter. Halperin did his best to work with Weingarten, including him in the small representative committee he set up to take care of civilian matters, but it was a losing game. Weingarten desperately wanted to recover his position by gaining control of the food sent in by convoys, and the British abetted him in this attitude. Finally, toward the end of March, when Halperin was at Weingarten's home at one of his regular meetings there the British officer in charge of that area, a Captain Faulkner, arrived. Weingarten received him in the adjoining room, where they were closeted a quarter of an hour. After Halperin's meeting ended, when he left the house he immediately realized something was wrong. The surrounding area was deserted, but British soldiers were standing at various points controlling the approaches. He knew that if he tried to escape he would certainly be caught. He might even be shot while trying to escape. An N.C.O. approached and informed him he was under arrest. A few minutes later Captain Faulkner appeared and ordered him removed under escort to the New City, where, after being interrogated, he was released. He did manage to appoint a successor, under the very eyes of the British captain.

Halperin tried repeatedly to get back to the Old City. Once he was taken out of a convoy when he was recognized by Weingarten's daughter, Yehudit, who helped the British check the personnel of convoys. Then he bribed a British sergeant to take him back in a command car. Unfortunately he was spotted, just as he reached the Jewish quarter, by Captain Faulkner, who, of course, knew him to be the Hagana commander who had been expelled.

Weingarten was an interesting example of the kind of person who emerges in any struggle between a popular revolt and an external tyranny. He was a complex character, ambitious, evidently eager to play the role of savior of the Old City for the Jews. He was apparently convinced that the Arabs could beat Hagana, and he was certain the British would never leave Palestine. He possibly justified his dealings with the British as a way of winning a gratitude he could later exploit to save the Jews in the Old City, who, he was sure, would then forgive him.

Every Thursday afternoon, as Halperin's men observed from their lookouts, it was Weingarten's custom to spend some hours with a British government officer who used to come to Weingarten's house laden with wine and white bread for the Sabbath.

Hagana tested the special protection given him by the British by putting an empty gasoline drum on his roof and telling him it was a bomb. Within minutes, a squad of British soldiers was on the roof to take care of their friend.

Aware of the role Weingarten was playing, we decided on March 23 to inform the British that we must boycott him. The result was that the British held up convoys to the Old City for nearly two weeks, until a compromise was worked out. We were at this time trying to arrange for special allocations of food to be allowed into the Jewish quarter for Passover, and for a regular supply of kerosene. In the absence of Halperin, a committee was appointed to deal with civil affairs. It never achieved the same control of the situation. Its members included Rabbi Yitzhak Ornstein, Rabbi Shlomo Min-Hahar and Yaacov Tangye. Moshe Russnak, Halperin's nominee, was appointed Hagana commander in the quarter.

At this time I met with these civilian representatives of the Old City to discuss their problems. They wanted a special official of the Jerusalem Emergency Committee to deal with their needs, and a liaison officer from Hagana to spend most of his time in the Old City. We arranged for both. My notes show that I gave instructions for detailed reports to be furnished of the Old City's need for security men, for daily supplies, and for reserve stocks. Three weeks later I find an entry on arrangements we made to increase reserve supplies, as well as a special financial allocation we made toward the cost of celebrating Passover there.

It was fortunate that Halperin's reorganization of civilian and Hagana affairs took place in good time, for the month of March ushered in a period of violent attacks by the Arabs, sometimes openly assisted by the British. Before this, the pattern of Old City fighting, as in the battle for the Warsaw Houses on January 3, had brought British intervention after Jews and Arabs were already involved in fighting. In that battle, for example, the British were fired on heavily by the Arabs and took cover inside the Hagana defenses of the Warsaw Houses. By the following morning, they insisted that the Hagana men evacuate. Hagana arms and the synagogue scrolls were smuggled out. In spite of a British promise to return the building within three or four days, it was not recovered by us until May 13.

By the end of March we found ourselves often fighting the British. One of the worst incidents began on March 28 when a British major accompanied by one soldier entered a Hagana position and confiscated Hagana's 2-inch mortar. As he was leaving, the Hagana Old City command gave instructions that the seizure should be resisted by force. Two of the defenders grappled with the Britishers and disarmed them; in the scuffle the soldier was killed and the major wounded. Both British and Hagana reinforcements arrived quickly and a general scattered engagement broke out in the immediate neighborhood. Hagana covering scouts were able to block all but a few British reinforcements. Word of the fighting reached Hagana headquarters in Jerusalem, where it was possible to persuade British headquarters to order their men to cease fire. A British major came out with his hands up and asked for a parley.

The Hagana conditions for a local cease-fire here were that the British should withdraw, returning all arms and ammunition they had taken from the Jewish posts and allowing Hagana men in the future to move about openly with their weapons. Hagana undertook to return weapons they had taken from the British. Three British had been killed and three wounded, while Hagana had lost one killed and four wounded in addition to four wounded civilians, of whom one woman later died.

It was an uneasy truce, broken within a half hour when British soldiers shot a Hagana man in the back after he had walked up to them and accepted a cigarette. But a kind of truce lasted for three days, until the British guard changed at that position. The officer in charge of the relief unit refused to be bound by the terms agreed on, and the situation returned to its former tenseness.

As March faded into April, the number of attacks made by the British exceeded those made by Arabs. One inexcusable outrage was the shelling of the Hurva Synagogue. Arab attacks reached a climax with a mass attack on the quarter on April 9 following the tremendous funeral at the Mosque of Omar of Abdul Kader el Husseini, the most popular Arab commander, who had been killed in fighting at Kastel, and with the shelling of the children's club in Maddan Street on April 13, when more than twenty children were injured.

In April a special officer of Hagana, Menachem Meyer, was appointed for liaison with the British. He went into the Old City on April 21. He reported:

I had been well briefed on the situation . . . I was therefore not surprised to find on arrival that relations with the British were exceedingly tense. The relations between the Hagana command and the civilians suffered from lack of attention and misunderstanding. My marching orders were to do everything possible to avoid clashes and to enable Hagana to operate with the minimum interference from the British. There were only three weeks left till the date fixed for the British evacuation. I arranged daily meetings with the Army commander whether there were important or routine matters to be discussed. I think this enabled me to remove a number of causes of friction.

I hoped for the replacement of the sitting garrison by a new one, as this would start us off with a clean sheet without old scores awaiting payment on both sides.

The change did not take place until May 3, when the Highland Light Infantry left after a final shelling of some of our buildings and were replaced by a company of the Suffolk Regiment, newly arrived from England and therefore not so badly envenomed against the Jews as those who had been a long time in Palestine and subject to anti-Jewish indoctrination. During all the fighting we had the additional handicap that our men were under orders not to hit any Moslem or Christian religious site, while the Arabs had no such inhibition; nor were there any Christian sites in the Jewish quarter.

It was only a week before the British evacuation that a full working agreement was reached between Hagana and the Etzel. The Etzel was to accept fully the discipline and authority of the Hagana command although continuing to be organized as a separate unit. Their co-operation since January had been of the sketchiest kind. Four young members of the Stern Gang, who really operated alone, had not co-operated at all. Even the Etzel men, who had won recruits among the Old City residents, exaggerated every action in which they took part and splashed their claims in posters in new Jerusalem and the Old City. They also published groundless complaints that Hagana was starving them and interfering with their punitive operations.

On April 3, the Security Council of the United Nations had ordered the Jewish Agency and the Arab Higher Committee to cease all aggressive activities and to meet with the Security Council to agree upon an armistice, which was to include freedom of access to the Old City. While negotiations were still in progress, King Abdullah of Transjordan on April 26 declared war on the Jewish community of Palestine. A cessation of fighting did not materialize, but on April 28 Moshe Shertok for the Jews and Jamal Husseini for the Arabs agreed to a three-day cease-fire in the Old City to enable negotiations to take place. On May 2, the Hagana commander in the Old City announced that orders had been given the preceding day to cease fire during the period of negotiations. The truce was intended to remain in force in the Old City until the British left on May 15.

We were not at all sure that the British would in fact depart on the date set and were afraid that they might find some excuse to remain at least in the Old City or retain some other foothold in Jerusalem. Nevertheless, Hagana made preparations for the British evacuation and a detailed plan was elaborated for the Old City. This included the take-over of the British positions and those Arab positions which had the Jewish quarter in their field of fire. The object of the plan was to establish physical contact between the Old City and Jewish new Jerusalem.

The last few days passed in great suspense. From their observation posts Hagana men kept the British under close surveillance, hoping to gain some satisfactory hint of their intentions. On May 13, significant movements were observed. There was much coming and going of military transport. Then men were seen taking tea kettles and cooking stoves through the alleys to the waiting trucks. There seemed to be no doubt about it. The British were leaving.

The departure was undramatic enough. At noon that day the Hagana stood to. They took their weapons out of concealment, cleaned them and waited. At two o'clock, a British officer appeared in the Jewish quarter with two rifles, which he gave to the two local Jewish policemen. The same routine was followed with every Jewish and Arab policeman in Jerusalem.

Hagana sent out a cautious scouting party toward Zion Gate and saw the British apparently digging in. The information was conveyed to the liaison officer, who went to the British officer and asked him, "What are you doing here?" The latter looked at his watch, gave a quiet order to his men and marched them off.

At 6:15 P.M. young Hagana messengers were on the move busily running to all the positions with the order "Prepare to move." The British meanwhile began to march out in orderly files, the men staring directly ahead of them, not looking to right or left. Each squad had two men who marched with guns at the ready and kept looking around. Everyone held his breath; one wrong or impulsive action could still mean trouble.

The British commander stopped at the door of Weingarten's house. Characteristically, the British still recognized him as *mukhtar* of the Jewish quarter despite the fact that the Jewish authorities in Jerusalem had told them that they had disowned him. He handed him the keys to Zion Gate and said with emotion, "From the year 70 A.D. until today the keys of Jerusalem have never been in the hands of Jews. This is the first time for eighteen centuries that you are so privileged."

He then gave him a Sten gun and a few magazines of ammunition and said, "Our relations have not always been too smooth lately, but I personally did what I could for you. Your fighters are first-class. Let us part as friends. I hope that you will have a complete victory. Good luck and goodbye."

One solitary cry of "Good luck" burst in response from a Hagana man. For the rest there was grim business that had to be started immediately. Six defenders in civilian dress but heavily armed and wearing steel helmets immediately took over the nearest British position, and Operation *Shfifon* got under way. Within a few minutes the 150 Hagana defenders were in possession of all the British positions which had overlooked the Jewish quarter. It was just after 6:30 P.M.

A census of the military supply position had been taken two days earlier. To oppose 20,000 well-armed Arabs in the Old City there were 1,700 Jews, of whom 150 were fighting personnel. Their arms consisted of two machine guns, one Bren and one Lewis; 2,000 rounds of ammunition; one 2-inch mortar and ninety-three shells; 100 ballistic bullets; seventeen British-type rifles and 5,500 bullets; forty-two submachine guns, Thompson or Sten type, and five Finnish submachine guns with 21,600 rounds of ammunition; three grenade rifles with twenty-seven grenades; forty-five pistols of twelve varying makes with 1,724 bullets; 324 defensive grenades plus fifty primitive homemade ones; 126 attack grenades; 200 kilograms of explosive material and 1,000 fuses.

IV

THE CRUEL MONTH

ЛЛЛЛЛЛЛЛЛЛЛЛ

JEWISH SUCCESSES at this stage of the campaign outside Jerusalem were sporadic and rare. The end of March found Jerusalem besieged, the Negev cut off, our settlements in Galilee under continuing attack. During the next six weeks, before the mandate was to end, there was no possibility of a general offensive by the Jews, and both the Arab volunteer armies and the chances of eventual intervention by regular Arab troops were growing steadily. April was the cruel and testing month.

None of the beleaguered settlements across the country were watched by Jerusalem with the same attention and anxiety as Kfar Etzion and the adjoining Jewish settlements, high in the mountains near Hebron. Dominating the main route from Jerusalem to the Negev, they had always been a lonely outpost of Jewish farmers in a region which was heavily populated by bellicose Arabs. For months now they had been under constant attack by Arab bands.

On January 18, a group of thirty-five volunteers had set out from Jerusalem to try to break the Arab blockade and bring help to Etzion. The group included some of the finest young Jews in Palestine, top students at the Hebrew University and a few young scientists who were already well enough known to be considered national assets. It was a tragically small force to send deep into enemy country, but they were all trained in patrol and reconnaissance techniques and in night fighting. They were commanded by an experienced and able officer.

The first night they started from Bet Hakerem, along a mountain path which had been carefully planned. But they failed to reach their goal before daylight, and the commander brought them back unharmed. The second night they went as far as Hartuv in armored cars, taking full equipment, arms and ammunition, and proceeded by a route the Arabs were not likely to expect Jews to take. But they must have been spotted too early. The Arabs put in a *fazaag*, their own form of grapevine alarm, to the villages of the neighborhood. Some hundreds of armed Arabs were assembled, and the Jewish force was intercepted in a ravine not far from its objective. Arabs say the critical battle was in daylight. For some unknown reason it was not on a ridge, where the Jewish group's tactical training should have put them. They fought until their ammunition was exhausted. Every one of the thirty-five was killed. In death one of the men held a stone in his hand, a last desperate effort to fight the enemy. Despite military assurances that the risk had been calculated and warranted, there was strong feeling in Jerusalem that it had been greater even than in the operations normally mounted by Hagana.

We suffered a reverse of a different nature on April 9 when combined Etzel and Stern Gang units mounted a deliberate and unprovoked attack on the Arab village of Deir Yassin on the western edge of Jerusalem. There was no reason for the attack. It was a quiet village, which had denied entry to the volunteer Arab units from across the frontier and which had not been involved in any attacks on Jewish areas. The dissident groups chose it for strictly political reasons. It was a deliberate act of terrorism.

For once their plans had leaked, and two senior Hagana officers tried to dissuade them, asking them instead to help in our fight for Kastel. However, their techniques were such that, apart from arguing with them, there was not much we could have done to stop them. The attack was launched from Bet Hakerem at dawn, with a Stern Gang officer in command. Fighting which should have taken an hour went on all morning; the attackers were incompetently directed and a few Arab marksmen in one house held them up for a long time. Women and children had not been given time enough to evacuate the village, although warned to do so by loudspeaker, and there were many of them among the 254 persons reported by the Arab Higher Committee as killed.

The event was a disaster in every way. The dissidents held the village for two days and then abandoned it. They earned the contempt of most Jews in Jerusalem, and an unequivocal public repudiation by the Jewish Agency. But they gave the Arabs a strong charge against us, and the words "Deir Yassin" were used over and over again both to justify their own atrocities and to persuade Arab villagers to join the mass flight which was now taking place all over Palestine.

The effect of acts of terrorism by the dissident Etzel and Lehi have been grossly exaggerated. Terrorism may aggravate a situation. It cannot create. It can provoke authority which is the target of its activity and so bring matters more hastily to a head. But constructive action when the climactic moment is reached requires the support of the people as a whole, disciplined to follow its leaders, and a foundation of moral principles upon which to base what must be built.

It was in the second week of April that the inhabitants of Jerusalem, who had by now become used to incessant machine gun and mortar fire, first learned what it is to live under heavy artillery bombardment. In the Valley of Jezreel a major offensive by the Arab Liberation Army had been repulsed at Mishmar Haemek, and Fawzi el Kawkji, the Arab guerrilla leader, sent four French 75-mm. cannon, under the command of an Iraqi officer, to the hills around Jerusalem on April 10. From emplacements near Bet Iksa, these cannon could shell all of the Kastel area. Our only possible counter was the desperate course, which was tried and sometimes successfully, of sending men close enough to the batteries with medium machine guns to force them to withdraw.

This artillery now shelling the Holy City had been sold to the Arabs by Western powers, chiefly Great Britain. Chief Rabbi Herzog cabled word of this new barbarism to the Pope, the United Nations and religious leaders of the five Great Powers. This produced appropriate public statements by the Vatican, the Archbishop of York and scores of other Christian religious dignitaries who were shocked by the news, but the Christian world did not raise a finger to stop the shelling.

There is a fine line between panic and the capacity of a civilian population to endure hardship. A constant watch has to be maintained on morale and the factors that build it in order to keep people on the right side of this line. One of the ways is to encourage a spirit of improvisation and self-help, for it is the mounting effect of the feeling of being unable to hit back, of being unable to do anything to improve the situation, which leads to the utter frustration that turns to panic. This shelling of the city was a case in point.

The rain of projectiles came over day after day for weeks on end at the rate of one shell every two minutes, striking indiscriminately and all over the city. In addition to the casualties and the damage, which were both heavy, the shelling produced a dangerous feeling of helplessness.

Eventually a young Jewish engineer, David Leibovitch, invented a homemade weapon which was fondly called a "Davidka" and which has been much compared to David's slingshot. It was basically a kind of mortar which used a six-inch drainpipe. It fired a bomb of nails and metal scrap which exploded with some force and —what was more important—with tremendous noise and fury. Its effect on the Arabs was sometimes considerable, notably at Safad, where they mistook it for an atomic weapon when they abandoned the city. But its noise frightened them almost as much as its projectiles hurt them, and it gave great heart to the people of Jerusalem when real artillery shells were falling on them. In one of Jerusalem's squares there stands today a modest monument on which is mounted a replica of the Davidka.

During these April weeks we withdrew part of the Jewish population from mixed quarters and Arabs left areas which were almost entirely Jewish. We were still trying to achieve some contiguity between the center of the city and our outlying suburbs. To the west, this came when the Arabs had been cleared out of Sheikh Bader and Upper Lifta. To the south, we still had a number of quarters strung out as far as Ramat Rahel which could not be approached except by passing through Arab areas like Katamon and Talbieh which were also centers for Arab firing and attacks against us.

St. Simon's Monastery, a massive and ancient building on a hilltop, was the key to Katamon. It served the Arabs as an arms supply dump and a liaison center with the volunteer forces from neighboring countries. On April 30, the eve of the seventh day of Passover, a Palmach battalion launched a night attack. The two priests who were still living there were uninjured, but the Iraqi and Arab Legion soldiers who held it were driven out after we captured two of their armored cars. By morning the monastery had been taken, and after another day's fighting it became clear that we could hold it and eventually take all of the Katamon quarter which it controlled.

To the north we were still cut off from Mount Scopus, where stood the Hebrew University and Hadassah Hospital, by the Arab position at Sheikh Jarrah, which we had already captured once on January 13 but which the British had taken from us and handed back to the Arabs. On April 25 we took it again after a full night's fighting by another Palmach battalion supported by other units. For the first time in months unarmored vehicles had an open road to Mount Scopus.

Again the British demanded that we withdraw. At first we refused, and our troops who were mopping up a small Arab group on the roof of the Nashashibi house, commanding the road to Mount Scopus, were then fired on by British artillery and armored cars. This went on for a whole day while we negotiated with British officers who were determined to keep this quarter to protect their eventual line of withdrawal from Jerusalem. Finally a deal was made at their headquarters at the Damascus Gate. Our troops were to evacuate at night with their arms; the British would give us the arms of the Arabs still on the roof as spoils; the British would return Sheikh Jarrah to us when the last British soldier passed this point on their evacuation of the city. This time they kept their promise and handed Sheikh Jarrah over to us free of Arabs.

If we had needed proof of its importance, it was provided in the Hadassah massacre, when seventy-seven Jewish doctors, nurses and teachers were killed or burned alive on the road to Mount Scopus. We had been sending relief units to the Hebrew University and the Hadassah Hospital in regular convoys on the basis of assurances given personally by the High Commissioner and the British Secretary of State for Colonies, Arthur Creech-Jones, that medical and civilian traffic to Mount Scopus would be protected by their Army and police forces. The Hadassah convoy massacre of April 14 was one of the many reasons for the bitter feelings with which Jerusalem lived through the final days of British rule.

The convoy started at 9:30 A.M., made up of two ambulances, three armored buses, three trucks with food and hospital supplies and two small escort cars. The responsible British police officer had given the usual assurance that the road was clear. On the way from Sheikh Jarrah to Mount Scopus, the convoy struck a mine. One ambulance and two buses were damaged and could not be operated. The rear car turned around and managed to get away. A hail of fire, including grenades and Molotov cocktails, hit the cars from both sides of the road. The firing continued throughout the morning.

The attack took place less than two hundred yards from the British military post responsible for the safety of the road. The soldiers watched the attack, but did nothing. At 9:45 General Gordon H. A. Macmillan, who was the ranking British officer in Jerusalem, passed nearby in his car; later he said he had the impression the attack was ending. Twice later, at 1 P.M. and at 2 P.M., British military cars passed and were hailed by Dr. Chaim Yassky, director of the hospital. Neither of them stopped.

When the Jewish Agency liaison officer appealed to British military headquarters to let us send Hagana men to the scene, he was told the Army had the situation in hand and would extricate the convoy. A Hagana intervention would only make the fighting worse. Finally, two Hagana cars which tried to reach the convoy were ambushed and two cars which tried to come down to help from Mount Scopus were mined, but all their occupants engaged the attacking Arabs. At noon the Arabs were reinforced. By 1:45 Dr. Judah Magnes, president of the university, telephoned General Macmillan with a desperate plea for help. The reply was that military vehicles were trying to reach the scene but that a large battle had developed. By three o'clock the two buses were set on fire and most of the passengers who had not already been killed were burned alive.

The attack had lasted for seven hours. It was 4:30 P.M. before the Arabs were finally driven off and the killed and wounded taken out. Only twenty-eight persons were saved, eight of these unhurt. The seventy-seven dead included Drs. Chaim Yassky, Leonid Doljansky and Moshe Ben-David, who were the founders of the new faculty of medicine at the university, Dr. Guenther Wolfsohn, the physicist, and Professor Enzo Bonaventura, head of the university's department of psychology.

The attack had been commanded by an Iraqi officer, it was claimed by the Arab Higher Committee, which praised the massacre as a heroic exploit. It censured the British for their last-minute intervention: "Had it not been for Army interference, not a single Jewish passenger would have remained alive." Considering what their delay had cost us, this was small comfort.

As if to remind Jerusalem that its affairs had once been the concern of the world and the United Nations, in March six officials of the Implementation Commission arrived in Jerusalem headed by Dr. Pablo de Azcarate, who had been the Spanish Republican Ambassador to Great Britain. They sought to initiate talks with the government, the Jewish Agency and the Arabs concerning the transfer of governmental authority to the commission—the "five lonely pilgrims," as they were described by their chairman. They were still being refused permission by the British to come to Palestine and implement the partition of the country and the transfer of power.

Both the government and the Arabs ignored their existence. As honorary legal adviser to the Jewish Agency, I was glad to meet the Greek lawyer Constantin Stavropoulos and explain to him the complicated system of law which would be left in Palestine at the end of the mandate.

The Implementation Commission itself continued to struggle at Lake Success with its own defeatism, the British refusal to co-operate and the unwillingness of the Security Council to vote for an international force to carry out partition. Dr. Ralph Bunche was its secretary, and he learned much in the unhappy process which was to help him later when the time came to end the fighting. But even if the members of the commission had been stronger men they could have done nothing without some help from the mandatory power. In a report to the Assembly on April 13, it gave the Jewish Agency a clean bill of health for co-operating with it and blamed its own failure on Great Britain for not permitting it to work out plans for the transfer of power, and on the Security Council for not giving it an armed contingent to enforce its conclusions.

The British policy since November 29 was beginning to bear fruit. The violence and confusion inside Palestine seemed from a distance to have been produced solely by the partition decision and not by deliberate British steps to sabotage the plan. Many members of the United Nations were beginning to think a second time about the situation. The long-term British political aim had been aided substantially by the United States embargo on arms shipments to Palestine. This embargo applied to Jews and Arabs alike but was clearly discriminatory, since the neighboring Arab countries continued to get arms and munitions from British sources. The die-hards among the British must have felt their victory was close when, on March 19, the United States told the Security Council it was now convinced that Palestine could not be partitioned without violence and recommended a temporary trusteeship over Palestine while the General Assembly reviewed the entire problem.

This United States bombshell hit us hard. It represented a real triumph for the State Department, for Secretary of Defense James V. Forrestal, and for American oil interests in the Middle East. There is no doubt in my own mind that the cold war played a major part in the decision to reverse American policy. If a choice had to be made between Arabs and Jews, the great land areas of the Arab countries and the oil they held seemed to many Americans to dictate a pro-Arab position as part of national defense in any East-West conflict. Even President Truman, who may not have realized in advance what the decision involved, backed the State Department and tried to explain his curious change of mind to a bewildered world.

We did our best, through Zionists and friends of Zionism, to make it hard to explain or to continue the new policy. In Palestine the American statement was regarded by the Jews as a direct betrayal.

In Jerusalem, I could see no despair over the *volte-face*. The city had met the brunt of the Arab attack so far, and its people seemed to me to recognize that the new development only confirmed the inevitability of a bigger and more bitter military struggle. A school principal I knew, sixty-five years old, told a friend who had asked how he received the United States announcement, "After that, I went to Hagana and asked them to teach me how to use a rifle. From this moment, knowledge of the rifle became the chief learning any of us needed."

The American plan was devoid of serious content, and it never got off the ground. By the end of April, the U.S. representatives at the U.N. had whittled the proposal down to a trusteeship for Jerusalem alone and by May 4 they were proposing to the Trusteeship Council that even this attempt to protect the city be abandoned. But the harm done by the proposal was real and serious. It encouraged the Arabs to continue their refusal to agree to a truce or to accept partition and it gave support to those British elements who were still determined at the eleventh hour to nullify the United Nations decision.

In trying to rally our friends abroad, the greatest help came from the Soviet Union, for reasons which are less understandable now than they were then. Andrei Gromyko pressed constantly at the United Nations for implementation of the partition resolution. Some of his statements make interesting reading now, in the light of the violent attacks on Israel which have followed recent Soviet intervention in Middle East affairs. "Acts of violence will not prevent final execution of the U.N. decisions," he said. The partition plan was not directed against the Arabs. It was in the basic interests of both Jews and Arabs. It was the only practicable solution of the Palestine problem. "The partition decision satisfied the legitimate aspirations of the Jewish people to establish a state of its own in

Palestine," he went on. "It would be a dreadful injustice if we do not take into account these Jewish aspirations, especially after the suffering which was the lot of the Jews in Europe under Nazi rule.''

There was very little we could do, granted the international situation, except to press forward our own plans to take over our part of the country. Ben Gurion spoke for all the Jews in Palestine when he said, at the end of March:

We are the determining factor in the fate of the land. We are the foundation stone of the Jewish state and we shall set it up . . . We will not agree to any trusteeship, neither temporary nor permanent, even for the shortest time. We shall no longer accept foreign rule over us. We shall insist on the speediest possible liquidation of the British administration and its evacuation without delay.

The Jewish state exists and will continue to exist as long as we know how to defend it. The Jewish state will find a way to mutual understanding with the Arab peoples. We never had a quarrel with the Arab people and if the Arabs want peace—the hand of the Jewish state is stretched out to them.

By the beginning of April, Ben Gurion's position was endorsed by the Zionist General Council, composed of delegates from all sections of the World Zionist Organization, which directed the activities of the Jewish Agency.

Probably the last hope of international help to expire in our minds was the thin chance of an international police force to implement partition. As early as January, Canada had proposed such a force, to be made up of volunteers. Public opinion throughout the world welcomed the idea. Toward the end of March the Jewish Agency proposed to the Implementation Commission the use of Scandinavian troops who had completed a tour of duty in Germany and who could have served as a police force in Jerusalem. The commission itself pressed constantly for an international force. Many responsible persons believed that a relatively small force could have put down and scattered the Arab bands inside Palestine and deterred the neighboring Arab countries from sending in their regular troops. And everyone knew by now that without such a force there could only be full-scale war.

But another war, the cold war, had already stacked the cards against us in the United Nations. The United States and Great

Britain, on the one hand, and the Soviet Union and its satellites, on the other, distrusted each other far too bitterly now for any such co-operative effort. How far the die-hards on both sides actively worked for a worsening of the situation in Palestine through the spring of 1948, in order to prosecute the cold war, and how far this bigger conflict developed on its own momentum are questions over which generations of historians will still have to work. The conclusion we drew was short and simple: We would have to fight for our existence.

One of the first things I did after Ben Gurion asked me on April 10 to take over full powers in Jerusalem was to write down on a sheet of paper a sort of agenda of what I knew must be done at once. The scrap of paper was preserved in my files and it lies before me as I write. It lists, in no sort of order, fifty-nine items. They range from ration cards to tin for water tanks, from edible oils to postal services, from moving cows to making sure that a small mosque in a Jewish area was not damaged.

It was a formidable agenda, and I was sure it was not complete. All the preparations, I knew, would have to be made while the British were still nominally in control of the city and the country. Many things would have to be done in secret so that the British should not interfere and sabotage our efforts. Many matters we in Jerusalem knew were vital would have to be harangued for with the authorities in Tel Aviv while they were busy organizing and directing the struggle for survival for the whole country. Like the Psalmist of old, I determined that for the sake of Jerusalem I would neither be silent nor hold my peace.

Fortunately, I could mobilize able men. Zvi Leibowitz, water engineer of the Jerusalem municipality, was a lean and wiry man, jerky in his movements, with the meticulous attention to detail of a gifted public servant. Hayim Solomon, who was chairman of the Jewish Community Council, was a gentle and deeply religious septuagenarian, a wealthy pharmaceutical wholesaler. Adolf Suess, a gigantic Austrian Jew, was very correct in protecting the interests of his employers, the Shell Oil Company, but also ready to do everything in his power to help us. Michael Lubarsky (later Bar), of the Jewish Agency's transport department, was a cheerful, easygoing Russian Jew who could turn as hard as nails when he had to handle tough truck drivers. Henry Becker, a district engineer in the Public Works

Department under the British, was an Irish Jew with Jewish wit and Irish temper who could denounce British officials to their faces in a sound Irish brogue. Hayim Yaffet was a Vaad Leumi official who had learned social-service work under Henrietta Szold, the founder of Hadassah. Dr. Gershon Cyderovitch, a Polish economist, knew the food situation of the city thoroughly. Professor Saul Adler, a scientist from England, had been the leading parasitologist at the Hebrew University for many years. Shmuel Dudkevitch (later Dudayi), an agile, round-the-clock worker, managed the Jerusalem branch of Tnuva, the Histadrut organization for marketing dairy and agricultural produce, and Arieh Belkind, a competent Russian-Jewish intellectual, was experienced in handling supply problems. The list could be much longer, but these were typical of the men who rallied to the defense of Jerusalem.

Food came first of all. At the end of January it had been estimated that Jewish Jerusalem possessed about one fortnight's supply of standard flour—about 300 tons—ten days' supply of white flour, and a month's supply of sugar. There were also rather meager stocks of rice and sardines. There was practically no tinned milk, a little powdered milk, six weeks' supply of lentils, beans and peas and two months' supply of groats. Egg supplies were down by 35 per cent, milk by 66 per cent, and in general the food consumption standard of the Jewish population had fallen by about a third in quantities consumed, and in nutrition even lower because of the lack of proteins in the diet.

At a meeting of the Jerusalem Emergency Committee in January, we had concluded that the quantity of food and agricultural products which would have to be transported from Tel Aviv to Jerusalem would amount to 4,500 tons per month on a minimal basis. In the hope of building up some reserve stocks, I arranged for the Jewish Agency to furnish Hamashbir Hamerkazi, the wholesale supply company of the Histadrut, or General Federation of Jewish Labor, with a credit of fifty thousand Palestine pounds with which to purchase foodstuffs as a reserve supply for emergency needs. It was stipulated that these supplies were to be available not only to the co-operative stores, owned by Histadrut, but to all the inhabitants of the city. This arrangement was made just in the nick of time, as a report came through from intelligence sources in Tel Aviv that the Arabs intended to close the Tel Aviv-Jerusalem road within the next few days.

The privately organized merchants grumbled about the credit

given to the Hamashbir organization, and attempts were made throughout the next few weeks to add their representatives to the supply subcommittee. Later, when I had taken over responsibility for Jerusalem's civilian population, I proposed that the merchants set up a consortium together with Hamashbir Hamerkazi, to bring in food to supply the whole population. I offered to ensure them against loss and to provide warehousing space for the goods. They failed to take advantage of this offer, and this left the Jerusalem Emergency Committee with no option but to obtain and distribute the food ourselves through local shopkeepers.

This question of warehousing had been under anxious consideration for a long time. In the middle of February we had taken over the basements of the former Rothschild Hospital for this purpose. The basement of the Alliance School was another center. It had the advantage of standing in large grounds surrounded by high walls. Trucks could drive in and be unloaded without being harassed by snipers' bullets. After the British left and the Arabs began to shell the New City, no area was safe. On June 1 a shell fell right in the Alliance School courtyard. Later on we added the Schneller Compound to our warehouse space. This was in the middle of a military camp and therefore an active target for Arab guns, but we had no alternative; the number of large buildings in the city which met the requirements was very limited. We also pressed into service some unoccupied shops in the Mahaneh Yehuda quarter and the ground floors of a number of schools. This had the advantage of putting shoppers in that densely populated neighborhood into close contact with their daily supplies. This was an important consideration, as by then the city was under constant bombardment so that all movement in the streets was highly dangerous.

We instituted a strict system of checks over all supplies entering the city and coming in and going out of our warehouses. In the warehouses, we kept daily stock sheets showing the quantity of every commodity and details of all goods taken out and all replenishments. In this difficult task I had the valuable assistance of a young architect, Dan Ben Dor, who had served as garrison engineer in the British Army during World War II. He displayed remarkable ingenuity in evolving methods of handling and storing our supplies.

As a further check, wholesalers were required to submit weekly reports of the quantities of essential foodstuffs and other commodities they had in stock. In this way, by totaling these returns and adding them to our stock sheets we knew where we were at any given moment. The system also served as a check on distribution and ensured that the goods were not withheld from the public after a distribution had been ordered by us. We had a small corps of inspectors for this as for other control duties. There was little need to check quantities in retail stores. The shortage was so great that their stocks were negligible.

One of our problems in warehousing was the lack of cold-storage facilities. In all, we could store only 980 tons, of which 550 were in the Tel Arza plant, which was on the outskirts of the city and exposed to enemy fire. Our cold-storage facilities were in eight different places and these were powered by generators which operated refrigerating motors of quite small horsepower. Considerable skill was required of the engineer in charge of warehouses in fitting them for their purpose. He had to see that supplies were guarded against theft and pilfering and that they were so stored as to make careful and frequent stocktaking possible.

After storage came the problem of distribution. Technically there was still rationing of a number of vital commodities in Palestine for which the British Food Controller was responsible. Every citizen had a ration book, but by the beginning of 1948 the arrival of foodstuffs to honor the ration was entirely desultory and the system had largely broken down. However, we made use of the ration cards issued by the British. Later, as the situation became even more strained and just before the final departure of the British, we introduced a linking system. Just as each customer was linked to a specific grocery shop, he was now to be linked to a specific butcher and a fishmonger and to the local Tnuva, a Histadrut dairy produce shop, for children's special rations.

One of our most serious problems was to maintain the supply of bread for the population, for the backbone of the whole feeding program rested on the daily loaf. At the beginning of April we had twenty-six bakeries operating in the city. This large number of small bakeries meant the consumption of unnecessary amounts of fuel. Only two bakeries had any fuel reserves, one for four weeks and the other for ten days. We decided to restrict the number to five, and this step cut fuel consumption from twenty-two tons per week to fifteen. It also entailed savings in gasoline in transporting the bread to distribution centers, and better inspection of the quality and quantity of flour used. At the end of April we were baking 28,000 loaves per day, just under a third of a loaf of bread per person.

The bakers had proven obstreperous and disinclined to accept the discipline required by these drastic measures. So on April 29 I wrote to them that the committee would not tolerate their threats to close down if our reorganization schemes were carried through. "Please understand," I said, "that it is your duty to supply bread to all the inhabitants of the city and if you display unwillingness to perform this duty, we shall take over all the bakeries and ourselves arrange for the supply of bread."

One large biscuit factory owned by a wealthy and influential industrialist refused to comply with the committee's decision fixing prices for its goods. We therefore requisitioned the factory's supply of fuel and applied it to baking bread. This was a healthy object lesson to other establishments that in a state of emergency the interests of the public came first and that decisions taken in the public interest would have to be respected by all, rich and poor alike.

Side by side with the organization of warehouses, bakeries and other depots for vital commodities, we had to proceed with the setting up of enforcement machinery. We had no legal powers to set up our own courts, but we did so in disregard of the rapidly disintegrating mandatory government. The self-discipline of the Jewish community was such that their authority was effective.

Our enforcement tribunals dealt with contraventions of our rationing regulations, the punishment of profiteers and speculators. Later, when the state came into being on May 15, these courts continued to try rationing offenses, and imprisonment was added to the warnings, rebukes and fines which had been the earlier penalties. The offenses included speculative prices, failure to comply with instructions of the national institutions, and unfair practices. The courts were usually composed of one lawyer, one army officer and one member of the public. Members served without remuneration.

We felt it preferable to bring such cases before these courts rather than the ordinary courts of the new state, because we wished to give the greatest publicity to profiteering, which affected all the public. This lent the weight of public opinion to the condemnation of those found guilty. Moreover, procedure was speedy, unhampered by the rules and formalities of ordinary courts. Another sanction we imposed was to remove a dealer who contravened regulations from the list of persons authorized to operate establishments where any kind of food was sold.

A certain amount of trouble was caused by soldiers who purloined food found in Arab areas. Our committee was responsible

for the army's food supplies; we allocated to the army 12.5 per cent
of all supplies coming into the area. This enabled the army to give
soldiers a double portion of bread and a 50 per cent increment of
all other foods allocated to civilians. But I insisted that all foodstuffs seized by the army should be handed over to the common
stock. I was able to effect an agreement, on May 30, with Halamish
—the army branch supplying the armed forces—confirming the
practice of a common pool of foodstuffs. My committee would
henceforth check the lists of enlisted persons and remove their
names from civilian lists in order to prevent duplication. The
armed forces would receive from the committee daily their agreed
share of all food we made available to the civilians. In addition we
distributed small rations of cigarettes and chocolate to the soldiers.
Arrangements were made in case of need to drop food to the troops
by parachute.

Many Jewish officials in the British administration found themselves in an awkward dilemma as regards food supplies for their
families. The Arab officials, who had plenty of food that came in
freely from the hinterland, used to offer them eggs, bananas and
other tempting items which they would have been eager to take
home for their children. The Arabs wished in this way to prove
how badly off the Jewish population were. The Jewish officials soon
realized this and agreed that as a matter of principle none of them
would accept any such food, even from Arab friends.

By the beginning of March, the food supply had become very
bad. We lacked animal proteins, and apart from flour we had vital
foods for only four to fifteen days. From the last week in February
the city was entirely without meat or fish, eggs or milk (except for
children). There were no vegetables or butter. Three weeks later
we did manage to squeeze out an allowance of 125 grams of fresh
meat per soul with a little extra for hospitals.

In an effort to improve our prospects of keeping alive, we in-
augurated a campaign encouraging people to plant vegetables in
their gardens and to use their waste water for watering them. We
distributed seed and seedlings from the stores of the British administration. We also started hydroponics on roofs with money I made
available for the purpose. We set up a seedling nursery in the heart
of Rehaviah, and also got large supplies of seedlings from Mrs.
Rahel Ben Zvi's farm school near Government House. Every few
days, Mrs. Ben Zvi would come to town, running the gantlet of the
Arab quarters on the way, to bring us seedlings. Several thousand

people planted these vegetables. We also sent children into the fields to collect *halamith,* weeds which spring up toward the end of the winter rains with leaves which taste a little like spinach, and sold it to the public for making soups. (Later we had to stop this when we feared they would tread on a mine or be hit by Arab sniping.) Dan Ben Dor pointed out that the advice to gather and cook *halamith* was scoffed at by the dietitians, who reminded the authorities that this weed is nonexistent after February. But during the winter months of 1947-48 there was such heavy rainfall that the fields were full of *halamith* much longer than usual. And the people considered this too a sort of minor miracle.

Well before our real troubles began, I was under constant pressure from numerous community leaders whom the shortage of food began to frighten. They considered, for reasons which still baffle me, that they would help matters by warning me of the consequences to the city's morale if the people were hungry. It was obvious they would have to overcome their fears and harden their spirits. This they all did when the time came.

On April 4, when ordinary food convoys had been discontinued and the city was already cut off, we had on hand thirty days' supply of flour, two days' supply of noodles, 50 tons of white flour, 2.5 tons of corn flour, 13 tons of beans, 2.8 tons of dry peas, 12.5 tons of sugar, 69 tons of edible and frying oils, 15 tons of coffee (sixty days' minimal supply), 3.5 tons of tea (forty-one days), 15 tons of salt, 7.5 tons of herrings, and 1.5 tons of powdered milk. Two days after Ben Gurion gave me full powers over the situation, I learned by radio in Tel Aviv that we were already drawing on our iron rations of flour in Jerusalem after ten days without any meat, fish, eggs or milk except for children.

Water was almost as important to us as food. Jerusalem's main water supply came from springs at Ras el Ein, some forty miles away in the coastal plain near Lydda, through a sixteen-inch pipeline with three pumping stations all of which were in Arab areas. In the 1936-39 troubles, Arabs had damaged this water supply, even when British authorities were trying to maintain order. It was clear that this time it would be easy for the Arabs to cut off our supply. They and the British each took only 15 per cent of the water pumped through this line, having alternative supplies of their own in the Ein Farah springs in the wilderness of Judaea on the way to

Jericho, as well as a very large supply in the 60,000-cubic-meter cistern in the Mosque of Omar and the famous King Solomon's pools just beyond Bethlehem. It was an ironic fate which gave a water system built by a Jewish king nearly three thousand years ago to the enemies of his people at a supreme crisis in their history.

The only fairly large reservoir in Jewish hands was the municipal cistern in Romema, with a capacity of 20,000 cubic meters. On the basis of normal usage, this would have lasted the Jewish population of Jerusalem for exactly two days. We could, and did, urge the British authorities to replace the Arab guards at the three pumping stations and to set up a patrol to guard the pipeline. But we knew the authorities well enough by now to realize that we must also prepare for the worst kind of emergency.

Thanks to the help of some Jewish officials in the British-administered Municipal Water Department, we were able to make some clandestine preparations without the knowledge of the British. On December 19, a secret request was sent to all citizens to clean out their home cisterns as quickly as possible in order to make them ready to receive rain water when the rainy season began. But this was only a camouflage. We had no intention of relying upon the caprice of the weather and intended to fill these cisterns with water from municipal sources. We simultaneously made arrangements to seal these cisterns when full so as to have them available as a source of supply in case of need.

Cisterns are an old device in Jerusalem, dating from the times when rain water was used by all except the very poor, who bought water in small quantities delivered in goatskins by water carriers. These cisterns were built of stone or concrete in the ground next to each house and were often three or four yards deep, ten yards long and five yards wide. Water flowed into them from gutters on the roofs, and was drawn up for use by buckets or with pumps. Most of these cisterns had been in disuse for many years.

We organized a group of some forty Jewish engineers who volunteered to examine every unused cistern in Jewish-occupied premises to ascertain what repairs they required to render them fit for storing water, and to make a general survey of our total potential water capacity, to know what would be the maximum supply of water we could arrange for.

We also decided to bring to Jerusalem a large supply of tin for making water tanks and to supply as many householders as possible with such tanks, which they would be able to purchase cheaply and fill with water from the municipal supply as an extra reserve for future use.

Our survey showed us that the use of the cisterns would give us a supply of 30,000 cubic meters. This took into account only the cisterns already available. By repairing and filling all cisterns of 100 cubic meters' capacity and more, we could gain another 30,000 cubic meters. If we used cisterns of 50 to 100 cubic meters' capacity, we could gain yet another 25,000. Cisterns of less than 50 cubic meters would give us 15,000 cubic meters, and the Romema reservoir could be counted on for at least 15,000 cubic meters. Each 1,000 cubic meters would enable us to supply the inhabitants with ten liters (approximately ten quarts) per day. We would thus be able to hold out for 115 days if we brought our plans to fruition. If we cut the ration down to seven liters per day for drinking, cooking, washing and all other requirements, we could hold out for 164 days, and if we were forced down to five liters per person per day we could hold out for 250 days.

The British had to be kept in ignorance of the fact that extra water would be pumped into their main water line, through Arab territory, in order to prepare the Jewish community for a possible siege. They would certainly have taken steps to prevent this unauthorized operation had they got wind of it. My experts reported to me that the preparatory work of cleaning, repairing and filling the cisterns would take five to seven weeks and that thereafter they would have to be sealed and guarded day and night to ensure that they were not broken into and water purloined. I insisted that the period must be five weeks, not seven, and I was confident that the Mishmar Ha'am, the Home Guard, would be capable of looking after the supply. They had done an excellent and swift preliminary job in going through the Jewish quarters house by house, in order to draw up the list of all cisterns. They had then been followed by engineers who inspected every cistern and prepared detailed reports on their condition. The survey had also disclosed that Hadassah Hospital had a reserve of twenty-five days, which could be stretched to thirty days in an emergency. The other hospitals also had some reserves.

Our committee had no funds to pay for what was needed. I went to Ben Gurion and told him that of an estimated total cost of twenty thousand Palestine pounds, I needed five thousand right away. To my surprise, Ben Gurion, who never handled money matters, wrote out a check at once for the amount I had asked for.

With this money we started our secret work. Much of the credit should go to the municipal water engineer Zvi Leibowitz. He began to hold back some of the city's regular water supply, without the knowledge of his superiors, in order to enable us to fill our cisterns during the night.

I eagerly examined the day-by-day reports of the buildup of our supply. I made myself thoroughly unpopular with the engineers by my constantly urging them to go even faster and faster. I may have seemed unreasonable to them. I knew they were held up in their efforts by the need to supply the city with its regular supply and they could not control the amount of water reaching the city. But no excuse was acceptable. My colleagues on the committee considered the whole project unrealistic and impossible. They looked ahead darkly to the not distant day when we would be without water. They genuinely believed that our only hope was for our troubles to be over before the pipeline was cut. The British, finally, were a constant danger to the plan; at one time their military authorities complained sharply to the municipality that they were not getting their regular water supply. Little did they know where it was going!

The shape of things to come was seen on March 1 when three hundred Arab irregulars seized the British Army camp adjoining the Ras el Ein water works. There they stayed, poised to cut our water supply when they wanted to. At the beginning of May, I sent Ben Gurion a radio message that Iraqi troops were preventing Arab employees from pumping water. Complaint to the British brought the reply that they would take over the station, but they never did. When the fateful day of British evacuation came, the Arabs immediately cut the pipeline, and on August 12 they blew up the Latrun pumping station. But we had secretly accumulated a reserve of 115,000 cubic meters of water, including what was in the Romema reservoir. We had enough to last us 115 days on a daily per capita ration of ten liters, enough for eight months if we cut the ration in half. This latter figure would entail severe hardship. With care we could hold out until the winter rains.

After food and water came fuel. Palestine was almost completely dependent on oil products refined in Haifa from Iraqi supplies. Jerusalem's fuel came normally by rail. Without it the city would be without heat, without electricity, without ovens to bake bread, without vehicles to move, without hospitals, without means of cooking food.

Until the end of February, Jerusalem received some 80 per cent of its normal requirements. With self-imposed economies this should have sufficed, but the deficiency of 20 per cent was enough to produce a scare, and this in turn precipitated hoarding. The situation might have deteriorated rapidly. It was met by the immediate institution of a rationing system for kerosene which secured at first to every family sufficient fuel for cooking but not for heating. As it is very cold indeed in Jerusalem at this time of the year, this entailed some hardship. Our anxieties were increased by the fact that, with deliveries by rail very vulnerable, we might have to resort to road deliveries of fuel from Tel Aviv. This meant that this highly inflammable commodity, like all the other things we needed, would have to run the gantlet of enemy fire.

Nor was our anxiety caused merely by the fact that the oil was in Haifa and transportation to Jerusalem depended on the good will of the British. When it arrived in Jerusalem it still had to be brought to the Jewish quarters from the railhead, which lay in a thickly populated Arab area. Soon after the troubles started, the Jewish employees at the railway station and the oil storage dumps were forced to leave. Their lives were endangered by Arab attacks, and the British failed to provide protection for them. The oil companies were left entirely dependent on Arab labor. It was possible for Jewish lorry tankers to reach the station only if accompanied by armed British escorts, and on numerous occasions these were not provided. Finally, on April 10, the British suddenly refused to provide any further escort at all. We tried once to send a lorry to the station without an escort to get fuel, but the driver was kidnaped and taken captive to the Old City. A few days later the British stopped all shipments of fuel by rail from Haifa because of the disruption of the railway services. These were now being used almost exclusively to evacuate British Army equipment and supplies to the port.

Minutes of a meeting we held on May 12 disclose that the Jerusalem Electric Corporation's manager, Alexander Singer, a Hungarian who was a first-class engineer and a champion fencer, informed me that his fuel supply would last for only eight more days, eighteen hours per day, for our already drastically restricted use of electricity. We decided to cut the use of electricity to twelve hours per day so that we could spread the supply to last twelve days. To save gasoline we had from the very beginning of the fuel scarcity prohibited bread deliveries to the home.

The Jerusalem Electric Corporation, on which both Arabs and Jews depended, presented special problems. It used twenty-five tons of fuel oil a day, holding a three-week supply in reserve. But we knew that supply of electricity to Jewish areas could be cut off almost at will. The company's security officer was an Arab in close touch with the Arab Higher Committee. On alleged grounds of economy, the company had consistently cut down the number of its Jewish employees, and the British refused police protection to the few who managed to keep their jobs. The station was surrounded by Arab armed posts whose men were never searched or disarmed by the British.

That was our problem. Our first act to meet possible siege conditions was to draw up a list of vital institutions that would be supplied electric current from auxiliary stations where we could set up small diesel engines and generators to be brought from Tel Aviv. We elaborated a detailed plan of the weekly requirements of fuel of all kinds for all the city's essential needs, for bakeries, hospitals, cold-storage plants, water supply, and some other vital industries and establishments. We appealed to the public to hand over to our committee all reserve supplies they had, against payment. I then ordered the Mishmar Ha'am to make a house-to-house collection of all fuel oil remaining in central heating tanks and to scour every abandoned house in the city for fuel. The oil was pumped out into fuel lorries and taken to our storage centers. We stopped supplying gasoline to all vehicles operating out of Jerusalem, requiring them to fill up in Tel Aviv. Restaurants were ordered to go over to cooking on stoves burning wood. Bus services were cut to a bare minimum and later were stopped entirely and people went on foot. Use of private cars was prohibited. Taxi service was also stopped except for two taxis for emergency purposes.

The extent of our fuel problem may be gauged from a report on the situation of our supply need in March. On March 3 the economic adviser of the Jewish Agency, Dr. Alfred Bonne, informed me that the city had supplies of gasoline for two or three days only and that the large users like the Egged Bus Company had no storage facilities. That meant that if the railway stopped running for five consecutive days we would be completely out of gasoline.

One of our earliest steps had been to tighten up kerosene rationing for homes. Distribution was undertaken by the Mishmar Ha'am, and cards for this domestic fuel were issued on the basis of the ordinary wartime ration cards held by all consumers. Nevertheless, as the isolation of Jerusalem continued, people were reduced to cooking in their gardens and back yards over campfires of sticks and waste wood and in other improvised ways. We also taught the public to build box ovens to keep food warm without applying heat. As there was soon very little left to cook, this domestic hardship was not too serious a problem. Our greatest concern was to find sufficient fuel to generate electricity for vital services, to keep essential transport running, for the Hagana vehicles, ambulances, the delivery of bread and food, and for a few very severely restricted undertakings.

Our position was improved somewhat when, in the fighting several days after the British withdrawal, we were able to lay hands on a considerable quantity of fuel in the Shell Company's premises in the Arab zone. There was rejoicing when the trucks carrying this fuel passed through the streets. People thought the siege had been broken.

The main problems were always to obtain additional supplies and then to store them. We planned to arrange for the keeping of iron rations of fuel in barrels and tanks, some of which we hoped to acquire from the British Army salvage section. In this we had little success. We could not use the barrels in which some supplies came from Tel Aviv, because they too were very short of storage receptacles and wanted them returned. Finally we hit on the idea of trying to keep fuel in small cisterns normally used for holding water. The experts told us that there would be seepage and that the idea was impracticable. However, we tried it with certain modifications and this unique method of storage worked. All these arrangements were financed by a tax which our committee imposed on all fuel used.

In order to maintain morale and the will to resist, it was almost as important to keep people busy as it was to feed and supply them. Jerusalem had been the center of the British mandatory government as well as a trade center for the Middle East. Suddenly, its people were cut off from any kind of free access to other parts of the country. Business came to a standstill. A great city, with an energetic life of its own, was transformed within a few weeks into a conglomeration of people, cut off from the world, with little to do except go hungry and thirsty and cold, repel the assaults of their foes and await the outcome of events.

Some reasonable facsimile of life as usual had to be contrived. As the long winter months followed each other, it became clearer and clearer that an important element in the British strategy of refusing to implement partition was their conviction that siege would lead in turn to chaos, to despair, to panic and to abandonment of our plans to found a state. So we had to make sure that people were occupied, that they had a chance to work their passage into the future.

The manpower problem held many of the germs of its own solution. There were public works to be constructed, for example, for defense, which could occupy many breadwinners. We made a survey of all industrial raw materials within the boundaries of Jerusalem and drew up a list of priorities. As early as February, we set up a gravel plant near Bet Hakerem for material with which to build fortifications. One of these was a defense wall on Princess Mary Road to protect pedestrians from sniping, another was a similar rampart to shield parts of King George V Avenue from Arab firing positions on the Old City walls. There were shelters to be built, and equipment for rescue squads. We built new roads, some new housing, even an airfield near the Givat Shaul section of the city which could handle Piper Cub airplanes.

By April, such work was in full blast. We called in the directors of Solel Boneh, the construction company belonging to the Histadrut, which had set up a special company for the British Army to build fortifications during World War II. The workers had confidence in this company, since they owned it, and it had a staff of experienced engineers and foremen. At first it used volunteers, but by April we conscripted older men, many in their fifties and some of them of the ultra-religious type who wear the long traditional *payoth*, or earlocks. Among the works built by this company was a cable trolley from our isolated position on Mount Zion across the valley to the Ophthalmic Hospital. It was lowered in the daytime so that it could not be seen; at night it was raised to carry supplies and ammunition and to bring down wounded soldiers. The line was three hundred yards long. The Arabs must have wondered how we could hold out without any means of obtaining supplies or reinforcements.

Work under direct enemy fire was often unavoidable. In one

place the company tunneled through the rock under an existing road. It fortified houses as strong points, blasted out defense positions, dug communication trenches and built pillboxes and roadblocks. These men worked over the whole extent of the Jerusalem front. How dangerous was their task is told by the roll of honor. Out of three hundred men, six were killed and sixteen wounded.

Directly under our Emergency Committee, and later under my control as Military Governor, was the Mishmar Ha'am, or Home Guard, which had been set up in November. Sometimes these men were engaged in front-line fighting, but more often they did the vast auxiliary and reserve jobs required by modern war. As the British mandatory government disintegrated in its "Operation Chaos," this new organization gradually took over, too, most of the duties which usually fall to municipal or local government bodies.

By June 1948 it numbered some 3,200 men and women in Jerusalem alone. Its duties included an enormous range of practical activities: registering all citizens; issuing identity tags to children; organizing blood donors for Magen David Adom, the Jewish Red Cross; air defense; fire fighting; erection and care of shelters; lookout duties in observation posts; checking the blackout; supervision of water cisterns; warden duties; guard duty at roadblocks; first-aid instruction; care of refugees; auxiliary work in hospitals and army kitchens; public information. There was a Mishmar Ha'am warden responsible for every building in the city. He conveyed our instructions to the householders and saw to it that they were carried out.

When the disturbances first began, the Hagana set up a secret radio station, Kol Hamagen, to keep contact with the Jewish population. This was our principal means of contact with the people. The British police tried unsuccessfully to discover the station. It was set up in a private home which had no regular electricity supply. We arranged for a special cable to be drawn from one of the hospitals, from house to house, and the connecting line to the final house was rigged up to look like a clothesline, on which a few pieces of washing were hung daily to keep up appearances.

Kol Hamagen used to broadcast the notices of the Jerusalem Emergency Committee, as well as reports and programs in English, Hebrew and Arabic. The Arabic program was the longest. The station was on the sixth floor and artillery fire frequently made it necessary for the operators to go down to a lower floor. When this happened one of the staff remained on duty broadcasting the signature tune till the bombing ended. This continued until after the state was established and we set up the Kol Jerusalem radio broadcaster at Schneller's.

We set up some twenty-six loudspeakers linked to radios in houses and institutions provided with electricity, so that in various parts of the city the public could be informed of what was happening. This was important for morale. Sometimes when shelling would begin the listeners in the street would run to safety and the loudspeakers would go on talking into empty space.

We broadcast instances of bravery and good conduct, for their psychological effect on the public. Lectures were organized on the maximum utilization of food and simple methods of preparing food under siege conditions.

In December a special department had been set up in Mishmar Ha'am to deal with those who suffered in the Jerusalem disorders. Its purpose was to prepare dwelling places for those who had lost their homes and to care for their primary needs. Children were moved from danger spots to places of relative safety. The victims of the Ben Yehuda Street explosion, for example, were housed in a nearby synagogue until homes were found for them in private houses. In the second stage of its work, the volunteers dealt with those who had to leave their homes in the battle areas. Old people, women and children who came into Jerusalem from the surrounding settlements were cared for. When the Old City was evacuated on May 28, the Mishmar Ha'am dealt with the hundreds of refugees. At first they were given full food requirements and medical and hygienic care. Later they set up their own kitchens and prepared their own meals, but food kitchens were still needed for many. In this work, conducted under a heavy and constant bombardment from the Arab side, hundreds of women members of Mishmar Ha'am were prominent.

The uniform which was subsequently made available was extremely simple. It consisted of a raincoat, a beret, a baton and an armband bearing the words "Mishmar Ha'am."

The recruits were trained not only in their duties but for the total war that we felt might come upon us. They were given intensive drill in the use of small arms and hand grenades, field exercises and fire fighting. The cadre of N.C.O.s received even more intensive preparation.

This body of devoted citizens were a model of selfless devotion to duty, day and night. Their unflinching performance of the tasks assigned to them under fire and regardless of personal safety encouraged others to take the shelling and face the danger in their stride. They not only rendered public service in all walks of life but by their exemplary conduct helped to build and maintain the high spirit of our people that was so vital to our success.

For over a generation the key to Jerusalem's medical services had been the Hadassah Medical Organization, with its great modern hospital on Mount Scopus, the Hadassah University Medical School, the Nurses' Training School, the medical clinics and the Strauss Health Center. Other hospital and health services in Jerusalem were the Histadrut Workers' Sick Fund, Kupat Holim, which relied upon Hadassah for specialization and hospital services, and the older hospitals like Bikur Holim and Shaarai Zedek. To co-ordinate all medical and hygiene services, I set up a Health Council on which these bodies were represented. But at the center of the whole effort was Hadassah, which had in fact pioneered the medical services for the whole of Palestine with hospitals in key points throughout the country, with its introduction of preventive medicine, with its nurses' school, its school feeding services in Jerusalem, its infant "Drop of Milk" stations and other benefits.

Long before the April 14 massacre, access to the Mount Scopus hospital had become highly uncertain. By the middle of January, Dr. Yassky, who was himself killed in the later massacre, was reporting to New York that one student nurse had been killed and over a score of hospital workers wounded. "If we regarded complete security as an essential condition for our work in Palestine," he wrote, "we would have to give up all ideas of nationhood." But the difficulties of getting there had led to the setting up, in January, of emergency operating theaters in a clinic in Hassolel Street in the center of new Jerusalem.

On March 15 I met with Dr. Shaul Ziman of Hadassah's Strauss Health Center, where we had set up a joint body with the Vaad Leumi Health Department and Kupat Holim to look after hygiene services. I asked the body to accept responsibility for supervision of all matters of public health and for organizing on our behalf sanitary and hygienic activities essential for the Jewish community. I outlined some of their special duties: a campaign against contagious diseases; quarantine and preventive measures; preparing a supply of serums and organizing inoculation; general sanitation; examination and control of drinking water; a method of using toilets when there would be no water for flushing; destruction of refuse; maintaining a sewage system; and educating the public as to how to keep healthy during the emergency. They undertook these tasks.

At this time, too, Hadassah established two more hospitals in the center of Jerusalem. It had been maintaining a full team in the Old City and provided experienced physicians and invaluable surgical equipment to isolated settlements on the Jewish fronts. It extended its preventive services and made appropriate adjustments to its home medical service to meet siege conditions. On April 9, it transferred its casualty clearing station to Hadassah Hospital A, which began work in the premises of the former English Mission Hospital. Hadassah managed somehow to assure the city and its defenders adequate, well-organized medical services despite the trying wartime conditions under which they had to work. Hadassah's doctors, nurses and staff workers served Jerusalem with selfless devotion.

The organization which had functioned in Jewish Palestine since 1935 in the field normally occupied in other lands by voluntary first-aid and ambulance services was called Magen David Adom, the Red Shield of David (the shield of David is the symbol on the Israel flag). In the emergency, this body performed heroic and indispensable services. It supplied the city with an ambulance service, and its drivers and doctors displayed the courage expected of such organizations. From the outset it formed part of the framework of the defense service, serving the Hagana wounded just as the Red Cross of any country serves its armed forces. Since Hagana was not a legally recognized force, the Magen David Adom members were in constant jeopardy when aiding Hagana wounded.

A blood bank was opened on December 17, in two small rooms in the Kupat Holim building. Within two months it possessed 1,200 doses of plasma. During the whole war there was never a case when a person needing a blood transfusion could not get it. Donations of blood were voluntary. When the thousandth donor, a woman, was offered the not inconsiderable gift in those days of a bottle of kerosene and an egg, she refused and felt insulted.

At the beginning of the disturbances, Magen David Adom supplied first-aid outfits and supplies to all points of settlement in the Jerusalem area and set up a special surgical section at Bikur Holim

Hospital. It also supplied the surgical equipment needed for an operating theater in the field, at Kiryat Anavim, as it did for all Hagana units.

Even before the U.N. resolution of November 29, 1947, steps had been taken by the Jewish Agency to prepare plans for the legal and administrative structure of the state-to-be. Committees were set up to deal with finance and economic problems, communications, police, local administration, public works and social services. A legal council of some twenty-nine members was established, which I headed. We were to examine existing laws, to advise on the structure of the state's legal system and to prepare plans for the administration of justice and the organization of the courts in the state and also in the Jerusalem area. On April 27, 1948, I was able to submit a final report on the legal council's activities.

In spite of the difficulties of working under the conditions prevailing at that time, we managed to elaborate a detailed blueprint of the organization of the various departments of government and the administrative machinery of the state. This task was carried out conscientiously under the direction of Ze'ev Sherf, a Jewish Agency official who was later appointed secretary to the Cabinet.

The establishment of the Minhalat Ha'am (People's Directorate) before the British withdrawal helped avoid chaos and ensured the orderly taking over of government functions. To secure full utilization of our manpower for national service, a census of the population was carried out in February 1948. Postal services were organized, but in Jerusalem at the beginning we used Jewish National Fund stamps, which normally were not postage stamps at all. Arrangements were made for the printing of currency notes, which were available by the middle of August.

There was a great earnestness in the way the entire Jewish population tackled the problem of setting up the state, as shown by the serious discussion in the newspapers of innumerable questions affecting the nature of the state and the principles that should guide us in determining its forms. The unwritten law that difficulties and setbacks should never deter us in our main work of attaining nationhood served us well at this time.

Every preparation we could make was in the long run dependent on one thing: a steady flow of supplies from other parts of Jewish Palestine to Jerusalem. Without this we knew we could hold out for days, even for weeks, but not for longer. The railroad was hopeless, and by the end of March 'the highway from Tel Aviv to Jerusalem was closed, apparently for good. The most decisive event in the last agonizing weeks of the British mandate was a major campaign, called Operation Nachshon, by which we managed to open the road for a few short days, squeezing a few desperately needed convoys through the mountain road before it was closed again and the siege and the war took on new, bigger and more terrifying dimensions.

This road had not been really open since December, and by the end of February it had been virtually closed. In January my committee had tried desperately to double the thirty trucks which were still working the route; all we had to show for our trouble by the beginning of March was a shrinkage of the daily average to six. Days passed without a single vehicle getting through. On March 27 a small convoy was utterly wiped out, and for a solid week not a single Jewish vehicle reached Jerusalem. The heavy March rains had made swamps of the few alternate dirt roads which might have been risked. On March 31, a convoy set out from Hulda preceded by a fairly strong force of riflemen to clear the way. But the trucks bogged down in the mud and were immobilized for several hours. This gave the Arabs the time they needed to concentrate Iraqi and trained Arab reinforcements and to attack the convoy with overwhelming firepower. Some of the trucks managed to extricate themselves and get back to Hulda, but our losses in men, trucks and armored cars were very heavy.

It was at this point that the Hagana command was forced to the decision to fight larger-scale battles and to oppose the British by force if necessary. The convoy system clearly could not work. From the start it had been more psychological warfare than solid defense, putting heart into the Jews who had to travel, and discouraging some Arab attacks. But the Arabs soon learned that it was simple to outnumber any defenders we could send with a convoy, especially when these had to conceal their weapons from British patrols. They developed a system of solid roadblocks, flanked by a wall of small-arms fire extending several hundred yards on both sides of the steep and narrow road. The trucks were hard to turn around, and the Arabs booby-trapped the sides of the road to discourage drivers from getting out of their trucks.

This tough situation was made far worse by the British. There were instances when British police contented themselves with perfunctory search for weapons, realizing that this traffic was carrying

food for the civilian population of Jerusalem. But these were exceptions. Usually they carried out most meticulous searches, giving the
local Arabs plenty of time to mount an ambush or an attack. Arab
members of the police force deserted from these control points in
even heavier numbers than elsewhere, taking their weapons with
them as well as information as to which British personnel were prepared to sell confiscated arms to other Arabs. Sometimes the British
intervened directly. On March 17, for example, a small Palmach
section on convoy duty was attacked by a much bigger Arab force
near Kastel. It defended itself with skill and courage, and inflicted
heavy casualties on the attackers. Then the British moved in,
opened fire and killed six Jewish soldiers.

We were uncertain how the British would react to our decision
at the end of March to resist arms searches. It was a calculated risk
we had to take. We confronted them with a risk of their own, that
of clearly showing the United Nations and world public opinion,
on the very eve of their withdrawal from the country, that they
were engaged as participants in a full-scale war, and on the side of
the Arabs. As it worked out, except for individual engagements, the
British chose to give way before the Jewish determination to defend
themselves.

There were nine major points of danger along the road from the
coastal plain of Palestine to Jerusalem in the mountains. We managed to neutralize some of these by diversionary routes, but there
was at that time no way around the two desperate Arab bottlenecks
on the eastward and mountainous portion of the road. One of
these was around Bab el Wad, which means literally "the gate to the
valley," leading into the foothills from our supply base at Hulda in
the fringes of the plain. The other was at Kastel, an ancient Roman
encampment and crusaders' castle, which dominates the closest approaches to the city. This was completely Arab territory, and it was
at these two bottlenecks that most of the attacks on convoys took
place.

During this period, the Jewish arms position had improved somewhat by the arrival of weapons from Czechoslovakia. These consisted of light arms, light cannon and some antitank and antiair-
craft weapons. But we still had no fighter planes or artillery. The
problem of relieving Jerusalem was complicated by this shortage of
heavy war material, the nature of the terrain and the density of the
Arab population in the region. To this had to be added the fact
that there was practically no Jewish settlement in the area except

for a sprinkling of isolated points near the capital. Most of this region was under the direct control of one of the most powerful and popular of all the Arab leaders, Abdul Kader el Husseini. He had large family and clan connections all through the district and could call on their help to attack convoys at short notice. We turned to the vital task of relieving the city by gaining control of the road and the area which dominated it. This entailed some of the bitterest fighting during our War of Independence. The order of the day published to our men ended: "If Jerusalem remains cut off this will have a fateful effect on the whole war."

The first large-scale battle involved 1,500 Jewish soldiers, the largest contingent yet to be engaged in any single operation of the war. Its name, Operation Nachshon, was symbolic. Legend tells us that when the Jews were departing from Pharoah's Egypt they were caught at the shores of the Red Sea between the angry waters and the advancing Egyptian chariots. They stood trembling on the shore until Nachshon, the head of one of the tribes, broke the hesitation by plunging into the sea. He was immediately followed by the rest of the people, and the waters parted. The effort to free Jerusalem was equally desperate but had to be made, and so it was called Operation Nachshon.

The battle began on April 3 when the Haportzim Battalion took Kastel from its base at Kiryat Anavim, only six miles from Jerusalem. Abdul Kader was in command of large Arab forces which compelled us to abandon the flat-topped ridge of Suba about a mile away. Our forces—under the command of a young officer, Alexander Shapir, who later married my elder daughter—took the Arab stronghold at Deir Muhesin. But the Arabs launched heavy counterattacks and we were forced to withdraw from Kastel, with heavy losses. The fighting continued for days, with a few convoys getting through while we held the commanding heights. We retook Kastel on April 9 and an important hill village, Kolonia, on April 10. At the other major bottleneck, around Bab el Wad, we managed to take Saris, the Arab village which commanded the winding road, but here the British intervened against us with 3-inch mortars. Strong reaction by us soon forced the British troops to resume their policy of "neutrality."

The turning point at the Jerusalem end of the road, around Kastel, came when some Palmach soldiers in our command post fired on three Arabs approaching them. One of the Arabs killed was found from papers in his pocket to be Abdul Kader. The Arabs recovered his body and took it to Ramallah and then to the Old City of Jerusalem, where it was buried in the courtyard of the Mosque of Omar, in the presence of thirty thousand Arabs. His fellaheen supporters, discouraged by the loss of their leader, went back to their homes, and Kawkji's Liberation Army, angry at this desertion, retreated too.

The long battle had been won at the Jerusalem end of the road, and our reward was the breakthrough of three of the largest convoys ever to reach the city. I had been in Tel Aviv making preparations, and there was no delay. A convoy of 131 trucks with 550 tons of food left on April 15. On April 17, some 300 trucks, bringing 1,000 tons, reached Jerusalem. The trucks ran bumper to bumper, stretching out over six miles of road. They were attacked and we had some casualties, but the trucks got through, some of them being towed by others after they had been hit. I returned to Jerusalem in this convoy. It was an unforgettable experience to witness the exuberance, the self-confidence and the fearlessness of our drivers. Although this convoy arrived on the Sabbath, when orthodox Jews do not work or travel, an old rabbi blessed the trucks in the street, crying out, "These men hallow heaven and earth!" Even religious Jews left their synagogues, still wearing their prayer shawls, to do their assigned tasks of checking quantities and unloading the trucks.

Among my records is a list of what one of these convoys, that of April 15, carried. It contained 107 tons of white flour, 41 tons of barley flour, 9 tons of flour for matzoth, 25 tons of oil, 5 tons of soap, 100 tons of sugar, 470 cases of tinned milk, 38 tons of potatoes, 6.5 tons of syrup, 0.4 tons of chocolate, 4 tons of halva, 180,000 eggs, 6.5 tons of fruit and vegetables, 13 tons of cheese, 4 tons of miscellaneous foods, 21 tons of canned vegetables, 11 tons of beans, 4 tons of lentils, 3.5 tons of fodder and 0.6 tons of assorted groceries, to which had been added 80 tons of flour at Hulda and 60 tons of powdered milk and miscellaneous foods at Bilu, a former British Army camp east of Rehovot on the road from Ramleh.

We had managed to round up the trucks thanks to a group of young officers who had had experience in the Jewish transport units of the British Army in World War II. Their leader was a young South African Jew, Major Harry Jaffe, who brought the convoy in though badly wounded in the leg, and his assistant was Major Ber Shemer. They had secured 150 trucks from Solel Boneh and the Shelev Transport Co-operative; they brought the figure up to

300 by taking a Hagana field force out on the roads and requisitioning trucks with their drivers.

They had rounded up 1,000 men to service the trucks—drivers, assistant drivers and mechanics. They set up headquarters at Bilu, with warehouses in which we stored, at one time, 10,000 tons of supplies. They organized a small army of porters with the help of Benny Meyer, the head Jewish stevedore at the port of Jaffa. The catering for this extraordinary camp was undertaken by Yechezkel Ish-Kassit, the owner of a popular café in Tel Aviv called the Kassit.

Some fifty veterans of British Army Transport organized and ran the whole complicated business. Some of the drivers took their conscription in good part; others had to be recruited for such dangerous work at the point of Sten guns. There were tense moments when a thousand disgruntled men, most of them middle-aged and taken from their families without warning, were being rounded up. In those days almost every driver carried a weapon of some kind; here were hundreds of them to be faced down by a few officers. The drivers knew better than anyone else the odds on their getting a sniper's bullet or being burned to death on the long winding spirals of the road to Jerusalem. Yet we got them.

But the third convoy, on April 20, had a rough passage. It was a special Passover convoy bringing chickens, eggs, sugar and unleavened bread for the great Jewish festival. Its three hundred trucks were attacked at Bab el Wad, where Operation Nachshon had failed to establish control of the road. Three Jews were killed and thirty wounded. Six trucks had to be abandoned, their burned-out chassis lying to this day beside the road as silent reminders of the struggle for Jerusalem. The battle lasted all day. Some of the drivers volunteered to go up the hill to engage the Arabs at close quarters; they killed some thirty but lost their own commander, Maccabi Mosseri, son of one of the leading Egyptian Jewish families, who had already distinguished himself in the fighting around Jerusalem.

After this, the road was impassable again. Three times we sent the empty trucks back from Jerusalem to try to break through at Bab el Wad, but they never made it. I sent Shemer to Tel Aviv by Piper Cub to explain the situation to Ben Gurion and urge him to find an alternative road through the hills. On May 17 our army managed to get a small convoy of a dozen trucks through to Jerusalem. They contained army supplies, but no food for the civilians.

The men who fought our third convoy through were the drivers who only a few days before, when their vehicles had been requisitioned, had been conscripted and forced to make the journey to Jerusalem. When they eventually got through to the city and saw what their journey meant to the inhabitants, a miraculous transformation took place. They became different men, proud of having been in the convoy and eager to continue to help. When they had first arrived at the Bilu camp they had not realized that they would be confined behind barbed wire and not even be allowed to go home to see their families. While the third convoy was being organized, we had allowed them twelve hours' leave to go home, see their families and then report for the journey. Ninety per cent returned of their own free will to Bilu. They had ceased to be a band of unwilling and disgruntled men and became a team willing to work and dare together.

We now knew that we would have to subsist on the supplies which had been brought in during the weeks of anxious but meticulous preparation, and it can be said that Jerusalem is Jewish today because those preparations were made. The laying in of stocks of food, water and fuel to withstand a siege was only one part of the effort to save Jerusalem for the state of Israel. But it was a vital part. Without food and water, everything else that we also designed and planned would have gone by the board.

As that historic Passover passed into history we now began our final effort to withstand the storm that we knew would break when the British finally evacuated the country. In Jewish tradition, Passover is a "night of watchfulness," commemorating the great vigil when the children of Israel waited in Egypt for the Redemption. We felt the impact of that historic association. With us in the city were the drivers of the last convoy. There were 280 of them who were cut off in Jerusalem and could not get back to their families. They had to spend Passover and, as it turned out, some months more with us. Their presence was a symbol of how utterly we were besieged.

We arranged a special *seder,* the Passover repast, for these drivers, in the workers' co-operative restaurant in Jerusalem, at which I was present. I felt that if these men, for the sake of Jerusalem, had been forced to forego the pleasure of sitting down at this most significant festival of freedom with their families—for the Eve of Passover meal is the outstanding and most sacred family ceremonial of the Jewish year—then the least I could do would be to leave my family as well and be with them. I spoke to them in praise of their sacrifice, explaining how great a contribution they had made to enable the city to hold out. They were sad to be parted from their families, but their pride of achievement soon got the better of their longing to be home, and the ceremonial feast of liberation, though sober (despite the four glasses of wine they were enjoined by religious injunction to drink), was celebrated in a spirit of comradeship and good will.

That year, we in Jerusalem varied the traditional greeting of "Hag Sameach—a happy holiday" to "Hag Shaket—a quiet holiday." That particular Passover night was beautiful and quiet. Somehow this great festival of freedom brought with it a note of deep solemnity at the beginning of the siege. It was a kind of formal marking of the upsurge of solidarity among the most unexpected circles of the population. There was to come the day when five hundred of the ultra-orthodox, who spent their whole lives in prayer and study and who never knew manual work or the affairs of this world, came forth and insisted on being given an opportunity to help in the work of fortification. There was instant and unswerving obedience from all sections of the community to the orders issued by the Jerusalem Emergency Committee, although until the actual departure of the British the powers we had were solely those which we had assumed with the acquiescent consent of the people.

From time to time I broadcast over the radio to the people of Jerusalem in order to keep them informed about the situation. I followed the principle that the best could be got out of people if they were given a stark picture of affairs as they were and if they knew what they had to face and do. In making these broadcasts, one had to be conscious of the fact that the enemy was listening. It was often a ticklish job to find the correct language to emphasize the shortages and the need for the utmost economy and at the same time not give encouragement to the enemy, who monitored every word.

However, when this third convoy arrived, I spoke frankly: "Two weeks ago I told you briefly of the food and water situation in Jerusalem. At that time the city was cut off . . . Now the position has changed for the better. After a courageous struggle by hundreds of Jewish young men for the right of the inhabitants of the country to travel along the roads without interference, within one week three large convoys have reached us, bringing various food supplies.

"If a shortage was felt before these convoys arrived it was because those responsible for our iron rations had not considered the time had come to use them, and rightly so. Now after we have managed at one stroke to bring thousands of tons of food into the city the situation has altered completely and we may look to the future with more confidence as regards the supply of food to the public. Even now there will not be plenty and certainly no luxuries . . . The public must remember that the bringing of food to Jerusalem still entails danger, great effort and the sacrifice of precious lives . . .

"In times like these the public must be content with little. To ensure fair distribution of what we have and to cut down queuing up for food we shall, from next week, introduce rationing of all the essential foods . . ."

This convoy was the last to get through for some considerable time. No more supplies were to reach us by normal means for seven weeks. The Arabs had not been dislodged from their key point at Bab el Wad and they had also rendered the road impassable by mining and blowing up several hundred yards in a place where an alternative passage could not be found.

We were completely besieged. We would now have to make the most of our supplies while awaiting the departure of the British and the outcome of the battles which would follow. At the same time preparations were set on foot to find an alternative route to Jerusalem from the coastal plain. We were now engaged in a desperate race against time. Would our supplies hold out, or would the city be forced to surrender through hunger?

V

THE BRITISH EVACUATION

ЛГЛГЛГЛГЛГЛГЛГ

As THE END of the mandate approached, both our military and our supply problems grew more bewildering as well as more urgent. By the end of April there were three organized armies in the country: the British, the Arab Legion and the Hagana. There were three other armed groups: the irregular Arab forces, which recognized, if only nominally, the Arab Higher Committee, and the Irgun Zvai Leumi and the Stern Gang, which recognized no authority. The armies of six Arab states which were members of the Arab League were mobilized on the frontiers. The United Nations, which had voted the end of the mandate and the setting up of two new states to partition Palestine, was far away and paralyzed by the creeping terrors of the cold war. Finally, Great Britain, the mandatory power, was closing out its thirty-year trusteeship of the Holy Land in a mood compounded of bitterness, defeatism, and die-hard vengefulness. So each of these twelve armed forces, some of them big, some small, all in dead earnest, was improvising its strategy as events developed, playing by ear, and creating out of the chaos a tension so highly charged that a serious upheaval in international affairs might well have grown out of the fighting.

We tried from the outset to impress upon the High Commissioner that these disorders were not merely acts of Arab terrorism. Now war had been declared upon us publicly by the Arab states at the United Nations. The British administration should vigorously suppress this Arab design. Our exhortations evoked oral assurances of good intentions but no action. The Arabs were left free to carry out their military plans against us.

The tension was basically as old as human history, and as tangled in dark questions of right and wrong. The chaos was something new, and it was produced by British policy. The determination to maintain a formal posture of government while abdicating its most essential functions was its starting point. Through the hard winter and the harder spring, the lines of cleavage inside British policy became steadily clearer, and their capacity to operate the mandate or to end it dwindled as quickly as their desire to do either. The result was a maelstrom of legality and illegality, a daytime nightmare of clinging to formalism and protocol as order fell apart.

By April 26, the Central Post Office had closed down for good. Three days later, the stores of Jerusalem were empty again. The Jerusalem municipality, controlled by the British High Commissioner's office, had quietly ceased to meet. Both Arabs and Jews had long since stopped paying all taxes, and officials did nothing to collect them. By the end of the month the six Jewish ex-members of the municipality formed themselves into a council; the British turned a blind eye to this without surrendering the tiniest portion of their sovereignty. Large numbers of British had already been evacuated from Palestine. In many areas of life, illegally improvised Jewish authorities were functioning in the open. Yet the British clung so firmly to their refusal to co-operate in the transfer of power that many of us were not sure until the final, fateful day that they would leave the country in the end.

Even with the Arabs, we at least knew where we stood. As far back as December 24 the Hagana distributed a pamphlet in all Arab villages assuring their people that it had no aggressive intentions against them and urging them not to be drawn into a fight with the Jews. At the same time, the Histadrut made a similar appeal in the name of Jewish labor. "At this hour," it said, "when bloodshed and strife have been forced upon us, we turn to the Arabs in the area of the proposed Jewish state and to our neighbors in adjacent territories with an appeal for brotherhood, co-operation and peace. We are a peaceful people, and we are here to build in peace. Let us build our state together, as equal citizens with equal rights and obligations, with mutual trust and respect, each with a true understanding of the other's needs." The appeal was rejected. Tens of thousands of Palestine Arabs subsequently heeded the orders of the Arab Higher Committee and fled the country under the assurance that they had only to go for a little while until the Jews would be driven into the sea.

With the British, we operated in a fog of enmity and confusion. From the very beginning there had been good reason to suspect ulterior designs in their reaction to the United Nations vote for partition. As early as December 7, the High Commissioner, General Sir Alan Cunningham, had summoned our representatives to make an official statement on evacuation. His Majesty's Government, he said, desired to evacuate the country as soon as possible, and they desired the evacuation to be as smooth, as quiet and as rapid as they could make it. "You already know," he continued, "that the Army intends to leave by August 1, and if possible sooner." But he always used the term "intend." His words did not include an express undertaking that they would in fact leave by that date. He explained that it was a difficult task to evacuate all the troops. They had large warehouses. He left us puzzled and suspicious as to his real intention.

There are still knowledgeable men who believe that this original declaration was a bluff, at least on the part of important elements in London, in the British Army and in the High Commissioner's office. Their plan, it can be argued, was to produce the chaos which they expected would come about, to wait for an appeal by the United Nations to stop the bloodshed by remaining on their own terms, and thus to retain their imperial position free of the burden of the pro-Jewish provisions of the mandate. This analysis of British policy would help to explain their sullen, stubborn refusal to cooperate in any United Nations implementation of partition. It would make sense out of their unrealistic and illegal refusal to recognize any Jewish attempts to organize a new state on the grounds that the Arabs refused to make parallel efforts on their side. Finally, this explanation jibes with the open anti-Semitism of Ernest Bevin, British Foreign Secretary, and with the curious grudge against Israel which could lead the far more urbane and cultivated Lord Attlee, who was Prime Minister in 1948, to charge ten years later that the creation of Israel was a mistake responsible for all the ills of the Middle East. Recent revolutions and assassinations in Arab states and acrimonious feuds between them conclusively demonstrate the invalidity of this opinion.

Yet it seems to me now that this portrayal is too black and white. Jews who had lived in Palestine as long as I knew that there were many elements in British policy, that there were, in fact, several British policies. There were bulky files on Palestine in London in the Foreign Office, in the War Office, in the Colonial Office, in the Treasury, and in a dozen other departments. There was a continent between London and Jerusalem. Inside Palestine, we had daily evidence, in the most concrete and believable terms, of important differences between the British Army and the police force, between the High Commissioner and his Chief Secretary, between senior officers and enlisted men. Our tragedy was that our final fight for freedom, after two thousand years of exile, came at a moment when a war-weary nation, unwilling to go on paying the price of empire and unwilling to give it up, was capable only of a kind of massive, wavering indecision. This may well be a special failing of democracies. It produces chaos quickly, and in this chaos all kinds of sullen or bitter men find scope for the evil and the despair that are in them. Under circumstances like these an army or an athletic team or a mandatory administration becomes less than the sum total of the men who make it up. Something very much like this, it seems to me, lay behind the evacuation of the 6,208 British civilians and close to 100,000 British soldiers from Palestine in the spring of 1948. There was a world of difference between the days of Field Marshal Lord Plumer, High Commissioner in 1927, who when warned by the Arabs of the danger of disturbances replied that he did not need their help to maintain order in the country, to the final days of the mandate, when Arabs and Jews alike ironically referred to the *High* Commissioner and the *Higher* Arab Committee.

In the chaotic breakdown of British administration it was impossible to be sure what London wanted its officials on the spot to do or what these latter wished to do themselves. The uncertainty of British policy was its most baffling and, to us, one of its most costly aspects. We could be certain only of what they did *not* want, and this was chiefly three things: no Jewish immigration in excess of the 1,500 permitted every month; no constructive help by anyone else, including the United Nations, toward implementing partition; and no creation of even a shadow Jewish state, at least while they remained in the country.

The ban on the so-called "illegal" immigration was especially galling to the Jews. The full might of the British Navy was placed

behind this ban. The British candidly admitted their inability to
prevent the Arabs from bringing arms and men across Palestine's
land frontiers. They made not even a token effort to police the
borders against Arab infiltrators. Yet they hunted down every ship
bringing Jews from the D.P. camps of Europe. Week after week, the
British published proudly the record of their captures, sometimes
on the Mediterranean, sometimes on the beaches when men managed to land under cover of darkness. All those captured were im-
prisoned in detention camps in Cyprus. The Jews protested, world
public opinion was aroused, but to no avail. Even our need for
manpower, which was great, was secondary in our minds to the
overriding necessity to rescue such Jews as could still be saved from
the Europe Hitler had destroyed. But the British stuck grimly to
their ancient quota of 1,500 immigrants a month, long after the
Arabs themselves had given up complaining about Jewish immigration, having weightier problems to worry about.

British policy remained equally clear-cut in its opposition to any
international help in the transfer of power. They were blunt about
this both in London and in Jerusalem. The United Nations, for
example, had explicitly called for the freeing of a port for Jewish
immigration by February 1. The British refused to do this. The
Secretary of State for Colonies, Creech-Jones, had made fair promises in December, it is true, about British co-operation with the
United Nations Implementation Commission. "We do not wish to
cause difficulties for the U.N.," he told Parliament, "nor to encourage violence in Palestine, nor do we wish disorder to prevail
there and ruin what our administration created during the mandate. We wish for orderly transfer of jurisdiction to our successors
and that both sides so far as possible will respect the decision of the
international authority. . . . The British Government will wind
up its affairs in Palestine in a fair manner. The U.N. Commission
will have difficulties since the Arab Higher Committee refuse to co-
operate with it."

The Arabs never had a chance to co-operate or not to co-operate.
By January, Sir Alexander Cadogan told the United Nations
bluntly that his government would maintain undivided control
over Palestine until May 15, that British troops would leave by
August 1, that His Majesty's Government would look with disfavor
on any plan of the Implementation Commission to arrive in Palestine sooner than a fortnight before the mandate was to end on May
15. In reply to questions, he added that the commission would not

be permitted to travel in Palestine, to fix boundaries, to borrow any officials from the British mandatory administration, or to supervise the setting up of any armed militia while the mandate was still in force. A government spokesman in Jerusalem declared at the end of December that evacuation would be in a form which would not give ground for the accusation (*sic!*) that they were implementing the plan of the United Nations.

Finally, it was clear that the British were adamantly opposed to our building even the skeleton of an administration while they were still in Palestine. This harmed us more, of course, than either their ban on immigration or their refusal to co-operate with the United Nations. On the one hand, it required the Hagana forces at our disposal to continue far too long to operate underground, hiding their weapons and powerless to prevent Arab attacks. On the other hand, it produced a breakdown of normal economic life, in measure as the British administrative machine disintegrated or disappeared, which almost cost us Jerusalem itself in the long and bitter siege. In the irregular and unsatisfactory contacts we had with British top officials between December and May, they first justified this policy by arguing that a show of Jewish restraint would lead the Arabs to call off their disorders and their attacks. We had learned expensively the falsity of this argument in the 1936-39 riots, and we had good reason not to trust the British security forces to do anything but encourage Arab troublemakers. Then the British retreated behind the argument that since the Arabs were determined not to accept partition or set up a state, they could not help us to do so. The illegality of this argument was as potent as its immorality, once the United Nations had called on Great Britain to take the necessary steps to make partition work. But the British stuck to it, and on it was founded the entire policy of "neutrality" which served only to penalize the Jews and to leave the Arabs free to carry on a war which—at least some Britishers apparently hoped —would finally liquidate the old and unhappy problem of Palestine by liquidating the Jews.

So this led directly to their discriminatory handling of all the problems of government, at least during the months when they made even a pretense of enforcing law and order. British official pronouncements during this period came close in their unreality to what George Orwell has called "doublespeak": "The government opposes retaliation." "We will protect the Jerusalem-Tel Aviv road at all costs." "We are not prepared to provide escorts for convoys to Jerusalem." "The decision not to recognize Hagana is final. Hagana members caught with arms will be tried by military courts." The High Commissioner at an interview he gave Ben Gurion: "I tell you again it is not our policy to search Hagana members or to confiscate their arms." "The army will shoot at any side firing." "The police will arrest any person in possession of arms." Since the Jews were the only party to the dispute trying to carry out the United Nations injunction that militias should be ready to take over responsibility for law and order when the mandate ended, each of these announcements was a direct blow at us, and there were always men available to interpret them as savagely as they could.

I have tried, as dispassionately as I could, to describe how this "neutrality" worked to our disadvantage in the military operations which led up to all-out war. But only someone who lived through it can fully understand the resentment it caused among Jews who were trying to make partition work. The British allowed the Arabs, for example, to set up check posts at five entrances to the Old City. This barred all Jewish traffic, including milk or medical supplies for the Jewish quarter except when convoyed; even British soldiers had to show their credentials to the Arab guards before they could go in or out. Moslems could continue to visit their mosques in the Old City and Christians their churches, but the Jews were completely blocked from access to the Wailing Wall, a privilege which had never been denied them before, even by Moslem rulers of the country. The British allocated 300,000 Palestine pounds to the Supreme Moslem Council, an organization they had earlier disbanded and which was known by every child to be working hand in glove with the Arab Higher Committee. Yet, at the end of February, without even consulting the Jewish Agency, they excluded Palestine from the sterling bloc and released only seven million pounds in sterling to pay for all the country's essential imports until May 15. Most of the money Britain was freezing in this way had been brought to the country by Jews. In January the lawyer defending some young Jews charged before a military court with carrying firearms asserted without contradiction that tens of Hagana members had been put on trial before the courts while not one of the Arab attackers had been brought to trial. The British authorities were aware that large supplies of Arab arms were streaming into the country with an arrogant contempt for frontiers. Yet they took no effective measures to stop this wholesale arming of the Arabs against the Jews. At the same time they meticulously searched for and confiscated arms shipped to the Jews from abroad.

Under the pressure of acts like these, relations between the Jews and the British deteriorated rapidly. They had not been excellent, even before the fateful Black Saturday in 1946 when the British made their all-out attack on the Jewish community and its leaders in the foolhardy attempt to break their spirit. I know that we were never easy to get along with. We kept up a constant pressure on British officials which must have tried their patience sorely; we were in a hurry to found our state, and we hoped that our insistence would speed them up.

Personally, as a natural result of my upbringing and training in Canada I had started out in fullest sympathy with the British in Palestine, eager to foster the closest co-operation between the Jews and Great Britain. Only after their anti-Jewish policy as applied by Bevin was I regretfully forced to the conclusion that we Jews must sever our ties with the British. Christopher Sykes in his book *Orde Wingate* quotes a long letter I wrote to Dr. Weizmann about a conversation with Wingate during which he had said, "You must realize once and for all that the present British government does not care one bit for you." To this I had replied, I reported to Dr. Weizmann, "that it would not be an easy matter for us to break with the British, that they were one of the few peoples who had been friends to us, and that we had a sense of loyalty to them . . ." This severance of our ties with the British remains one of the painful memories of my life. I can understand the feelings of "one of the better Palestine officials" who once explained to the historian Sir Lewis B. Namier his preference for the Arabs by saying, "When I go to an Arab village and give an order, they obey; in a Jewish village, they argue." But by 1948 we seldom had a chance even to argue, in the rare, often tense, always uncordial meetings which took place between officials of the Jewish Agency or the Jerusalem Emergency Committee—and I served on both—and the High Commissioner or his senior officers.

On one occasion, an interview with the Chief Secretary was requested by the late E. Z. Hoofien, an outstanding personality in the Jewish community who was general manager of the leading Jewish bank in the country as well as Consul General of the Netherlands. He was told the meeting would take place in the street outside government offices. The implication was that he might have terrorist intentions and could not be trusted to enter the building.

With regard to Jerusalem, the British were obviously determined
to prevent its inclusion in a Jewish state even if one should ultimately be set up. This seemed evident from their military policy on
the roads, aimed at isolating the city so that it might be starved into
surrender, their efforts to bring about the Old City's evacuation by
the Jews and their attempts to undermine the Hagana.

There were many Britishers who behaved correctly, and some
who went out of their way to prove their sympathy for what we
were trying to do. Eric Mills, for example, who was the intellectual in the British administration of the mandate for many years,
became Commissioner on Special Duty in charge of the burial arrangements for the mandate; he was an old friend of ours, and he
had our sympathy in his unhappy job. Another senior British official, Richard Graves, who was named to head the municipality
when it was about to go out of existence, wrote publicly that the
Arabs were responsible for starting the disorders and that the
British must share the blame for their failure to check the violence
at the outset and to ensure the orderly transfer of powers when they
gave up the mandate. The High Commissioner himself, Sir Alan
Cunningham, we felt to be a fair-minded gentleman of high integrity, critical of Bevin's stubborn immigration policy, helpless under the orders he received from London.

The Chief Secretary, however, who held the real power in the administration, was Sir Henry Gurney, completely a Bevin man in his
relations with Jews. He was a very shrewd and careful civil servant,
reactionary in his bones, with that respect for physical power which
went hand in hand with anti-Semitism in the thinking of fascists in
the 1940s. He was later assassinated by terrorists in Malaya.

But by the spring of 1948, forces were at work which dwarfed personalities. Not more than a dozen non-Jewish British citizens stayed
on in Jerusalem to share our siege, half of those because of mar-
riage ties. I can think of only three or four Arabs of any promi-
nence who did, in spite of our efforts to persuade them. Fear of our
dissident terrorists and of Arab reprisals against those remaining led
to the flight even of Arabs who genuinely and deeply believed in
Arab-Jewish co-operation. Individuals had little choice, no matter
what their convictions. One could say, with some justice, that the
British Army was not as anti-Jewish as the police; that they had
shorter enlistments and fewer chances to become friendly with individual Arabs. Some Army officers behaved very badly, while
many rank-and-file soldiers wanted simply to finish their job and go

home. Some educated Englishmen, especially those with Colonel T. E. Lawrence's desert fixation or nostalgic memories of Kipling's Empire, were among the worst; a few of these men, especially in the Palestine police force, were open adherents of Sir Oswald Mosley. Some of these either deserted to the Arab side or transferred their allegiance immediately after the evacuation.

Only a decade before, Orde Wingate had written on December 31, 1937, to his cousin, Sir Reginald Wingate: "The administration of Palestine and Transjordan is, to a man, anti-Jew and pro-Arab. This is largely due to the fact that we seem to send only the worst type of British official to Palestine. They hate the Jew and like the Arab who, although he shoots at them, toadies to them and takes care to flatter their sense of importance."

Finally, there is no doubt in my mind that the Jewish cause was seriously hurt by the terrible hangover from Hitler's war. Sometimes ugly truths are better said than left unsaid; one of these is that even rational, decent non-Jews, before the establishment of Israel, could calmly contemplate the possibility of the Arabs' physically wiping out the Jews of Palestine.

Again, as in quoting Wingate, it is better for me to cite non-Jewish sources on this point. On July 20, just after the second truce began, another Englishman wrote, in the *Palestine Post:* "The thing to ponder on is what the Jews have done: they have made a revolution, they have revolted against a classic tyranny, they have torn off the vestments of the anti-Semitic witch-doctor to which the world, in medieval nostalgia, has been dancing. That is one meaning, the universal meaning: a sort of absolution. Glory be to God, it will do men's souls good when they feel the burden of their antique prejudice lifted."

It was hard to explain at the time, but this was precisely why we cared so passionately for the nation whose future we were molding.

No picture of Jewish relations with Great Britain at the time the mandate ended can be complete without an explanation of the ugliest single legacy the British left behind—the Arab Legion. This was originally the Transjordan Frontier Force, troops many of whom Colonel Lawrence had helped to train during World War I to help the British campaign against the Turks in the Middle East. British secret treaties with France, and not—as is widely but falsely believed—the Balfour Declaration of 1917, made it impossible to reward King Hussein of the Hejaz, after that war, as richly as he wanted. Much of the fumbling of British Middle Eastern policy for a generation can be explained by their feelings of guilt, and the constant Arab blackmail which kept those feelings alive, over British failure to give King Hussein's sons the Syrian empire which they believed had been promised to them. This was why, in 1922, the British unilaterally carved off from the territory entrusted to them under mandate by the League of Nations all the area west of the Jordan River, which was in part within the historic boundaries of ancient Israel, and set up one of Hussein's sons, Abdullah, as Emir, which is Arabic for Prince, of Transjordan. In effect, this served to buttress the entire British imperial position and its lifeline to India, and when they permitted Abdullah to proclaim himself King they kept the Transjordan Frontier Force, later renamed the Arab Legion, to safeguard this key bastion of their empire.

This force was composed of Arabs of Transjordan and Palestine, partly Bedouin, partly Circassian. They were easily the best-trained and best-equipped Arab soldiers in the world. But their officers were British. Their commander was General Sir John Bagot Glubb, known to newspaper readers as Glubb Pasha, indubitably an Englishman. They were paid by grants of the British exchequer to Transjordan. The Legion was directly controlled by the War Office in London and did not become an independent force even in name until after the Jewish state had been proclaimed. It became one in fact only in 1956 when Glubb was ignominiously expelled from Jordan by Abdullah's grandson, King Hussein.

This force took an active part in the War of Liberation. Questions asked about this in the House of Commons were evaded by the reply that the Legion was independent and that the British officers who served in it were employed by King Abdullah. The commander of the Jerusalem area was a Britisher, Brigadier Norman Olive Lash. On certain occasions before May 15, this officer had threatened to fire on our food convoys. It was the British who took the decisions and gave the orders. King Abdullah took some decisions of his own on political policy. It is unlikely that the British would have used the Legion to fight the Jews in Palestine if Abdullah had objected; but it is equally unlikely that Abdullah would have sent the force into Palestine to engage in fighting us if the British had objected, or even if they had advised against it.

In private conversations with representatives of the Jews, whom he trusted not to disclose the contents of his conversations, Abdullah had often professed his friendship and his concern for the welfare of the Jews. As with so many Arab leaders, an entire world separated his publicly declared views regarding the Jews from his private and confidential protestations of friendship to them made under circumstances which would leave him free to deny any Jewish leakage. For example, in 1933 this Arab patriot wandered so far from the accepted policy of Arab nationalism not to dispose of land to Jews that he agreed to rent a large area of his territory in Transjordan to the Jewish Agency. I drafted the lease agreement and met the Emir at his winter palace at Shuna. He was full of affability and good will, and hoped that the Jews would develop the land agriculturally so that it would be a model to Arab farmers in Transjordan. While he accepted his regular payments of rent, he managed to find all sorts of excuses to put off the date when we could take occupation of the land.

When partition was agreed on by the U.N., Abdullah was pleased, for he saw that this gave him an opportunity of grasping at the Arab-designated portion of Palestine. Therefore he was at first deliberately vague in his attitude to the plan and did not oppose it with the same rancor as the other Arab leaders. But when he saw himself isolated in a fury of Arab nationalist opposition, he fell in line with their views. He then hoped that he would fall heir to the whole territory, including the Jewish part, when the Israelis had been wiped off the face of the earth by the concerted Arab invasion. Many British saw this as at least a second-best possibility. They believed that the Jews, under the threat of defeat and annihilation, would in desperation call for their help at any price. In this event, they would come back to a shattered Palestine on their own terms. Alternatively, they would be almost as well off with the Jews crushed and all Palestine in the hands of their puppet King of Transjordan. The British proved as consistently wrong in this calculation as in so many other aspects of their Middle Eastern policy, but it was a strategy which made sense in 1948 to the diehards of the British Empire.

None of this, of course, was openly stated at the time. One explanation given to us by the British was that the Arab Legion was a foreign force, and that British officers in it were in the same position as Englishmen taking up employment in any foreign country. British consular officials in Jerusalem assured me personally, no doubt with tongue in cheek, that in the long run the Jews would stand to gain from the presence and influence of these British officers, even if in the immediate sense they might add to our military difficulties. The gain would be in their humanizing the war. While British officers were directing the shelling of Jerusalem, before they were withdrawn, the officials asserted, the shelling was much less indiscriminate than later on.

However, when the Jewish Agency asked why the authorities had brought the Legion into Palestine, the High Commissioner stated (in an interview with Ben Gurion early in December 1947) that it was a British force and that they were responsible for it. The Legion would do nothing without British approval. When Ben Gurion observed that the BBC had reported the night before that the Legion had already entered into combat with the Jews, the High Commissioner replied that he had more trouble with the BBC than we had, and he could not be responsible for their statements. He declared that the Legion would leave the country before the British did. This corresponded to the assurance previously given to the House of Commons by the Foreign Secretary. Bevin had declared flatly that the Arab Legion would be withdrawn together with the British troops.

In fact, they took an active part in the fighting against the Jews before the British left, in the Etzion settlements, where their intervention was decisive, and in sporadic incidents elsewhere. When the authorities finally yielded to pressure to withdraw them from the Palestine Broadcasting Studios, where they were stationed, they were posted in the Russian Compound in the very heart of Jerusalem. On the eve of the termination of the mandate, Transjordan received for its Legion three shiploads of British arms at Aqaba.

These were the complicated factors which made it so hard for us to be sure, during the entire winter and spring, just what the British would eventually do. It was clear that the officials were planning to leave and that many Army units were already being evacuated. But the refusal to co-operate with our plans to take over administrative functions, plus the announced plan to keep some troops until at least August, led many of us to suspect that they were still hoping that the Arab assault would leave all of Palestine in such a state of collapse and exhaustion that they would have to change their plans and stay.

Already by the end of December there were indications of active steps to evacuate. Some troops and equipment began leaving the country and camps were wound up. The Air Force was the first to move. The Criminal Investigation Department of the police began closing down certain sections.

In January, seven hundred British residents were moved to Cyprus. The emptying of Army warehouses began. Troops started to evacuate certain Jewish areas. In the middle of January, the Chief Secretary advised heads of departments that they must be ready to wind up their departments and leave at a month's notice, but that this did not mean a full month's notice would necessarily be given.

By the middle of January, half the thirty-two government departments were immobilized. The administration of justice was greatly restricted, with the courts not functioning properly, and it had become evident that the whole machine was running down. The Postmaster General announced he could not maintain the postal services. Yet no other authority would be admitted and Hagana remained illegal.

At first, the British plan was to hand over governmental functions to municipalities and local councils in Jewish areas, and in Arab areas to committees controlled by the Arab Higher Committee. They resolutely resisted all our proposals that these functions should be turned over either to the U.N. Implementation Commission or, in Jewish areas, to our national institutions, the Jewish Agency and the Vaad Leumi. In the end, they followed no plan. On the stubborn refusal of the Jews to collapse, "Operation Chaos" had to be carried out in a general spirit of scuttle and run.

A total of six weekly meetings of the heads of government departments were held, chaired either by the Chief Secretary or by Eric Mills, who had been named, but not really empowered, to deal with the liquidation of the mandate. There was only one non-Britisher at these meetings, Amihud Goor, a Jew who was the head of the Forestry Department. There was no discussion at these meetings, but instructions, sometimes in written form, were given by the chairman.

It is impossible, even now, to make sense out of these instructions. At one meeting, the Chief Secretary announced that all persons in prisons would be released on the day of evacuation. When asked if this might not lead to trouble, he said this could not be helped. (As it turned out, they were not released.)

In effect, most officials took independent action. One Jewish department head, after he had openly transferred his allegiance to the

Jewish Agency, telephoned the chief of the Government Printing Office with a request for stationery. A truckful was sent to a point in no man's land between the British zones and the Jewish-controlled area. The next day he called back and said that we had lost the stationery. "Send your truck again," was the reply, "and I'll give you a second lot." None of the paper carried British headings on it; the supplies lasted the new government of Israel for nearly a year.

A British official of the Lands Department, who had never been regarded as friendly to the Jews, allowed us to take all maps that could possibly be useful. We also took from the Survey Department, in the Russian Compound, two truckloads of aerial photographs of the country. No comment was made by the Britisher in charge when he saw that they were gone; they were kept in a private house for a few days and then turned over to those who were already at work at setting up a survey department for the future Israel government. In the Forestry Department, in the first days of May, we simply packed up all the contents of the office, files and furniture, and moved them into warehouses. The head of the department drew out all the official funds from Barclay's Bank and redeposited them in the names of three senior Jewish officials. Within a week of the proclamation of the new state, this department was functioning normally.

Jewish officials in the British administration were told nothing by their superiors except to come to work regularly, to protect government property, to act as if nothing momentous were about to happen. They were asked no questions. Jewish authorities told them to stay at their posts, too, and to try to minimize the disorganization of services. Most of them were members of Hagana; all of them, almost without exception, now took orders from the Jewish Agency. They came over in a body to the new government of Israel, and it was their courage and loyalty which made it possible to set up the nucleus of a new administration almost overnight when the British left. Credit for this must be shared by the many well-trained officials of the Jewish Agency who went over to the service of the state.

It was officially announced on March 15 that evacuation of troops was proceeding according to plan and "if continued at the same speed" should be completed by August 1. Several thousand troops had already left. Early in April, Army headquarters was moved from Jerusalem to Haifa, the port of departure. It was announced that the Jerusalem Military Court would be wound up on April 20 and that Sir Hugh Daw would be the British representative in Palestine as from May 15. All civilian officials received notice of termination of their services. The Import Department closed down. Foreign airlines stopped their traffic to Lydda. It began to look even to the skeptics as if the British were really going.

By April 15 all British officials had left Jaffa and the British staff of the Chief Secretary's office began to leave Jerusalem for home. Before the end of the month all British civilians, officials and police had been evacuated except some two thousand police and twenty senior officials who were to remain with the High Commissioner until he left. Censorship on press and broadcasts came to an end after twelve long years.

By May 5 Jewish officials took over the Central Post Office, since all the British and most Arab officials had gone for good. A few days before leaving, the administration handed over all government offices in Tel Aviv to the municipality "on trust"; anything was better than to admit the possibility of a Jewish state coming into being by handing over to the Jewish national institutions already engaged in setting up that state. The same was done in Haifa, except for the port, which was entrusted to the management of three Jews, one Britisher and one Arab.

Finally, on the morning of Friday, May 14, Sir Alan Cunningham drove out of Jerusalem in his bulletproof Daimler. The last British civilians and troops followed him, and within ten minutes Hagana men were in their evacuated offices and control posts. The thirty-year British rule of Palestine had ended. The Jews were not sorry to see them leave. Only later were the practical benefits of the British administration in Palestine properly appraised and given due credit; but the policy they followed in the last years of their mandate must remain a blot on the record of British rule in the Holy Land.

A fortnight later, in a speech in Scotland, Winston Churchill, the man who had once declared to the world that he did not intend to preside over the liquidation of His Majesty's empire, made a summary of the last chapter with which no Jew in Palestine could quarrel. He said, according to the newspaper report which reached us in besieged and embattled Jerusalem, that

the Socialist handling of the Palestine problem had been an extraordinary failure. As soon as they came to power they turned their backs on their election promises of 1945 and thus caused much disappointment and anger among the Jews. It was possible to carry out a fair partition of Palestine right after victory with the help of the army we then had and with the influence and good name of Britain. When we had seen how bad things were in Palestine and how helpless the Government was he had advised the Government in August 1946 to return the mandate to the United Nations and to leave Palestine from which they were unable to derive any benefit nor receive any honor. But the government waited eighteen months, during which time numerous British soldiers were killed. . . . Now they had reached a situation when the whole effort, which gave much promise, lasting some thirty years, was ending in dishonor . . .

VI

THE ALL-OUT WAR

ᴨᴜᴨᴜᴨᴜᴨᴜᴨᴜᴨᴜᴨᴜ

Aᴄʀᴏss ᴍᴏsᴛ of the hills and plains of Palestine, the war had become a full-scale military operation for both the Jews and the Arabs some weeks before the end of the mandate. The proclamation of the new state of Israel on May 15, however, transformed it into an official, all-out war.

On Friday, May 14, at 4:30 P.M. in the Tel Aviv Museum the members of the People's Council, the Jewish Agency Executive and a select group of veteran Zionists assembled to hear Ben Gurion read the Declaration of Independence and the establishment as from midnight of a Jewish state to be called Israel.

The true situation in Jerusalem was such that we could not celebrate the great day of the proclamation of the state. We were concerned mostly with the fact that the British were leaving the country, that we would no longer be hampered and harassed in our national efforts and would now be able to tackle the tasks in hand freely. We could not even think of getting to Tel Aviv to take part in the actual ceremony for which we had striven for so many long years, although it was arranged for the oldest member of the Jewish Agency Executive, Rabbi Yehuda Fishman (later Maimon), to be present at this historic and solemn occasion.

Every word of the proclamation meant something to us all, but it was only months later that we could think of it as a document which future generations of Israelis would treasure. We did not even receive the special newspaper published collectively by all the newspapers in Tel Aviv, called *The Day of the State*. Our reading

matter was confined to the circular published by the Bureau for
National Service proclaiming men in Jerusalem from eighteen to
forty-five years of age, regardless of family status, to be at the disposal of the security forces. On paper the dream had come true.
The first President of the state had been elected, the Zionist emblem
was selected as the flag of Israel, a temporary seat of government
chosen. But for us in Jerusalem, as the state was proclaimed the
battle for Jerusalem raged, while the battle for the Jerusalem-Tel
Aviv road was still in full force. We anxiously thought of the morrow and what it had in store for us.

Five foreign nations, Syria, Lebanon, Iraq, Jordan and Egypt, began at once to move columns across the frontiers of Palestine. The
Arab Legion, far from evacuating as the British had promised,
moved into strategic positions in and around Jerusalem. There
could now be no turning back for the Jews. We had to win, alone,
or perish.

The end of April and the first two weeks of May had seen our
positions strengthened across almost the entire country except for
Jerusalem. In the Valley of Jezreel, the Arab Liberation Army under Fawzi el Kawkji had been defeated at Mishmar Haemek and
forced to withdraw to the Jenin area. Another battle at Ramat
Yohanan eliminated the Druse mercenaries who had been hired
by Kawkji; ever since that time the Druses have been the most loyal
of all Israel's minorities.

On April 18, Tiberias was cut in two by the Golani Brigade, and
a few days later the Arab population fled and the city became Jewish. In Haifa, the British, with less than a month to go, were concentrating their forces, equipment and evacuable supplies in the
harbor area and were no longer seriously concerned with the
fate of the city. The crucial battle for Haifa, which took place on
April 21-22, was over within twenty-four hours. Most of its Arabs
left by sea or land, although some thousands believed the Jewish
offer to protect them and their property, and remained.

These successes in Galilee gave the Jewish forces a finger of territory right up to the Syrian and Lebanese borders. With a Palmach
unit (in which our younger daughter Leila served) successfully
penetrating into Safad, the fate of that city was also determined, although it was nearly a month before the city fell, after savage fighting in which the Jews could only oppose their new mortar, the
Davidka, to artillery and heavy automatic weapons and armor. The
fall of Safad and the subsequent mopping-up operations cleared

Galilee right up to Lake Hula, and by May 16 the Jewish positions and holdings in this area were linked up. An Arab Legion counterthrust in the region of Zemah and Gesher was successfully repulsed. These places had strong points built around former British police fortresses. At the beginning of May, too, a Lebanese armored column and an Arab attack assisted by heavy artillery in the vicinity of Ramat Naftali were repulsed. In the east, Beisan in the Jordan Valley fell to the Jews on May 12, as did the Arab villages in the region of Mount Tabor, Sejera, Bethlehem of Galilee, the former German colony of Waldheim and Umme Zinaat on southern Carmel. On the western Galilee coast, the Carmeli Brigade of Hagana took Acre, Ez-Ziv and Batzat, breaking the siege of Yehiam and the Hanita bloc. This series of operations was completed by May 17.

The front in the Sharon plain and in the region of Tel Aviv also showed quick successes. Three Hagana brigades, the Alexandroni, Kiryati and Givati, were involved and they mopped up Arab villages in the vicinity of Tel Aviv and Jaffa. These included Hiriya, Sakiya, Salame and Yazur. This was the eve of Passover and the operation was called *"Hametz,"* which refers to the cleansing of the home of leaven. A premature attack on Jaffa by the Irgun Zvai Leumi was frustrated by British intervention on April 26, on the grounds that this city was a designated Arab area. But the city was encircled on April 29, and when the British left on May 13 it fell to the Jews.

Closer to Jerusalem the news was not so good. By May 4 and 5 the Arab Legion was mounting a sustained drive on the Jewish villages in the mountains known as the Etzion bloc, which had been besieged for months. The settlers there were ill-provided with weapons but held out until May 13, when they succumbed to a combined attack by local Arab irregulars and the Arab Legion. Those who survived a general massacre by the irregulars surrendered to the Legion forces.

The brave resistance of the Etzion bloc delayed the arrival of part of the Arab Legion in Jerusalem and gave the capital more time to consolidate its position. But seen in retrospect, the view that by their stand they saved Jerusalem does not appear to be justified. The plain truth of the matter is that Jerusalem was saved by its own defenders and residents. The hordes of Arabs who had been attacking the Etzion settlements for so long did not even join the later assault on Jerusalem. Most of them were villagers of that area who resented the existence of Jewish villages on their mountain. They

wanted to wipe them out, and they wanted loot. Having gained
both objectives, most of them went home to their villages.

As for the Arab Legion, after Etzion fell they did not constitute
the main force in attacking the south of Jerusalem. This task was
entrusted to Egyptian troops, which did not take part in the
Etzion fighting. Indeed, from the military point of view, had they
wished to join in the attack on Jerusalem before Etzion fell, the
Legion could have done so and ignored the existence of the Etzion
bloc, since the Etzion settlements could not prevent the Legion
from reaching Jerusalem by other roads entirely open to them. The
settlers would have had all they could do to hold out against the
attacks of the Arab irregular forces alone. They were certainly in
no position to have come to the help of Jerusalem. It would be his-
torically more accurate to say that in their struggle the Jews of
Jerusalem were defending not only themselves but also the state
of Israel. Were it not for the prolonged and successful defense of
Jerusalem the Arab Legion and other units with their armor and
artillery would have been free to join the general attack in the
other areas of war.

It was on May 18 that the Legion wheeled southward until its
right wing reached Latrun. The next day, its forces appeared inside
Jerusalem. This was the one area in which the tactics and training
of the Legion were least likely to prove of any avail. The Legion
was a highly mobile force which would have been difficult to oppose in open fighting with our inferiority in armor and artillery,
as our subsequent experience around Latrun showed. That our
forces could meet it and take its measure was also shown on some
fronts, although these were hard-fought and costly battles. But
street fighting was one place where tanks, tracked vehicles, armored
cars and even heavy artillery were of least use. The Germans had
learned this in Stalingrad, where the world realized that a people
fighting inside their own homes, with a stubborn determination
never to surrender, is as nearly invincible as any force can be in
modern warfare.

It was a blow to us, nevertheless, to find the Arab Legion in
Jerusalem a few days after the British Army had left. We had
made careful plans to take over the British security zones, which
had been used by Arabs as lookout posts and where British soldiers
had joined Arabs over many weeks in firing at our positions and
sniping down our streets. If the Arabs had gained control of these
zones, forming a line through the Italian Hospital, Abyssinia

House, the Russian Compound, the Generali Building, the King David Hotel district, the security zone in the eastern part of Rehaviah and Talbieh, the railway station and the German Colony, the position of Jerusalem would have been catastrophic. Apart from the fact that this line would have cut across Jewish Jerusalem, it would have meant complete isolation for Ramat Rahel, Talpiot and Mekor Hayim. Yemin Moshe would have been cut off and we had already paid a great price to hold it in the hope that it might prove a springboard to link us up with the Jewish quarter of the Old City. The Sheikh Jarrah quarter would have passed finally to the Arabs, and with it would go access to Mount Scopus, the Hebrew University and the Hadassah Hospital.

These positions had to be taken for another reason too. We just did not have enough fighters and arms and ammunition to protect such a scattered area as Jerusalem would have become without these positions. If we were to survive, we had to join up our isolated areas, straighten and shorten our defense lines, and move our front from the inhabited central areas which also held our food and equipment concentrations and the heart of our civilian and military communication facilities.

It was only *force majeure*—the presence of the British—which compelled us to hold off the implementation of this plan. But we had nevertheless been able to achieve certain elements of our plan even before they left. By the beginning of May, we had taken most of Katamon and carved out a narrow corridor through the Greek Colony to Mekor Hayim. This could be traversed only by night. On the west, our situation had improved with the evacuation of Lifta by the Arabs. The Schneller Camp and several other little end bits of territory of security zones were in the event peacefully and officially joined to our area.

Our plans, which had been completed in the afternoon of Thursday, May 13, called for a three-pronged movement, known as Operation Pitchfork, to create the solid Jewish area within Jerusalem which we so sorely needed. One arc movement was to advance from Katamon to link up with Mekor Hayim and Talpiot. A second was aimed straight through the center of the city toward Jaffa Gate. The third was to be another arc movement from Bet Israel to link up with the university on Mount Scopus.

Our logistic difficulties were great. We were short of men and ammunition. Pitchfork entailed a series of operations undertaken simultaneously and in sufficient strength to strike immediate and crippling blows. But we could not detach the necessary manpower from covering our long and ragged line, mustering fighting patrols and repairing Arab breaches in the line. Since we had practically no reserves, our static troops had to move from their positions into new ones as they were captured in order to release troops effecting the capture to go on to new objectives. Shortage of arms also dictated a kind of poor man's technique in the use of our troops. Men took turns in using the arms we had; while one group of men was engaged in armed duties, another would be manning searchlights or working on fortifications.

The following standard inventory of arms available for a rifle platoon indicates our position. It consisted of ten rifles, fifteen Sten guns and one Bren or Lewis machine gun. In all, we had in Jerusalem some two dozen 2-inch mortars with a small supply of shells; five 3-inch mortars, including those isolated at Talpiot and the university on Mount Scopus and therefore not switchable from front to front; five machine guns of the Browning or Schwartzlose type; three Davidkas of Jerusalem manufacture; and two 2-pounder cannon mounted on ex-British armored cars which also had Beza machine guns. As things turned out, no additional supply of arms could be moved to us in time.

Hagana intelligence brought us the news only on May 13 that the British evacuation had been advanced a day from the original date of May 15. That night, Kol Hamagen, the Hagana station, broadcast an order to all the people of Jerusalem to be prepared "to protect our future." A special message was included to the defenders of the Old City:

On the eve of the day of proclamation of the Jewish State, we send you greetings. We believe that the day is near when the dawn of redemption will shine forth for Jerusalem, and our ancient city, now besieged, will have its full reward.

On the morning of May 14, the British moved out and Operation Pitchfork began. Our forces, which had been concentrated during the night in the stretch adjoining the British security zones, advanced in four columns. One turned down the Street of the Prophets and seized the Italian Hospital area. The Italians had agreed to entrust the hospital to Jewish guards. The second column turned down to Sheikh Jarrah, the third continued from the Generali Building into the heart of Security Zone 3, and the fourth from the gate of Security Zone 2 to the railway and the crossroads to southern Jerusalem.

Zone 2 was the first to be liberated. Hagana forces entered the zone when it was still night, and on the British departure at dawn the Hagana were already in the lookout posts that overlooked the zone. Arab attempts to penetrate were in vain and when these failed the few Arabs in the zone fled.

The Arabs had prepared for this decisive battle, concentrating troops at Jaffa Gate and Damascus Gate and in the Old City. Five hundred Arabs in armored cars and on foot entered El Alamein Camp on the Jerusalem-Bethlehem road a few minutes after the British evacuated it.

We gained our first objectives with comparative rapidity. Key buildings were captured one by one. Bevingrad was taken almost without a shot being fired. This was the main fortress of the British Criminal Investigation Department, which symbolized in the center of the city the foreign character and tyranny of the emergency rule introduced by the British to maintain by force the anti-Jewish policy of the 1939 White Paper. It was universally called Bevingrad, in contempt for the British Foreign Secretary. Some two hundred shops, offices and businesses had been seized by the authorities and formed into a fortified enclave, surrounded by barbed-wire fences several times the height of a man, concrete emplacements, and dragons' teeth. They included the Bank Leumi, the General Post Office, the Generali Building. My former law offices had been obliged to move from this building on twenty-four hours' notice with all its other occupants. I later returned to this same building to set up my offices as Military Governor. In this fortress had been centralized the main strength of the British police and their stores. They did not realize that by shutting others out they were shutting themselves into a prison of their own making.

At 8 A.M. a British Army officer appeared on the balcony of one of the buildings in the Russian Compound and told a Jewish police officer that he would hand over the buildings only to unarmed Jewish police officers. He assured them there were no armed Arabs in the buildings. The Jewish police entered the building of the district police and speedily sensed the presence of an armed Arab gang. They left and informed the British officer that if the Arabs did not leave, an armed Jewish squad would enter the building. The Brit-

ish evacuated twenty armed Arabs and the Jews took over. They
also took over the other buildings in quick succession. The Israel
flag was hoisted over the Generali Building; the British officer
saluted it smartly and left. Police headquarters were seized by armed
contingents of Hagana and Irgun Zvai Leumi; so was the District
Officer's building. Work parties of Jews at once began removing the
barbed wire around Bevingrad. Thousands of uniforms, boots and
other police equipment in the police storehouses passed into our
hands.

In the General Post Office a number of Jewish officials had been
in constant residence for ten days, their arms hidden in the building. Arab workers who were there on May 14 were captured. By
8:15 A.M., Israel forces were in control of the Post Office and the
telephone exchanges.

In the Russian Compound there was deathly silence. But after an
hour Jewish forces arrived and in military formation advanced and
took control of all the buildings in the compound. The Russian
church was wide open. A week later the priests and nuns left their
lodgings in the compound for the Old City, having been frightened
by the Arabs with tales of what the Jewish "Bolsheviks" might do
to them.

The column which carried out these operations then turned to
join up with that which had taken the Italian Hospital, and both
turned down to the Musrara quarter. They took the Meah Shearim
police station and the adjoining police dwelling quarters and found
themselves faced by hundreds of Arabs who were pouring out of the
Old City through the Damascus Gate. The Notre Dame Hostel,
only seven yards from the Old City wall, was also taken.

On the eastern front, Jewish forces set out to the Police Training
School, overlooking Mount Scopus, on the road to Neveh Yaacov.
They seized the building and grounds. They found much equipment and arms. When they had consolidated their positions they began the encirclement of Sheikh Jarrah, which was speedily captured. The Rockefeller Museum was showing a large red cross and
though the Israelis were fired on from one of its roofs they did not
return the fire, because of the Red Cross flag, nor did they attempt
to seize it.

In the south of the city, our men took Talbieh and the David
Building on King George V Avenue, which had also constituted a
British security zone. The Jews moved in as the British left and the
Arabs fled in fear. There was no real fighting here, only some snip-

ing. The same day we attempted to send a convoy through to Talpiot. This area was cut off; it was necessary to get arms and ammunition to the defenders and to evacuate the women and children. The convoy was attacked near Deir Abu Tor and compelled to turn back. An important decision had then to be made. Should the attempt to get through be deferred till the evening or should the main burden of battle be moved at once from the center of the city to the southern area?

It was decided to move two companies through the area held by the enemy around St. Simon's Monastery in Katamon and to reach Mekor Hayim, cut across the El Alamein Camp and so reach Talpiot. It was feared that having helped to subdue the Etzion block, the Arab Legion might approach Jerusalem from the south.

If this proved correct, it would be met at Ramat Rahel. If the Legion did not attack there, our force would turn inward and try to take Bakaa, Katamon south, and the Greek and German colonies, joining up with another force that would advance from Talbieh.

This latter force moved forward at midnight on Friday armed with a Davidka, ammunition and explosive materials, under cover of darkness. It reached Talpiot early on Saturday morning without having had to fight. Meanwhile, news was received that the Arabs had seized Allenby Barracks adjoining Talpiot. The company that reached Talpiot was ordered to attack in daylight. Two attempts to penetrate were repelled by heavy fire, several of our men being killed. Orders were then received to shell the camp with the Davidka and it was also shelled by 3-inch mortars stationed at Kiryat Shmuel. At midday, it became clear that the prospects of penetrating the camp were slight. As the Israeli troops were getting ready to break off the engagement, our intelligence reported overhearing a telephone conversation between the camp commandant, who had three hundred Iraqi troops, and the Old City commander, complaining that he was being shelled and would not be able to hold out. He asked for help, which was refused. This news encouraged the Israeli troops to attack again and by dusk the camp was captured. The victory was important because enough arms and ammunition were taken to equip a company. Part of the haul was a British antitank gun. The way was now open for Jewish forces to move from Katamon to clear the area of the German colony and to join up with Talpiot.

After some slight fighting this objective was attained on Saturday night. We now had a contiguous area, but it did not include Deir

Abu Tor nor the Government Printing Office. The power station, under the control of three foreign consuls, was also in this area, as well as the railway station. The southern command was ordered to make a diversionary attack here Saturday night, to cover a major attempt to break through the Jaffa Gate into the Old City. The attack on Jaffa Gate failed, but the printing presses, the railway station and the entire region of Deir Abu Tor fell into our hands, giving us at last all of the southern part of the New City.

The first day of independence, Saturday, May 15, came to an end with Mount Zion still in the possession of Arab snipers, who poured fire on Yemin Moshe and the closest outposts we had to the Jaffa Gate. In Musrara the Arabs began to counterattack in two directions: toward the Israel position near the Meah Shearim police station and toward our positions close to Barclay's Bank and the New Gate. That Saturday night there was heavy shelling from the Arab cannon situated in Nebi Samuel, Bet Hanina and Bir Nabala. All day Sunday, hand-to-hand fighting occurred in buildings throughout the city against a background of incessant shelling which the civilian population took very well.

For the sixty hours from Friday morning until Sunday night the entire city was like a single front, with firing throughout the area, fighting being fiercer first at one point, then at another, and shells bursting throughout the day and night. Many buildings changed hands numerous times. This was no small ordeal for a civilian population, but people were not panicky, many went into their shelters, the streets were kept clear of civilians not on duty, while every able-bodied man and woman did his assigned duty resolutely and courageously. They were a people's army, if ever there was one, for all who could be were in it and of it. Everybody sensed that these few days would be crucial in deciding the city's fate.

Things did not go so well for the Israelis at Atarot. We knew we could not hold this isolated settlement to the north of the city, and it was evacuated. The Arabs set it on fire. Neveh Yaacov was also evacuated according to plan. That Saturday morning, men, women and children, undeterred by the danger of snipers and shelling, went out to work on the fortifications in the north of the city. In a few hours, roadblocks and other defenses were completed.

The fighting around Notre Dame and the French convent had been very bitter. The British had suddenly left this building, which they had occupied, without handing it back to the convent authorities. Doors and gates were left wide open. Hundreds of Arabs at once rushed in. They were armed with mortars, rifles and machine guns. Many began looting. Others told the priest in charge that they had come to "protect the priests against the Zionists." They remained and continued their looting even after he told them that the building was French, under the French flag, and that he did not need their protection.

They had been in the building less than an hour when a group of twenty young armed Jews belonging to one of the dissident organizations broke in and drove the Arabs out. The Arabs, realizing how few they were, counterattacked and drove them out. On May 19, a force of Palmach fighters, having captured the French hospital adjoining the convent, again took the building. It then became a focus of savage counterattack by Arab Legion troops who had by this time poured into the Old City.

The Notre Dame buildings command the New Gate and the Damascus Gate. They were an important objective because the Legion could break through from them into the New City. The Arabs brought up armored cars mounting machine guns and cannon, but after a struggle which lasted eight hours they were decisively beaten. Twenty of their men were killed and many wounded. The defense of Notre Dame was by no means passive. The Israelis within made sorties, destroyed armored cars near the Damascus Gate and blew up a two-story building opposite Notre Dame which served as a snipers' nest. The Legion made several more attempts during the next few days to advance from the Damascus Gate by Notre Dame and thus to break into the center of the city. They also made repeated efforts to advance from Sheikh Jarrah with the same objective. All these attacks were beaten back in fierce fighting. In one day's fighting at Sheikh Jarrah, five armored cars were put out of action. Arab reaction to such setbacks was to intensify their general shelling of the city. They also spared some of their shells to attack the Hadassah Hospital on Mount Scopus.

Yemin Moshe, the most advanced Jewish position in this sector, had been a source of steady irritation to the Arabs for months because, despite persistent attempts, they had been unable to dislodge its defenders from their positions facing the Old City walls. Here the Jews could keep a sharp lookout on attempts to break out toward the New City. The British had, early in the fighting, ordered the Jews to evacuate this stronghold because it "threatened Arab traffic," but we refused to budge. It withstood so many determined Arab attacks and beat them back so ignominiously that the very name became an insult to the Arabs.

In time it also served as the springboard for the leap to Mount Zion and the breaching of the Zion Gate in a spectacular operation to relieve the Old City Jews. This attack took place on the night of May 18 and was mounted by the Haportzim Battalion of Palmach. Defeated almost everywhere in Jerusalem, the enemy was concentrating his attack on the Jewish quarter in the Old City, using mortars and keeping up relentless house-to-house fighting. Shortly after dawn on May 19, the Old City wall was breached by Haportzim and contact was made with the Hagana defenders inside the Old City.

The news of the breach was heralded by a tremendous explosion which drowned out the noise of the fighting going on at the New, Damascus and Jaffa gates. This was at 3:35 A.M. The Israeli forces entered cautiously, watching for Arab machine gun fire. Only 150 yards separated them from the defenders of the Jewish quarter and this distance was traversed in three minutes. Evacuation of the wounded began at once, and the attacking unit handed over their weapons and ammunition to replenish the dwindling supplies of the Jewish defenders.

That day the Arab Legion, which had moved into the city, began an immediate counterattack and sealed the breach in the walls. The engagement ended with the Jews in possession of Mount Zion. This gave us a position overlooking the Old City. Arab counterattacks to recover Mount Zion all failed, just as we failed to hold our link with the Old City.

By May 22, the Arab Legion opened an offensive against Ramat Rahel, a kibbutz south of new Jerusalem which was defended by the farmers who were its members, with a battalion of Hagana troops holding the settlement of Givat Eliahu, a little beyond Ramat Rahel. By 6 P.M. the superior Arab forces had driven out the defenders; four hours later it was recovered. The next day Egyptian troops entered the fighting here. From positions in Mar Elias, facing Givat Eliahu, they poured shrapnel fire into the kibbutz. Our men suffered serious casualties, the command was temporarily demoralized, and retreat began in broad daylight. But the force at Givat Eliahu held its ground, and reserves were brought up. By 9 P.M. the kibbutz had been recovered again, partly because the Arabs had been too busy looting to dig in.

The pattern was repeated the next day. There was heavy daylight shelling followed by a strong enemy attack, then a retreat of our men to Givat Eliahu and Arnona, with the reserves recovering, going into the attack and retaking the position by evening. On May 25 the enemy attacked again, driving the Hagana men out of all positions except the dining room. Palmach reinforcements came up, expelled the enemy and mined the Mar Elias area. The enemy suffered heavy losses and now gave up the attempt. Altogether Ramat Rahel had changed hands seven times within ten days.

In this fighting for Jerusalem, the Israeli Air Force, such as it was at that time, also came into action. On May 21 the Arab village of Shaafat, which served as a base for Arab Legion concentrations to the north of Jerusalem, was bombed during the night and fires broke out. The sight of several Jewish planes flying over Jerusalem that same day was very heartening. Two days later, the Air Force was again heard from in action over the front along the Jordan. On May 24 they made a night raid on Arab positions near Jerusalem, and a day or so later they bombed the artillery post at Nebi Samuel and the Ramallah and Hartuv roads.

It was not just over the Jerusalem front that the small Israeli Air Force was in action. By the end of the month Amman was bombed; two days later the British airfield there received a strafing, and on June 3 the planes attacked the Arab stronghold of Nablus. They finished that week by flying over Damascus and dropping three tons of bombs. Off Tel Aviv an Egyptian corvette getting into position to shell the city was driven off by shore batteries and Israeli Air Force planes. These attacks were trifling in comparison to what a well-equipped modern plane could do, but they had a real effect on the enemy. The news that there was now a menace from the skies helped to increase the Arab demoralization already begun by the strength and unexpectedness of the Jewish resistance.

Against these successes, the early fighting of the all-out war brought us two major setbacks. The first was at Sheikh Jarrah, which we had orginally taken in April but had been forced to give back to the British, who held it until their evacuation. We had taken it again on May 14, but four days later it was overrun by heavily armored Arab Legion troops attacking from the Ramallah road to the northeast, after the Etzel unit stationed in the Police Training School on that road failed to hold this strong point. We

kept enough troops on Mount Scopus to hold the university and
the hospital buildings, but the loss of Sheikh Jarrah deprived us of
our only access to them. The most modern and best-equipped hospital in the Middle East, together with all the laboratories and li-
braries of a great university, have remained unused and derelict
ever since as a result of this defeat and the stubborn, dog-in-the-
manger policy of the Arabs.

The second failure was at Latrun. Here, too, it was the Arab
Legion which we failed to dislodge. Two attempts were made to
storm this village, which commands the vital stretch of the highway
where it begins its final ascent to Jerusalem. The attacks drew off
Arab Legion forces from the fighting inside Jerusalem, but they
could do no more than dent the enemy's iron grip on the road
which was the city's lifeline. The first few days of all-out war had
proved that the Jews in Jerusalem would not be defeated easily in
hand-to-hand fighting, but we could still be shelled or starved into
surrender.

The shelling of the city, which had started on April 10, was
sharply intensified after the departure of the British. Not all of
them had left; vital cadres of officers had stayed behind with the
Arab Legion and it was these who directed the bombardment of
new Jerusalem. This helped to account for the greater damage
caused. According to some, it also explained a curious lull in the
firing for about half an hour every afternoon, when it was pre-
sumed the British artillery experts were having their tea.

Day after day and night after night, throughout the siege, the
Arabs continued indiscriminate shelling of the city almost without
respite, frequently using incendiary shells which caused fires. Sometimes the firing was at irregular intervals. On some occasions the
shells came with enervating regularity every two minutes, a kind of
Chinese torture as one waited for the next shell to explode. The
fact that there was no letup made the shelling difficult to endure,
quite apart from the suffering and the damage caused.

Shells were fired from positions in Sheikh Jarrah and the Old
City which especially damaged the northern end of new Jerusalem,
and civilian casualties were heavy. The Egyptian army fired 4.2-
inch shells from a hill near Mar Elias. Hagana was unable to retali-
ate, as they had no cannon. The best that could be done was to hurl
a few mortar shells into the Old City and at Sheikh Jarrah.

This, strange as it may seem, was one of the most disconcerting of all our experiences during the siege. Our public was able to bear news of a setback in battle in the hope that the loss would be made good in another attempt. But to have to sit helplessly by while the Arabs cannonaded the city day after day and night after night, killing and wounding hundreds of civilians, in the knowledge that we had no comparable cannon with which to hit back, caused more chagrin and did more to undermine public morale than almost any other single hardship our public were called upon to endure.

Direct hits were scored by the Arabs on the French, Greek and Spanish consulates. Shells fell in the Red Cross zone near Government House. Ramat Rahel and Talpiot were heavily bombarded and the barrage rolled along through Yemin Moshe as far as the Street of the Prophets. The Hadassah Hospital on Mount Scopus, whose services had always been available to Jews and Arabs alike, was heavily shelled, as were the Hebrew University buildings. In addition to the shelling, enemy planes occasionally flew over the city dropping incendiaries. We were now literally in the front line, not just the men in the fighting units but every man, woman and child in the city, for the fire was indiscriminate, searching out, sometimes in turn and sometimes simultaneously, every quarter of the capital.

One can grow used to anything. My own feeling is that those of us who had a lot of work to do were luckier, as far as this shelling was concerned, than persons with time to worry about it. One day, when I was talking with three officials in a conference room of the Sansur Building on Zion Square, where the Jerusalem Emergency Committee was then located, a shell exploded near the window and pieces of shrapnel flew into the room. We went on with our business, although one of my assistants pressed me to go to my own room on the other side of the corridor. I told him it was impossible to guess where the next shell might land, so we might just as well carry on. Eventually, our business concluded, I went into my office and sat down at my desk. Just as I did so, a shell burst below the window and peppered the room with shrapnel. I have seldom been proved right so quickly.

From December 1 to May 14, Hadassah had handled 2,800 casualties, a large proportion of all the Jews wounded in the entire country. Total casualties were much higher. On May 3 the *Palestine Post* published casualty figures covering the preceding five months

which showed 5,014 dead, including 1,256 Jews, 3,569 Arabs and
152 British, with an additional 6,632 wounded. These figures, like
all wartime casualty figures, were at best approximations.

But we had better statistics on the casualties inside Jerusalem,
and these showed that the city suffered, in one year's fighting, pro-
portionately five times as many casualties as London during one
year of World War II. The Central Bureau of Medical Statistics reported to me over 1,700 casualties by enemy action in Jerusalem
and its environs in the four weeks of the shelling between May 15
and June 11. The following are the figures they furnished:

	Killed	Wounded	Total Casualties
CIVILIANS	199	658	857
SOLDIERS NOT IN ACTION	52	345	397
SOLDIERS IN ACTION	65	419	484
Total	316	1,422	1,738

These figures were progressively radioed by me to Ben Gurion in
Tel Aviv. My reason for doing so was more than informative. I
wished to impress upon him the strain under which the people of
Jerusalem were suffering. There was a feeling in the city that more
men and material might have been spared by the central authorities in Tel Aviv to help lift the blockade on the roads to Jerusalem
and prevent the siege from developing. The facts as they subsequently became known conclusively belied this belief, but at the
time it was understandable.

The facts that the proportion of dead to wounded was not higher
than it was and that the morale of the people was not shattered by
the shelling were due in a very important measure to the medical
services improvised by the Hadassah, the Kupat Holim and other
hospitals in the city and maintained without interruption despite
the bombing of the hospitals. It soon became apparent that evacuation of the Mount Scopus Hospital must take place, and there were
six hundred patients to bring down into the New City. The first
thing that had to be done was to secure the co-operation of the British Army authorities at a time when official permission was granted
for not more than three food convoys of three trucks each to
reach the hospital weekly. We had previously made a request for

the transfer of equipment and personnel, but it had been postponed indefinitely.

Fortunately the major in charge of the area was prepared to make an unofficial arrangement which did not involve the High Commissioner or the higher Army authorities. Despite hitches, by the beginning of May the six hundred had been transferred to the hospitals that had been prepared in the New City. These had been arranged for after complex negotiations. The St. Joseph Convent, which had no Arab children left in their school, was acquired on lease. This hospital dealt mainly with Hagana casualties, and the surgeons and nurses were available around the clock. Most of the cases were very grave. There were wounded with several bullets in their chests and abdomens, with ruptured inner organs equivalent to the most serious cases seen in World War II. Treatment was on a par with that given under similar conditions in the American Army corps in that struggle. The reason was that Hadassah had supplied penicillin, streptomycin and first-rate equipment in operating theaters, wards and laboratories and had trained many young doctors to become competent surgeons able to work in emergency conditions. This meant that the Hagana in Jerusalem could go into battle knowing it could rely on a well-trained and well-equipped medical organization. By the time the all-out war was less than a week old, Hadassah was able to report that the St. Joseph Hospital was functioning at full capacity; so was that in the former English Mission buildings in the Street of the Prophets. There was also a maternity hospital with 100 normal births per month. This was of great importance, since there was not a sickbed to be had in Jerusalem. Hotels, pensions and schools were crowded with wounded. Hadassah also set up a subterranean operating theater and helped overcome the nursing shortage by organizing courses for nurses' aids.

With the intensification of the attacks after May 14, we acquired the operating-theater equipment from the retiring British at their Talbieh Hospital and all the medical supplies of the Palestine Health Department, after we captured the Russian Compound. This enabled the opening of the Ziv (mainly surgical) Hospital in Jerusalem.

Parallel to the work of Hadassah was that of the Magen David Adom. One of the most vital tasks performed by the Magen David Adom in its capacity as medical unit of the Hagana was to set up a field hospital in the monastery at Abu Ghosh. This hospital was organized within seventy-two hours. The ambulance service of the

Magen David Adom reached its peak during the shelling of Jerusalem and was mainly staffed by volunteer drivers, most of them bus
drivers of the Jerusalem Hamekasher co-operative, which was not
functioning because of lack of gasoline and oil. Hundreds of
women and girls volunteered for round-the-clock service in the hospitals and clinics, and a number of them set up first-aid stations in
their own homes.

One of the outstanding examples of initiative was that of Made-
leine Lewin-Epstein, a trained nurse and the wife of an outstanding dentist. They had both come from America as Zionists; her
younger son, serving in the A.A.F., lost his life in an air battle
over Germany. Her home was in the danger spot on the Princess
Mary Road from which most of the inhabitants had been evacuated. But Mrs. Lewin-Epstein turned her home into a first-aid station, using her husband's store of medical supplies and often going
out into the street, under fire, to bring the wounded into her home
for treatment. For a short while her home was more than a first-aid
station. The wounded were hospitalized until they could be moved.
Her training and selfless devotion proved an invaluable combina-
tion.

During the three weeks after May 14, Jerusalem was hit by more
than ten thousand shells. In the period of the first truce, which began on June 11, we had an opportunity to investigate the damage.
A preliminary report showed that two thousand families had suffered from the bombardment. We endeavored to arrange for loans
to enable the repair of such buildings as could be repaired without
too great expense. We settled disputes between landlords and ten-
ants arising out of damage to leased premises and we tried to provide alternative accommodation for evacuees who were bombed out
of their homes.

We had good reason during these days to follow closely what was
happening to Jewish forces in other parts of Palestine. For we knew
that the capture of Jerusalem was only one of the three major objectives of the invading Arab armies. The second was the occupation of the coast line, which was the only contact with the world of
our small nation landlocked on all other sides by hostile Arab countries. The third was capture of the harbor and refineries at Haifa,
which would have meant paralysis for all transportation and industry in a country completely dependent on imported fuel.

Syrian and Lebanese troops were assigned a southward advance on a line between Zemah and Beisan. This began on May 16 with a heavy artillery attack on Ein Gev, Massada and Shaar Hagolan. The Jordan Valley settlements were also attacked, the main Syrian infantry being deployed against Zemah after attacking Massada and Shaar Hagolan en route. The campaign began with an assault on the two kibbutzim at Degania with light tanks, infantry and armor. These were the oldest and most famous of the agricultural co-operative settlements established by Jews in Palestine, near the Sea of Galilee. Degania A repulsed the attackers, who withdrew to Zemah; Degania B also stood firm. The Israeli forces brought up light artillery by surprise and this compelled the Syrians to withdraw from the entire area.

Meanwhile, in the finger of Galilee, our Yiftah Brigade attacked at Malkiya and the Nebi Yusha strongpoint, capturing the latter. The same force sabotaged bridges over the Litany River on the Lebanese border and the Baniyas Wadi Bridge and blew up a large ammunition dump which had been prepared at this point for the invasion. We took Malkiya on May 29.

On May 14 the Arab Legion captured the power station on the Jordan border. Iraq entered the struggle in the region of the Kochav el Hawa Bridge, and failing to take the village of that name, they diverted their forces to the Triangle. This was the area between Nablus, Tulkarem and Jenin, in Samaria, where Fawzi el Kawkji's forces were already concentrated. The Yiftah Brigade had handed over their positions in the north to the rather raw Oded group and this facilitated the second Syrian invasion attempt, which hinged on B'not Yaacov Bridge. One of our oldest settlements in Galilee, Mishmar Hayarden, was taken after six days' fighting. There was no prospect of a counterattack by our forces, as this coincided with the beginning of the first truce. However, the Syrian attempt to take Ein Gev on the eve of the truce failed. On June 6, the Lebanese recaptured Malkiya, which opened the way for Fawzi el Kawkji's forces to enter central Galilee, but his troops did not succeed in their main objective, which was to take Sejera.

The arrival of the Iraqi forces in the center of the country activated the central front. On May 25, Israel forces attacked Jenin, thus holding down three Iraqi brigades, who counterattacked, forcing our withdrawal. On June 6, our Alexandroni Brigade took Karkur on the western edge of the Triangle.

In the Negev the defense rested on the Negev Brigade, based on the twenty-seven Jewish settlements scattered through this extensive territory. Also important was the work of the Givati Brigade, which had spent the period immediately preceding the eve of liberation in cleaning up Arab villages which threatened Israel's Negev communications. The seizure of the Negev and the opening of the direct route to Tel Aviv was entrusted by the Arabs to the Egyptian army, whose advance moved along two main lines: the coastal road and the Nitzana-Beersheba road. The Egyptians at first used light forces which included Moslem Brotherhood volunteers. They reached Bet Govrin, Hebron, Bethlehem and Hartuv and thus became a factor in the threat to Jerusalem.

On May 11, Egyptian regular forces were thrown in, and they attacked Kfar Darom. The assault was repulsed but the settlement was cut off. Between May 23 and 29, the Egyptians took the offensive with their regular Army, armor and planes. They attacked Yad Mordechai and captured it after three days' fighting. They then turned north and joined up with their volunteer forces at Migdal. On May 29 a mobile Egyptian force reached Ashdod, which is only twenty-one miles from Tel Aviv. The Israel forces reacted strongly and held the Egyptians down to their strongpoints. Part of our success in stopping the Egyptian penetration was thanks to our use of Messerschmitt planes obtained through Czechoslovakia. An Egyptian attack on Negba, a settlement which was subject to intense and continuous artillery bombardment but which dug in and was successfully defended by its own settlers, held the line of the Egyptians from reaching Ashkelon and Bet Govrin. A counterattack on June 3 by the Givati Brigade failed to take Ashdod, but the operation forced the Egyptians to give up their drive on Tel Aviv by way of the southern villages. Both sides now took a number of points, but most important was the success of the Negev Brigade in storming the police station at Bir Asluj. Our attack on another police station which dominated the flank of Negba did not succeed at this time.

On May 28, our fledgling state acquired at last a legal army. The Hagana, its striking arm, the Palmach troops, and the dissident Irgun Zvai Leumi and Stern Gang forces were abolished as separate units and incorporated into the new Israel Defense Force, henceforth called Zahal, the Hebrew initials of its full name, Zva Hagana Le-Yisrael. It took a long time to work out real integration of the dissident terrorists, but we had at last the structure of a unified command of all land, sea and air forces.

In his order of the day to the fighters of Israel on that historic occasion, Major General Yaacov Dostrovsky (now Yaacov Dori, president of the Technion-Israel Institute of Technology at Haifa) said:

Soldiers and officers! With a deep sense of the responsibility and sanctity of the occasion we are about to take the oath of loyalty to the State of Israel, which arose and was established in our lifetime through the sacred blood of myriads of our people and their age-old longing for freedom, redemption and salvation . . .

May the purity of our arms, faithfulness and dedication to the purposes of the nation, and zealous attachment to the moral principle of Hebrew self-defense be the pillar of fire that will go before the formations of the Israel Defense Force.

In another order of the day dated "22 Iyyar 5708: May 31, 1948, Year 1 of the Freedom of Israel," David Ben Gurion, as Prime Minister and Minister of Defense, prescribed:

Every man and woman soldier will be required to take the following oath:

"I swear solemnly to be loyal to the State of Israel, its laws and proper authorities; to accept the discipline of the Israel Defense Forces unconditionally and without reservation; to obey all orders and instructions given to me by my duly appointed officers and to devote myself utterly even unto death to the defense of my country and the freedom of Israel."

The development of the war now brought some specific problems to Jerusalem which had to be handled immediately. The refugees from the Old City, which fell on May 28, had to be accommodated in new quarters. Their number was swelled by those who had lost their homes through bombing or because they were in areas where the Hagana wanted freedom to maneuver. Accommodation was made available by the capture of quarters previously held by the Arabs, in Katamon and Bakaa. In these latter areas we had to stop looting both by the defense forces and by civilians. This often took the form of the removal of doors and window frames for use as cooking fuel or the purloining of taps and other household fittings. It was serious enough in itself, for looting undermines the spirit of the soldier and takes his mind off his main objective. But it had much more important practical consequences. It meant that accommodation of our own refugees in the newly captured houses could take place only after expensive and time-consuming repairs.

We were also building public shelters against air raids and shelling. These were intended to serve by day as refuges for passersby and for the inmates of nearby homes at night. In the absence of other accommodation, these shelters began to be taken over by refugee squatters who had no other place to live. Their presence raised grave questions of cleanliness and sanitation, which the Mishmar Ha'am had to deal with.

There were other pressures on these shelters. For example, in one district the local synagogue had been converted for the purpose. During the day it was used as a school for the children and at night as a shelter. Sometimes when there was shelling at night people would go down from their homes only to find the accommodation taken by refugees. It was interesting that the religious refugees seemed less perturbed by the dangers of the shelling and bombing than others. They had a deep faith in the God of Israel and were confident that He would not allow any ultimate harm to befall His Holy City.

At a first glance three weeks after its capture, Katamon looked as though normal life would never return. Doors hung askew from broken hinges in damaged doorframes. Windows were shattered or hung drunkenly from one hinge. Great holes gaped from broken walls. Many streets were still shut off by barbed wire or littered with the remains of tank traps, with the debris of strongpoints, sandbags spewing their contents and jagged masses of broken stone and masonry. Yet close inspection showed that little grave damage had been done to the houses in the whole periphery, because as soon as Katamon fell the Syrian and Iraqi gangs that had held the neighborhood realized that their position was untenable and moved out quickly and without much resistance.

On June 2 I was able to report to the Jerusalem Emergency Committee that the area had been handed over to us by the military authorities. It was being guarded by thirty policemen, who had been able in large measure to stop the looting. Within days the evacuees from the Old City began to move in. This was the beginning of our handling the problem. It was to take years before it was finally solved. I had arranged with the Vaad Leumi, under whose jurisdiction education continued, to take over ten school buildings for temporary accommodation of evacuees. By May 27 the Housing Committee of the Jerusalem Emergency Committee had accommodated 784 families in temporary homes. Apart from evacuees from the Old City we had to provide housing for women and children evacuated from Ramat Rahel, the kibbutz near Jerusalem which had been the scene of bitter fighting and attack and counterattack, and from the Etzion bloc and other nearby agricultural settlements.

Later, at a meeting of the committee held on July 7, we took further drastic steps to relieve the shortage of accommodation by permitting the requisition of homes left vacant by residents who had gone to Tel Aviv.

Another problem which could not be postponed was the need for a more closely knit internal security than the Mishmar Ha'am could provide. Until my appointment as Military Governor in August, I had no legal authority to set up a police force in a city which considered itself *de facto* a part of the new state of Israel but which had been set aside for internationalization by the United Nations resolution on partition. The members of the old police force had been released from their oath of loyalty to the British authorities on May 12.

We moved cautiously but quickly. On May 12, the Jerusalem Emergency Committee decided to take over on probation the four hundred regular Jewish police who had worked under the mandate. They were organized in four districts and two substations, with a prison or lockup. This force was placed under the joint control of the Jerusalem municipality, which was now functioning again, and the state of Israel's Police Ministry, with a watch committee made up of experts and members of my committee headed by the indefatigable Reuven Shreibman (later Shari).

Five Jewish post-office officials had undertaken, on May 1, to draw up a plan for a new postal system. We opened three post offices for the tiny amount of mail we could hope to send out by Piper Cub airplane. Schools were easier, because they had always been the concern of the Vaad Leumi, with only a meager grant of funds and some sketchy pedagogical inspection from the British. Teachers were exempted from war duties and a number of schools were transferred to air raid shelters.

A supply of information was essential for morale, and for this we depended chiefly on the Voice of Jerusalem broadcasting station. With no electricity during most hours of the day, we had to set up a network of battery-operated loudspeakers at points throughout the city. When the Arab Legion were posted to guard the Palestine Broadcasting Station on Queen Melisande Street in December, with the help of the British authorities, we had managed to salvage three grand pianos, 8,000 records of classical and Israeli music, and 6,000 sheets of music, much of it in manuscript. With this and some technical equipment, and the skill of a few young engineers who had been testing clandestine transmitters while the British still ran the city, we improvised a radio station which functioned throughout the war.

At first it was hidden in the house of the late Rabbi Simcha Assaf, whose weekly radio lessons on the Talmud had been a great attraction. When these quarters proved too small, we moved to the Bet Hahalutzot of the American Women's League for Israel, a building in which land lines had already been installed for musical programs. Even this was too small, and the station's newsroom had to be set up in the Rehaviah Café down the street. Throughout the siege, this newsroom transmitted newscasts in Hebrew, Arabic, French and English. Sometimes the announcer panted hard, because he had run to the microphone through a curtain of shells and bullets. Enemy gunners scored one direct hit, killing a number of the station's staff. The small radio orchestra never missed its weekly concert, usually played by the light of kerosene lamps because all available current was needed for the transmitter. On one occasion, when electricity failed, the residents of the area around the station crowded near the building and asked the announcer to finish his news by means of a loudspeaker.

The *Palestine Post,* edited courageously by Gershon Agronsky (later Agron, the mayor of Jerusalem), never failed to appear, although twice it had to resort to a mimeographed edition. Our Emergency Committee put out a daily news bulletin, first of two pages and then a single page, which was distributed free of charge at noon. This gave ration news as well as information about what was happening on other fronts. For several weeks, a small sheet called *Yediot Yerushalayim* was published by the Jerusalem staffs of the major Hebrew newspapers of the country. There was also a mimeographed sheet put out by the Jerusalem Workers' Council.

In addition to these regular channels of communication the Jerusalem Emergency Committee from time to time issued stenciled appeals to all citizens of Jerusalem. On June 6, at the height of the shelling, it published a statement reading in part as follows:

We have been besieged now for seven weeks and have had to restrict our food and water rations and to make do with the bare minimum. The enemy's shells have taken toll of many loved ones among us in.his effort to break our spirit. But the days of siege and stress found us united in our determination to beat off the attack and to hit back. In want and hardship we guard the borders of our capital and shall continue our efforts to assure the Jewish future. . . .

Jews of Jerusalem! Deeply conscious of the justice of our struggle, let us dedicate ourselves to it until the day of liberation dawns. May He that has chosen Jerusalem spread His tabernacle of peace over the City of Peace.

The primary problem of food, water and fuel was a constant threat which overshadowed all others. Without water we could hold out only for a couple of days. Without food we might last a little longer, but everything that we might subsequently do would depend on giving the Army and the people food and drink. The next vital essential was fuel to generate power. To save what we had and make it last, we needed tight controls.

Paradoxically, our desire to introduce a strict rationing was helped by the breakdown of British administration at the end of April. At that time the senior British officials of the Food Controller's Office left the country. Jewish employees in the office volunteered to assist us in setting up controls.

But by the time we introduced the stricter controls we still had no accurate and complete list of consumers, and we had to use the British list. This had been drawn up in 1942 and amended in 1947. By the end of September 1948 we had issued 78,000 books to adults and 28,400 to children, a total of 106,400. By October 16, 1948, the public held 90,000 ration books; 3,000 were held for inmates of institutions; we had canceled 13,400 in respect of persons who had died or left the city.

Applications for ration books were filled in at the grocery store to which every consumer was linked. Each grocer kept a list of his registered customers and these lists were also used for allocations of other foods such as meat, fish and vegetables. Pregnant women, whose number varied between 500 and 700, had special rations.

Profits were kept down to a minimum in order to ensure that

what we had was within reach of all. By the end of September we had on our lists 721 provision stores. We tried to distribute the consumers fairly among all the shopkeepers. We also sought, because of transportation difficulties, to have customers shop near their homes.

We had trouble at first with some of the shopkeepers in exposed areas who did not keep their shops open regularly. This meant that housewives had to expose themselves unnecessarily to shelling. Some women were killed on such journeys. Offending shopkeepers were threatened with cancellation of their licenses. We insisted on grocery shops being kept open during four fixed hours every day. Supervision of this situation was put into the hands of Mishmar Ha'am. We made a selective transfer of customers in danger areas to shops in safer areas. The general planning and control of rations was in the hands of a department of supply which I set up.

One of the points I watched personally was that there should not be any distinction between rich and poor. Thus the comfortable Rehaviah quarter never received its rations until supplies had reached the exposed districts like Meah Shearim and Bet Israel, or the poorer districts like Mahaneh Yehuda and the Nachlaot. In the more prosperous quarters, householders were assumed to have some small supplies in stock. They had money on hand with which to forage and look for supplies and they knew better how to make good meals out of the type of rations distributed; these were unfamiliar foods to some of the Oriental communities.

It might be interesting to give here a sample of a week's supply of rations per person as an indication of the scarcity that existed during the siege. On June 11 this was the list in quantities per person for the entire week: groats, 100 grams (three and a half ounces); beans, 100 grams; processed cheese, 40 grams; coffee for adults, 100 grams; powdered milk (for children), 100 grams; bread (per day), 160 grams (barely six ounces); and margarine, 50 grams. In addition, sick persons got an egg or two from Tnuva.

At the Strauss Health Center demonstrations were regularly given on how to make the most of the rations and a health exhibit was set up. This display demonstrated how to cook without electricity or kerosene, how to make primitive stoves out of blocks of wood, and how to cook with all sorts of twigs, chips, and other makeshift combustible material. Sometimes, when there was no bread, shopkeepers would receive an allocation of matzoth which we had in stock. Thus, on May 25, the Jerusalem Committee published a notice that a ration of 200 grams of matzoth was to be issued instead of bread, which was not forthcoming that day.

At this time (on June 1) we put into operation the plans we had made for the establishment of seven public restaurants where meals would be sold at minimum prices in order to make sure that those who had no alternative could get as good a meal as our meager resources would allow, at a cost they could afford. We estimated that we could supply 5,000 three-course meals per day. The cost was 6.5 piasters (about 31 cents) and the meal included 200 grams of bread. Before the siege was over we opened four public kitchens where we distributed simple cooked food.

The commercial restaurants were having their troubles. At the end of March their association had written to our Supplies Committee complaining they had been given only half the 250 cans of kerosene promised them. They had asked for flour and were informed that all flour was needed for bread. They were offered 1,500 eggs to be divided among 200 restaurants. They asked us how they could divide them. They received no meat allocations; poultry was practically nonexistent. They claimed that they would have to shut down altogether unless they were helped. There was little we could do for them and in fact many of them eventually did close down.

The main staple was bread, and one of our greatest headaches was caused by the selfish attitude of some of the bakers. We fixed the wholesale price and the bakers sent the committee a letter in which they threatened to shut down unless they got more money. I summoned their representatives to my house and informed them that if they did not wish to bake bread for the community on the conditions laid down by the authorities we would take over the bakeries. If they didn't want to bake bread for us I was confident their workers would. My plans were all ready for the take-over, but it was not necessary to put them into execution. When the bakers realized that I meant what I said, they accepted our ruling.

We nevertheless prepared a supply of matzoth which could be distributed if at any time the supply of bread ran out or the bakeries' work was interrupted for a day or so. I had to veto a proposal to deliver bread throughout the city only every second day, to save fuel and transport. The supply was irregular enough as it was in some districts, because of problems of transportation and electricity failures in bakeries. To have regular deliveries scheduled every two days would only have been an added hardship. In the many problems of bread production I could rely upon several experts, headed by a zealous young member of the Agudat Israel, Chaim Stern, and Yaacov Picker, an able economist with considerable experience in factory management.

Despite all the precautions taken, on June 9, two days before the first truce came into effect, the stock records showed that we were down to a potential of 42,600 loaves for the whole city. This meant less than half a loaf per person, or, at a minimum distribution of barely some six ounces per day, a three-day ration. This calculation took into account all the flour in Army stores and loaves held in stock which had not been distributed that day due to a transport breakdown. If the Arabs had known how critically low our supplies of flour were on the eve of the truce, it is doubtful whether they would have agreed to it. Indeed, the specter of starvation was never absent. We were able to hold out only because we had kept our average daily ration of food distributed down to the dangerously low figure of 900 calories.

Water no longer flowed through the pipes into the houses and we needed tankers to bring it to the householders. It was found that tanks mounted on trucks could do the job. The people who drove them showed real heroism. Despite shell fire and sniping, they went daily on their rounds into every suburb. People soon learned to queue up with their containers at fixed places at fixed times, despite the sniping to which they were exposed, and sure enough the water tankers never failed them. We did not open the cisterns at first, as these contained our iron ration of water. As Arabs fled from their houses, almost all of which had cisterns, we first used up these supplies for local needs. Instructions were issued on how to save water and how to cook, drink, wash and keep clean on the ration, started on May 12, of two gallons of water per person per day, of which barely four pints was drinking water. Eventually our water ration was cut to six quarts per day. People found their own means of using and reusing their supply. One favorite device was to remove the stopper from the kitchen sink and place a bucket underneath the vent. The water thus trapped was used to wash floors and then to flush the toilet.

Fuel was a greater problem. With the complete stoppage of fuel supplies toward the end of April, we had to resort to desperate expedients in order to keep essential services going. By May 16, when water trucks had to be replaced (in part) by donkey carts, no bus had run in Jerusalem for five days for lack of fuel. All bus traffic and private motoring ceased in the city. The fuel now left was used for Hagana and ambulances. The remaining stocks of crude and fuel oil were restricted to the following essential enterprises: hospitals and clinics of Hadassah, Kupat Holim and other bodies, Jewish and non-Jewish; bakeries; only three of the city's printing presses—the most important being the *Palestine Post;* certain vital factories; the workers' restaurant; one matzoth factory; the Teva pharmaceutical plant; Tnuva dairy products and a food-processing plant; cold-storage plants; the water works; the Voice of Jerusalem and Hagana radio stations; the Post Office; and a few rooms in the Jewish Agency offices where Hagana headquarters were situated.

We had practically no fuel whatsoever for domestic use. How catastrophic our fuel position was during the siege can be gauged from the following record I find in my diary for May 19: "Today was a lucky day. After the Legionaires retreated from the Allenby Barracks, we entered and found several barrels of fuel oil and many jerry-cans of gasoline. The Legionaires had tried to destroy all the fuel by firing at hundreds of jerry-cans and piercing others with bayonets. As they had to leave in a hurry we poured what remained into intact jerry-cans and found we had 62 full cans."

On June 3, our fuel supplies had diminished to only three tons of fuel oil, six hundred gallons of gasoline and thirty-seven tins of kerosene for all the needs of the entire city.

The fact that people had to walk had its positive effects on morale, for they felt, in walking calmly through the streets when there was constant sniping and imminent danger of a shell exploding near them, that they were asserting their courage and their manliness. Sometimes it would take a good half hour to go a distance normally covered in five or six minutes, depending on how frequently one had to take shelter in doorways from exploding shells. People walked; they did not run.

For domestic cooking, Jerusalemites were forced to use Boy Scout methods. The trick of lighting a fire without using more than two matches became an important economic necessity. At the Jerusalem Emergency Committee we took steps to provide 5,000 tons of firewood by pruning all the trees in the city and centralizing the collection of all deadwood. We also managed to bring in some wood from the nearby Jewish settlement Kiryat Anavim. There were few candles for the Sabbath by the middle of June; some were bor-

rowed from the Ratisbonne Catholic monastery. But all these im-
provisations were secondary to our main tasks: to keep the public
fed, to find them a small ration of water, to supply electricity at
least for our principal public institutions, to provide some economic
basis for their livelihood so that they would not sit in idle-
ness, and to maintain essential services, including the grim duty of
burying the dead.

The main user of fuel was the electricity company, which was
still supplying power to both the Jewish and Jordanian parts of
Jerusalem. The International Red Cross representative offered to
put the power station under Red Cross supervision and bring it
fuel in a Red Cross train, a move to which the Jewish authorities
did, but the Arabs did not, agree.

After the conquest by Jewish forces of the area in which the
power station was situated, the dangers were still great. Special
lines had to be laid to vital undertakings. Otherwise, there was
nothing to prevent unauthorized persons from using current which
passed on the regular channels. The linesmen who had to repair
transformer stations and maintain connections acted with great
heroism, as they were under constant fire and the lines were frequently cut. The one which passed along King George V Avenue,
for example, was severed no less than twelve times in one night
and was restored to service just as often.

Since linesmen trying to make repairs were exposed in many
areas to enemy snipers and would be perfect sitting birds for their
marksmen, we adopted the practice of noting in the daytime the
places where the lines needed repairing and sending men to execute the repairs at night. Auxiliary generators were brought into
service, but these could deal with only a fraction of the problem.
Singer, the manager of the Jerusalem Electric Corporation, proudly
boasted that during the whole period of the siege and the emergency there was only one occasion when electricity was interrupted
completely for a continuous period of twenty hours. When the
company's supply of fuel was giving out he used an ingenious
method of drilling holes in the hard sludge at the bottom of their
fuel oil containers and filling them with kerosene. This made a fuel
that could be used to run their diesel engines to generate power. It
was not until August 1948 that he was able to reorganize the electricity supply to give a fairly regular service to all of Jerusalem's
inhabitants.

When the last convoy had reached Jerusalem on the eve of Pass-over, April 20, it was estimated by men who knew the facts that the city could survive, with severe rationing, for four weeks. In fact, we stretched the rations over eight. Because of security reasons, only a few persons in Jerusalem knew that a desperate effort was being made to cut a new road through the mountains. And it was a few days short of two full months before new supplies of food or fuel could reach the city.

There was little point in pleading with Ben Gurion, with the Jewish Agency, or with Nahum Verlinsky, who was representing us in Tel Aviv. But I did plead, with all the anxiety and persuasive-ness of which I was capable. The members of our committee kept worrying me with repeated expressions of alarm at our fate if food did not reach us quickly. I could only read them the radio messages I had been sending. In simple fact, there was very little more that anyone could do.

A few driblets came in by air, since we now had contrived an airstrip of sorts in the valley to the west of Rehaviah. The work was done by cutting away part of one side of the slope down to the bed of the valley. We used a bulldozer backed by scores of men who moved the earth to fill in and widen the base of the valley. The ground was then flattened and hardened by a road roller and by watering it. The strip was not really level; because of the terrain and the difficulty of completely leveling it, it rose slightly from south to north. It was only some three hundred yards long and twenty-five wide and could be used by Piper Cub planes.

In an emergency skilled pilots could land slightly larger aircraft. We set up a signals section which tried without great success to maintain radio contact with headquarters in Tel Aviv. Lack of adequate equipment made this contact very uncertain. There was no air-to-ground contact and the pilots had to land according to visual instructions, at night with the aid of lamps and flares.

On one occasion word was received that a plane had left Tel Aviv after dark. As there were no facilities as yet for a proper flare path, the neighboring householders were asked to provide lamps with which the landing path was lit after a fashion.

The planes were often attacked by Spitfires on their way to Jeru-salem. They flew spasmodically two or three times a week and served mainly to transport small quantities of vital arms and ammunition.

When all my radio messages proved ineffective, I decided to try to talk to Ben Gurion by means of a walkie-talkie radio-telephone. The best we had was designed for a range of about four miles and could not be expected to work at all for more than nine. The straight-line distance to Tel Aviv was twenty-four miles. But by aiming the instrument carefully when the wind was right, our technicians could sometimes establish contact with Tel Aviv. So I went to the radio hut, on the roof of the military camp at Schneller's. It was under constant observation by Arab snipers, and the girl sergeant in charge told me to crawl to the pillbox. It was a deep-blue, starlit night and I did not feel like crawling under that mysterious, beautiful Jerusalem night sky. I ignored her warning and walked across the roof to the pillbox hut.

Luck was with me and contact was made. I was careful at first to use language which could not be readily understood by others, lest the Arabs listen in to our talk. But Ben Gurion's replies were so guarded that I wondered whether I had sufficiently impressed him with the seriousness of the situation. I threw caution to the winds and told him bluntly and forcefully that if we did not get fresh supplies very quickly the city's position would be most grave.

I left after that, hoping that Ben Gurion had heard and been convinced of our plight. His last words to me sounded like "Good, very good. Be strong and of good courage."

The girl who had operated the walkie-talkie for me was coming off duty. Walking down the stairs she said to me, "I thought the severe rationing and the few groats in our Army soup ration were because you were stretching supplies. Now I see that we really have nothing."

I changed the conversation and talked of lighter matters. My intention was to disabuse her mind of the seriousness of the situation. Later she told my son, who had interrupted his studies in London to do his duty at home, that she thought I had just exaggerated to Ben Gurion to make sure he hurried and sent us supplies. It was important that this impression should remain with her. A besieged city is as full of rumors as a prison. The grapevine is incredibly fast and nothing could have been worse for a city facing starvation than to spread the fear that there would be no food on the morrow.

By June 4, word began to get about inside Jerusalem of a new road to the coast. Actually, it had been started on May 18, in great secrecy, and it became Israel's Burma Road. It was not to be open for any important supplies for some weeks, but it is not too much to say that it helped save Jerusalem.

As early as Operation Nachshon, in April, we had been planning the road, ever since a single jeep, called "the Orphan Convoy" by our soldiers because it was all alone in the world, had made its way across country to that engagement. What one vehicle could do others could. Then three young men, fighting in Jerusalem, were given leave to visit their home on the coastal plain when they claimed they could make their way there on foot. They proved that they were right. Our failure to capture Latrun left the old road blocked at Bab el Wad, but we had taken the two small villages of Bet Jiz and Bet Susin, which made it theoretically possible to skirt the Arab roadblock.

There was only a gap of slightly more than four miles to be traversed to Bet Susin. This distance was again explored by jeep and most of it presented no special difficulties. But a little less than a mile and a half of this route, down to the Jerusalem-Hartuv road a little east of Bab el Wad, was not even a track, incredibly steep, and covered with boulders. It was obvious that no jeep could survive a second trip along this stretch. But engineers went to work, and two precious weeks went by while an attempt was made to improve the situation with bulldozers.

We could not wait. So we worked out a new method of operation. Jerusalem trucks were sent after dark to the ravine near the present settlement of Mesillat Zion, about a mile from Bab el Wad. From the other end supplies were trucked through Hulda to Bet Susin. From there we used forty mules to move the supplies a little farther. Then for five nights every one of two hundred men of Jerusalem's Mishmar Ha'am carried a forty-five-pound sack of flour over this three-mile stretch to the Jerusalem road. They were mostly men of fifty or over and were able to make two trips per night. They worked grimly, efficiently, and were not fazed by mortar fire from nearby Latrun. They walked down the hillside in the dark, each man holding the shirttails of the one ahead.

After the bulldozers did their difficult leveling work for five weeks and we spread wire netting on the ground, we risked sending some vehicles down the steepest point. The bulldozers helped them make the ascent back. We had also sent several hundred experienced Jerusalem quarry men every night to help build the road. A pipeline was laid down the hill and fuel was sent from vehicles at the top to vehicles waiting on the Jerusalem road. The road, on which dust was axle-deep, rising in clouds around every truck, was gradually improved, and by the time the first truce came it had already broken the siege of Jerusalem. It was used thereafter to convoy supplies into the city. It was our artery to the coast for several months until we built the road called Kvish Hagevurah, the Valor Road, which is now the main road from Jerusalem to Tel Aviv. But the Burma Road was still in use at the end of June to send night convoys over to Jerusalem. It was necessary to use a tractor to haul the trucks over difficult parts of the road, although they were loaded only to part of their capacity. The usual convoy was 100 tons per night.

From Tel Aviv came Ben Gurion's message: "The whole country is alive to what is happening in Jerusalem. The country is full of pride at the firm stand of Jerusalem and the bravery of its defenders. The Government of Israel is doing everything possible to redeem Jerusalem . . . Jerusalem will be freed by the combined moral effort of the Jews of Jerusalem and the physical effort of our troops."

Speaking at a ceremony much later, on December 8, 1948, the Prime Minister said, "The road we are dedicating today embodies the height of our war effort for homeland and independence, for it is bound up inextricably with the most glorious chapter of our struggle—that for Jerusalem. This was the focal point of the War of Liberation."

This was in the future. There was much agony and toil to go through before the opening of that road could be seen to have heralded the final turning point of the war to complete victory.

What did Jerusalem look like during the siege? The streets were empty; to venture out of doors was dangerous because of the constant shelling. A great stillness pervaded the city in between the explosions of shells and the detonation of our answering mortars, which greeted our ears all too infrequently. The rattle of gunfire broke the silence of the beleaguered city. The daytime sky was filled with blue wisps of smoke from wood fires in the gardens. At night the city was dark and gloomy. There was no life in the cafés, no cinemas were open. The large restaurants were closed. The only eating places were the public restaurants set up by our committee.

In our house as in all others, we learned the old tricks of resisting siege: that one can eat off plates and not wash them, and that one should go through the motions of eating a meal, even when there was almost nothing to eat, for the sake of one's morale.

Most of the factories were closed. Thousands of workers and employees in industries like quarrying or the Dead Sea Works and in the former government offices were without work other than their public service. This enforced unemployment reduced purchasing power in the city, thus facilitating our control of prices and our successful effort to eliminate black-marketeering. People off duty had no option but to sit at home. Reading was mostly confined to the newssheets. It is the unusual person who can concentrate on a book, especially to the light of a kerosene lamp, with his ears keyed to the music of explosions. But even in such circumstances much of the best in human nature often comes to the fore. A friend of my wife's who had lost her only child—a girl—in the fighting at Neveh Yaacov risked her life time and again to obtain a little milk from a nearby convent for a neighbor's ailing baby.

Business was almost completely paralyzed. Shops were open for only short periods of each day, and this involved risks for both shopkeepers and customers. The youth clubs were closed, as most of the members were enlisted in the Army. Now and again a district came to life for a few·minutes when the water carts arrived and people stood quietly in line waiting for their daily ration.

Especially depressing was our being cut off from the Yishuv outside Jerusalem, the impossibility of contact with relatives and friends, or of reading one's paper in the morning. To be offered a cigarette was a rare treat by a real friend. It was most difficult to buy cigarettes, and then very few. They had become a new medium of exchange—ten cigarettes were worth half a bottle of kerosene.

Quite early in the siege, I formed the conclusion that, despite the danger to life involved, it was vital to the well-being of the community as a whole for life to go on as normally as possible. If people sat idly at home a feeling of depression might become general. I therefore called together some thirty of the leading Mishmar Ha'am officers, whose job it was to keep contact with the public. I asked them to persuade people to try to maintain every possible vestige of ordinary life and to urge men to go to their offices daily and keep their businesses open even if there was little for them to do. It was these men and women I relied on to scotch harmful rumors spread by "experts" in the science of warfare who had the habit of holding forth, with little or no genuine information, as to what was happening from day to day. The only prohibition I proposed was upon children continuing to play in the streets or people assembling in groups as they were wont to do at their street corners.

Yet, despite everything, the spirit of the people was something which one looks back on today as nothing but a miracle of courage and fortitude. The columns of one newssheet, *Davar Yerushalayim,* one day published the obituary notice of Avner Lichtenstein, who fell in the fighting. Following the announcement of the name was the declaration by his dear ones, "The entire family will continue to fight until victory." Avner was the second son of the Lichtenstein family to fall. All the sons were enlisted as front-line fighters. When the first son, Yankele, fell as a Palmach fighter, the family had announced, "He fell a hero; we shall continue the struggle until victory." Little square obituary notices were posted up to record casualties.

The Army pointed out that there were no shirkers in Jerusalem. There may have been an objective reason for this. The city was surrounded by enemies, and every man, woman and child was actively involved in the defense—the children as messengers, the men in the fighting ranks if they were young, in the labor battalions or Mishmar Ha'am if they were older, and even the over-fifties going out in their hundreds to work on building the new road or creeping down the ridge from the Burma Road by night, humping flour and supplies on their shoulders over the gap where wheels could not turn. There was also the sense that there was no alternative but to stand and fight, and General "Ein Brera" ("There is no alternative"), as he was called, was an inexorable moral disciplinarian.

The most popular jocular expression among the young people in those days of trial was "To the devil with life, the important thing is to keep well." The inevitable rebuke to a grumbler was the Hebrew equivalent of "Keep a cheerful heart." The nine-year-old son of a caretaker at the Jewish Agency, around the corner from my house, used to bring us messages during heavy shelling. When my wife scolded him for taking risks he said, "But I'm still far from *bar mitzvah,* and I'm so small that when I crawl on my belly the big shells don't even see me."

I also like to believe that the fine spirit of the people was due to some extent to the arrangements made to feed and care for the population even with the minimum that was given them and by the principle we applied of fair shares for all, rich and poor alike, without any exception or favor. Because of this, they felt they all stood together in trying to save the city from surrender. Each Jew killed by the shelling only hardened the determination of all the people to see the struggle through. Their unity was in sharp contrast to the conduct of the Jews of Jerusalem who failed to withstand siege some 1,900 years previously because of their differences, their constant quarreling and the absence of unity.

During most of the period of the siege the orthodox Jews living in Meah Shearim, in addition to their daily prayers, recited the Psalms all through the day and night, praying for salvation. The story went the rounds that a group of young soldiers who were in the vicinity listened intently to the prayers. When the soldiers began to leave the synagogue a rabbi pulled one by the sleeve and said, "We shall go on praying, but you must not depend only on our prayers. Provide yourselves with good rifles too!"

Chief Rabbi Herzog was a source of strength to many, who were encouraged by his example of steadfast faith in the outcome of our struggle. He quietly continued in the day-to-day performance of his rabbinical duties and demonstrated his devout belief that "the Lord shall yet comfort Zion and shall yet choose Jerusalem."

Before the war was over, one could see even the ultra-religious Jews, with their long earlocks and beards blowing in the breeze, working side by side with free-thinkers, new immigrants, people with whom they would never have associated before the siege began. For the war changed everyone in important ways. For religious Jews, the change was fantastic.

One day, after the British had left, I was asked by Chief Rabbi Herzog to come to his home. I found quite a gathering of people, including the Sephardic Chief Rabbi BenZion Uziel and a group of Jews of the ultra-orthodox type.

I was offered a seat, and for some minutes dead silence prevailed. I looked politely at the rabbis and they looked back at me somewhat uncomfortably, embarrassed. I wondered what all this was about until finally Rabbi Herzog turned to an elderly gray-bearded gentleman and said, "Well, Reb Alter, you wanted to speak to Dr. Joseph. Here he is—speak."

After some hesitation, the old man turned to me and began explaining how fundamental it was to Jewish religious precepts to save life, to prevent the loss of a human soul. He went on to say that their quarter had been badly shelled and fired at day and night for weeks now. The men could stand it, but it was too much for the women and children, and quite a number of people had already been killed, so they thought something should be done about it. They knew we would not think of giving up the fight with the Arabs, but— Here he paused and looked cautiously at me from the corner of his somewhat downcast eyes. I sensed what was coming and looked straight at him. At last he continued: They thought that perhaps they could go out to the Arabs and arrange that their particular quarter should be excluded from the fighting. We could go on fighting, but their women and children would not have to endure any more firing and there would be no more killing of innocent souls.

Again silence reigned. Finally he mustered up the courage to ask, "Well, what say you?"

I said, "You do what you believe to be right, and I shall do what I believe to be right."

Again silence, followed by another question: "And what do you think to be right?"

I replied, "I think that if anyone attempts to raise the white flag, he will be shot." With this, I rose, told the rabbis that I had nothing more to say, and left.

Many months later I learned the epilogue of that strange meeting, from Rabbi Herzog's younger son, today Israel's Ambassador in Ottawa. The rabbi asked his son to accompany the old gentleman and his friends and help get them safely back to their quarter. As they were walking along, hugging the buildings to avoid being hit by snipers' bullets, all except the old man carried on a heated argument as to whether or not they should go ahead with their intention, until he turned to them, saying, "That's enough of all your talk; we are not going to raise any white flag. He is a tough customer; he will shoot." With this they all became silent. The incident was closed.

VII

THE FALL OF THE OLD CITY

⎍⎍⎍⎍⎍⎍⎍⎍⎍⎍⎍

W HEN THE BRITISH pulled out of the Old City on May 14, a cease-fire had theoretically been in force since May 1, but it had not stopped continued sporadic attacks by Arab irregulars on the Jewish quarter. The Jews had good reasons to observe the truce. A few hours before the evacuation began, David Shaltiel, who was Hagana district commander for Jerusalem, sent instructions to Moshe Russnak, who was in command inside the Old City, to seize the British positions but not to be the first to shoot. He was to observe the cease-fire rules strictly, as the continuation of Red Cross convoys depended on this. Shaltiel warned him there was no prospect of his receiving reinforcements or more arms for the present and his plan would have to take into account only such forces as he now had.

Taking over the posts held by the British was the first of three steps planned in Operation *Shfifon,* by which we hoped to hold our Old City positions. It was the only one we accomplished. The second had been to occupy certain key positions in enemy territory; we had too little manpower for this. The third was to blow up a clear area around the Jewish quarter to deprive the attacking enemy of cover. This turned out to be completely impractical: a total supply of 400 pounds of dynamite was hopelessly inadequate for any such demolition.

At this point the attack was being made by gangs of Arab irregulars and by the Arab National Guard. They were helped by some Arab Legion noncommissioned officers and some British soldiers, but the Arab Legion itself did not enter the Old City fighting until May 18. The enemy had 2-inch mortars, machine guns and submachine guns, hand grenades and bags of explosives which were slung by centrifugal force at the end of short pieces of string. But the early firing was chiefly in short, sharp bursts of rifle fire, each followed by a sudden assault on a specific building. One of the gang leaders, Fadel Bek, a follower of the ex-Mufti, Haj Amin el Husseini, and a former assistant superintendent of police in Jerusalem, predicted confidently that this kind of attack would be all that was needed to force surrender, when, he said, the inhabitants would be "put up against the wall to teach these Jews a lesson."

On Saturday, May 15, both sides were informed of an extension of the cease-fire, and the fighting stayed on a sporadic level through most of the day. At seven-thirty in the evening the Arabs began a mortar bombardment of the whole quarter, followed up by grenade attacks. By the end of that night, it was clear that the Arabs were violating the cease-fire in a major and systematic way, and Hagana instructed its men in the Old City to return the fire.

When the mortar bombardment began, about 1,200 of the Jewish civilians left their homes and concentrated in two places of refuge: the subterranean synagogues and the basements of the Batai Machse, a large block of solidly built stone tenements close to the city wall, inhabited by poor families and Yeshiva students. By Sunday all civilians living on upper floors had to be evacuated. As the bombardment was stepped up, many of them began to run about in panic. Strong measures had to be taken; sometimes they could be persuaded to return to their houses only by threatening them with weapons.

Our unilateral observance of the cease-fire agreement cost us valuable positions. We also lost seriously by trusting a promise of neutrality given us by the Armenian ecclesiastics, which kept us from occupying the Armenian quarter. The Arabs had fewer scruples; they occupied the quarter at once, and this forced us to evacuate our positions near the wall and in the matzoth factory close to the Zion Gate. It also gave them a field of fire over the Sefardi Talmud Torah and the Karliner Synagogue which completely isolated one of our positions.

On Sunday, May 16, help was promised the Old City within an hour and a half. The tone of the next messages showed that nerves were badly frayed. The next day, which was one of unrelieved disaster, saw the enemy beginning to penetrate close to the center of the Jewish quarter. By 5:55 P.M. on May 17, the Jewish defenders reported to Hagana in new Jerusalem: "There will be no use soon. The need is now. The hour and a half has already continued thirty-six hours. By what watch are you going?"

The enemy had broken into the Street of the Jews, but were forced back toward evening. The Arabs began to broadcast warnings in Hebrew through loudspeakers, calling on the Jews to surrender. Many of the Jewish civilians gathered inside one of the larger synagogues and began to pray. Only three factors saved the Jewish quarter that day: The enemy did not push his advantage, looting each captured building and then burning it, thus setting up effective blocks to his own advance. The Hagana defense was stubborn and bitter, with almost no place left for retreat. Finally, a homemade grenade was being manufactured quickly enough and in some quantity, and it was highly effective in repelling frontal assaults.

At dawn on May 18 came the news that Palmach units from new Jerusalem had taken Mount Zion and were preparing an attempt to break through into the Old City. The story of a crucial day's fighting can be told from messages exchanged during the day.

The morning began with a message that the Arabs were fortifying themselves and the defenders needed more ammunition to be able to hold out. Soon after came a more urgent cry for help to be rushed and a plea for the area to be shelled, as the Arabs were mounting a heavy attack. Before noon came a message that the Arabs had presented an ultimatum: they would repeat the Kfar Etzion massacre if the Jews did not surrender. The Old City command kept advising the Hagana in the New City what to do, suggesting they try to come through the Armenian quarter. They reported that the Old City was being penetrated from all directions in a general attack on the Jewish quarter, which was being shelled constantly. The language of their messages was such that they were urged by New City headquarters to keep control of their nerves, the Arabs knew that the Jewish quarter was not isolated in its defense. Early in the afternoon Hagana headquarters tried to reassure the defenders, informing them that the attack on the Old City would begin in an hour's time and that everything would be done to reach them. Several hours later, since no attack materialized, the Old City resumed their pressure, reporting that the Arabs were in the Street of the Jews, that they were demolishing Habad Street house by house and had blown up the Armenian Church of the Cross and if help did not come at once it would be too late. They were told to hold out a little longer and they would be saved.

By this time the morale of the civilians was broken and the rabbis insisted on a message being sent to the Red Cross requesting an arrangement for a cease-fire. They also wished to go out with a white flag, but the defenders forcibly restrained them from doing so. They proposed that the women and children be concentrated in the Misgav Ledah hospital building under the Red Cross flag.

Toward evening a series of further hysterical messages was received in the New City that the Jewish quarter was being attacked with bombs and the Arabs were coming up from Silwan; their situation was hopeless. Again came pleas to rush help and to shell the surrounding Arab area so as to enable them to hold out.

Finally came a message that it was a matter of minutes for the Old City, to which the Hagana commander replied that our forces would enter the Old City from the south that night.

Communication was then lost with the Old City for over an hour and a half. When it was restored the frantic pleas continued until past midnight. The district command replied only that they were doing their best to send help and were mortaring the battlefield.

After diversionary attacks had been made on the Jaffa and Damascus gates, a tremendous explosion shook the Zion Gate at two-forty in the morning on May 19. A Palmach force broke in almost simultaneously and quickly forced the 150 yards which separated the Jewish quarter from the gate. Its meeting with the defenders was undramatic. Wounded had to be evacuated, together with some old men and women. A few soldiers who had not been out for four months were relieved. Some reinforcements, boxes of ammunition, medical and other supplies and stretchers for the wounded were hurried in. One girl defender was offered the chance to go out, after months inside the Jewish quarter. "Why should I go?" she asked. "I'm used to it by now. The devil won't get me here."

The breakthrough was not followed up, and no bridgehead was established. The Palmach unit withdrew, and an Arab counterattack quickly sealed off the break in the Old City wall. The Jews were in firm possession of Mount Zion, the point from which most successful attacks on the Old City have been mounted throughout history. But the days of the Jewish quarter were numbered, for the Arab Legion had now moved into action in full strength, and this was one place where an Arab victory would bring the kind of resounding propaganda which they badly needed.

For the next nine days, radio messages from the Old City showed an unmistakable growth in panic. This started in the ambivalence felt even by seasoned fighters when help was only a few hundred yards away but powerless to break through to them. It grew on the terror of a frightened civilian population, most of whom were prepared, some eager, to surrender. The tone of panic, finally, grew shriller from the knowledge that the enemy outnumbered the fighting defenders by a twenty-to-one ratio and was backed by a savage mob of Arab civilians who had been shouting for weeks their determination to massacre every Jew inside the Old City.

What delayed the surrender for nine days was the tigerish ferocity with which the defenders fought for every house and the total moral effect of a series of acts of courage performed by individual soldiers or groups of two or three. The fighting had ceased to be an organized battle on the Jewish side. Most of the unit commanders had been killed or wounded, and there was little effective command from above. Yet a series of lonely battles, fought in daylight and at night, gave the Arabs a completely false impression of the strength of Jewish resistance and almost kept the fighting going until a new breakthrough could be accomplished.

Many accounts of these lonely battles have been preserved. Early one morning three young defenders, one of them wounded in his left leg, suddenly encountered five Arabs poking about the ashes of a still-smoldering house, looking for booty. They immediately attacked although their only weapon was one revolver. Two of the Arabs were killed by the first two shots and the other three fled, one of them wounded from a third shot. The trio of defenders returned to their post with two submachine guns—one Jewish, the fruit of a confiscation which had been turned over or sold to the Arabs, and one British. They also had three belts of ammunition and a loaded sack of high explosives. "And I still had two bullets left in the pistol," said the member of the trio who was armed.

Here is another picture: A group of defenders sit in a cellar surrounded by old cans and sticks of gelignite, busily manufacturing homemade bombs while one of their number stands on guard at a lattice watching for the next assault of the enemy. They are short of cans, and a couple of them go from house to house asking the women for any containers they might have. A pious old lady runs to her kitchen cupboard and starts emptying coffee, tea and other pitiful remnants of food from the canisters and hands them over. As she does so she mumbles a prayer, "Please, God, let my bomb be the one that will drive back the enemy and make him leave our Holy City." Another younger woman with a child in her arms gives the defenders all the matches she has in her possession. "Dear God," she says, "for the sake of the innocent children who have not known sin, help us and save us from the Arabs." The word gets around the Jewish quarter that the Hagana are collecting materials for the final stand. An ancient crone hobbles dizzily to the nearest command post clutching four rusty nails, needed to fill the bombs with a kind of makeshift shrapnel.

Still another picture: Communications have broken down. The only contact is by child messengers, boys running or crawling through the rubble from one ruined post to another, bearing small sacks of homemade grenades or some bullets, or reporting how other posts are holding out. They fly from post to post with a childish enthusiasm and absolute disregard of the danger involved.

The other side of the picture: An old man, greedily holding back a whole kilogram of nails until he gets paid, and a young smoke-begrimed defender screaming at him, "The bombs are to defend you just as much as to defend us." With difficulty he restrains himself from shooting the old man and chokes out, "Get away from here as fast as you can—you and your nails!"

By May 20, the defenders reported that they were down to their last 100 grenades and that shelling had started from the Jericho Road and the heights above Silwan village. Headquarters replied that the new cannon fire was being aimed at new Jerusalem and not at the Old City. The Old City staff reported that they no longer held any commanding position and that one more shelling would be the end of everything. As we learned later, they were in fact being attacked heavily on all sides. The system of intercommunication between posts that had been worked out was of little use, since no post could spare men to answer a call for reinforcement elsewhere. There was an urgent appeal for Jewish bombardment of the Nissan Bak position, into which the Arabs were breaking, but it came too late. The enemy carried the position after it had changed hands three times in desperate hand-to-hand fighting, and began to attack Misgav Ledah. The defenders lost five men killed and ten wounded in this action. By now the messages reported that the civilians were rebelling. The answer from new Jerusalem was:

"Hold out. Reinforcements will come in due course. Be strong and of good courage."

If the messages from the Old City were increasingly hysterical, the record shows that they were answered chiefly by vague reassurances or by silence. There is now no doubt that this sapped the morale of the defenders. Hagana headquarters in new Jerusalem was clearly worried over the possibility that the Arabs would break our code and learn how desperate our Old City position was. In fact, the enemy was not getting our messages. For days the Old City radio continued to warn of imminent collapse, to beg for ammunition to be dropped by parachute, and to plead for some kind of cease-fire before the civilians inside the quarter got completely out of control.

Nothing could be delivered by plane. On May 25 the Old City reported that there were no commanders left, that ammunition had given out and that there was demoralization among some soldiers, who were abandoning their posts. In the early morning of May 26, a plane flew low over the area four times and parachuted bundles into the Old City. One fell just outside the wall near the Zion Gate, another between the matzoth factory and the Wailing Wall, both into Arab hands. The Old City reported at 5 A.M. that it had received nothing. By this time the Nissan Bak position had been blown up by the Arabs and the Legion had pushed an armored car almost to the center of the Jewish quarter. The defenders had 170 machine gun bullets left, and no grenades at all.

Efforts to work out a temporary truce were equally futile, as the Arabs refused to accept the Red Cross conditions. When the Old City staff pressed for these efforts to be renewed, new-Jerusalem headquarters maintained that any further request for a truce would only reveal our weakness and prompt the Arabs to more vigorous attacks on them. Everything possible was being done to break through and bring them help. It appears that some civilians in the Old City who held French citizenship, headed by their rabbi, Haham Chamo, were demanding contact with the French consulate in order to arrange their evacuation. An attempt was made to use this as a lever to obtain a one-day truce, but this took time.

That day the Arab Legion notified the Red Cross that it would permit evacuation of Jewish women and children from the Old City on condition that the Hagana surrender its positions on Mount Zion. The Old City was informed of this and was told that the condition was unacceptable, as a comprehensive action was being prepared to extricate them. To assure its success approximately two days were needed. They were ordered to organize their forces and ensure a very strict regime so as completely to control the population. Fire was to be opened only at sure targets. A few minutes later, the Old City reported that the Arabs had just raised their flag over the Great Synagogue (the Hurva).

At ten o'clock that night the Arabs began broadcasting to the Old City in English, Hebrew and Arabic that the rest of the Jews in Jerusalem were about to surrender and that it would go hard with them if they did not yield too. So the Hagana commander in the Old City told headquarters the next morning that the civilians were about to open negotiations for surrender. This was about ten o'clock on May 27. "We shall be unable to hold them back. We have no ammunition." Shortly after noon, the Jerusalem area commander sent a message: "You must act according to my instructions." The reply came immediately: "There is no possibility from a military point of view of holding out here."

Hagana headquarters began to consider again the possibility of parachuting ammunition, but the defenders now replied that no parachuting of ammunition would help, as there was no longer anyone to use it. The only hope was a breakthrough at midnight. The district commander answered curtly: "Answer my questions. Radio the co-ordinates, the boundaries and the light signals. We shall parachute tonight." Later the news was flashed that bread had given out, that the bakery was in the line of fire, that only forty soldiers were left. This information, like numerous other messages they sent, proved not to be correct.

The fateful May 28 dawned. At nine-fifteen the representatives of the inhabitants went out under a white flag to Zion Gate to arrange for a cease-fire. They had received permission for this move from the local command in the Old City. Had they obeyed Shaltiel's orders and held out for another day till the breakthrough materialized there would have been no surrender then, and perhaps none at all.

Later it became possible to piece together from the stories of survivors a much more credible account of what had happened than would appear from the frantic messages from the Old City. Evidence presented before a formal commission of inquiry which first met on June 22 produced a record which modifies substantially the picture of events we had had before, and in some respects flatly contradicts it. Debate still continues in Jerusalem, more than a decade later, about the precise allocation of blame for the loss of the Old City. But nothing changes the conviction which was real in our minds even then—the Old City had surrendered to forces which in some degree were operating against new Jerusalem and all of Israel, and it was desperately important for us to try to understand them if we were to survive.

It became clear fairly quickly that there had been some exaggeration in the alarmist messages sent out by the Hagana command in the Old City. They were trying to produce a quicker response from district headquarters in the New City. There had been, it turned out, enough food until the very end. Moshe Wolfenhaut, who was in charge of food warehouses when the Old City fell, testified that the final reserves were enough for a month. The bread difficulties in the final days had developed because the approach to the bakery was under constant fire and the bakers sometimes ran away rather than face the danger. The civilians had more food than the soldiers. There was enough water, and chlorine brought in during the May 19 breakthrough had been placed in the cisterns.

The medical situation was very grave but had not got out of hand. Dr. Avraham Laufer, in his account of the work of the Hadassah medical unit in the Old City, did not minimize the difficulties, but made it clear they had been coped with. The top floors of the hospital had been evacuated as early as May 17, under heavy shelling. Mattresses and blankets were simply thrown down into the courtyards, but the wounded were carried down as carefully as possible into three small basement rooms. In a few days there were seventy patients, bedded down close to each other, sometimes two on a single mattress. The single window in the adjoining synagogue, which had to be used as a hospital also, had to be walled up to half its height because of enemy shooting. There the wounded lay in the ancient holy building in semidarkness, the walls around them lined with great sacred tomes of the Talmud. Some of the shelves were emptied, and in between the large yellowing volumes were bandages, bottles and surgical supplies, clean shirts and pajamas for new patients.

The wooden benches of the synagogue, where people had prayed a few days before, served as hard, narrow couches for wounded men waiting their turn to be operated on. All that could be done for them as they were brought in was to administer morphine and antitetanus. The lightly wounded were given first aid and a cup of coffee, allowed to rest a few hours and then sent back to the front. Some went to their posts in splints and plaster casts.

I saw several men who were in and out of the casualty clinic two or three times in the same day and still went back each time to fight [Dr. Laufer wrote]. I have to admit that men who would have been hospitalized under normal battle conditions were sent back to the front after being bandaged. We did this because we were so short of men and because while they were receiving treatment their places were being taken in the posts by children. . . . There were men back at the loopholes whose fingers had been amputated a few days previously, or whose wounds were inflamed and suppurating, or who had one eye bandaged up.

There was one case I shall never forget. A handsome boy about twenty years old was brought in. A piece of shrapnel had penetrated his eye.

"How long will the operation take?" he asked.

"About fifteen to twenty minutes," I answered.

"Too long," he said. "The situation at our post is desperate right now. Just put a few drops of something in to kill the pain and bandage it. I'll be back as soon as we have driven them off." An hour later they brought him back. His handsome face was blown away by a shell. There was no need to trouble any further about his eye. He was dead.

When the electricity supply failed, the blood bank spoiled. Even the supplies of plasma which had been brought in on May 19 were lost. Operations were then performed by pocket flashlights and, when their batteries gave out, by the light of kerosene lamps. When there was no ether, or no way of administering it, operations were performed without it.

Another witness, David Eisen, who had joined the defenders in the May 19 breakthrough, stated that a message of May 22 that ammunition had given out had been exaggerated. There were still grenades at the posts, but no reserve supply. On May 26, machine gun ammunition had been exhausted and attempts were made to use rifle bullets. These jammed the guns. The reports of desertion required serious revision, according to Eisen. Men left one position for another, sometimes without orders, and then could not get back to their original posts.

On May 25, this witness said, there had been a serious rising of some of the inhabitants, demanding surrender. He was emphatic that at this point the demonstrators did not include any of the civilian leaders. He had already testified that Russnak, the Hagana commander in the Old City, had suffered what amounted to a nervous breakdown and had abandoned his command to his deputy, Mordechai Pinkus. The dispersal of this first demonstration had not required arms, according to Eisen, although Pinkus had announced that he would shoot anyone disobeying his orders.

On May 26, Eisen said, he was asked by Rabbi Ze'ev Mintzberg, who was his uncle, to arrange a meeting with the Hagana commander. Pinkus saw the rabbi and explained the situation to him. It was virtually agreed between the two men that contact should be established with the Arabs the next morning, but Eisen insisted that it was contact and not surrender that was spoken of. Questioned about a radio message that evening that they would surrender if help was not forthcoming by five o'clock the next morning, Eisen said that at several fighting positions soldiers had stated that they would not go out on duty the next morning if help had not arrived.

A meeting on Thursday, May 27, brought together in Rabbi Mintzberg's house most of the leaders of the Jewish quarter. They included Rabbis Mintzberg, Hazan, Yungreis, Meir Chamo and another Sephardic rabbi. For Hagana, Pinkus, Shlomo Bergman and the witness, Eisen, were present. Weingarten appeared but was asked to leave. He was told, "If it is a religious problem, we have rabbis, and if it is a military problem, we have our own experts." Eisen tried, in his testimony, to draw a distinction between contact and surrender, but he stated that a bitter difference of opinion developed between the rabbis and the Hagana staff over negotiations of any kind. The staff did not want to make any move without having consulted Hagana headquarters. The rabbis objected to this. It was during this meeting that the message came in from the district commander in new Jerusalem, "You must act according to my instructions," with a repeated promise of an extricating action to be launched within two days.

The timing was bad. An action on this very day had given the Arabs the Bethel section and all of the Street of the Jews. In twenty minutes of heavy assault, forty-two of the defenders had been hit, four of them fatally. A third of the Jewish territory had been lost. Why the Arabs failed to cross the street, about two yards wide, into the Yohanan ben Zakkai Synagogue, where eight hundred frightened men and women were cowering, remains a mystery. There was nothing to hold them back; the result would have been the kind of massacre which the Arabs had been planning.

If this action made it difficult for the defenders to heed the exhortations to further resistance they were getting from headquarters, it also made it impossible to negotiate with the enemy. For it was local Arabs who made this assault, gangs which were all but leaderless and without any military discipline. Hagana headquarters postponed the breaching of the wall for Thursday night. So it was decided to try to make contact with the Arab legion at once. The civilian spokesmen feared that if an Arab assault took place next morning the Jews would be slaughtered before any cease-fire could be arranged. On Friday morning, Rabbis Mintzberg and Hazan, equipped with a note by Eisen saying they had the permission of the staff, went out carrying a sheet tied between two poles, as a white flag. At first some soldiers would not let them pass until Russnak and Eisen accompanied them to the last outpost. Rabbi Hazan was wounded; it is possible but not certain that the bullet was fired by one of the defenders.

At this point in his story, Eisen was asked why the district command in new Jerusalem had been urged to shell the Old City after the rabbis had been escorted on their mission. His answer was that there had still been no agreement on the objective of the negotiations, and that the Old City staff was still playing for time. They hoped the rabbis would ask for a truce to bring out the dead and wounded. This would entail finding Red Cross, Magen David Adom and Red Crescent representatives, and a cease-fire might be stretched out until the evening. It was a gamble with very long odds, because the Arabs were extremely unlikely to agree to a truce for the evacuation of wounded men, but the odds against any other plan were also formidable.

The rabbis were led to the commander of the Arab Legion in the Old City, a typical urban Arab of the upper class named Abdullah el Tel. Between thirty and thirty-five, somewhat foppish and lithe in his movements, a little effeminate, Abdullah el Tel had no strong personality of his own and was known to us to be completely under British influence. There were no Britishers actually in the room where the first negotiations took place, but all notes sent in and out of the room were written in English. At the very outset Rabbi Mintzberg was held as a hostage while Rabbi Hazan was sent back to the Jewish positions with a note saying there could be no negotiations without Hagana representatives. An effort was made to persuade Dr. Laufer to go as staff representative, but he refused on the grounds that there were no killed lying in no man's land and that the condition of his wounded was as good as circumstances permitted. So the new delegation was made up of Shaul Tawil for the Hagana staff, Eisen as chaplain and Weingarten for the inhabitants. Yehudit Weingarten insisted that she would not allow her father to go alone, so she was included as secretary of the delegation.

By now it was nearly noon. The Jewish negotiators were taken to a house in the Armenian quarter. There was no cease-fire, but shelling went on with less intensity. The first requests on the Jewish side were that a Red Cross representative be present, as well as Dr. Pablo de Azcarate, the Palestine representative of the United Nations Implementation Commission. Abdullah el Tel agreed, but said these requests must not hold up the negotiations. Tawil then proposed the evacuation of the wounded. Abdullah refused this at once, stating that it would be extremely hard for the Arab Legion to protect a free passage for the wounded against the Old City Arabs who wished to avenge the massacre perpetrated at Deir Yassin nearly two months before. That act of inhumanity and violence, which had been carried out by the dissident Jewish factions to break Arab morale, was once again used, and effectively used, against the Jews.

The Jewish negotiators then made it clear they had no authority from the Hagana commander in new Jerusalem to negotiate. They later claimed they were eager to keep Abdullah from making retirement from Mount Zion one of his conditions for surrender. The two rabbis stayed, so as not to break off contact with the Legion, while the rest of the party began to make their way back to the Jewish quarter. But at the first vaulted roof in the Street of the Jews they were fired on and seized by an Arab mob, and they were taken to an Arab headquarters in the northern part of the Old City. Several times they were threatened with death. A Legion sergeant took them in custody, but they were beaten there. When contact was established with Abdullah, they were taken back to Arab Legion headquarters in a car. The time limit, which had been set at three o'clock, had already expired and Abdullah agreed to extend it by an hour. The intervention by the Arab mob had gained a little time, but not enough, and it had tipped the scales for the Arabs in convincing the Jewish representatives that the only alternative to immediate surrender was the massacre of all the Jews in the Old City by the Arab irregulars. So events moved quickly. The debate in the staff was short and uncomplicated. No effort was even made to communicate with Hagana headquarters in new Jerusalem. The negotiators were authorized to surrender the area and all arms, to try to secure the right of all men to leave the Old City, but to settle even if this were denied. They returned to Abdullah, and he dictated the terms at once, with no discussion except about the wounded. His terms were:

1. All arms and ammunition were to be handed over.

2. All men capable of bearing arms were to be taken prisoners of war. It was agreed orally that these prisoners would be transferred to Amman, the capital of Transjordan, under the supervision of the Red Cross and of Dr. Azcarate.

3. All the other inhabitants, women and children and wounded soldiers, were to be sent into new Jerusalem under the supervision of Dr. Azcarate.

4. Abdullah el Tel was to guarantee, on behalf of King Abdullah, the safety of all Jews until they reached their destinations.

5. The Jewish quarter in the Old City was to be occupied by Arab Legion troops.

The surrender was signed at five o'clock. The staff assembled the soldiers and collected their arms. When the Legion troops saw only forty soldiers and a pitiful collection of weapons, one of them exclaimed, "You dogs! If we had known this, we would have marched in with sticks in our hands!" They insisted on searching every house to see if other men were hiding. During the delay, while Dr. Azcarate was being sent for, a member of the former Grand Mufti's fanatically anti-Jewish family named Moussa Husseini appeared. By this time the Arabs were determined to take a maximum number of prisoners to help explain the Jewish resistance, and the Legion representative included some men in their seventies among the prisoners of war when the population had been lined up in the square of Batai Machse, over which the Arab Legion flag was now flying.

In evidence given before the official inquiry later in new Jerusalem, Isaac Degani claimed that his father-in-law, Weingarten, protested against civilian inhabitants being made prisoners of war. "I estimate," he said, "that he succeeded in rescuing some fifty to sixty men." The witness added, "I was allowed to leave on the intervention of Mr. Weingarten, who said I was his son-in-law and had just got married. I was stopped several times on the way out and they wanted to take me prisoner. Yehudit [Weingarten's daughter] went and spoke to Abdullah el Tel, who sent a corporal to accompany me to Zion Gate." Apparently Weingarten himself begged to be allowed to remain with the prisoners; the witness, Eisen, said Weingarten feared to go into new Jerusalem. .

The evacuees marched to the Zion Gate between two lines of Legionaires. Behind them they could see pillars of smoke rising from the Jewish quarter. The Hadassah welfare station had been set on fire, and a wholesale destruction of Jewish property was in progress. The Arab crowds were angry and excited, stones were thrown, the Legionaires were cursed out loud by Arabs who still wanted a massacre. The Arab Legion, according to all our evidence, behaved extremely well. Some of their officers were Arab, some British, but all of them treated the Jews correctly and even courteously. At one stage, they opened rifle fire against the Arab mob to protect the Jewish wounded while they were being given a quick check by an Arab doctor who decided which were to be kept back as prisoners of war. The three Hadassah doctors, Dr. Laufer, Dr. Egon Reis and Dr. Eli Peiser, and four nurses, one of them a daughter of Weingarten's, refused to be evacuated and chose to go into captivity with the wounded prisoners. Dr. Reis's wife, unknown to him, had been killed while he was besieged in the Old City.

It was not until the next morning that the wounded were finally classified and the serious cases transferred to new Jerusalem. A two-hour cease-fire was arranged to make this possible. The rest were sent with the prisoners of war to Amman. The Red Cross reported that there were in all 340 prisoners, including 54 listed as lightly wounded. In the final week of fighting, we had lost 62 killed and 200 wounded. The entire armament that fell into Arab hands consisted of 100 rifles, five Bren guns, three of which were damaged and useless, forty Sten guns, fourteen tommy guns, two mortars, and five thousand 9-mm. bullets.

News of the surrender had reached my office in the New City shortly after noon on Friday, May 28. I had to arrange immediately for the reception and housing of some 1,300 old men, wounded men, women and children in a city which was itself under siege and fighting around its whole periphery. The obvious solution was to take over the Arab houses vacated in Katamon. My secretary, Haim Haller, set out at once with two large trucks and ten workers to assemble blankets and mattresses. In some houses they found the tables still set, with pots standing on burned-out stoves. In five hours, they had prepared temporary accommodation for all the evacuees. By ten o'clock that night more than half of them had been safely transferred through Zion Gate, some of the older men being carried by Legionaires on their shoulders.

Their faces showed their mixed emotions: relief at their deliverance, mingled with grief at having to desecrate the Sabbath. They looked gaunt and worn out; they kept starting and glancing around in fear. Now and again some of the women would break into bitter sobbing, crying out loud the name of a son or husband who had been kept behind, for the Arabs had detained all able-bodied men between fifteen and sixty. Some of the women begged our officials to provide them with candles so that, late though it was, they could still bless the Sabbath lights. A few pairs of candlesticks were found and the sight of them helped to lift the blanket of gloom which hung over most of the evacuees. Yet it is hard to forget a twelve-year-old girl who threw her ration of bread at the volunteer distributing the first meal, screaming, "Why didn't you send us arms before instead of giving us bread now?"

I called a meeting of the Jerusalem Emergency Committee on Sunday, May 30, to deal with the technical problems raised by the Old City evacuation. Charles Passman, the American Jewish Joint Distribution Committee's representative in Palestine, and an old friend, was put in charge, helped by experienced officials of the Jewish Agency's immigration department who had no regular duties at that time. They set up food kitchens, arranged for water trucks and field sanitation, distributed new ration books, lined up jobs for those who could work. I allocated thirty special police to the Katamon area, and later, as Military Governor, I was able to order the confiscation of goods and furniture left behind by Arabs for distribution among the refugees.

At first we cared for 1,500 persons in Katamon. By July, this number had been reduced to 800. By then we had also arranged for the appropriate bodies to set up schools, kindergartens, a Talmud Torah (for the very orthodox), a baby clinic, a hospital (Misgav Ledah) and a home for the aged. We also arranged for school luncheons. The wives of men who were not soldiers but who had been taken prisoner in the Old City eventually received the same benefits as the wives of soldiers who were prisoners of war.

There was, of course, little we could do for the Old City. Twenty-two of its twenty-seven synagogues had been reduced to ruins, the ancient and historic Hurva Synagogue having been burned by the Arabs on the day before the surrender. But we assumed that the Scrolls of the Law and other sacred books in the Jewish quarter would be placed in safety, since they were not covered in the surrender agreement, and as reports reached us that hundreds were being destroyed, we tried again and again to make contact with the Arab authorities in the hope of saving some of them. One of these contacts, made on July 9, the day the first truce was to end, provided an interesting epilogue to the tragic story of the Old City and of the role of Weingarten in its last chapter.

By July 9, Weingarten was already the subject of an official investigation by Israeli authorities, but, as we knew him to be the only Jew who was *persona grata* with the Arabs, we decided to ask him to contact Abdullah el Tel so that a deputation could meet to discuss outstanding complaints regarding the nonfulfillment by the Arabs of surrender conditions. Abdullah el Tel agreed at once to receive Weingarten. We sent along a trusted representative, A. Lutzky. Colonel Frank Begley of the United States Army, chief U.N. observer, arranged for the deputation to cross the lines to the Arab side. Lutzky reported that a Legion lieutenant, about forty, a Bedouin, conducted the group to Arab area headquarters, keeping up a running conversation about the affinity between Jews and Arabs, that there seemed to be no sense in the determination of both sides to fill the land with graveyards, that both nations could live in peace, and expressed the opinion that the *Inglesi* were the cause of all the trouble.

Abdullah el Tel received the deputation politely enough but, in answer to a question as to their taking nonfighting inhabitants prisoner, said that he had received instructions from Amman to transfer all male inhabitants. He finally agreed in principle to release noncombatants from the prisoner-of-war camp and that Weingarten should go to Transjordan to pick the noncombatants. They learned from Abdullah el Tel that Jews killed in the Old City had not yet been buried. After some discussion it was decided, upon our insistence, that the dead be buried by Jewish prisoners of war who would be brought up from Mafrak for the purpose. When

it came to the subject of the Scrolls of the Law, although Weingarten said that there had been hundreds it transpired that only a
few scrolls had been saved.

This interview raised once again the question of Weingarten.
What was his true role in the collapse of the Old City? He had
gone into captivity with the others on the fall of the Jewish quarter
and was returned with his family from Transjordan on June 7.
He was at once taken into custody pending an investigation. On
June 9, an order was made permitting them to be kept under house
arrest. An investigating commission was set up, consisting of a
lawyer, Gideon Hausner, Hanoch Givton and Avraham Arest. It
began hearings on June 22. After a number of witnesses had been
heard, the commission reported on July 7 that Weingarten refused to testify until he had been permitted to see the Chief Rabbi
and other personages. He finally appeared before the commission
on August 17.

His own evidence was a long indictment of the defenders of the
Old City. He claimed he had used his influence to stiffen their resistance and he cited instances of desertion where he had stepped
in to persuade soldiers to return to their positions. He declined to
name the men, and his stories could not be checked from any other
source. He claimed there had been complete confusion through
the final week of fighting, with no military effort to maintain contact with the civilians. "Few of the men fought valiantly," he said.
"Others hid themselves. In effect, there was no command. I do not
accuse Russnak. There should have been a man of stature . . ."
This was unmitigated effrontery on his part, in view of the expulsion from the Old City in March of Halperin, who had been a commander of real stature.

The inquiry dragged on. When the last defenders came back
from captivity, their evidence made sorry reading. They agreed that
they did not think Weingarten was a "hater of Israel," but they
all termed him pretentious, power-greedy and in suspiciously close
contact with the British. He had wanted his son-in-law, Isaac Degani, to be named Hagana commander, a proposal which Hagana
had found ridiculous. The Jerusalem Emergency Committee's decision to boycott Weingarten after an investigation by one of the
members of our committee had led him to redouble his intrigues.

A reliable senior officer who served in the Old City told me that
when their position was bad, about May 23, Weingarten spoke to
him several times, urging him to persuade our people to surrender

and not to allow matters to drag. This, the officer added, may have
been only fear, which seized many people then. When the negotiations with the Arabs began, it was Weingarten who urged that the
terms of surrender be accepted at once and without arguing.

You càn see Weingarten today walking about Jerusalem. The
self-important strut has been rendered a little less emphatic by a
decade of years during which his life has been one of utter unim-
portance. As you pass him, his sly, rubicund face turns sharply and
expectantly in your direction as though he were eager to converse
with you at your pleasure. But it is a fleeting glance which a
shadow of disappointment quickly subdues, and he goes on his
way. Matters of greater import than his peculiar and questionable
conduct have since come up. It is now clear that while he may have
been of considerable use to the British in helping them nibble away
at the Hagana resistance, Weingarten was not a big enough factor
to have caused the fall and surrender of the Old City. There were
objective factors involved which had nothing to do with him.

It is still difficult to say whether the Old City was doomed from
the start of the war or could have been saved by different decisions
or different leaders. The odds against it had been formidable from
the beginning. And nothing handicapped us as much as the character of the Jewish population there. The two thousand Jews in
the Old City when the siege began included too many old and in-
firm, too many Yeshiva students incapable either of working or of
fighting, too many mystics of all shades of orthodoxy who lived for
weeks praying at the graveside of their saintly but departed prede-
cessors. Chief among these were the members of the Neturei Karta
sect, a large group of ultra-orthodox Jews to whom the whole idea
of national independence was a blasphemy. The most that could be
got from them was agreement to train ten of their men in exchange
for a promise to take our girl soldiers out of the synagogues, and
even these ten did not fight. The Yeshiva students refused even
to help bury the dead when more than forty bodies had piled up
on the top floor of the hospital and the defense feared an outbreak
of plague. Although the argument took place in the Stambuli Synagogue, the Hagana officer drew his revolver and forced them to
help dig the common grave. "I believe their refusal was based
simply on fear," the officer later testified. "They did not regard
themselves as part of us, and could not overcome their fear as we

did from time to time. They just stood there reciting the Psalms until I drew my revolver."

They helped to spread alarm and defeatism. In this they were backed by several prominent, well-known members of leading Oriental families. The head of one of these families deliberately started a false rumor that there would be no more bread baked in the Old City. But this was not typical of the Oriental Jews, who generally bore their full share in the struggle. One young Yemenite girl was a nurse in the hospital during the final days. As soon as an attack began, she used calmly to take off her white apron, hang it neatly on a nail, pick up a Sten gun and go out to shoot. As soon as the Legionaires withdrew, she washed her hands, put on her apron and returned to her duties. There was another simple Yemenite called Hajji, who went on with his work as usual when Bethel Street became a no man's land with its houses evacuated and even fighting men traversing it only when absolutely necessary. In that street was our only remaining bakery. Hajji remained there all alone steadily baking pitta, a form of unleavened bread, for the population.

Considering their background, many civilians behaved admirably. They received the Hagana men with typical Jewish generosity, offered them food and such small services as were within their power and looked up to them as their defenders. Some of them even volunteered and asked to be trained to help in the fighting. Among the Ashkenazim, some consulted their rabbis, who ordained that the war was a *milhemet mitzva,* or holy battle. These enlisted and a few were killed fighting. Indeed, apart from the Neturei Karta, the young people as a whole did their duty. They made up a main part of the fighting force, contributing sixty-five of the fighters, as compared to 120 Hagana men who came in at first and eighty more who were left behind when the Palmach broke in on May 19.

Nor can it be stated that the battle was lost only because of a lack of ammunition. Some of the men still had hand grenades and Mills bombs in their belts, although there was no reserve stock. There was a little explosive material left with which to make grenades. The men had at least some ten bullets each when the fighting stopped. There was also a small reserve of ammunition at headquarters. The ammunition position was clearly so precarious as to have prompted some to surrender before it was too late, but the fact is that there was enough ammunition left to go through one

more fight. This may be said to have been the case only because of
the terrain and nature of the fighting in the Old City. Standing
behind stone walls difficult to assault, our men could husband
their negligible supply of ammunition, not replying to indiscriminate shooting at them but firing only when some of the enemy actually tried to go forward. In this way almost all of the limited supply of bullets could have been preserved for an Arab assault which
might be made on the crucial last day. Carefully utilized, their
small supply could, it was thought, have sufficed to hold back an attack. Such fine calculations would be utterly impossible in open
warfare, but in the conditions prevailing in the Old City fighting
they could nevertheless be valid.

Just before the decision was taken on Friday morning to meet
with the Arabs, the commander of the northern section of the
quarter, Avraham Ornstein, was asked what the position was in his
area. He replied that they could still hold out along a part of his
front, but he could not be sure that the Legion would not break
through into the synagogues where the civilians were concentrated. If they gave him reinforcements, he might be able to hold
that area as well. The trouble was, he said, that by then there was
no one he could talk to. If a trusted leader in whom they had
confidence had appealed to them then to go on fighting for another day, as help was being organized, he was confident they
would have gone on. Other reliable officers expressed the same
opinion to me. Ornstein added, "In retrospect, I can say that objectively we could still have held out, at least twenty-four hours, by
using our last ounce of strength and nerves. It was not necessary to
surrender that morning. Those who took the decision had an er-
roneous assessment of the situation because they were not in control, and did not influence events, which took their own course."

It is certain beyond any doubt that when the question of surrender arose it was not the soldiers who faltered. They did nothing
to urge their superiors to seek a cease-fire, although by the morning
of the surrender it was their general feeling that H.Q. had abandoned them to their fate and that it was imperative to save the
civilian population from slaughter. This was clear when the two
rabbis first went forth and the soldiers tore their white sheet and
escorted them back to the command post. Had the matter depended upon them, exhausted and disappointed as they were,
they would have fought on. No blame whatever attaches to them.

On the other hand, there was one platoon which the Palmach

brought in as reinforcement on May 19 which turned out to be worse than useless. Some did not know how to use their rifles and they lowered the morale of the others with their bitter grumbling. They said they had been deceived and told that they were being sent into the Old City only to carry ammunition and not to fight. These were older men who were not fit for fighting. This platoon's commander lay on a couch protesting that he couldn't carry on. The behavior of the commander of the other platoon, Baruch Gal, was beyond reproach, but he was a quartermaster officer and not a fighting officer and should never have been sent to a front like the Old City.

The Jerusalem area commander, Shaltiel, apparently attached insufficient importance to who was in command of the Old City. At any rate, no attempt was made to replace the officer who was patently unsuitable for so responsible a post. It is not always possible to know beforehand who will make a good commander in battle, but the inadequacy of the Old City's responsible commanders was known well before the May 19 breakthrough, when they could have been replaced. Possibly this was because Shaltiel had other plans for its defense. At one time, he is said to have envisaged the Old City holding out until an outflanking and encirclement plan could be mounted for the whole area, after which the Old City would have fallen into our hands like a ripe plum. Even if that were the case, it showed poor judgment to have weighted the odds against the Jewish quarter's holding out until then by the attitude which he took with regard to its commanders. As an old Hagana officer he should have remembered that the success of Hagana actions depended almost entirely on the kind of men who led the action.

The very first Hagana commander in the Old City was ineffectual. He kept holding meetings where everyone sat and talked over problems instead of tackling them. He was replaced by Halperin, who was a real commander and who contributed heavily to what resistance the Old City put up. Even after he had been expelled by the British, Halperin worked out on his own initiative a plan for the Hagana in the Old City to capture position after position through the Armenian quarter until the Jaffa Gate was reached. This would have opened the city to our forces. Halperin was convinced that this could have been done, and this was the view expressed to him by the people in the Old City with whom he privately maintained contact by wireless. But when they captured a vital point, an Armenian holy place, they were ordered by Shaltiel to withdraw, on the basis of an agreement he had made with the Consular Truce Commission. No sooner had Hagana withdrawn, after receiving an assurance of complete neutrality from the Armenians, than Arab forces entered the building in violation of Shaltiel's agreement with the Truce Commission. As will be shown in a subsequent chapter, it was not in the nature of the Truce Commission to take action in the case of Arab violations.

The officer whom Halperin himself asked to replace him when he was arrested near Weingarten's house was not of the requisite caliber. This man, Moshe Russnak, knew it, and appealed to Shaltiel several times to relieve him of his command. Russnak was a good civilian administrator and, because of his nature, and also probably because it was an escape from responsibility which he disliked and feared, allowed himself to be snowed under with administrative matters dealing with civilians.

The consensus of opinion about Russnak was that he was a loyal and devoted officer who did his best. But he lacked powers of decision, was unable to assert and impose his authority, and failed to maintain discipline among his subordinates. His fault was not in making tactical errors of judgment, but in not exercising his judgment at all. In consequence, the various zone commanders under him were free to act as they saw fit, without co-ordination. The result was, to quote one of the very responsible and effective officers in the Old City, "none of us knew we had a commander." Eventually Russnak cracked under the strain and in the last days of the siege was hardly in the picture at all.

Now there is a romantic notion attached to the tough commander of men, that when a weak commander asks to be relieved, the general grimly sets his jaw and forces him to carry on at his post until the hidden qualities of leadership assert themselves and all is well. But at this stage of the war, Hagana was not yet that sort of military organization; there was much camaraderie between all ranks, and certainly a good deal of give and take among the officers. And the hidden qualities were just not there so far as Russnak was concerned.

In the last stages of the siege Russnak was assisted in his command duties by two other officers, Mordechai Wager, who came in the last convoy that reached the Old City, with the appointment as deputy commander, and Pinkus. These three leaders, Russnak, Wager and Pinkus, stayed in their offices sending desperate calls for help and notifications of imminent disaster to district H.Q., and alternating these with orders to others to go out and continue the fight. This was hardly a leadership which would build or maintain morale. The other, more junior commanders were brave men who stuck to their posts. They had no part in the decision to surrender.

The Etzel commander, Issar Nathanson, personally appears to have behaved courageously, to have fought together with his handful of men, although he was wounded in the hand, and to have maintained control of them to the end.

The planning for the Old City would also seem to have left a good deal to be desired. The breakthrough on May 19 lost most of its effect because plans were not made to follow it up. A group of the Harel Brigade of Palmach which had been sent to the Jerusalem Corridor had been brought back to prepare for this assault. In addition, a company of the Hagana field forces was also readied. But the operations of the two units were never really co-ordinated. They made separate attempts. Harel tried from the direction of Yemin Moshe across Mount Zion, with the intention of breaking in through Zion Gate. The field force of Shaltiel's Etzioni Brigade assembled in the old Commercial Center with the idea of breaking in through the Jaffa Gate.

The Etzioni operation was timed for the night before May 17. A breakdown in staff work first delayed it until the early hours of May 17. This delay gave the Arabs time to get wind of the operation, and when the Etzioni finally made their attack on the night of the seventeenth a hot reception had been prepared for them. The saboteurs who were to have blown open the gate were killed; the armored vehicles were scattered to the four winds; the commander was badly wounded; it took the unit all night to extricate itself from what turned out to be nothing less than an ambush.

It did have the effect of creating a diversion for the Palmach attack, and this, proceeding on May 18 from the Deir Abu Tor side and going by the steepest slope of Mount Zion, surprised the Arabs from the rear. Mount Zion was taken with few losses and in the early hours of May 19 we penetrated into the Old City. Why were these forces withdrawn? This was very likely in keeping with the general policy, for which Shaltiel was not responsible, to use the Palmach units as a striking force to be withdrawn immediately their objective was achieved, leaving it to other troops to hold what Palmach gained. It should, however, have been clear that if the Jewish quarter was to be saved, even if enough seasoned men were not available to be left in the Old City as adequate reinforcements there, at least a bridgehead should have been held between the Jewish quarter and the Zion Gate and the Arabs prevented from seizing the Zion Gate again, so that our link with the Old City might be kept.

After the event, it was the opinion of several of the senior officers that if, instead of a strong force of men being kept on the other side of the wall, on Mount Zion, part of them had been sent inside to hold the bridgehead and the connecting corridor to the matzoth factory, we could have held the Jewish quarter of the Old City. Those who were in the Old City contend that if they had been told beforehand that the Palmach would be withdrawn they could themselves have held a bridgehead with a dozen men. They would certainly have made the effort in view of the vital importance they attached to maintaining a link with new Jerusalem.

For Shaltiel it must be said that positions which were tenable at night, following a surprise attack, were not so good in the light of day and in full view of the enemy, who could see exactly what was involved. Nor did he have at his disposal as many men of fighting quality or such supplies of ammunition as he must have wished. The men who broke in were immediately faced by fresh Arab troops, and this was the day the Legion arrived. The Israelis in the Old City were battle-weary and the quality of nearly half the men who were left in the Old City was so poor that they were not really fit to serve as replacements. But, whatever the reasons, the fighters in the Old City did not receive the help they had been promised, and they were again left to their own resources. What was more, they now had to face the best Arab troops, well trained and officered by the British, when the Arab Legion entered the Old City from the north and the east, with the set task of crushing Jewish resistance.

Avraham Ornstein, the commander of the northern area, a man who had lived most of his life in the Old City, a mathematician, lanky, serious-looking and scrupulously honest, said:

I would summarize the reasons for our surrender as follows:
a. Lack of ammunition.
b. Lack of proper command and failure to control the situation. The decision to make the surrender was in effect theirs, for the rabbis would not have gone to commence the negotiations had the local army command opposed their doing so.
c. The feeling prevalent among fighters in the Old City that

there was lack of adequate regard for the Old City struggle on the part of Shaltiel or his headquarters, either because they felt there would be no struggle for the Old City and it would be arranged by political action, or because they thought the Old City would not be able to hold out anyway.

d. Pangs of conscience that we were jeopardizing the lives of the civilians, who might be slaughtered if we did not come to terms with the Arabs.

e. The fact that many of our men were wounded and all were physically weary to the point of exhaustion. We were left at the end with some thirty-five men fit to fight. This was due to lack of proper command. In fact, we had more men, but they were not all utilized properly by the command and for practical purposes they were not available as fighting men.

f. The enemy had a tremendous superiority of forces. They had many more men, and their men were replaced in the fighting from time to time.

Wolfenhaut, also a solid, reliable eyewitness, asserted:

I would say that the Old City fell because of the following factors:

a. In general, the military training of the men was hardly adequate for such a struggle. The best of our men were not above the average of our weakest battalions elsewhere. The officers had no organizing ability and were not competent to assess the situation properly from a military point of view. For example, I did not come on military duty, but I set up defenses on my own authority. They had no proper military plan. Shaltiel did not send a proper engineer or other competent officer to prepare a detailed defense plan for the Old City. At first, when the attackers were untrained Arabs, we stood against them, but when we were later confronted by a well-trained military force our position deteriorated.

b. Absence of a competent commander.

c. Failure to fulfill promises to send help, and the consequent feeling that got about that the people outside had no particular concern that we succeed, as if we had been sent there only for the sake of history.

d. Absence of reserves. Inadequate forces. The Arabs were amazed when they saw how few men had held out. Our position was so bad

*that the doctors had to urge men in hospitals that they were well
enough to go out and fight again.*

  e. Great superiority of the enemy in manpower and equipment.
  f. Chaos and demoralization during the last few days.

Although he was making thorough and serious preparations for
his promised breakthrough into the Old City, what steps did Shaltiel take to ensure that the defenders and the inhabitants could be
stiffened to hold out a little longer? One of the best officers in the
Old City wrote later that "the men were without sleep, very weary,
they saw their comrades fall before their eyes. They had no command, and no reserves to replace men who were at the end of their
strength. Nevertheless, if on that Thursday night, leading representatives of the nation had appealed to the men in the Old City to
hold out another twenty-four hours and had promised that help
would then surely come, I firmly believe they would have agreed to
hold on and that they could have done so."

I consider it one of Shaltiel's fundamental mistakes that he did
not keep the civilian authorities sufficiently informed of the progress of events. He did not mention a word of the final messages of
desperation from the Old City to us who were in charge of civil
affairs in new Jerusalem. He never informed us how critical their
position was. The successes our forces under his command were
having in the New City deluded us into believing that our men in
the Old City would also manage to hold out until we could relieve
them by breaking through again. I have always felt it was most re-
grettable that we were not asked to intervene and urge the civilian
leaders in the Old City to hold fast a little longer till help reached
them. I felt that if several of us, like Ben Zvi, Hayim Solomon and
myself, had appealed to them and reminded them how much was at
stake for the Jewish people as a whole, and what it would mean to
us if the Old City of Jerusalem fell, they would have heeded our appeal and not pressed the issue of surrender with the Hagana men in
the Jewish quarter on that fateful day. Had Shaltiel spoken to me
about the situation, I would have appealed to Ben Gurion directly
to do all in his power to pare off a small number of competent
armed men from the Tel Aviv area to go into the Old City with the
Palmach group on May 19 in order to remain there to help hold it.

But this reserve of Shaltiel was not just expressed in his silence
toward us (a not unusual reaction of military to civilian authorities). It was also his attitude toward his own officers. He had

been an officer in the French Foreign Legion, and his tough, hard-boiled manner compounded his sureness that his opinions were the right ones. When the commander of the northern area of Jerusalem, into whose sector the Old City might be said to fall, told him three days before the fall that its collapse was only a matter of hours and that it was clear that the help of the Palmach would be too late, his reply was that this commander was "pessimistic." They had men and arms and he "had given instructions." He had. His reply to their calls for help on May 26 were, it will be remembered, "to organize your forces, ensure a very strict 'regime so as to completely control the civilian population." When Pinkus asked to speak to him by radio-telephone, he refused, on the ground that the enemy might listen in. One witness testified, "The refusal (to speak to Pinkus) sealed the fate of the Old City. It may be that it was impossible to prevent the fall of the Old City, but it was clear that the spirit of the Old City commander was broken when the district commander refused to speak to him . . ."

In his own defense, Shaltiel urged that a wide outflanking movement to cut off the whole of the Old City was in preparation, and that only the entry into force of the first truce prevented us from realizing this objective. "My first duty," he stated, "was to protect the one hundred thousand Jews of Jerusalem; only after that was I to try to capture the Old City." There is no gainsaying that in this he was right. It should be added that in his primary duty to protect the Jews of Jerusalem and hold Jewish-occupied territory in the New City he and the forces under his command were eminently successful. Full credit is due to Shaltiel as the commander of the area during most of the struggle.

Shaltiel may also have hoped that political action would come in time to save the Jewish quarter of the Old City. In fact there was little ground for hoping that we could accomplish anything through political agreements. Israel has nothing which we did not hold physically; none of the agreements made by Arabs on other matters have ever been kept. However, Shaltiel could not know this then, and it cannot be held against him.

And so again Jews were driven out of the Old City of Jerusalem. All this has happened before in worse circumstances, but the dreams and longings of generations cannot be destroyed by shell fire. Though not a single Jew remained after May 1948, the struggle for Jewish rights there did not end with the fall of the Jewish Quarter Old City.

VIII

ARABS VERSUS ARABS

பு.ப.ப.ப.ப.ப.ப.ப.ப.ப.ப

T HE FALL of the Old City, which was our biggest military loss,
showed almost as clearly as our victories the disunity within
the Arab camp which was to prove one of the truly decisive factors
in the outcome of the war. For the Jewish quarter in the Old City
fell to the Arab Legion, King Abdullah's army, and it is small exaggeration to say that both Abdullah's allies in the other nations of
the Arab League and the irregular armed mobs within the Old
City were also defeated when the Jews surrendered. Differences between rival groups of Arabs which had been growing steadily
sharper for six months became clear for all to see when the first big
prize of war to fall to the Arab side went to King Abdullah, a man
most unlikely to share it with his allies.

Those of us who had lived in Palestine for many years were not
surprised by Arab disunity in the war. Some of us, including myself, had had business or legal dealings with individual Arab leaders
over nearly three decades. In private conversations with them we
had confirmed three truths about the Arabs which we had learned
from living with them. The first of these was their bitter personal
and clan rivalry for leadership of the still fledgling Arab movement.
The second was the almost disarming duplicity with which every
Arab leader could whip up public feeling against the Jews, as part
of his struggle with other Arab leaders, while privately admitting
that he felt no more real enmity toward us than the great majority
of our friendly Arab neighbors. The third was the degree to which

Arab-Jewish troubles had been compounded by the divide-and-rule techniques of the British.

These truths were not understood by all Jews, and to the rest of the world the Arab side looked both united and massive. There were seven countries arrayed against one, and the manpower ratio was something like forty to one. Spokesmen for the Arab League could always talk in big numbers and impressive sentences. It was easy to believe, in 1948, that simple size and momentum would hold the Arab alliance together at least until military victory had been achieved. Events were to prove that there was no true Arab unity either at the beginning of the war or at its end. Had it been otherwise, we might not have survived. The notion that there is Arab unity was no less a legend in 1948 than it is today.

The basic division within the Arab world was, of course, between the ordinary people and their leaders. This exists to some degree in every nation, but it becomes of major importance when there are no democratic forms of government, almost no literacy, a frighteningly low standard of living, and a primitive pattern of clan authority based on family and village hierarchies of great antiquity. All these conditions prevailed among the Arabs, and they made it possible for their leaders to provoke a struggle for which the great mass of the people had little heart. The overwhelming majority of Arabs living in Palestine paid no taxes, expected little from whoever ruled over them, and talked or thought of politics almost entirely on a local level.

After forty years of living in this region, I am convinced that Jews and Arabs have a great deal in common with each other, and that we can live at peace. I have never found among Moslems, who made up the great majority of the Arabs of Palestine, any trace of feeling against Jews comparable to anti-Semitism. As people, Jews and Arabs have always got along well and liked each other. When there was no political agitation or religious incitement by fanatics, we lived together on terms of amity.

Even when the political issue came to a head, Arab reaction to it was by no means unanimous. The mass of the Arab population, in all probability, would have preferred that the matter not be forced to a showdown between the Jews and themselves. They were not eager to take up arms and fight the matter out. They would have preferred an amicable solution. Had it not been for the political agitators they would have preferred, I still believe, to give partition and economic union between the Jewish and Arab states a trial,

since this would have meant Arab independence in a large part of
the country, peace with their neighbors, and an end to the constant
political turmoil of the preceding generation.

This view found expression not only in the declarations made by
hundreds of Arabs to their Jewish friends or by Arab *mukhtars*
(village headmen) to neighboring Jewish mayors, but also in the
Arabic press. Thus, for example, the Palestine *Al-Ittihad* asserted:

*The unity of Palestine will not be achieved by instigating racial
hatred nor by threats of religious massacres. All this is only calculated to strengthen and perpetuate partition. To achieve unity we
must fight against the heritage of blood and tears left behind by the
Mandatory, we must remove the tension between Jews and Arabs,
raise the latter's standard of living, promote their social and economic progress. We must work for peace and freedom lest the im-
perialists take advantage of the disturbances and try to dominate
the country again. We must, in a word, bring about full co-operation between Jews and Arabs for the good of all.*

Similarly, the Egyptian *Al-Mokattam* declared:

*We stand for partition because we believe that it is the best final
solution for the problem of Palestine. If rejection of partition
would solve the problem we would have welcomed it, but, in fact,
it will lead to further complications and will give the Zionists another space of time to complete their plans of defense and attack.*

I do not mean to claim that there was no strain or conflict between Jews and Arabs except what was provoked for political reasons. A measure of conflict was inherent in the situation; the Arabs
seemed intransigent to many of the Jews, and in many Arab eyes the
Jews were interlopers. For more than twenty-five years, Arabs and
Jews had dreamed separate dreams about the future of a self-
governing country free of the rule of a mandatory power. The Jews
would not forego their right to large-scale immigration in fulfillment of the Biblical prophecy of the ingathering of the exiles, and
to renew their national life in their ancient homeland. They were
devoutly convinced they could not surrender these rights, which the
nations of the world had recognized, without betraying their heritage and their sacred trust to their fellow Jews abroad. The Arabs
of Palestine were still far from being a distinct national group, but

they were gradually acquiring an aspiration to nationhood in the confused political constellation left in the Middle East by World War I. They were politically separated from their fellow Arabs in neighboring areas which had been turned into separate and independent states. This engendered in many Arabs of Palestine a desire to become independent themselves and to hold the whole of Palestine. It also prompted them to object to further Jewish immigration so that the Jews, whose enterprise and technical and intellectual superiority they feared, might remain a permanent minority ruled by them.

But the Arab aspiration to nationhood was most importantly blocked by British interests. The Middle East contained huge oil reserves vital to British industry and to its war machine. The Middle East lay across Britain's connections with its vast African, Indian and Far Eastern empires. This area had been regarded as of major strategic importance by the British from the time of Napoleon. They were not prepared to yield to the pressure of Arab demands to turn over to them the control of Palestine. Here was the link which could connect or break, depending on who held it, the great imperial highways between Egypt and the African continent and the Lebanon, Syria, Transjordan and Iraq to the north and the east, as well as those from the Mediterranean to India and the Far East.

One of the very few matters on which most Arab nationalist leaders were agreed was their desire to escape from British rule, but their timetables were very different. Oil revenues, subsidies or the physical presence of British troops led some Arab states to adopt a less belligerent posture than others toward Great Britain, and the Jews were a convenient enemy who could be denounced by all Arab leaders with equal fervor. This was stated clearly as early as March 21, 1948, by the Arab newspaper *Falastin:*

We have always maintained that the British withdrawal from Palestine is to be regarded as a purely Arab victory. The little that will be left to the Jews afterward could easily be eliminated. In their political immaturity, the Jews keep on bragging that it is they who have forced the British to give up what they have held for the last thirty years. Be that as it may, the British withdrawal gives the Arabs the longed-for opportunity to stamp out Jewish dreams once and for all.

Far more important than their differences in basic attitudes toward the Jews and the British, however, were the differences among Arabs about each other. From the beginning of the war until long after its end, the Jews were in the advantageous military position of fighting against a coalition of jealous and suspicious allies. We knew a good deal about their quarrels before the war started. We learned more from the course of the fighting. Arab recriminations after the war, and especially a careful post-mortem launched in February 1949, by a parliamentary commission in Iraq, completed the picture. This is a good place in my story to summarize the deep cleavages within the Arab camp which helped our victory. They were many; the most important were between rival factions of Palestinian Arabs, and between King Abdullah and his partners in the Arab League.

Even a dozen years after the events, it is hard to fit the complicated details of Arab disunity into a narrative which does not oversimplify them, and while we were being shelled in Jerusalem by soldiers in a dozen different kinds of uniform it was still more bewildering. But every day's fighting brought us evidence that Haj Amin el Husseini, who called himself the Grand Mufti of Jerusalem and who was the head of the Arab Higher Committee, was on bad and worsening terms with other prominent Arab families in Jerusalem, chiefly that of Ragheb Bey Nashashibi, former mayor of Jerusalem. It also became steadily clearer, as the fighting went on, that King Abdullah of Transjordan, whose Arab Legion was the most efficient fighting force against us, was at serious odds with the former Grand Mufti, while Egypt and Syria, which controlled the two largest invading armies, were backing the ex-Mufti chiefly out of suspicion and distrust of Abdullah. Each of these factions is worth a short description.

The former Grand Mufti was the leader of a powerful family which had come to dominate the local affairs of entire areas of Jerusalem and many villages in the Judaean hills. Of medium height, with a blond and somewhat graying square beard, he was suave, polished in manners, and spoke both little and quietly. In his blue-and-red turban and long, flowing black robe, he always impressed me as too weak to be the intriguing politician and organizer of riots and violence which he had been for two decades in Palestine. In the 1936-39 riots he had accepted Nazi subsidies, and during World War II he had been Hitler's guest in Berlin and a radio propagandist against the British in the Middle East. His announced ambition was to be the ruler of Palestine, but as a descendant of the family of Mohammed he may have aspired to even greater heights.

I knew leading members of his family well. One of his kinsmen, Jamil Husseini, had once engaged my services in land litigation which went as high as the Privy Council in London. He was the effendi overlord of the Arab village in which Moshe Shertok lived for several years as a boy and learned to speak Arabic. The Mufti's brother was my colleague in the practice of law, and we were on most friendly terms. Arab nationalist feelings were never allowed to harm the interests of the Husseini family. For years one of the Mufti's close relations prospered mightily by forcing Arab small-holders to sell land, at niggardly prices, which he then resold to Jews at a handsome profit. The Grand Mufti himself lived outside Palestine during the Arab-Jewish war. But his kinsmen were thick in Jerusalem and its suburbs; one of them, Abdel Kader el Husseini, led the attacks on Kfar Etzion, Yemin Moshe and Kastel, where he was killed on April 8.

The Nashashibis were almost as numerous as the Husseinis, equally wealthy, and even more widely connected with other influential landowning families who dominated Arab village life throughout Palestine. During the years of the mandate they had, however, usually taken second rank to their rivals in control of the religious affairs of the Moslem community—an important source of the patronage and the funds for bribery which held together the loose-knit Arab world. The feud between these two families was old and bitter, but the growing power of the Jews had led them to combine, together with some other Moslem elements and representatives of the Christian Arabs, in the Arab Higher Committee. This was originally set up to counterbalance the Vaad Leumi and the Jewish Agency, and the British authorities, when it suited them, treated with the committee on Arab affairs. They did not hesitate, however, to take advantage of the constant enmity of the two major groups in the committee to play one off against the other and to deal separately with each when the occasion required. Generally the influence of the Mufti predominated in the committee, which was accordingly extremist in character.

The committee, although not democratically elected as were the Jewish national institutions, enjoyed fairly general acceptance by the Arabs of Palestine as their political spokesman. This did not prevent moderate Arab leaders from ignoring and speaking out against extremist decisions of the committee from time to time. When there were differences within the committee, different groups of Arabs acted in fact according to the advice of whichever member of the committee they normally supported. The members of the committee were agreed chiefly on the policy of opposing the partition of Palestine and the establishment of a Jewish state. The Arab Higher Committee, purporting to speak in the name of the Palestine Arabs, had met on the day following the adoption by the United Nations of the November 29 resolution, to consider their attitude to it. It was they who decided to call the three-day general strike of Arabs throughout Palestine and to boycott all plans connected with the partition of the country.

The difference between Jewish institutions and the Arab Higher Committee can best be seen in the fact, soon realized by the Arab masses themselves, that while the Jewish leaders personally directed the struggle for independence, the members of the Arab Higher Committee sought safety in neighboring Arab countries when the fighting began. By the beginning of May, not a single one of them remained in Palestine. So oblivious were the committee of the duty of national leaders that they announced publicly, as reported in *Haaretz* on April 7, 1948, that the committee would continue to sit in Damascus while it prepared to take over the administration of Palestine on the termination of the mandate. The committee had earlier decided on principles for the establishment of a provisional Arab government for Palestine under the presidency of the Grand Mufti, Haj Amin el Husseini, to be proclaimed on May 15, with its capital in Jerusalem, and if that were not possible, in Nablus. The government was also to include representatives of Arab states which were members of the Arab League.

On paper, this Arab Higher Committee was in control of the Arab National Guard, an armed force set up to defend Arab interests illegally, like the Hagana. But, unlike the Hagana, this force accepted no higher command, had no fixed system of training, and in practice operated independently in each locality. The factions struggling for power at the top had used terror and assassination for many years to liquidate any Arab group or individual suspected of readiness to come to terms with the Jews. The campaign of incitement was always more anti-Jewish than pro-Arab for the simple reason that there was no universally recognized political authority among the Arabs in Palestine. So the Grand Mufti, the Nashashibis and other chieftains organized their henchmen in fighting groups headed by men loyal to them. The so-called national committees, organized by mayors or other leaders in Arab villages, were in reality little more than fronts or covers for the factions, which were as suspicious of each other as they were hostile to the Jews. The course taken by all these leaders was not determined by the interests and inclination of the little men who made up the masses of the Arab population, although the latter footed the bill in loss of life and suffering.

The earliest plans of the Arab Higher Committee to set up an Arab administration for all of Palestine or for whatever part of the country they could win and hold in war ran into strictly non-Jewish trouble. The Arab League knew the Grand Mufti too well, and its member nations had too many vested interests and ambitions of their own, to give him the leverage and the control which would have come through his establishment of a government in exile. None of its members trusted him any more than his rivals among the Palestinian Arabs. None of them opposed him as frontally or as powerfully as King Abdullah of Transjordan.

All the Arabs in the area subject to partition in 1948 numbered 1,174,000. Immediately to the east in Transjordan lived 325,000 other Arabs. Until 1917 there had been no frontier dividing these Arabs. Abdullah was one of the sons of the ill-fated Hussein, who had helped the British in their war against the Turks on the promise that another son, Feisal, would be made ruler of Syria. The French, to whom the British had also promised Syria in one of the famous secret treaties of World War I, threw Feisal out, and he was later given Iraq as a consolation prize in the strange game of empire building as it was then played. Abdullah had first shown up in Transjordan, a tract of some 34,000 square miles, most of it desert wilderness, with the announced aim of rescuing Syria from the French for his brother. Just how he managed to stay there, to become first Emir and then King, is a secret still buried in the files of Whitehall. All anyone knows is that the British unilaterally carved the area out of what had been entrusted to them under mandate by the League of Nations and gave it to Abdullah as another consolation prize. Winston Churchill, when Colonial Secretary in 1921, against the evidence of British administrators on the spot like

Sir Alec Kirkbride, acted on the advice of Colonel T. E. Lawrence, he has said, in setting up Abdullah in Transjordan, "where I put him one Sunday afternoon in Jerusalem." The French had been complaining about raids into Syria and Abdullah had "undertaken to maintain order in Transjordan and to prevent any hostile action against the French. That was the indispensable stipulation which I made," according to Churchill.

Abdullah served the British well and loyally until July 20, 1951, when he was shot and killed while at prayer in the Mosque of Omar in the Old City by assassins who were widely known to be in the pay of his old enemy, the former Grand Mufti. It was no easy task to be loyal. British subsidies kept his kingdom going, and British officers and arms made his Arab Legion an effective fighting force. But to follow British political directives in 1947 and 1948, while the mandate in Palestine was being surrendered in "Operation Chaos," would have required an even more agile tightrope walker than Abdullah.

When the U.N. decided on the partition of the country, it was thought by those familiar with Arab affairs that Abdullah was rather pleased, since this created a possibility for him later to join the Arab part of the country to Transjordan and thus to expand his kingdom. So his public utterances were at first vague on the subject. Later, when it was apparent that Arab public opinion was opposed to the partition plan and when the other Arab states made it clear they would help prevent by force the establishment of a Jewish state, he fell into line with the popular Arab nationalist policy. No doubt he hoped he would be able, in the event of Arab success, to acquire control of the entire area and put it under his rule. Possibly he also hoped that somehow he would ultimately persuade the Jews to acquiesce and accept his rule, particularly if they suffered a few reverses at the hands of the Arabs.

The commander of his Arab Legion, General Sir John Bagot Glubb, has published in his book *A Soldier with the Arabs* an interesting story of an interview in London in the spring of 1948 between Ernest Bevin, British Foreign Secretary, and Abdullah's Prime Minister, Taufiq Pasha Abu el Huda. It throws a curious light on both the British and Abdullah as each was struggling in those bitter final months to salvage something from the imperial structure which was crashing down around their ears.

"Taufiq Pasha explained the reason for his request for an interview," Glubb writes, "while I translated for him, sentence by sentence." The British mandate for Palestine, he said, was about to come to an end. The Jews had prepared a government which would be able to assume power as soon as the mandate was terminated on May 15. But the Palestine Arabs had made no preparations to govern themselves. They had no leaders in the country capable of organizing an administration. In the same way, the Jews had prepared a police force from the Jewish members of the Palestine police. But, what was more important still, the Jews had an army in the form of the Hagana. The Arabs had no armed forces, and no means of creating an army. Consequently, Taufiq Pasha explained, if the situation were left as it was, one of two things would happen. Either the Jews would neglect the United Nations partition plan and would seize the whole of Palestine up to the River Jordan; or else the Mufti would return and endeavor to make himself ruler of Arab Palestine. Neither of these alternatives would suit either Britain or Transjordan. The Mufti was the bitterest enemy of Britain and had spent the war with Hitler in Berlin. He was also an irreconcilable enemy of Transjordan and considered himself to be the personal rival of King Abdullah.

During recent weeks, King Abdullah and the government of Transjordan had received, and were still receiving, many requests and petitions from Palestine Arab notables. In all these communications, the Palestinians begged for the help and protection of the Arab Legion as soon as the British forces withdrew. The Transjordan government accordingly proposed to send the Arab Legion across the Jordan when the British mandate ended, and to occupy that part of Palestine awarded to the Arabs which was contiguous with the frontier of Transjordan.

"I can to this day almost see Mr. Bevin sitting at his table in that splendid room. When I had finished my translation thus far, he interrupted Taufiq Pasha's statement by saying: 'It seems the obvious thing to do.'"

Abdullah wanted as much of Palestine as he could get, but he had to move with extreme care in order not to offend the British until they finally evacuated, and in order not to destroy in public the myth of solidarity with his Arab allies. In private he pleaded earnestly for a negotiated peace. At the end of April 1948 he sent a telegram to Elias Sasson, now Israel's Ambassador to Italy, then the Jewish Agency's expert on Arab affairs, a man who knew Arabic and Arab politics from years of study. Abdullah urged on him a proposal he had earlier made that the Jews content themselves with autonomy in the areas where they were a majority, leaving sovereignty vested in Great Britain. Abdullah was ready for any compromise which would secure for him *de facto* rule over the Arabs of Palestine and deny this to the former Grand Mufti.

His assassins were at least correct in thinking him prepared to betray the extreme Arab nationalist position. He was not even discreet in his private talk about this, although in public he was forced to give lip service to his alliance with the former Grand Mufti, the Egyptians and other Arab die-hards. Count Folke Bernadotte saw a good deal of him in the spring and summer of 1948, and he wrote in his book *To Jerusalem*:

King Abdullah has more at stake in the Palestine conflict than any of the other interested parties. If he succeeds in incorporating the Arab parts of Palestine in his dominions, he will expand his country's economic resources and make himself more independent of his protectors. That will also be the case if he brings about a political and economic agreement with the Jews. Transjordan troops have occupied the central parts of Palestine and set up a military administration there.

General Glubb remains the best source on Abdullah, whose army he commanded. Some Arabs of the Mufti's party in Haifa once told one of his officers, "We reckon the Arab Legion to be a greater danger to us than are the Jews!" These twelve thousand well-trained and disciplined men, commanded by British officers and well equipped with British arms, were the most formidable enemy we faced, and it is probable that only our victory kept them from turning on and defeating the mercenaries, the irregulars and the private Arab armies who were their allies.

The Arab Legion moved into action long before the British left. As early as December 14, 1947, it was responsible for an attack on a guard escorting a Jewish convoy of trucks on its way to Ben Shemen, a children's agricultural village near Lod (then Lydda). Fourteen Jews were killed and twelve wounded. On February 16, Arab Legion troopers dragged two Jewish men and a girl out of their car in Haifa and killed them. A detailed list of similar attacks was reported on April 19 by the Jewish Agency to the Security Council of the United Nations. The British authorities had promised us faithfully that the Legion would leave the country before the British evacuation, but it had been clear from the start that nothing would be done to keep the Legion from re-entering immediately as the army of Transjordan. This is exactly what happened.

The strange story of the Legion's part in the Arab invasion of Palestine can best be told by excerpts from General Glubb's own memoirs:

When, however, hostilities in Palestine became inevitable, I sent a personal signal direct to the Commander-in-Chief, Middle-East, asking him to dispatch immediately to Aqaba a ship containing certain specified types of ammunition. The C.-in-C. rose to the occasion and the ship was duly loaded and steamed out of Suez for Aqaba.

The four regiments of the Arab Legion which were to cross to Palestine on May 15th had been camped in the desert just north of Zerqa. They were to move on May 14th from Zerqa to Amman and thence down the long twisting road to the Jordan valley, four thousand feet below. They were to bivouac on the east bank of the Jordan and cross the Allenby Bridge at dawn on May 15th. The Mandate was to end officially at midnight, May 14th-15th, though the British in practice evacuated Jerusalem on the morning of May 14th.

On May 16th, 1948, the day after the Arab Legion crossed the Jordan, the Belgian Consul-General in Jerusalem called on King Abdullah in Amman. He came in the name of the Security Council to protest to King Abdullah against the "unilateral aggression" committed by the Arab armies by their entry into Palestine.

With regard to the Arab Legion's participation in the attack on Jerusalem, Glubb wrote:

I went back to my house, full of anxious forebodings. I knew the extent of Jewish preparations. I knew that the Arabs had no plan and that there was no co-operation between them. We still had received no ammunition. The people expected us in two or three days to take Tel Aviv. How was I to act amid so much folly?

There seemed to be no alternative but to break into Jerusalem from the north, clear the Sheikh Jarrah and establish contact with the Old City. Then a continuous line of defense could be built up across the city and the Jewish offensive halted.

As soon as I reached home, I went to my room and wrote out the signal myself. "I have decided to intervene in force in Jerusalem." Divisional headquarters were ordered to attack Sheikh Jarrah at dawn on the 19th and break through, so as to establish contact with the Old City. The 8th Infantry Company on the Mount of Olives was to move forward across the Kidron and join in the defense of the Old City. The die was cast.

With regard to the important role the British officers filled in the Arab Legion, Glubb makes the following admissions:

On May 30th orders were received from the British government that all British Army seconded officers were immediately to leave their commands and withdraw from battle. The reason for this order was that the Security Council, at a meeting on May 29th, had adopted a British resolution calling for a four weeks' truce in Palestine. . . .

The withdrawal of the British officers was a shattering blow. They included all operational staff officers, both the brigade commanders, and the commanding officers of three out of the four infantry regiments, and all the trained artillery officers. The artillery having only been raised three months before, none of the Jordanian officers were yet really competent to direct the fire of the guns. . . . The British regular officers were therefore the keystone to the whole edifice in 1948.

Although the Arabs were favorably placed at the end of the first month of fighting, we knew that they had in reality shot their bolt. If on May 15th they had rapidly brought their full forces to bear, and had then advanced energetically, they might have succeeded in over-running the new Jewish State. But they were far from doing this. Most of them completely underestimated the task, despatched quite inadequate forces, and came to a halt as soon as they met resolute opposition. Transjordan alone had thrown all her available forces into the struggle on the first day.

The first military aid contributed by Palestine's neighbors other than Transjordan was the recruitment of volunteers, chiefly as mercenaries, and their training at camps in Syria. This was the plan

which the Arab League originally believed would suffice to break
the resistance of the Jews. These soldiers infiltrated across the frontiers in larger and larger contingents as the winter war developed
and were formed, inside Palestine, into so-called Liberation Armies.
The Jewish Agency submitted two long and detailed memoranda
about them to the Security Council of the United Nations, the first
on February 2, and the second on March 13. These gave the names
of the retired or pensioned army officers from Arab countries who
commanded these troops, the numbers of the "volunteers" and
the dates of their crossings of the frontier, descriptions of their uniforms, and direct quotations from the Arab leaders who were
organizing the recruitment. These were direct acts of aggression
openly carried out by member states of the United Nations, but
there was clearly nothing that could or would be done at Lake Success to stop them.

At first these liberation armies attacked only unprotected Jewish
settlements, chiefly in Galilee, looking for loot. Except for what
they could plunder, these armies depended on allocation of funds
raised by the Arab League for the defense of Palestine. Long after
the war, in July 1953, Mohammed Hussein Haykal, editor of the
Cairo weekly *Ahar Sa'ah,* published a series of articles which
showed that rivalry for these funds was the cause of fantastic ex-
aggerations of the bravery and the achievements of these Liberation
Armies.

This was not hard for us to believe in respect of the most notorious of them, which was led by Fawzi el Kawkji, a braggart Arab
adventurer who had been a kind of freebooter in the Middle East
for nearly a quarter of a century since taking part in the Syrian rising against the French in 1925. He had been prominent in the
1936-39 Arab disorders in Palestine, a minor leader in the Raschid
Ali revolt in Iraq against the British, a grateful recipient of the
Iron Cross from Adolf Hitler in Berlin. His followers called him "the
Lion of Damascus," but his roar was worse than his bite. Abdullah
disliked him; the other members of the Arab League came early
to distrust him; in the end he quarreled even with the Grand Mufti.

There is good reason to believe that, like Fawzi, the Arab League
and the British both expected these Liberation Armies to overrun
the country before May 15, to shatter Jewish morale, and to make
an all-out war unnecessary. By April they had infiltrated deeply
into Palestine and looted some Jewish settlements. They enormously
complicated our communications and supply problems. They

played a major and immensely costly part in whipping up the
emotional and political fanaticism on the Arab side which so envenomed the war and its aftermath. But they never broke Jewish
morale. They mobilized too many mercenaries and riffraff, some
in uniform and some not, to be an effective military force. There
were plenty of Palestinian Arabs among the rank and file, but by
the end of April every Arab commander in the country, except in
the Jerusalem and Lod areas, was a non-Palestinian. In the supreme
command in Palestine, such as it was, there was not a single Palestinian Arab. Friends of the Arabs, like General Glubb, have un-
equivocally laid the blame for the fate which befell the Palestine
Arabs at the door of the Arab governments who irresponsibly raised
hopes among them. Several opportunities for compromise were offered them, but they were intransigent and, as a result, lost out.

In the middle of May, Kawkji's army withdrew from the central
part of the country and the regular Arab armies took over. In General Glubb's words, at this point "the politicians, the demagogues,
the press and the mob were in charge—not the soldiers." They
operated through the Arab League.

This body had been set up in 1943, largely by the British Foreign
Office under Anthony Eden. It was designed originally as a consul-
tative political body representative of all Arab states, to foster close
ties between them and to erect a common political front in foreign
relations. Two of the Arab states are known to have joined the
Arab League only because of British advice, if not pressure. It has
never created real unity among the Arabs and it has served chiefly
as an arena for the competitive struggle and intrigues of Arab states
and their rulers. But it did unite the Arabs in opposition to Jewish
immigration into Palestine and the establishment of Israel. Count
Bernadotte wrote, in his *To Jerusalem:*

*The unifying force in the Arab world is the Arab League. Lan-
guage, religion and culture are the factors that bind the Arab states
together, but their economic, political and geographical structure
are so widely different thay they can only achieve real unity to a
very limited extent. In the struggle for Palestine they stand against
the Jews. But they have not been able to find a solution to their
problem that would be acceptable to them all.*

This was not for want of trying. The Political Committee of the Arab League held a long series of meetings on the Palestine problem in the Lebanon, in Bludan in May 1946 and June 1947, in Sofar, a small summer resort, in September 1947 and in Aley in October 1947; in Cairo in December 1947 and February 1948; in Amman at the end of April; and in Damascus in May. Thanks to the post-mortem investigation carried out by the Iraq parliament, we now know a great deal about what went on at these meetings. It confirms the summary given by Salah Jabr, the Iraqi Prime Minister, on December 24, 1948: "It is my duty to declare and reveal that the attitude of the members of the Political Committee confirmed my fear and suspicion which arose at the meetings in Sofar and Aley. From their attitude it was clear to me that the Arab States were not prepared to solve the Palestine problem finally and with success. The League is not even honest in its decisions arrived at and published with the declarations of its Secretary-General or certain of its members."

As early as the October 1947 meeting, the Political Committee had called for unified military command and an agreed quota system for delivery of arms and equipment. But no meeting of the chiefs of staff took place until the end of April 1948, in Amman, fifteen days before the expected British evacuation. Field Marshal Ismail Safwat, of the Iraqi Army, had been named supreme commander of all Arab fighting forces in Palestine as early as the Cairo meeting in December 1947, but he could get agreement neither on the objectives of the war nor on the means of fighting it.

Azzam Pasha, the secretary general of the Arab League, stated on the day before the United Nations resolution was approved that partition would make war in the Middle East inevitable. All the Arab countries were prepared to carry out the decisions of the Arab League. It was a great injustice, he added, to partition a country where the Arabs formed a majority. The Arabs would never accept partition. Though they were not armed, they were not afraid of Jewish terrorists. The Palestine Arabs would receive every material and moral assistance from the Arab countries. "This will be a war of annihilation and dreadful slaughter, reminiscent of the Mongol slaughter and the Crusades," he said.

Similar public statements continued for months. On March 8 the Syrian Minister of Defense, Ahmed Sharabati, declared, "We have obtained superior weapons with which to fight the Jews. As soon as the British Army withdraws from Palestine the big fight will start."

At the end of April the Egyptian daily newspaper *Al Ahram* reported King Abdullah as stating he would shortly send his forces into Palestine. Abdullah at that time informed foreign newsmen, "The only course now open to us is to solve the Palestine problem by military means. The Jews instead of waiting till May 15 attacked Arab settlements. This in itself suffices to impel the Arab states to send troops there. I doubt whether a single Arab state will be able to withstand the will of the Arab people to proffer help to the Arabs of Palestine." He repeated his proposal that Jews should be citizens with equal rights in a single Palestine state.

In an order of the day soon after, Abdullah said to his troops: "Prepare for service to save Palestine. Prepare for the struggle for our honor, for it is our duty to join in the holy war, a war in which the neighboring Arab states will participate."

In an interview with the Associated Press at the end of April, General Ismail Safwat declared that the armies of the Arab states would enter Palestine on May 16, the day after the British mandate was scheduled to terminate, while King Ibn Saud of Saudi Arabia promised to send Saudi troops to take part in any military action by the Arab League.

Actually, only five Arab states took part directly in the war: Iraq, Egypt, Syria, the Lebanon and Jordan. Of the other two Saudi Arabia provided a solitary company of soldiers, while Yemen contributed nothing but statements to the press. The participating states fought as individual armies, paying no attention to General Safwat's unified command. All of them delivered fewer soldiers and smaller quantities of arms and equipment than were promised. The Iraqi parliamentary commission in 1949 published the answers of the Iraq Ministry of Defense to twelve questions it asked about the conduct of the war, and the document, which was translated into Hebrew in 1954 under the title "Behind the Scenes," makes curious reading to those who remember the public statements made in 1948 by Arab leaders. One of its conclusions ran:

The meeting of the Political Committee in Sofar, the session of the League Council at Aley on October 7, 1947, and of the Political Committee in Cairo in December 1947, were the most important meetings which the League had on the Palestine question. Their importance derived from the discovery of the very serious rifts between the Arab states which they could not bridge. It became clear that the participation of some of the Arab states in these meet-

*ings was only intended to satisfy public opinion in their countries.
They did not believe that the situation in Palestine was serious, and
it was necessary tò persuade them and to implore that they should
be prepared for some measure of sacrifice for Palestine. They were
apparently infected with the general enthusiasm, but secretly they
struggled to delay and gain time and see what would happen. As
a result it was not difficult for the Zionist enemy to discover the
main weakness, to foresee the split in the Arab camp and to exploit the time gained to fortify its positions in. the whole area, with
wonderful patience. Against this foe the Arab states and their
leaders remained calm and wasted valuable time which could not
be regained.*

The report went on to state:

*From the beginning of the campaign in Palestine the Mufti of
Jerusalem, Haj Amin el Husseini, tried to interfere, to establish his
influence, and to organize a force subject to his command. General
Safwat raised this question on various occasions at the meetings of
the Political Committee and in the Palestine Committee and explained the difficulties and lack of co-ordination caused by the Mufti's interference. In spite of the Mufti's assurances that he would
leave military operations in the hands of the General Staff and that
he had instructed his men to obey its commands and to co-operate
with it, his actions have been proved to be diametrically opposed
to his promises. In fact, not a day passed without some action on the
part of the Mufti intended to increase his following, to weaken his
opponents and to entrench his influence. Since his activities were not
carried out with any regard for military reasons, but completely
otherwise, he interfered with the war effort.*

*Following the receipt of Safwat's report, the Palestine Committee
instructed the Mufti to suspend his separatist activities. The Mufti
paid no attention and continued, as was usual with him, to promise
and not to obey. This embarrassed the military forces and caused
considerable difficulties.*

If the Grand Mufti proved hard to control, the Egyptians were
even more difficult. There are many experts on the Middle East
who claim that it is a mistake to call Egyptians Arabs at all, as
most of them are descendants of the Egyptians of Pharaonic times.
Literally all authorities are agreed that in the last few generations

the Egyptians have had to wrestle with a host of problems which concerned Egypt alone and not the Arab world. Chief among these, of course, have been the struggle to recover independence from the British and the deep popular revolt against the Egyptian monarchy. Both of these were in acute phases in 1948, and both led Egyptian representatives to play contradictory roles in the public and private meetings of the Arab League.

One of the best witnesses to this is Mohammed Hussein Haykal, a close friend of General Nasser. In 1953, when he was editor of *Ahar Sa'ah,* he admitted that in 1948 he had not expected the regular Arab armies to invade Palestine and that he was sure the Egyptian Army would not move.

This was for several reasons [he wrote on March 13, 1953]: (a) The Egyptian Prime Minister, Nokrashy Pasha, said at the conference of Prime Ministers at Aley, in the Lebanon, at the beginning of 1948, that Egypt could not enter into a formal war in Palestine. It would help as much as it could with money, arms and volunteers, but not more. (b) On a short trip to Cairo I met Nokrashy and told him what I had seen in Palestine. He replied: "Our armies will not embark upon open warfare in Palestine, for our fight was primarily against the British; I assured the Security Council that the Egyptian Army was capable of filling the void that could be created by the British evacuation of the Suez Canal, and how can I put this army to any other trial, even though the risk involved be the slightest. . . ?"

On the same visit I met General Mohammed Kheidar, the Minister of War in those days. . . . I told him what I had seen with my own eyes in Palestine and he replied, banging on the table: "We shall never enter into a formal war . . . are we mad? But we shall enable soldiers and officers to volunteer and we shall equip them with arms, as much as they want." . . .

Let us now return to my hasty visit to Cairo, after which I returned to Jordan . . . I dined with King Abdullah, who told me that at a secret session of the Egyptian Parliament Nokrashy had explained that he would not permit the Egyptian Army to intervene in the war . . . In the same period I met in Amman with Azzam Pasha, then the Secretary General of the Arab League, who said to me: "All that is requested of Egypt is money and volunteers." . . . All this strengthened my belief in the nonintervention of my country in the war.

Haykal reports, quoting General Ahmed Ali el Mawawy, who was the first commander of the Egyptian Army in the Palestine war, about a meeting of the Egyptian headquarters staff at the beginning of May 1948: "Nokrashy, the Prime Minister, also participated in the meeting. He told me frankly: 'Our standing among the Arab states obliges us to enter the war.' He subsequently expressed the opinion that the battle would end quickly, as the U.N. would certainly intervene. He also contended that the encounters would be in the nature of a political demonstration and not fighting operations. This was the evidence of Mawawy."

Contrary to everything Egyptian leaders said publicly and to the Arab League, it is now clear that they wanted desperately to limit their contribution to the volunteers who were recruited largely by the Moslem Brotherhood, a fanatical religious society with grandiose political aims, and to definite amounts of arms and money. It took the winter war to prove to them that the wish had been father to the thought in their minds that this would be enough to defeat the Jews. By May it had become evident that either the Jews or King Abdullah would win, and they were forced to invade in strength.

King Farouk was jealous of King Abdullah, and there is no doubt that he coveted the Negev for himself as a link with the Arab lands of the Middle East. But his press, under strict censorship, had been allowed to report only victories throughout the winter. Egyptian public opinion would not have tolerated a decision to cut his losses when it became obvious that the Jews would not collapse without a major campaign. Count Bernadotte, in his book *To Jerusalem,* showed that he shared the opinion that the final decision to invade in force was dictated "chiefly by considerations of home policy. Egypt is the largest and economically the strongest of the Arab states. But there are dangerous divisions in the country. From this point of view the Palestine affair was a welcome distraction—it has the support of a united popular opinion."

From this point on, and up to the present time, Egypt has been forced by the pressure of unresolved domestic problems to double and redouble its losses in Palestine. Even by the end of the first truce in the fighting, Egyptian leaders had backed themselves into a position from which they could see no escape except through fighting for which they had neither the heart nor the muscle. General Glubb is again the most credible witness on this, since he was clearly no friend of the Jews. This is his conclusion:

The real fact was that the Egyptian government had led the Arab League to war in May 1948 against the advice of Jordan. Egyptian leadership had ended in a fiasco, whereas the Arab Legion had gained in prestige and had actually saved a considerable part of Palestine. It was necessary for Egypt to find an excuse for her failure. She was also intensely jealous of Arab Legion successes, contrasted with her defeats. These two factors were further accentuated by King Farouk's jealousy of King Abdullah, and by the general anti-British trend of Egyptian policy. For the army which had outshone that of Egypt was the army of King Abdullah, and it had been trained and led by British officers. All these facts were intolerable to the dignity of Egypt . . .

During the period of the truce, criticism of the government increased in Egypt. To silence this criticism, the Egyptian Prime Minister decided to start hostilities once more. The future of the Arabs of Palestine was sacrificed to Egyptian politics.

The Syrians and the Lebanese were too weak in military terms to play decisive roles in the Arab League conferences, let alone in the actual fighting. The Syrians shared the Egyptian distrust of King Abdullah; they feared a revival of his old dynastic dream of a Greater Syria, to be ruled from Amman and to include the territory he believed had once been promised to his brother. Jamil Mardam, the Syrian Prime Minister, is now known to have made some of the most eloquent and belligerent speeches at meetings of the Arab League, promising an infantry division to fight on the battlements of Jerusalem and another to sweep the Jews into the sea, but their effect was tempered by knowledge, on the part of his colleagues in the Arab League, that the only Syrian division capable of taking the field was already heavily committed and in serious trouble in the fighting in Galilee. Sir Alec Kirkbride, reporting one of these meetings, writes: "Jerusalem was dismissed as saved, and the talk turned to more pleasant matters such as the final offensive which was to sweep the Jews into the sea, and how the Jewish property would be divided among the Arab governments that had sent armies."

I must admit disappointment that the Lebanese gave even lip service to the grandiose plans of the Arab League in 1948. There is serious ground, I believe, to think that the Christian Maronites, who make up a bare majority of the population of the Lebanon, would have preferred to keep out of the Palestine embroglio if it had not been for a few of their leaders and their fear of the Moslems who surround them. Maronite patriarchs were among the first of the world's religious leaders to speak out against the Nazi persecution of the Jews in 1933. The Maronite community gave evidence in our favor before the Anglo-American Commission in 1946. In September 1947 Bishop Ignatius Mubbarak declared in the name of the Maronite Church that the Lebanon wanted peace with the Jews and would be glad to see a Jewish state in Palestine. They saw in this a strengthening of the Lebanese Republic vis-à-vis the Moslem world. In the winter of 1948 many Syrian Jews found refuge in the Lebanon from Arab fanatics.

Long before the emergence of Israel, I came to know a former Lebanese President, Emile Edde, in Beirut. He was a Maronite and told me the Maronites were descended from the Phoenicians, who, like the ancestors of the Jews, were a Hebraic tribe. The Jews and the Maronites were consequently in the nature of cousins. They welcomed our return to Palestine because, coming back from our long sojourn in European countries, we would be able to help in the technical and industrial development of the Middle East for the benefit of all its inhabitants. He mentioned the wisdom of not exaggerating the scale of our immigration so as not to arouse the fears of the Palestinian Arabs. He also intimated that the Maronites would not be sorry to see an additional non-Moslem element in their neighborhood. He stressed the natural reasons for friendship between the Jews and the Maronites.

I also had the privilege of negotiating an agreement of friendship between the Maronites and the Jews with the Patriarch Arida, through his accredited representative. The document was signed on behalf of the Jewish Agency by its president, Dr. Weizmann, and by the Patriarch, whom I visited in that connection. The agreement stipulated that it should not be given publication, and I take the liberty of recording the fact now only because both the signatories have been dead for a considerable number of years.

The Lebanese had a tiny army and their participation in the Palestine war was of negligible significance. When the time came to sign an armistice, Israel was glad to offer unconditionally the evacuation of fourteen Lebanese villages which we had occupied in the course of repelling Arab attacks.

IX

THE FIRST TRUCE

꒐꒐꒐꒐꒐꒐꒐꒐꒐꒐꒐꒐

I N THE CAMP of the enemy, to use the famous phrase of the prophetess Deborah, great were the searchings of heart. By the end of May, neither the long winter war nor the all-out fighting which followed the British evacuation had broken the Jewish resistance. The forces of Israel were victorious on nearly every front. The areas assigned to us by the United Nations were largely in our hands. Even in Jerusalem it was clear that we were somehow surviving the siege and that our hold on the New City, at any rate, could not be broken by the Arab Legion. The rivalrous Arabs, the sullen British and an astounded world were all in their various ways trying to square the state of things as they were with the universal prediction which had been summed up by Field Marshal Bernard L. Montgomery, then Chief of the British Imperial General Staff, when he said in public, in the language and spirit of cricket, that the Arabs would "hit the Jews for six" into the Mediterranean.

Therefore, talk of a cease-fire began to spread widely in nations which had watched the anarchy of the preceding months with complacency. The chorus was led by Great Britain, where not only had dreams of a return to Palestine without the Zionists been shattered but also plans to retain an imperial position through King Abdullah looked uncertain. It was manifest that the refugee camps which they had prepared in Cyprus and in Greece would not be needed, at any rate for Jews. So, as early as May 22, the Security Council of the United Nations called for a cease-fire in Palestine, to become effective within thirty-six hours, and instructed its Consular Truce

Commission "to give the highest priority to the negotiation and maintenance of a truce in the city of Jerusalem."

This commission had been appointed by the Security Council on April 23 to try to arrange a truce in the city. It comprised the Jerusalem consuls of the United States, France and Belgium. At the time, this had seemed a shrewd diplomatic move; the fact that the Soviet Union had no consul in Jerusalem had eased the appointment over one of the obstacles of the cold war. The mandate of this commission, however, had been sharply defined (although the consuls themselves never understood the limitations on their authority), and on May 14 the Political Committee of the United Nations Assembly had voted to send a mediator to Palestine, with much wider powers. A week later Count Folke Bernadotte, vice-president of the Swedish Red Cross and a relative of the Swedish royal family, had been unanimously chosen to fill this post. The Consular Commission had held its first meeting on April 27; I was the man most directly involved with them, since I was chairman of the Jerusalem Emergency Committee and later Military Governor of Jerusalem. Count Bernadotte did not arrive in Tel Aviv until June 1.

Israel's acceptance of the May 22 call for a cease-fire was sent the following day. The Foreign Minister of the Provisional Government of the State of Israel reported to the Secretary General of the United Nations that an order had been issued to all fronts to cease fire at the stipulated hour, "provided that the other side acts likewise." The decision was also communicated to the Truce Commission and published in the press. But the proviso was the catch. King Abdullah declared on May 23, "My soldiers did not enter Palestine in order to stop the war to no purpose." His soldiers had the Jewish quarter of the Old City on the point of capitulation, his one success of any note since fighting had started. So he instructed his government not to reply to the Security Council.

A reply was made by other Arabs, requesting a postponement of the cease-fire. Shertok protested vigorously, "While the delay was granted on the plea of a need for consultation, the shelling of Jerusalem from outside by foreign Arab forces is proceeding with unabated fury and ancient Jewish synagogues in the Walled City are being destroyed one after the other as a result of Arab artillery fire directed from the inside." In fact the Arabs had without scruple used the Mosque of Omar area as a military base from which they fired at the Jewish quarters, just as the Egyptian troops had mounted their cannon in the courtyard of the Church of the Nativity in Bethlehem. But the British, acquiescing in the Arab tactic, now backed the postponement, and fighting continued on all fronts.

On May 29, the day after the fall of the Old City, the Security Council passed another resolution demanding a cease-fire. The text is worth reading because it formed the basis of the terms on which the first truce eventually came into force.

The Security Council:
Desiring to bring about a cessation of hostilities in Palestine without prejudice to the rights, claims and position of either Arabs or Jews:
Calls upon all Governments and authorities concerned to order a cessation of all acts of armed force for a period of four weeks;
Calls upon all Governments and authorities concerned to undertake that they will not introduce fighting personnel into Palestine, Egypt, Iraq, Lebanon, Saudi Arabia, Syria, Transjordan and Yemen during the cease-fire and
Calls upon all Governments and authorities concerned, should men of military age be introduced into countries or territories under their control, to undertake not to mobilize or submit them to military training during the cease-fire;
Calls upon all Governments and authorities concerned to refrain from importing war material into or to Palestine, Egypt, Iraq, Lebanon, Saudi Arabia, Syria, Transjordan and Yemen during the cease-fire;
Urges all Governments and authorities concerned to take every possible precaution for the protection of the Holy Places and of the City of Jerusalem, including access to all shrines and sanctuaries for the purpose of worship at them;
Instructs the U.N. Mediator for Palestine in concert with the Truce Commission to supervise the observance of the above provision, and decides that they shall be provided with a sufficient number of military observers;
Instructs the U.N. Mediator to make contact with all parties as soon as the cease-fire is in force with a view to carrying out his function as determined by the General Assembly;
Calls upon all concerned to give the greatest possible assistance to the U.N. Mediator;
Instructs the U.N. Mediator to make a weekly report to the Security Council during the cease-fire;
Invites the States members of the Arab League and the Jewish

*and Arab authorities in Palestine to communicate their acceptance
of this resolution to the Security Council not later than 6 P.M.
New York Standard Time on June 1, 1948.*

*Decides that if the present resolution is rejected by either party
or by both, or if, having been accepted, it is subsequently repudiated or violated, the situation in Palestine will be reconsidered
with a view to action under Chapter VII of the Charter. [This is
the chapter of the United Nations Charter which deals with sanctions.]*

*Calls upon all governments to take all possible steps to assist in
the implementation of this resolution.*

The Arabs still hesitated to accept the cease-fire. Each of the
Arab nations had whipped up a small but fanatical public opinion
at home on the question of Palestine and each had fed this public
with nothing but stories of sensational victories. In Egypt, Syria, and
Transjordan there were already tens of thousands of refugees who
had fled from their homes in Palestine on the assurance that they
would soon go back to take over what the Jews would leave behind
them. Even a cease-fire would be hard to explain. But by the beginning of June, the new Israeli Army was going over to the offensive on a large scale. It pierced the Triangle and broke into Jenin and Kakoun. Its chances looked good in the vital area around
Latrun. The Mediator was applying all the pressures he could to
stop the fighting. In a note sent on June 7, he fixed the hour of the
cease-fire at 6 A.M. on June 11, adding his own interpretation of
some of the clauses of the Security Council's resolution. For example, he claimed the right to restrict the immigration of men of
military age, although the resolution had forbidden only their mo-
bilization or training. The Israel government rejected this assumption. The Mediator also stated that he would control relief to populations in urban areas in such a way that stocks of essential supplies
would not be "substantially greater or less at the end of the truce
than they were at the beginning." To this we were careful to point
out that his control measures should not affect the areas of Jerusalem in Jewish hands "to the extent that the safety or passage to and
from them, and the supply of food to them, may have been secured
by the operation of the Jewish forces at the time of the commencement of the cease-fire and truce." We had no intention of giving up
the lifeline we had built in the Burma Road.

The Arabs, on their side, stipulated that they would resume the

war if the state of Israel were not wound up. Their reply made two
principal points: that ultimately Palestine must be a single political entity under Arab rule, and that Jewish immigration must be
restricted or stopped.

After nearly six and a half months of fighting, the Israeli forces
were ordered to cease fire at the hour named by the Mediator.
Ben Gurion published a call to all soldiers to observe the truce, and
declared that anyone violating it would be dealt with as an internal
enemy.

As soon as I could get away from the office, I went out on a stroll
through the streets of the city. For months one had walked quickly
to get to one's duty, but now for a few hours, I could look around
quietly to assess the damage caused by the fighting. My first thoughts
were for those who had paid with their lives or were in hospitals
and, strangely enough, for our Arab neighbors who had bombarded
the city in a futile effort to break the people's morale so that they
would force us to give up the struggle. I had to put out of my mind
the thought of the destruction I could not see in the Jewish Quarter
of the Old City of Jerusalem.

As one walked through the streets one's eye took note of broken
glass, bits of red tiles of roofs, pieces of wood of all description
strewn about, torn telephone and electric wires along the roadsides,
the parched dry earth of the open spaces, trees cut as though by a
giant saw, large branches of uprooted trees across the pavements
and in the road. Twisted shutters, broken windows and piles of
broken glass decorated a city crowned with broken tiled roofs and
splintered beams sticking out of the roofs. Where an outer staircase
had been blown away a ladder had been substituted. Fortunately
Jerusalem is a city of stone, so that most of the walls of the houses
stood up well to the shelling, but the walls had gaping holes in
them and as one entered the houses it was a different picture—
plaster, broken furniture, and pieces of shell still stuck in the walls
or the dusty floors. Many houses showed signs of direct hits, some
by incendiary bombs so that the outer walls were blackened and the
houses themselves burned out.

In the bright summer sunshine all this seemed like a modern abstract painting hanging crookedly on a nail in an open courtyard.
But I knew, only too well, that each physical sign of destruction had
been accompanied by human suffering. The shelling had been

heaviest during the last days when negotiations for the truce had been in process. The shelling had not let up at all. The punishment of Jerusalem had been by systematic mortar fire, a kind of combing out of the city from one end to the other. Not a single quarter had been spared. It had been the climax of the effort to wear down our resistance in the hope that surrender would take the place of the truce being negotiated.

To the surprise of all except the few who remembered how truly stiff-necked are the Jews, there had been no general panic and no widespread desire to surrender. After all the terrible days of tension and strain, of personal disaster and pain, I tried to forget what might come after this truce, and my mind was already busy with the work of rebuilding. At the same time my eyes followed with pleasure the sight of children venturing out, for the first time in many weeks, into the street, women hanging out their bedding for a much needed airing, boys trading in pieces of shrapnel. Men were conspicuous by their absence; slowly they would be given a chance to come home to see what had happened while they were on duty in other parts of the city. As the sights of destruction were filled in with human forms the picture changed, and I could say to myself, "How goodly are thy tents, O Jacob," even those smashed by the Arab Legion's fire.

I made many mental notes, besides filling my notebook with details of the great damage done to the city so that I would be prepared for the reports which would soon be reaching my desk. I was glad of the respite and ready, as were all these people, for the next round—political or military. As I approached the street on which I live, I was greeted by the sound of a bugle. This was the self-same bugle, very badly played by our neighbor's son, which had disturbed and annoyed us in other days; now the lad held it again in his hand and he blew with all his young strength a song of determination, courage and hope. It told me that no matter what lay in the future we could take it. We would not yield.

There was a certain amount of sporadic fighting just after the truce came into force, and only three hours after the cease-fire the Legion shelled Jerusalem. But it is still possible to argue that had the Arab Legion been left to follow its own bent there might have been a steady progression from truce to some permanent peace. Their behavior in the Old City surrender had been exemplary. They also co-operated in the first week following the truce. On June 16, for example, an agreement was signed by the Jewish commander, David Shaltiel, and the Arab Legion commander, Abdullah el Tel, in the presence of the Truce Commission and the U.N. Mediator's chief observer, regarding no man's land in the Deir Abu Tor quarter, fortifications and patrols there, entry of civilians into the area to remove personal belongings, examination by Arabs of municipal records in the Jewish area, recovery of Scrolls of the Law from the Old City, closing of the New Gate by the Arabs, and similar matters.

Meantime the Jewish soldiers and the Legionaires fraternized. The Arabs learned with surprise that the Jews were not starving. An Arab Legion officer expressed his gratification that this was so. He also observed that he was pleased at the cease-fire and claimed that British officers were pressing the Arabs to fight. He alleged that Arab Legionaires were fired at by their British officers when they would not attack Jewish positions.

A group of Arabs visited Ramat Rahel and invited several Jews to coffee. Three Jewish soldiers accompanied the Arabs to the neighboring Arab village, Sur Baher, and they were invited to lunch in Bethlehem. Some civilians there tried to bother them, but the Legionaires drove them away, telling the crowd that the Jews came as friends and that anyone harming them would be shot.

In the days that followed, people breathed a little more easily. Life returned to the streets. Young couples could be seen walking arm in arm. Just to go out in the bright sunshine of the high summer days was to gain a sense of freedom and release. People could be seen examining the damage caused to their houses with a view to repairing them. A limited number of scavengers were on duty collecting broken glass in the streets. Schools resumed their studies. Movies were reopened. Cigarettes and talk were exchanged by our defense men and Legionaires near the city walls. The cafés were now open at night, but they were still shrouded in darkness or semidarkness. All they could offer customers was a cup of coffee, sometimes a stale cake or pastry. One café was always noisy and full of heated discussion: the one commandeered by the convoy drivers who were still in the city. Convoys had resumed under strict U.N. supervision, but there was as yet no transportation for passengers. Newspapers still did not come from Tel Aviv.

There was a feeling abroad in Jerusalem that not all that could be done for the capital had been done. The tragedy of the convoy to Scopus of April 12, the annihilation of the thirty-five young men who had gone to the relief of the Etzion bloc and perished, the

loss of the Old City, the suffering that Jerusalem had experienced
—all these things weighed heavily on our spirits, and we wondered
if they were felt as deeply in Tel Aviv.

The thought found an echo in the debate of the Provisional Government Council in Tel Aviv on June 25, when Ben Gurion said in
reply to the discussion, "Jerusalem has not been neglected. The
problem of Jerusalem is a military problem and will not be solved
necessarily in Jerusalem itself. Everything is being done to widen
the corridor to Jerusalem and establish an economic basis for the
city. Tens of thousands of our youth are prepared to lay down
their lives for the sake of Jerusalem. Everything possible will be
done for Jerusalem. It is within the boundaries of the state of Israel
just as Tel Aviv is."

But this was by no means the dominant thought or feeling in the
minds and hearts of the Jews of Jerusalem. They were happy and
proud that they had withstood the siege. They had been struggling
not only for Jerusalem but for the newborn state of Israel. They
were gratified when subsequently the Prime Minister himself bore
witness to this. He declared at the formal celebration opening the
Valor Road, "Were it not for our victory in the struggle for Jerusalem, we would have lost the struggle in the country as a whole. . . .
Thanks to our victory in the struggle for Jerusalem, we can now
spread out and also settle in the hills."

It was during these early days of the truce that I first realized that
the Consular Truce Commission and the United Nations Mediator
would remain as living symbols of older relationships which the war
had made obsolete. For many months I was to see and confer with
these men more often than any other Jewish representative. As I
review the record now, it seems to me to make both a sorry story
and a tragic one. Some of the reasons for this are personal: the consuls were at best a poor team; the Mediator had been chosen partly
because he was innocent of any knowledge whatever of Palestine,
the Jews, or the Arabs; I am sure that I was sometimes impatient,
persistent and not too easy to do business with. But the true reasons
for our friction ran deeper. Neither the consuls nor the Mediator
were prepared to accept the legal definitions of their mandates as
given them by the United Nations, and this led them, in the climate which still persisted in Jerusalem for reasons old in history,

to clash almost constantly with a young nation which was in a hurry to change that history and begin a new one.

Our Arab neighbors had made the same mistake. They had known the curious make-up of the Jewish community in Jerusalem, ranging from orthodox rabbis to men trained at Belsen and at Tobruk. They knew that almost all the top leaders had left the city. They probably knew how short we were of arms and ammunition, and they certainly knew how easily the siege might have starved us into surrender. What they could not guess was that all these disparate and unhopeful elements could be welded together by the challenge of saving Jerusalem. They could not guess the experience we had gained from the days of illegal immigration and underground Hagana preparation. They never dreamed that Jews would fight not only for Jerusalem's historic past but for their homes and the homes their children were still to build, not only for the tombs of saints long dead but for the graveyards in which their own families were buried.

If it was difficult for the Arabs to realize this change, it was painful for the foreigners in Jerusalem to accept it. They had known us in the past as "notables"—representatives of one of Jerusalem's principal communities, who could be handled with vague promises, fair words and a careful observance of protocol. Once the truce began, they had to deal with us as a government, and one which threatened to hold that part of Jerusalem which it had won in war. As for myself and all those who worked with me, the thought that was always in our minds was to hold together another hour, another day, another night, another week, another month. Each hour that went by with us still on our feet was important. We had a one-sided attitude to every problem: if we thought it .was for the good of a Jewish Jerusalem, we were for it; if not, we were against it. I suspect that I became the personification of the whole community, tough and troublesome, constantly urging the commission to move faster, doggedly insisting on our rights. My job was to hold the city together so that it might remain Jewish, and the niceties of even normal human relations had to yield to the exigencies of this task, in what we knew was a life-and-death struggle for our future.

The three men who composed the Consular Truce Commission were Thomas C. Wesson of the United States, Jean Nieuwenhuys of Belgium, who was appointed chairman, and René Neuville of France. Unfortunately Mr. Wesson was shot on May 22 by an Arab sniper, and he was succeeded toward the end of June by the new U.S. Consul General, John J. Macdonald. From the start, our actions were not to their liking. They interfered in matters far outside their terms of reference. As early as the end of April, when they had just been named, the British High Commissioner had asked them whether they would take over responsibility for the Tel Aviv-Jerusalem road, although this was obviously a security task which could be executed only by a body responsible for the administration of the country. Yet the commission were quite ready to undertake it and asked the Security Council for orders, even indicating the number of U.N. men they would require for the purpose. The Security Council evidently had different views of this debonair readiness to undertake responsibilities they could not fulfill, for nothing came of the idea.

The Mediator, Count Bernadotte, had already built up the nucleus of his staff by the time the cease-fire took effect. Twenty-one United States officers had left for Palestine to serve as observers, and France and Belgium had also agreed to send officers to help him. On June 10, Shertok told me by radio from Tel Aviv that I had been appointed to represent the Provisional Government in maintaining contact with Count Bernadotte. I was to have the advice and assistance of Walter Eytan, now Israel's ambassador to France, Leo Kohn and any other officials of the Jewish Agency's Political Department who had remained in Jerusalem.

It is not easy, even a dozen years later, to define precisely and clearly either the authority or the responsibility which were mine. My appointment as Military Governor was not to come until August, and even then it defined my authority in terms of international law more than it changed the day-to-day operation of my job in Jerusalem. When Bernadotte arrived, I was still the head of the Jerusalem Emergency Committee, which had been set up in December 1947 by the Jewish Agency with the somewhat grudging consent of some of the leaders of the Jewish community in Jerusalem. On April 10 Ben Gurion had given me, on behalf of the Jewish Agency Executive, what amounted to an individual, carte-blanche mandate to run the city. But what I could do and what I could not do was still largely up to me to determine. There was neither a document nor a record of precedents in which I could discover how long my arm was. As things worked out, the problem never even occurred to me during 1948. I sensed then, and know

now, that my arm was as long or as short as the people of Jerusalem—who were all I had to work with—made it.

Now, from June 10 on, I had in addition this more official status. In relation to the Mediator, I was the legally appointed representative of a Provisional Government which was being recognized by a steadily growing number of nations. But even this authority was far from clear, granted the then uncertain status of the city of Jerusalem. Military forces were not under my command; although my duties required me to work intimately with the Army, I held no military rank and wore no uniform. There were some small splinter groups of civilians—chiefly the ultra-orthodox Jews—who did not accept me as they refused to accept any other symbol of temporal power. The underground sections of the dissident terrorists obviously worked with nobody. I held no elected post, and until August 2 I had no title from the government.

What saved this fragile situation was primarily the determination and single-mindedness of the Jews of Jerusalem. To the overwhelming majority of them, even the idea of questioning my authority or inquiring into its legal basis would have seemed fantastic. They were caught in the middle of a war they had not wanted but were determined to win. Behind me stood the prestige of the Jewish Agency, a nongovernmental body but one which all the Jews of Palestine trusted and supported. They knew me as a veteran leader of an organization in which they had invested their hopes and whose leadership they acknowledged. When Count Bernadotte and the United Nations authorities recognized my right to speak for the Jews of Jerusalem (and they were forced to do so by the absence of any alternative), these invested hopes became a powerful and legitimate reality in Jerusalem with which the world from then on had to deal.

These were my curious credentials for an assignment which brought me into contact with one of the most remarkable and enigmatic personalities connected with the birth pangs of the state of Israel, and which ended with one of the most tragic events of those dramatic times.

I looked forward to my first meeting with him, which took place on June 12. The main matters I would have to discuss with him or his political adviser would be the maintenance of the truce, security matters, the safeguarding of our positions, the prevention of violation of the frontiers by the Arabs, free access to the Holy

Places, and the supply of food and water for the population of
Jerusalem. The very fact of his appointment, I thought, held out
some hope of a more permanent arrangement with the Arabs. This
could obviate further loss of life and lead us to peace. Sweden was
certainly disinterested in Middle East politics, and Count Bernadotte
was one of his country's most illustrious public figures. I had heard
he was a great humanitarian and had done much to help save Jews
from the Nazis. I welcomed him cordially in the courtyard of the
Jewish Agency. I believed we could expect fair treatment by him
and objective consideration of the issues. I was not troubled by the
injunction which had been impressed on Jewish leaders again and
again in our efforts in the international arena: "Put not thy trust
in princes."

I talked with the utmost restraint, although I already had plenty
to complain about in the unsatisfactory manner in which the Truce
Commission had been treating us. It was not clear to what extent
his appearance on the scene would ultimately remove them from
active participation in supervising the truce, although the resolution
appointing the Mediator required him to co-operate with them.
(It was only later that it was agreed the Truce Commission would
assume direct responsibility for the supervision of the truce in the
Jerusalem area, assisted by the U.N. observers and the U.N. secre-
tariat personnel.) Our talk was primarily of a general character,
since this was more of a courtesy call than a business meeting. But
we did touch upon the practical problems that would have to be
dealt with. He left me with the impression that he was a shrewd,
astute person and a gentleman. I felt confident he would be anxious
to act objectively. He seemed full of energy, eager to get on with
his task and to make the most of it. I assured him of my readiness to
give him our fullest co-operation consonant with the protection of
our legitimate rights and interests.

His arrival in Jerusalem was well received by the Jewish public
at large, for the same reasons I felt when welcoming him. It was not
expected that he would pull easy solutions out of a magician's hat,
but it was thought he might help ease the tension and persuade the
Arabs to recognize the situation as it was, and to take a somewhat
more reasonable view of the future.

Count Bernadotte's public criticism of me later, for my alleged
unreasonableness in dealing with him, was in contrast with his own
impressions of our first meeting. He reported in his book *To Jerusalem*:

*My next visit was to the Jewish Agency Headquarters, where Dr.
Joseph and Dr. Kohn resided. They received me in the most de-
lightful manner: it was a pleasure to talk to them. To them the main
problem was how to ensure supplies to Jerusalem during the truce.
I explained my views to them: the supply system should be so organized that neither of the two parties would be in a more advantageous military position at the end of the truce than they had
been before; food stocks should therefore not be increased. We also
discussed the demilitarization of the Hebrew University and the
Arab Hospital, and they stated that the Jewish authorities were anxious to have a United Nations Observer quartered in these institutions, to make sure that no unnecessary acts of war took place.*

Infractions of the truce made up the great bulk of my subsequent
communications with the Mediator as with the Truce Commission.
After the truce ended, Shertok asked the Mediator to transmit to the
Security Council a report, dated July 12, which listed fifty-five violations. He added a reminder that "all these incidents were brought
to your attention or to that of members of your staff, but in hardly
a single case was a satisfactory reply received." He attached a list to
demonstrate the utter lack of sincerity which marked the attitude
and behavior of the Arab forces and governments during the truce
period.

The Iraqis were abetted in their breaches of the truce by their
British allies. On June 15 two British ships anchored at Basra with
vehicles, radio equipment, telescopes and motors, all destined for
the Iraqi Ministry of War. Many cases were not opened but just
initialed by the authorities.

The infractions by the Arab Legion formed the majority of all
the others which were listed in this note by Israel's Foreign Minister. They were collated in the main from particulars submitted by
myself and they concerned largely the Jerusalem area. It is impossible to list them all, so I shall summarize them briefly. There were
transfers of military supplies from Amman to Jericho and of six-
inch guns from Jericho to Jerusalem. The cemetery on the Mount
of Olives was desecrated and the gravestones were carried off on
donkeys and camels to be used as building blocks.

The day after the truce, I asked Nieuwenhuys, the Belgian Consul, to come with me to the Musrara quarter, where the Arabs were
"improving" their positions by moving forward into houses they had
not held. He did so, and we saw the Arabs *in flagrante delicto.*

On June 24 I reported thirty-six breaches of the peace in Jerusalem. Some were of a minor character, but together they added up to a total of general disrespect for the truce agreement, while the lack of U.N. action on the individual complaints encouraged the feeling among the Arabs that they could proceed with their military preparations to gain a considerable advantage in the Jerusalem area should hostilities be resumed. Thus rifle and machine gun fire was directed from Malha at Bait Vegan and from Bet Safafa at Mekor Hayim. New Arab fortified positions were established at Mar Elias, near the Tower of David, along the wall of the Old City, at Sheikh Jarrah, Bet Safafa, Deir Abu Tor, on the French Hill at Mount Scopus, in the no man's land between Bet Safafa and Mekor Hayim, near St. Simon's Monastery, near El Alamein Camp, at the flour mill at Bet Safafa. Roads and approaches were mined, continuous sniping took place which killed or wounded many persons, Issawiya—which was Jewish territory—was penetrated, houses in no man's land were entered in Musrara and Deir Abu Tor and not far from Ramat Rahel near the Bethlehem Road.

In one complaint we asserted that when we took Colonel B. L. P. Bonneau, a U.N. senior observer at the time, to Ramat Rahel, armed Egyptians continued, in his presence, to build fortifications and put up barbed-wire aprons in the area which had been demarcated as no man's land.

Further infiltration in the Musrara area was reported on June 25. On June 28, the Arabs were erecting a strong gun position on the wall of the Old City near the Citadel and fortifying further in Musrara. Two Jews were wounded by snipers.

On June 29, I reported another ten breaches of the truce. These included instances of fortification of the Old City wall along the Jaffa Road west of the Jaffa Gate, in the no-man's-land area of Musrara—this was a sensitive area in which the Legion was seeking to strengthen itself throughout the truce—and near David's Tower, while in Suleiman Road a bridge was built between the Italian school and the city wall.

The lists in my files seem endless. All that ever resulted from my reporting them to the commission was an answer, in some cases, that its members had investigated the complaints and made representations to the Arabs. But in most cases the infractions were simply noted and forgotten. It was hard to show the patience the commission requested of us. Even in London, the *Times* described on August 22 Jerusalem's "remarkable recovery from the effects of the siege" in spite of the continuing tense military situation, and added:

*United Nations Observers and the Consular Truce Commission,
in an endeavor to maintain some semblance of control, reimpose a
general cease-fire order and then have to declare special "no fire"
periods in order to be able to approach the front-line areas to arrange for further truce periods. The people of Jerusalem cynically
ask which will finish first: the so-called truce or the vocabulary of
the truce-makers.*

On the evening of the first day of the truce, I spoke to the people
of Jerusalem over the radio:

"This morning a cease-fire was proclaimed for the entire country.
Our government agreed to the cease-fire although it is obvious that
a number of the conditions fixed prejudice our rights. Despite this
we agreed to the truce principally because it was not we who
launched the war. It was the Arabs who began the war, refusing to
recognize the national rights of the Jewish people. When the war began we announced our readiness to cease firing the moment the
other side did so. It is not known how matters will develop and what
will be the consequences of the truce, or if, indeed, the Arabs will
fulfill the cease-fire or if they will do what they did only today, when
for six hours they violated their definite undertaking to cease fire.
Lack of clarity as to the behavior of the Arabs during the truce
obliges us to be particularly careful.

"After months of strenuous effort and long siege, it would be
natural to wish to ease the tension and to relax. But let us not permit ourselves any tranquillity or diminution of complete prepared-
ness. Our wish is for peace and we shall of course be glad if there
will be no need to renew the battle, but nothing is more dangerous than to assume that the truce is the end of the struggle. Consequently, so long as our government has not reached an agreement
as to lasting peace we must, despite the truce, remain deeply conscious of the fact that we are in the midst of a fateful struggle for
our freedom and our existence. We, the inhabitants of Jerusalem,
know how serious is the struggle and dare not slacken our constant
efforts to end our struggle successfully. Everyone is consequently
charged with the duty of remaining at his post and continuing to
perform his task.

"The past weeks were not easy ones. There is ground for assuming that if the truce is maintained there will be some lightening of our burden in a number of fields. If, up to the present, we restricted the food rations which we distributed, we did so to make our supplies last over a longer period of time. Also in the future and during the truce we shall continue the food-rationing system. It may be assumed the rations will be larger and more varied, but we shall make do with what we shall bring into the city and shall not draw on the iron rations that are left to us, for one cannot know how the truce will end.

"We still do not know what will be the arrangements for maintaining an ordered supply of water, but we shall make an effort also in this field, for that is our right. We shall endeavor to bring in the quantities of fuel we require. We shall try to ease the day-to-day life of the public during the period of the truce, but at the same time we call upon the Jews of Jerusalem to persevere in their efforts to guard our position in the city and to ensure to the maximum extent possible that at the end of the truce, if we should be compelled to renew the struggle, our position will be firm and our spirit strong so that the gain from the truce is not lost. Let us be prepared and alert, strong and of good courage."

The Arabs were determined to use the truce to build their strength for a resumption of the war. King Abdullah set off to make the rounds of the Arab capitals, trying to arrange general measures for a concerted offensive. General Glubb telegraphed the British forces in Egypt to send him spare parts and new equipment; he was wise enough to ask that they be sent to the port of Aqaba, where United Nations truce observers were not yet stationed. But the Egyptians confiscated his first shipload, and by the time he had secured a second shipment we had made sure that U.N. observers were in Aqaba to intercept them and that strong pressure was brought in London to stop such open violations of the truce.

We were determined to use the cease-fire ourselves to learn from our past mistakes and to co-ordinate a new strategy for future fighting. A conference was called in Tel Aviv by Ben Gurion to review the experience of the war to date and to work out ways of using internal resources which would not have to run the U.N. blockade. Its conclusions were interesting. It was decided to strengthen existing battalions rather than to set up new fighting units, to release as many seasoned troops as possible from defense assignments for offensive actions, to build our firepower against armored units rather than to try to supply armor for our own troops. A heavy emphasis was placed on morale; the representative of the Jerusalem command made a special plea for bigger rations.

Inside the Army, provision was made for leave for men who had not seen their families during months of fighting. New settlements were begun in what were known as stronghold areas. Here villages were to be established with stoutly built stone cabins so that their inhabitants could release regular units for service in the field elsewhere. A scheme of such new settlements was also worked out for the Jerusalem Corridor. Today when one travels between Jerusalem and Tel Aviv one sees the results of this endeavor. At night a satisfactory strip of country on both sides of the road is lit with the sparkling, starlike lights of many houses from numerous hill villages. Each light is not just a symbol that some wanderer has found a productive home on the soil of his fathers. It is also a lamp of reassurance to the wayfarer that the road on which he travels is no longer at the hazard of the Arabs, but is now inside well-protected Israel territory.

Nor was it against the terms of the truce to intensify our local arms industries. We now began to do this with a vengeance. More doubtful in its immediate value was the attempt to utilize new immigrant manpower above military age which had reached our shores.

The Jerusalem Emergency Committee appealed to the public to use the period of the truce to build more shelters. We levied a "shelters tax" which was collected by members of the Mishmar Ha'am. Large shelters were set up in hospitals to be available if shelling were renewed at the conclusion of the truce.

At this time too, I tried to get the Minister of Finance, Eliezer Kaplan, to transfer part of the financial burden Jerusalem had to bear to the shoulders of the state. We in Jerusalem had had to find considerable sums for the insurance of goods in convoy for losses sustained during the siege and for other extraordinary emergency expenditures. These imposts had been reflected in the price of certain rationed goods, for, since they formed part of the expense of bringing in the goods, it was only right that they be added to the price. The result, however, was that the rationed foods and other commodities were expensive, and this aroused criticism. I asked several members of the committee to examine the whole price structure afresh, with special attention to the influence of these uneconomic costs.

Kaplan, an old friend and colleague, an engineer by profession,

was a man with a cool head and much experience in both administration and finance. He had been treasurer of the Jewish Agency
for years before becoming Israel's first Minister of Finance. He
quickly saw the logic and the justice of our position, and a little
later we persuaded other government authorities in Tel Aviv to
readjust both taxes and prices on a national scale to lighten the
unfair burden which was carried throughout the siege by the Jerusalemites.

The Jerusalem municipality gained from the truce its first real
chance to get organized, and to take back gradually many functions
which had been carried out for months by the Jerusalem Emergency Committee. These included shelters, street cleaning, and
sanitation. The municipality also was concerned with setting up
a siren system of alarms, with the functioning of demolition and
rescue squads, with a municipal court and with an educational
committee. Urgent measures were taken to get householders to repair their water tanks.

The blackout was lifted during the truce period, and, as part of
the general contribution to morale, on the initiative of the Mishmar Ha'am a new club was set up in the Café Europa in Zion
Square for the public in general and for soldiers. The idea was to
give people an opportunity to leave their homes and meet other
people. This was very important, as people had lived such shut-in
lives during the siege. The city's bus traffic was resumed, although
on a reduced scale. The Ohel Theater Company arrived to give
two performances.

The electricity supply was poor and erratic, but it was restored
to some extent. At the beginning of July, two out of six high-ten-
sion lines damaged by shelling were repaired, and the plan then
was to give each quarter of the city current once every two nights,
for several hours a night. Telegraph services to other parts of the
country had been resumed a week before the truce came into force,
and on June 17 postal services to the rest of Israel were resumed,
while airmail abroad was instituted by Air France.

The city, for the first time since the fighting began, witnessed a
festive military parade through its streets on July 6, when the Jerusalem Brigade was presented with its colors at a ceremony in Rehaviah attended by the U.N. observers, the consular corps and
many notables. After the flag had been blessed by Chief Rabbi
Herzog, the troops marched through the main streets of the city
amid the enthusiasm of the crowds.

From the very first days of the truce, I pressed the Mediator and the Truce Commission to make arrangements to get water flowing again from the Ras el Ein pumping station to Jerusalem. My efforts were entirely without success. Count Bernadotte had become friendly with King Abdullah, but he could get nothing from him that would start the water flowing. On June 24 I told Shertok by radio that after two weeks of truce Jerusalem had not received a drop of water from normal sources. I added my conviction that the Arabs were dragging out the matter deliberately and with malice.

In a memorandum our government addressed to Count Bernadotte on June 25 for transmission to the Security Council, we referred to the failure to renew the supply of water to Jerusalem in the following terms:

On June 7, you agreed that, pursuant to the armistice conditions, the proper functioning of the Jerusalem water system must be ensured as part of the resumption of the normal supply of the necessities of life to the city. Yet by an elaborate system of obstruction and procrastination the Arabs succeeded in effectively preventing the implementation of this part of the truce conditions. They at first alleged that their machines (for pumping) at Ras el Ein were damaged beyond repair. When we insisted on their being inspected by our experts, they finally agreed that British engineers serving with the Arab Legion should carry out the inspection. After some further delay they reported that the machines themselves were in good order, but that certain minor spare parts were missing. They also opposed the repair by us of damaged parts of the pipe line, claiming that they would do it themselves. Days passed and nothing was done. It was only on June 23 that Jewish workers were allowed to repair the pipe. On the other hand access was denied to Jewish engineers to inspect the pumping machines at Latrun.

Finally, when it became evident that obstruction on technical grounds was no longer possible, the Arabs declared that the matter was a political issue to be discussed at top level. Bernadotte met with me on July 1 and I stressed most vehemently the failure of the U.N. to prevail upon the Arabs to allow the flow of water to Jerusalem to be resumed. He was no less emphatic in his denunciation of Arab conduct in this matter and promised to take energetic action. He expressed his readiness to go to Cairo to take the matter up with the Arab League should he fail to settle it in Rhodes.

In his diaries Bernadotte wrote of this interview with me:

> *I told him (Dr. Joseph) frankly that I completely shared his views; the attitude the Arabs tried to maintain was not in accordance with the truce agreement. The Arab military had made no difficulties whatever over the settlement of this question. But their politicians had raised obstacles. I promised Dr. Joseph that when I met the Arab representatives the following morning, I would tell them that they must try to persuade their government to agree to a settlement.*

The interview achieved little. On July 6, I wrote to the chairman of the U.N. Truce Commission: "It is now five days since I had the privilege of placing before Count Bernadotte and your Commission our grievance with regard to the consistent refusal of the Arab authorities to enable us to pump water through the Ras el Ein pumping system to Jerusalem. . . . Despite repeated applications to you, I have been unable to receive information as to the results of Count Bernadotte's efforts in this connection. Twenty-five days of the 28-day truce period have already elapsed without our having received a single drop of water, although for a considerable time now there has been no technical obstacle in the way to resumption of the flow of water . . ."

Fortunately, we did not rely on the successful outcome of these negotiations in order to ensure Jerusalem's water supply. Two of the pumping stations were in Arab hands, those at Ras el Ein and Latrun, and two were in ours, those at Bab el Wad and Saris. We also had the installations at Romema. Naturally we had begun at once to lay our own temporary pipeline, and on August 11 water began to flow through this new line into Jerusalem.

Nothing was as crucial to us during the truce as the organization of an adequate movement of food and other supplies to Jerusalem. Food distributed during the siege had been barely a third of the minimum calorie requirements; we were determined that this should not happen again. There were plenty of technical obstacles to be overcome. The Burma Road, for example, had to be improved enough to take normal trucks, for it would be fantastic to try to supply a city of 100,000 persons by mule traffic and jeep convoys.

There were other problems within our own control, chief among which was the transport of civilians. We might have simplified our task if we had allowed women and children to leave the city during the truce, but we were determined to keep the moral and political advantages of maintaining the city as much as possible a normal community. With the setting up of the government in Tel Aviv, many officials in Jerusalem feared for their livelihood; some thousands had already left before the siege, including all but two members of the Jewish Agency Executive and all but three of the Vaad Leumi Executive. I had, therefore, to decide on strict measures. No one was allowed to leave without a special permit issued by the Jerusalem Emergency Committee, and I took care that these permits should be issued only in exceptional circumstances.

But the toughest problems were those created by the Mediator and the Truce Commission. It seems a savage irony now that these United Nations officials, appointed for humanitarian purposes, should have devoted so much of their time and energies to trying to make sure that the people of Jerusalem should find themselves close to the starvation level when the truce ended. But this is what actually took place. It was the logical result of Count Bernadotte's strange determination that "stocks of essential supplies shall not be substantially greater or less at the end of the truce than they were at its beginning." I fought against this with two arguments: that we had the right to bring into the city food and materials measured by our consumption in normal times, and that roads which we had opened before the truce should not be subject to any control at all. All through the summer of 1948 I was involved in endless negotiations over these points. Sometimes the arguments became quite fantastic. I had a sharp exchange with Nieuwenhuys, the Belgian member of the Truce Commission, over a charge by him that the transfer by us of eighty-eight prisoners of war from Katamon to the Tel Aviv area had been in bad faith, since the eighty-eight had theoretically been included in the 118,000 persons for whom we were importing food. Were his incredible letters to me on this question not still in my files, I would find it hard to believe that he ever wrote them.

The most inveterate opposition to us came from the American member of the commission, John Macdonald, and his alternate, William C. Burdett, Jr. As early as June 22, Burdett was fighting to reduce our food quota in a long-drawn-out session to which he had brought a young Army doctor who later admitted that he was no expert on nutrition. I brought with me Dr. Sarah Bawly, Hadassah's chief dietitian. I contended that one could not deal with the Jews of Jerusalem as if we were refugees in a camp where every calorie of food was weighed. During the truce we were entitled to normal rations. I produced figures to show that in the U.S. the normal ration was 3,400 calories per day net, or 3,900 gross, and said that the Jews of Jerusalem were entitled to eat no less. We also claimed 15 per cent for loss in transportation and spoilage. The French Consul said that his conscience would not permit him to reduce the amount, lest women and children go hungry, and the Belgian Consul expressed a similar opinion. That is what they said, but not what they subsequently did. For Burdett was adamant. He said that we were entitled to only 2,800 calories per person. Later Macdonald produced a pamphlet on Jerusalem nutrition drawn up by Mrs. Bawly which pointed to undernourishment in 1943 to 1946. He said that in China there were millions of people who lived in a state of starvation. I replied that we preferred to model ourselves on the United States rather than on China. The Jews of Jerusalem were not inmates of a concentration camp nor objects of charity being fed at the expense of the United Nations.

As for Mrs. Bawly's brochure, it related to the food situation of Jerusalem during World War II and the years immediately following, when even the best year it dealt with, 1946, was still a subnormal year for food as a result of shipping-space limitations and world shortages. Most goods were still on ration then in Palestine. Her survey specifically pointed this out and also stated expressly that the intake of 2,800 calories and 30.4 grams of animal protein was inadequate. She, in fact, recommended 3,100 calories, as in 1947, plus 600 for unusually hard physical work, plus 500 for wastage in distribution, for spoilage and for edible and inedible waste at home—a total of 4,200, which would allow us an actual calorie intake of 3,700. She also pointed out that the malnutritional period prior to the truce made the need and craving for food greater than usual. People who had been losing weight should be given 600 to 800 calories and 60 grams of animal protein more per day.

The memorandum which she sent me on this subject was submitted to the commission, but they just ignored it. The majority on that body were not in agreement with the American Consul's stand; nevertheless, on June 25, the commission informed me that they could allow only 2,800 calories plus 5 per cent for loss and damage or 15 per cent in the case of vegetables. The view of Burdett had thus prevailed after all.

This tussle over calories was only the first round. It was followed by altercations over how many people were in Jerusalem at the time of the truce. The Truce Commission reduced my figure by 13,000, relying on a British estimate of 1946 although the British had not taken a census for fifteen years. Then we fought over the weight of packaging, which the commission had not allowed for in fixing permissible tonnages of food to be brought in. Finally, on July 1, the commission ruled that we could bring in enough food to give 3,100 calories, plus some percentages for spoilage, to 108,000 persons. This was not what I had tried to get, but it was 600 calories more than I had been offered.

It was not just food that the commission had under its parsimonious and unhumanitarian pedantic eye. It also cut down the quantities of clothing and shoes we had asked for from 700 to 150 tons. Even children's clothing was not allowed into Jerusalem without the Truce Commission's prior approval. I wondered at the time whether clothing too was a weapon dangerous to the peace.

Even before we began the battle on calories and numbers, negotiations had started on opening the road to Jerusalem. No sooner was the truce proclaimed than the Truce Commission, under Arab pressure, began their obstructive and needling tactics. An original agreement that convoys should be checked on reaching Jerusalem was reversed on June 13 by the commission, which wanted to please the Arabs by setting up the check point at Bab el Wad. I protested strongly, but Shertok requested me to give in "so as not to step on the corns of the consuls." Then the commission's promise to arrange for the convoys to be under Red Cross protection proved abortive, as the Red Cross refused to participate in food convoys on the grounds that their rules forbade them to operate under another body, especially a political organization like the United Nations. The Arabs next moved in with a refusal to let us provide armed escorts for the convoys or to allow any shipments by the main road unless they could control also shipments by our Burma Road. Each of these points had to be haggled over; the first week of the truce went by and the first convoy had not yet arrived. I stressed to the commission that the truce agreement did not merely impose a negative duty on them to control imports into Jerusalem. They also had a positive duty to facilitate the movement of convoys.

To add to our difficulties, we had to repair the section of the

main Jerusalem road between Bab el Wad and Latrun which had
been blown up by the Arabs. On June 17 I took two truckloads of
workers, some sixty men, to Bab el Wad, to begin this job. It was
here that I had one of my closest shaves of the war. I walked along
a narrow, winding path through tall grass some twenty yards from
the highway to a large Arab jar of water and took a drink. A few
minutes later one of the workers followed my example. Suddenly
there was an explosion; a booby trap, which I had miraculously
missed, had blown off one of his feet. We sent him back to Jerusalem at once and succeeded in saving his life.

Finally, on June 19, 140 trucks left Tel Aviv for Jerusalem in
two convoys. The vehicles traveled by the Burma Road to Bab el
Wad and thence by the main road to Jerusalem, which had been repaired by our men working day and night. After that the arrangement was that two convoys should leave Tel Aviv every day and
would be able to go all the way by the old road via Ramleh. It
was also agreed that the size of the convoys would be increased to
make up for the first week when none had gone up. The trucks were
checked on loading in Tel Aviv by U.N. observers, who recorded
exactly the number of the vehicles and the amount of each load.
There was a second check by two U.N. observers at Bab el Wad.

I visited Tel Aviv myself at this time to ensure the smooth flow
of convoys and the regular acquisition of supplies. I demanded that
the authorities in Tel Aviv completely discontinue for one week the
supply of eggs, vegetables and canned goods to other cities and
send them all to Jerusalem. One of the knotty problems was the
dispatch of private food parcels. We had decided in Jerusalem that
we would permit these only if they were not deducted from the total
amount of rations for Jerusalem. Meantime the Tel Aviv municipality had decided that every family in that city should send one
food parcel to Jerusalem.

As I anticipated, the Truce Commission did object to these food
parcels and insisted that they must be included in the total food
permitted to enter Jerusalem. I had to send a vigorous protest to
Verlinsky in which I asked, If Mayor Rokach of Tel Aviv could
procure the food that he did get for ten thousand food parcels, why
could not these commodities be made available for all the inhabitants of Jerusalem? I demanded that this food be handed over to
me for general distribution.

Once the convoys started moving, my difficulties became intensified. The U.N. and the Truce Commission continued to act with

maddening slowness and to put all sorts of technical and formal difficulties in our way. I had to fight with them every inch of the road. In addition, my problems in Tel Aviv itself were great. I had constantly to put pressure on suppliers to have supplies ready for shipment and with the drivers and trucking co-operatives to have their vehicles available.

In negotiations with the Truce Commission we had insisted that since the new road was open before the truce began we felt justified in using it for the conveyance of food and other nonmilitary supplies, as this would not be a breach of the status quo. Shipments began to arrive in a small but steady stream by this new avenue. They were essential, for the negotiations with the Consular Commission dragged on day after day and Jerusalem was hungry. Our stocks were almost exhausted, and to the danger of real hunger was added the frustration of the population, who, while all keyed up to endure while the fighting was going on, looked with increasing impatience on the failure of the truce to bring in supplies.

Not all the shipments gave us equal satisfaction. I was very annoyed on June 19 when five trucks containing watermelons arrived at a time when we were gasping for vital commodities. I cabled Verlinsky to remind him to concentrate on sending vital foodstuffs. It was not just any food we needed; we had to see that a proper nutritional standard was maintained. On June 23, I radioed to Eliezer Kaplan that I was worried at the lack of proteins in our Jerusalem diet, because of the absence of meat and the negligible quantities of eggs and milk. I asked him to get Tnuva, the wholesale dairy purveyors, to send us at once 400 tons of cheese, even at the expense of Tel Aviv and Haifa.

It should not be thought that very much came along the Burma Road at first. An indication of the traffic on this road is that from 11 P.M. on June 15 to the morning of June 17 only 130 tons arrived, and this was after I had had a conversation with Ben Gurion on the radiotelephone to try to expedite and increase supplies. The Red Cross did escort a convoy of twenty-four trucks laden with medical supplies which reached us from Tel Aviv via Rehovot, Latrun and Bab el Wad. We had our own difficulties with convoys as well. There was much bitterness in Jerusalem at drivers bringing in food parcels and trading them. I asked my transport officer to remove all such parcels and to report the drivers indulging in the practice.

The third week in June saw the alleviation of pressure on the inhabitants of Jerusalem as the convoys at last began to arrive regularly. We were able to distribute a can of kerosene per family through kerosene coupons. This ended the black market, where kerosene was being sold at £10 per can. What food was now coming in had been selected by a special nutrition committee. The sight of 200 grams of oranges per person was hailed with shouts of joy by the people, and in the butcher shops a generous ration of frozen fish was given out. A week previously we had increased the ration of bread by 25 per cent—to 200 grams (seven ounces) per day—and had improved its quality, with the arrival of additional shipments of flour.

There were no longer any queues for food. But it should not be imagined that the city already knew plenty. Thus on June 21, my records show, each inhabitant received one tomato, one cucumber, two onions, half a carrot, one green pepper and some string beans. There were also some unripe apricots, the first fruit in two months' time. Eggs were now added to the ration, each adult receiving one egg per day. The next day people were able to delight in a ration of fresh fish, also for the first time in two months. But we did not get everything we wanted. For example, at this time I radioed Tel Aviv: "The doctors inform me that children are dying of dysentery for want of rice. Ask Rokach to send us a ton for the hospitals."

The smooth passage of convoys lasted only a few days. The Truce Commission, determined that no stocks of food should be built up, had apparently decided that if Jewish Jerusalem was in a state of near starvation at the beginning of the truce, that is how they would have to be at the end of it. This attitude was also shared by the U.N. observers, who felt that food coming in by side roads, avoiding the check posts, was an infraction of the truce.

There was, in fact, a difference of opinion between our Foreign Minister, Shertok, and myself in connection with the use of the side roads to bring food over and above the quantities specified by the Truce Commission. He was very anxious to preserve the truce, in the hope that a permanent settlement could be reached. No one disagreed with this, but it seemed to me that he was anxious to satisfy the demands of the U.N. authorities, even when they were not juridically justified, in order to achieve an atmosphere of good will. In Jerusalem, I was forming quite a different judgment of the good will of the U.N. authorities. Moreover, the struggle for our food supplies was to my mind an important strategic question and one on which we had to take a firm stand.

On June 26 Shertok radioed me that we were not to send food

and supplies by the side road, as he had already informed the U.N. observers that we were using the side road for supplying only the outposts and not Jerusalem. Two days later I answered: "I do not know why you object to our bringing a convoy by the side road. My intention is that it shall come in by Bab el Wad and we shall inform the observer there that it is for Jerusalem. I shall base myself on my statement to the U.N. that we reserve the right to bring food by the side road, in addition to the quantities fixed by our agreement, until Count Bernadotte shall have discussed the matter with you as he promised to do, or until you come to an agreement with him or he decides. There will be no departure in this from your statement, since the act will be done overtly. This is most important to us because, unfortunately, attention was not paid to my request as to the order of shipment of commodities and apart from flour and sugar I received little basic commodities that can keep. This situation must be corrected before the end of the truce."

Of course, what we could not prevent, even though we may have been juridically correct, was the determination of the U.N. observers to haggle, delay and hold up the main convoys while they argued these matters. In the last analysis it boiled down to the point of view of the Truce Commission, and one regrettably had to recognize the fact that this body in practice showed partiality toward the Arab side and allowed them in effect to dictate the course the commission should follow. The Arabs for their part did everything in their power to slow down and hold up our supplies, and the pedantic attitude of the U.N. helped them.

On June 24 I again wrote to the Chairman of the Truce Commission about the Wailing Wall: "A fortnight has now passed since the commencement of the cease-fire agreement, and no arrangements have yet been made to afford Jews the access to the Holy Places in the Old City of Jerusalem to which they are entitled under the terms of the cease-fire agreement. . . ."

There were more than enough mistakes on our side during the truce. The same inexperience, impatience and fervor which we must have shown in our dealings with the Truce Commission cost us heavily, even when they were not compounded by the traditional preference of foreigners for doing business with the Arabs and by the unscrupulous pressure the Arabs could apply to United Nations personnel. We hurt our own cause in some incidents during the

truce, and in none more painfully than in the *Altalena* incident on
June 22, an incident with which I had a curious personal connection.

I was in Tel Aviv that morning, dealing with supply problems,
and I was having lunch in the dining room of the Kaete Dan Hotel, which had large glass doors opening onto a veranda on the shore
of the Mediterranean. I had been joined by a British acquaintance
now working for the United Nations. Some of us disapproved
strongly of the United Nations use of British personnel in a situation
where their objectivity could reasonably be suspect. But he was a
pleasant man and I could hardly refuse his suggestion that we lunch
together.

Before long we suddenly heard shots, obviously from rifles and
machine guns. Some bullets shattered the windows of the doors onto the veranda. Everyone in the room fell to the floor; the waiters
dropped their trays and did likewise. My English friend imperturba-
bly kept his seat and continued eating his food. I did likewise. The
bullets kept flying around us and it was a miracle that we were not
killed. The thought flashed through my mind that I was a fool not
to get down on the floor like everybody else, but at the same time
there came a second thought: I would see this Englishman in Hades
before I showed less *sang-froid* than he. And so we both sat calmly
through some five minutes of noise and firing and bullets whizzing
about us.

When the firing stopped, I called a police sergeant nearby and
learned that an Irgun Zvai Leumi ship had been engaged by our
forces and wrecked. Later I heard all the tragic details. A small die-
hard group of Etzel dissidents who had refused to join the Israel
Army on May 28 had secured a ship and loaded it with arms at a
French port. The Etzel had refused to turn over to the government
the ship, called the *Altalena,* and its cargo, later claimed by the
Etzel to include 5,000 rifles with ammunition, 250 submachine guns,
bombs, a few tanks and some eight hundred immigrants of military
age. United Nations observers had spotted the *Altalena* from a
plane. By the time one landing attempt had failed at Natanya and
the ship had anchored just off the Kaete Dan Hotel beach in Tel
Aviv, it was being awaited by Etzel detachments, regular Israel
Army units, United Nations observers, newspapermen and a crowd
of spectators.

Tel Aviv was then weakly garrisoned, most of the men being at

or near the front, and the Etzel quickly seized control of a small
section of the beach and began unloading in a small lighter. Reinforcements were hurried in by the Israel government, and in a sharp
engagement six Etzel members were killed and eighteen wounded,
while the Israel Army lost two men killed and six wounded. The
Altalena itself was shelled by a warning cannon shot after the Etzel
men had begun firing at Israeli Army positions with antitank guns
and other heavy weapons from the poop of the ship. A second warning shot hit the vessel, causing an explosion, and the ship burst into
flames. Its crew abandoned it and began to swim ashore. According
to the Israeli government account the Army tried to rescue some of
the swimmers; according to the U.N. observers, fire was directed at
the men in the water. Certainly there was crossfire between the
Israel Army forces and the Etzel men on the beach and in the streets
which led to the scene. In all, fourteen Etzel men lost their lives and
sixty-nine were wounded in the attempt.

The U.N. charged that arms had been unloaded at Natanya and
had found their way into the possession of the Israel government
and that hundreds of persons on the ship had got away into the
country. They also stated that their observers were delayed for several hours at the check posts leading to the scene near Natanya because an Israeli colonel said that he could not allow U.N. observers
to note Israel battle tactics or the types of weapon they had at their
disposal.

In his report on the incident to the Security Council, Count Bernadotte stated:

As regards the vital question as to how many men and how much
cargo may have been landed from the ship contrary to the terms of
the armistice agreement, Colonel Bonde has presented the following
appraisal: According to some reports there may have been tanks on
board; but tanks could not have been landed by the small barge
which was employed. If tanks were on board they were still there
when the ship burned. An Etzel broadcast had stated that a large
quantity of bombs was on the ship, but this appears to be greatly
exaggerated since, had bombs been on board, explosions would have
wrecked the city. The explosions which did occur did not greatly
damage the deck of the ship.

The evidence indicates that at Natanya the Etzel did land war
material, and that regular Jewish forces took this material over fol-

lowing the surrender of the Etzel forces. It must be assumed that this material remains in the possession of the regular Jewish forces. Its quantity is unknown.

It is established that at Tel Aviv there was heavy fighting and that the regular Jewish forces exerted strong efforts to overcome the Etzel operation.

The *Altalena* incident was one of the most painful experiences of the new nation of Israel, for by the force of grim circumstance brother had to turn arms against brother in the midst of a desperate war for survival. This was a case, however, which brooked no other methods. For a body of citizens to attempt to enforce a decision on a lawfully constituted government by force of arms is treason and rebellion, and it had to be dealt with as such. It was not simply a question of preventing a violation of the truce. There was also the need, at the very outset, not only to show our enemies that Israel was master in its own house, but also to serve notice on dissident revolutionary elements within our community that they would not be allowed to take control of the state except by the ordinary means of democratic persuasion.

It was not long before I realized that I had unwittingly been involved in one of the strange coincidences which fate sometimes contrives for man. The Kaete Dan Hotel stands close to the spot where years before, in 1933, the director of the Jewish Agency's Political Department, Dr. Chaim Arlosoroff, had been murdered one night while walking along the Tel Aviv sea front with his wife. I had been requested by the Jewish Agency and the family of Dr. Arlosoroff to act for them in the investigation of the murder in order to ensure that the guilty were brought to justice. On the day after that crime, I had visited the site with some police officers. Eventually two members of the extreme right Zionist Revisionist party, Abraham Stavsky and another, were tried for the crime. I had held a watching brief for the family in the trial. Stavsky was convicted and sentenced to death. He was later acquitted on appeal on a technical point of law. The case was a *cause célèbre* that agitated the Jewish community in Palestine for years, partisans of both sides violently arguing the question of whether Stavsky had really murdered Dr. Arlosoroff.

So it was with something of a shudder that I learned the next day that the Revisionist in charge of the *Altalena* had been Abraham Stavsky, that he was one of the people who had been killed during the encounter with our troops—and this had happened almost at the very spot where Dr. Arlosoroff had been murdered.

Excess of zeal cost us other tragedies during the truce. A Jerusalem Hagana officer, Major Meyer Tobiansky, was convicted of treasonable delivery of military information to the enemy by a makeshift military court. He was immediately executed by a firing squad. Two years later, the military judges and the prosecutor were themselves indicted for their conduct of the case. The victim of the tragedy was reburied with full military honors and Ben Gurion himself conducted the ceremony to rehabilitate the executed officer in the presence of his son and his son's schoolmates. The symbolic act also wiped from the record of the Israel Army the taint of having included even one traitor.

Another accident caused the death of one of our key officers, Colonel David ("Mickey") Marcus, a West Point graduate who had come to Israel to help in the Hagana command. On the night of June 13, while he was commanding a division at Abu Ghosh near Jerusalem, he returned late to his headquarters and went out about 3 A.M. enveloped in a white sheet. Our soldiers knew from intelligence reports that British officers were commanding Arab troops facing Maaleh Hahamisha, a kibbutz just above Abu Ghosh. When a sentry challenged Colonel Marcus in Hebrew, he answered something in English instead of giving the Hebrew password, and the sentry shot him. He was one of the finest men and one of the ablest and bravest officers in the service of the Hagana. An important street near the center of Jerusalem and an agricultural settlement near the Valor Road now bear his name.

X

THE TEN DAYS

ЛПЛЛЛЛЛЛЛЛЛЛЛ

BY THE BEGINNING of July Count Bernadotte was making strenuous efforts to arrange a prolongation of the cease-fire. Although our differences with him were multiplying, on a wider and wider range of questions, we were even more anxious than he to achieve a permanent truce. The government of Israel gave an unqualified affirmative to every inquiry he made on its readiness to extend the cease-fire. But his efforts in the Arab countries drew quite different answers.

At one point, Bernadotte was told by Nokrashy Pasha, the Egyptian Prime Minister, in a face-to-face interview alone with him, that the Arabs could never agree to anything that accepted the establishment of a Jewish state. Count Bernadotte retorted, as he later wrote the story:

For my own part I did not at all approve of the U.N. Resolution of November 29th, 1947. But I must remind him that the whole situation had been changed since then by the fact that the Jewish State was now in being and had been recognized by no less than 15 countries. Besides, I continued, in my opinion the Arabs were in an extremely precarious situation. If the war were to start up afresh and the Arabs were successful, the result would be that one or more of the Great Powers that had recognized Israel would give the Jews active military support, and that would inevitably turn the fortunes of war. If, on the other hand, the war took an unfavorable turn to the Arabs from the start, that would mean that they would find themselves in a far worse negotiating position than they were in at present.

Nokrashy Pasha admitted that my argument was logical and sound. Nevertheless, he felt it was the duty of the Arab world, for all that, to follow the dictates of its conscience and prevent the emergence of a Jewish State that would only lead to complications . . . And there was another thing to remember: thousands of Arabs had been driven out of their homes by the war. Was it just, then, that Jewish immigrants should be allowed to enter Palestine?

Instead of reminding Nokrashy that the war was begun by the Arabs and that the thousands had left their homes at the behest of Nokrashy and his colleagues, Bernadotte replied that he himself had

the interests of the Arab refugees in mind and my own proposal when we laid it down in one of our paragraphs as a matter of course that inhabitants of Palestine who had been forced to leave their normal places of residence should be allowed to return.

Either side which refused to prolong the truce, I pointed out in conclusion, would be exposing itself to a certain risk. Such a refusal would undoubtedly have the result that the Security Council would demand a prolongation in very definite terms.

Count Bernadotte turned to King Abdullah on July 1. Here he found a more sympathetic listener, but one who was by now all but powerless to help. Abdullah had already been urging the other Arab leaders to renew the truce, because he knew that any resumption of fighting was bound to weaken the Arab position. But his personal ambitions in respect to Palestine, which had never been a secret, had become only too public when Count Bernadotte made known, on June 28, his own plan for a final solution. This would have given Abdullah all the Arab areas of Palestine, plus the city of Jerusalem. The Jews would never have accepted Arab rule over Jerusalem, but Egypt, Syria and Iraq were equally determined that Abdullah should not have even the Arab parts of the country. Abdullah himself had journeyed to Cairo, Riadh and Baghdad during the truce, pleading for negotiations while the Arabs still had bargaining power. He had come to an open break with the Arab Higher Committee and had openly denied the right of the former Grand Mufti to speak for the Arabs of Palestine. There is some reason to think that the Egyptians listened to him at first, but they were the victims

of their own propaganda that the truce had been a trick to rob
them of certain victory. Rather than face a public outcry, the Arab
League's Political Committee voted to resume hostilities. Count Bernadotte flew back to Lake Success to make new proposals for United
Nations pressure on the Arab world.

In a cabled dispatch to the Security Council on July 5, the Mediator said that

*on the whole the truce has worked well. There have been com-
plaints from both sides as to the alleged violations of the terms of
the armistice agreement. There have been instances of violation,
but all fighting on a major scale has been stopped, and it can be
said quite confidently that the truce has worked well, and by July
9 [when it was due to terminate] neither state will have gained any
significant military advantages from its application. In the meantime through the operation of the truce, much bloodshed and destruction have been avoided and many lives spared.*

*The expiration of the truce is now imminent. The parties to the
truce must answer the question whether, in the absence of agreement on the procedure and substance of mediation, they will again
resort to armed conflict. There can be little doubt that a decision to
resume fighting in Palestine will be universally condemned and that
the party or parties taking such a decision will be assuming a responsibility which will be viewed by the world with the utmost
gravity . . .*

*In order that the efforts towards mediation of the dispute may
continue, and in the interests of a peaceful settlement of the problem by means of patient and tolerant effort and reciprocal good will,
I ask the U.N., as the U.N. Mediator on Palestine, to urgently
appeal to the interested parties to accept in principle the prolongation of the truce for such a period as may be decided upon in
consultation with the Mediator.*

The Security Council did precisely this on July 7. The Mediator
also asked on that day that both sides agree to at least a three-day
extension to give the United Nations observers a chance to leave the
country. Two days later another proposal was made for a ten-day
unconditional cease-fire. The Jews accepted and the Arabs rejected
both of them. On July 7 the Israel government gave notice of its
willingness to prolong the truce under substantially the same conditions as those governing the truce then in existence, and Count

Bernadotte reported this to the Security Council on July 12. At midnight on July 7 his representative in Cairo was informed orally by the Secretary General of the Arab League that the Arabs were not prepared to accept a prolongation of the truce. The following afternoon the formal note was delivered, reiterating with detailed reasons the Arab rejection of the appeal for prolongation.

At a press conference in Jerusalem on July 8, I said that we still hoped to avoid a renewal of the war but that we had to assume it would start again. I went on: "According to the opinion of our military, our position in Jerusalem is much better than it was when the truce began. In the last days prior to the commencement of the truce our situation began to improve consequent upon the opening of the new road by means of which a permanent connection with the coastal plain was established. We are today prepared to enter the fray with greater self-confidence and hope. An injustice was done to our military forces by describing their position, when the truce began, as difficult. The fact is that nearly all of Jerusalem is in the hands of our forces and a sense of self-confidence must pervade the civilian population as it exists in the ranks of the Army."

The fighting broke out again while Count Bernadotte was at Lake Success putting forward his proposals for peace in Palestine. Among them was a call by the Security Council for an immediate cease-fire on the lines of the Security Council resolution of May 29. Then he added, "In view of the prospect of the virtual destruction of this historic site which belongs to the world [there should be] an order for the demilitarization of the city of Jerusalem as a whole." He asked for these principles to be accompanied by an unequivocal threat of sanctions and hoped that such a cease-fire would lead to an armistice in which mediation could be hopefully employed.

Abba Eban, the Israel representative at the United Nations, attacked the tone of the Mediator's proposals and his failure to indicate who was the aggressor and who the victim in this fighting. He pointed out that running through the Arab answers there was a single theme—the Arab states harbored certain political ambitions which they regarded as legitimate but which could not be advanced if there were peace. He asked the Council whether this fact was not itself a reflection of these ambitions, and whether political aspirations which can be fostered only by successful war do not inherently disqualify themselves from the approval of the liberal world.

Gromyko, the Soviet delegate, was quite blunt about it. After describing how the Arabs had openly made preparations during the truce for a renewal of fighting and after pinning down the Arab guilt for starting the war, he said, "It is therefore odd to hear the Mediator's rather evasive reply to the question who, in his opinion, is responsible for the resumption of military operations in Palestine. Everyone knows who is responsible for it, and the Security Council ought to note the fact and place the burden of responsibility where it really belongs."

We were leaning over backward to keep the good will of the world. It was during this debate at the end of the first truce that Trygve Lie, Secretary General of the United Nations, first began to communicate with us as "the Provisional Government of the State of Israel." This was progress, and we wanted to hold our gains. When a proposal was made in the Security Council for an immediate and special cease-fire in Jerusalem, Eban declared that if the Security Council ordered it the forces of Israel in Jerusalem would cease fire at once.

He added a telling footnote to the whole debate when he said, "It has been suggested in the course of this debate that the Arabs must be given some reason for accepting a cease-fire. We confess that we see in this philosophy an attempt to condone the theory of aggression, for if we were to accept this theory . . . we should have to conclude that the political aspirations which can be fulfilled by methods of peace, and political aspirations which could only be fulfilled by methods of war, are theoretically equated, and from that it is a short step to proceed to the view that the objectives of aggressive war must be peacefully conceded. We were asked what alternative the Arab governments have to war. The answer is simple: The alternative is peace."

The first truce ended on July 9, and ten days of fighting followed before the United Nations ordered the second, or unlimited, truce on July 19. The ten days have a very special meaning in Israel history. We won a series of small, sharp, important victories on every front. We showed both discipline and power on a national scale and proved our right again to call ourselves a nation. Most important of all, we took the heart out of our enemies and sent them and their friends, especially Great Britain, scurrying to the United Nations to call off the war.

At the end of the first truce Israel was in a far better position morally, and to some extent from a purely military point of view, for the resumption of hostilities. The steps taken to train and reorganize our forces during the four weeks' respite had their effect; so had the measures for tightening up the command. In Jerusalem, the Arabs had calculated that the resumption of fighting, after the hope and relaxation of the truce, would break the spirit of the inhabitants, who would have to face a further apparently endless period of bombardment, privation and anxiety. In this they were completely mistaken. The Jerusalemite said to himself, "Well, I held out in spite of all that they could do to me when we were cut off, unprepared and almost without weapons. Now we have the Burma Road, our armies are stronger, we know the worst they can do and it is not enough to subdue us." Later, when it became known that we had cannon to fight back with, the boost in morale was even greater.

I spoke again over the radio as fighting was resumed. "Jews of Jerusalem," I said, "during the period of the first siege our enemies thought they would vanquish us by hunger and thirst. They failed in that and they shall fail this time as well. We would like to hope that the city will not remain beleaguered for a long time. But in war it is not always possible to know what the morrow may bring. But if, heaven forbid, our hopes be disappointed and we shall once more have to be cut off for a long time, even then the enemy will not be able to prevail over us because we are hungry or short of water. Now, as before, we have reserves of flour and other foods. We have fuel for the vital needs of the city. As regards water, I have grounds for saying that we shall give our enemies an unpleasant surprise.

"We have learned to know the difficulties to which the inhabitants of a besieged city must adapt themselves and how to overcome them. The Jerusalem Committee has taken all necessary measures to ease the task of the shopkeepers and of the consumers in the distribution of food. We believe we shall be able to continue to assure the public a fair distribution of the essential commodities and in larger rations.

"We call upon the Jerusalem public to stand fast together in the trial that we face, in the confident belief in victory.

"This time the sound of the cannon will not be only from enemy guns. If before the truce we succeeded in capturing almost all of the city, which the Arab inhabitants abandoned in their myriads, today, when we are much stronger in arms and ammunition, we may expect that our military forces will go forward from victory to victory.

"The city suffered, and will suffer, from enemy shelling. Dear comrades fell and will fall, but not by force will our enemies determine the fate of the city. The Jews of Jerusalem remained faithful to it and clung to it when others left it to its fate. One should not shut one's eyes to the fact that the inhabitants of Jerusalem are called upon to make a great sacrifice. I am certain that they will take upon themselves this heavy burden, realizing that a great privilege is granted us to defend the city from its attackers and to maintain the position of our people within it. Together let us meet whatever may come in the deep faith that the city will be ours and we shall be its builders."

A large Syrian force, equipped with artillery and armor, was poised along the east bank of the Jordan. It was based on Baniyas, Pik and Kuneitra, and its supplies hinged on the Kuneitra-Damascus road. Lebanon was arrayed along our northern frontier to Rosh Hanikra in the west. Its small forces had contact with the Liberation Army of Kawkji and covered the way for these forces to advance southward. The Iraqi forces were mainly concentrated in the Triangle, deployed from Beisan in the northeast down to Rosh Haayin to the southwest and occupying Jenin, Tulkarem and Kalkilya. The little triangle from the slopes of Mount Carmel southward was held by local Arab levies. The evacuation of the Haifa area by the British, which was completed by the end of the truce, now laid the city, its harbor and its refineries open to bombardment from the air or attack from the sea.

The Israel forces struck swiftly, and the Syrians fought back with equal tenacity. The Israel artillery range was too short to prove effective and our Air Force was brought into operation for the first time in this sector. After days of attack and bitterly contested counterattack, the end of the ten days found both armies on this front in very much the same positions they had held when the truce began.

In the center the Iraqis had a great superiority in armor, in firepower and in numbers. They succeeded in clearing the Triangle of Israelis, but were firmly held on the Gilboa ridge that protects the Valley of Jezreel. Here the Jewish inhabitants of a fertile region they had reclaimed from swamp and malaria during the previous twenty years fought like tigers for their homes and they held back the invaders. The most bitter fighting took place around Sejera, which we held and had to retain, for it was the key to control of the approaches to Nazareth, Tiberias and Kfar Tabor. Had this position been lost, communication would have been cut between the Israel territory in the center of the country and the Jordan Valley, and northward from there to Upper Galilee. It would also have entailed a large diversion of our forces to this front from other areas. On the other hand, Sejera in our hands would also mean that we could dominate with our fire the only hinge of Arab communications from Nazareth northward. So we held Sejera.

In Galilee, Kawkji attacked and in a bitter battle with much hand-to-hand fighting on both sides his artillery and armor were at last driven back after eight days of unceasing combat. He was unable to save his dwindling prestige by holding even one Israel village.

Until the first truce, the front in western Galilee had been comparatively quiescent. Now it flared up. The strip of coast from Haifa Bay to Rosh Hanikra had been in Israeli hands from June 11, but the heights farther inland were held by the Arab Liberation Army. In order to keep possession of the coastal strip, it was essential that we gain a foothold on the ridges farther inland. We had gained a number of strongholds on the eve of the truce, which Kawkji did not recognize, and these continually changed hands during the twenty-eight days. Our plan was therefore to smash Kawkji's bases, destroy his communications and give us a holding in depth on this front. One brigade advanced from the direction of Nahalal, took the village of Maalul and joined up with Kfar Hahoresh, which had been cut off. These advances of ours on Nazareth from several directions misled Kawkji as to the point where we intended to make our main attack. We continued for the next two days to probe at points around the city until, at 4:30 P.M. on July 16, we began our direct drive on the city. An Arab artillery barrage and the armored column which the Arab commander sent out from Nazareth both failed to stop our main column. At six-fifteen a delegation of Arab notables came out to surrender. Kawkji, who was in the fortress police station, managed to escape with a good portion of his forces, but we captured papers, plans, documents and reports.

On the eve of the attack on Nazareth the following order of the day was issued to the Israel Army.

OFFICERS AND MEN:

We are advancing on a city which Kawkji has used for his foul purposes but which is the cradle of Christianity. The city is sacred

*to millions. The eyes of all sects of Christians in all lands are turned
towards it. It has many churches, holy places and monasteries. You
will be met by gangs and units who will resist you fiercely and savagely, and whom you will combat. But you are ordered in the
strictest terms to refrain from doing any damage to the holy places.
Our soldiers will not enter churches, will not fight from them nor
fortify them except out of the direst necessity and only on a specific
order. No soldier will take any spoil whatsoever in this city. The
commanders have been ordered to take the strictest measures
against anyone infringing this order. Our fighters are enlightened
men who are expected to show respect and understanding for the
religious beliefs of others. If any offender be found among you he
will face summary trial and strict speedy punishment.*

Forward. Attack the enemy. Storm the city and conquer it!

This order was faithfully obeyed and no damage was done at
our instance to any sacred place or any civilian in Nazareth.

The fall of Nazareth led to the immediate crumbling of the
whole Arab war effort in western Galilee, which passed into Jewish hands in its entirety. There immediately followed the clearing
of the whole coastal belt between Haifa and Tel Aviv.

On the southern front the Egyptians anticipated the end of the
truce by twenty-four hours and attacked in an attempt to
strengthen the ring that they were trying to close around the Negev.
They were held back at Kfar Darom, which was subsequently
evacuated by our forces. An attack on Beerot Yitzhak was beaten
back only by the arrival of reinforcements. An all-out attempt
failed on the same day to seize Negba, the key Jewish settlement
which barred their way to the north. This settlement, with just
150 defenders, was surrounded on all sides by an Egyptian force
consisting of three battalions of infantry, one of tanks, a company
of field artillery, armored units, antitank guns, auxiliary units and
air support. Later when the attackers were all repulsed, an Egyptian officer who was captured claimed that four thousand shells had
been fired into the settlement at close range. Indeed, before they
were finally thrown back the Egyptians had got to within fifty yards
of the last defense line to the village.

The campaign in the Negev can be said to have resulted in a successful holding action by the Israelis, with the capture of a few
strategic points and the relinquishment of some positions. The
Negev was too big an area to be held in its entirety by the kind of

forces we could spare from the more vital fighting fronts, especially the front in Jerusalem itself.

We had two objectives inside Jerusalem which we wanted desperately, for old and tangled reasons: the recapture of the Old City, the citadel of our Biblical dreams and the symbol of so many ancient forces which had helped to make us a nation, and the capture of Sheikh Jarrah, the vital link which would re-establish contact for us with the Hebrew University and the Hadassah Hospital on Mount Scopus, two great symbols of the reborn strength of the Jewish people. We failed in both. This was because we chose deliberately to concentrate what strength we had on another objective: the clearing of a safe road from new Jerusalem to the sea. In this we succeeded. A hundred years from now historians may say that our choice, which assured the inclusion of Jerusalem in the State of Israel, was a major turning point in the history of the Middle East.

To create the safe road to the sea, we had to destroy four major bases of the Arab Legion, at Lydda, Ramleh, Latrun and Ramallah. This would open a wide, safe corridor from the Judean hills to the coastal plain; it would also give us the railroad line, and the great airfield at Lydda, and most of the water pipeline to Jerusalem. The important fighting took place on July 11 and 12. In these two days we took both Lydda, with its nearby airfield, and Ramleh. The airfield was within the area allocated to the Jews by the partition plan, but the British had handed it over to the Arabs. But by now it was clear from the newspapers that the United Nations would move to enforce a new truce, and we could not afford to be caught nibbling at too many fronts. So by July 14 we had concentrated on pushing out the sides of the corridor we held. A long list of small villages fell into our hands; some fifty thousand Arabs fled across the lines; we held the railroad line in its entirety and a fairly satisfactory corridor through which we could build a whole series of roads that would be safe from Arab attack.

At the Jerusalem end of the road, it was imperative that we take the villages of Malha and Ein Karem. The first was captured on July 13 by a youth unit of Hagana troops; it was one of the points from which the Arab Legion had bombarded Jerusalem and it closed the ring we were drawing tight around Ein Karem. This large village fell four days later. Most of the Arab Legion and Egyptian troops which held it managed to escape before the end; the rest had no choice but to surrender. This same operation won for us the heights now known as Mount Herzl, where the national military cemetery of Israel is located and where my younger daughter, killed in action in the Negev, is buried.

Inside Jerusalem we had less luck, largely because time was running out on us. As early as July 14 Colonel Begley, the senior United Nations observer, asked me if we were prepared to agree to an immediate truce in Jerusalem. Since the whole question was under discussion at Lake Success, I told him that I would refer his question to Shertok in Tel Aviv, but that I could not help wondering why he made such an urgent inquiry. He told me he was afraid that our attacks on the Arab Legion would force them to abandon their long lines and concentrate their forces within the city, and that he wanted to avoid the really major battle inside Jerusalem which would then follow.

Mount Scopus had already been demilitarized by a special agreement signed on July 7 by Brigadier Lash for the Arab Legion, Colonel Shaltiel for the Israel Army, Nieuwenhuys for the Consular Truce Commission and Colonel Nils Brunsson for the Mediator. The United Nations accepted responsibility for the security of the area, which was first defined as including the Hadassah Hospital, the Hebrew University, the Augusta Victoria Institute and the village of Issawiya. The agreement had never worked well. Sniping went on intermittently; neither the United Nations nor the Jordan government had ever managed to control unruly Arabs who encroached on the demilitarized area. The check posts to be established by the United Nations to control peaceful traffic were never set up as they should have been, and eventually Jewish supply convoys were allowed to go up only twice a month to relieve personnel. Our hopes that the Hebrew University and Hadassah Hospital could resume work in their proper buildings proved vain during the truce and for nearly a dozen years since then. Both institutions have been forced to rebuild elsewhere in New Jerusalem, and their old Mount Scopus buildings stand to this day as derelict monuments to the craven ineffectiveness of the United Nations in the face of Arab intransigence and violence.

The Old City had not been demilitarized, and we had made as careful preparations to capture it as our supply and manpower position permitted. But the first week of the renewed fighting had seen our forces concentrated on widening the corridor to the sea, and although our demolition squads broke through the Jaffa Gate twice and blew up snipers' buildings, it was not until Friday, July 16, that we could mount an attack on the scale necessary to have any chance against the new defenses organized by the Arab Legion. Even this was hurried; that same afternoon I had received instructions from Tel Aviv that we were to cease fire at 5:45 the next morning if the Arabs agreed to accept a new demand by the United Nations for a truce inside Jerusalem three days before the second truce became operative throughout the country.

So we had roughly five and a half hours. Shaltiel decided to make the try anyway, even though he was not completely ready and the time was too short. In this he was obviously right. We attacked at two points. Our troops broke into the Old City at the New Gate and established a bridgehead within the walls. We tried unsuccessfully to breach the wall near the Zion Gate with an unusually large charge of explosives, and our attacking unit had to withdraw. But this was as far as we could go in Operation *Kedem,* or Antiquity, which was the last Jewish attempt to recapture the Old City.

An unavoidable hitch had delayed the preliminary softening-up bombardment in this operation, which was a combined one, Hagana forces co-operating with Irgun Zvai Leumi and Lehi units. The enemy was expecting the attack and had concentrated large forces. The Arabs opened a violent bombardment along the whole length of the walls, since they did not know precisely where our attack would develop. At 3 A.M. New Gate was blown open by explosives, and our forces advanced 150 yards and seized ten buildings, which they held in expectation of a second wave of attack. This reinforcement did not materialize due to some failure in planning. Finally, at 5:45 A.M., the general order was given to all our troops to cease fire and break off the action, and those in the Old City were ordered to withdraw. One of the accidents which had delayed the commencement of the action and so conditioned the subsequent withdrawal was that an Arab shell scored a lucky hit on an ammunition vehicle which was in one of the rear bases of the Etzel detachment. Thousands of bullets were destroyed and two men were killed. The other incident was at the New Gate. There the Arabs had built a roadblock of wood and shavings. This was ignited by a shell, and it took twenty minutes before the blaze could be extinguished and our men could move forward. These were irrevocable, precious moments and it is on such flickers of fortune's eyelash that one can say the fate of the Old City was determined.

One other question arises now when we examine our failure to recapture the Old City. A memorandum I dictated at the time makes it evident that we would have had a legal right to continue the attack, which was going well for us, beyond the 5:45 deadline on Saturday morning. At 6 P.M. the evening before, Colonel Shaltiel and I had met the chairman of the Truce Commission and informed him that Shaltiel had been instructed by our government to order his troops to cease firing at 5:45 the next morning if we received information by midnight from the Truce Commission that the Arabs had also agreed. It was arranged between us that the Truce Commission would give this information directly to Shaltiel as soon as it was received.

At eleven o'clock that night I telephoned the chairman and learned that no word had yet come from the Arabs. A half hour later, he called at my home to give me the formal note from the Truce Commission to which we had answered orally some hours before. There was very heavy firing throughout the night, but all became quiet at about five-thirty in the morning and, apart from intermittent sniping and an occasional explosion, Saturday was a quiet day.

Only at about two-thirty on Saturday I learned that the Truce Commission had in fact received no official answer from the Arab side. According to my memorandum, I then telephoned Shaltiel, who confirmed that he had not been notified by midnight that the Arabs had consented to the cease-fire. When I asked him why, then, our forces had stopped firing at 5:45, he replied that his instruction was we were not to fire if the Arabs stopped firing, and in fact they had stopped firing. I expressed surprise at this and said my understanding from the explicit wording of Shertok's cable to me was that we would cease fire only if the Arabs had, at a fixed time, notified the commission that they would do likewise. I tried to get in touch with the chairman of the commission but succeeded in reaching him only at about six o'clock. I asked him, What was the formal position as to the cease-fire? Had the Arabs officially notified him that they had agreed to it? He replied that they had not informed him officially but, as I knew, it was difficult to establish contact with them. He had been unable to get in touch with Colonel Tel but it was clear that they were respecting the cease-fire. In support of this statement he said that, as I knew, it had been quiet the whole day except for a few incidents of firing. I replied that in fact it had been quiet throughout the day except for sporadic firing, but whatever was the factual situation it was necessary to deter-

mine clearly whether or not the Arabs agreed to the cease-fire. We
did not wish to be exposed to the danger of having to face a sudden
attack by the Arabs and to be told afterward that they had not
agreed to the cease-fire. Nieuwenhuys said he thought that they
could be regarded as having agreed. I said that the inference might
be correct, but it was merely an inference and I thought it was important that he should inform the Security Council of the actual
facts and that the Council should draw their own conclusions as to
the position.

It is apparent from my memorandum that the Arabs had not
given the commission any definite statement that they agreed to the
truce. All it had received was a statement at noon on Saturday from
Glubb Pasha, who had no authority to speak for all the Arab
forces, still less for the Arab governments, that it was "all right,"
that he had given the necessary instructions to his forces in Jerusalem. Clearly if we had gone on fighting that morning the Security
Council could not justifiably have held us to be at fault, since we
had made our acceptance of the truce dependent on similar acceptance by the Arabs and this did not exist at 5:45 A.M., when our
troops were ordered to cease fire. As on previous occasions, the
Israel authorities had been overscrupulously careful to comply
with the decisions of the U.N., to the detriment of our position.

If we failed in this major objective of penetrating the Old City,
we did succeed in frustrating all Arab attempts to take back any of
our gains in new Jerusalem or to breach our lines. The Arab Legion made such attempts from Damascus Gate along the Suleiman
Road toward Notre Dame and were thrown back. Two buildings
close to Jaffa Gate were blown up. This meant that the approaches
through Jaffa Gate, New Gate and Zion Gate were now closed. The
Arabs still had the free use of Damascus Gate, Dung Gate, Herod's
Gate and St. Stephen's Gate. We laid bare stretches of the Old City
wall by demolishing buildings, and this greatly diminished sniping.
Attacks on the Hungarian Houses quarter were driven off and the
recognition was forced on the Arabs that they could not penetrate
into new Jerusalem. All of Jerusalem was now in Jewish hands except the Old City, the American Colony quarter, Sheikh Jarrah and
part of the Musrara quarter.

As for Jerusalem's civilian population, the resumption of fighting
meant that they were again living in a theater of active warfare and
that siege conditions again governed their daily lives. They had
hastily to pass from an atmosphere of comparative quiet to constant

shelling and firing of which they were the target and the victims almost as much as the soldiers. In addition to the shells, mortars and machine gun fire they had endured before, there was now bombing from the air. Enemy planes had flown over the city before, but now they succeeded in dropping considerable loads of bombs. In broad daylight, Egyptian Spitfires dropped their bombs indiscriminately on the western quarters of the city two days after the renewal of fighting, killing and wounding a number of children. These planes returned a second time two nights later.

The second truce was forced by a United States threat in the Security Council to propose sanctions. On July 15 the Council ordered all belligerents in Palestine to cease hostilities within three days and demanded an unconditional cease-fire in Jerusalem within twenty-four hours. The Jews reluctantly agreed. It had become apparent to the entire world that any extension of the fighting could only mean further deterioration in the Arab position. Great Britain put real, if cynical, pressure on the Arabs by withholding arms shipments from the Arab Legion and threatening to support the sanctions proposal in the Security Council. The Arab League eventually announced that although it would not recognize the Jewish state it would accept the cease-fire and the truce.

The Arabs were slow to honor the truce after they had accepted it. All Saturday night they shelled the northwestern quarters of the city. Among the buildings hit were my home and the Jewish Agency offices. Only a threat that we would start shelling the Old City, conveyed through Colonel Begley, led Colonel Tel to give orders on Sunday to stop the shelling. From then on we had only intermittent sniping and shelling to worry about in Jerusalem.

During the ten days of fighting, the Consular Truce Commission had been busy mainly in its own private war, bombarding United Nations headquarters in New York with biased accounts of what was going on. These were the days when the last lingering doubt disappeared that the Jews could hold nine tenths of Jerusalem. For foreign diplomats living in the city, this was a shock more violent than can well be realized by anyone who did not know at first hand the intricate pattern of power in Jerusalem. When the British mandate had ended, it had seemed both right and inevitable to the consuls that they should inherit, under a United Nations cloak of legality, the subtle overlordship of the city which was based on acceptance of both the Arabs and the Jews as backward peoples who required some form of trusteeship. The Jews had broken suddenly out of tutelage. It was going to take time for even men of good will to learn to treat us as masters in our own house.

Under the circumstances, one can understand now why the Consular Truce Commission resented so bitterly our desperate struggle to survive: it challenged their traditional terms of reference in a thousand small but important ways. When we took over the King David Hotel, at a time when the consuls wanted to hold it, they reported that "the Jews appear to be increasingly inclined to ignore the most elementary rules of international war." When nonuniformed Arab gangs provoked retaliatory action by us, the consuls would report that "in view of the exhaustion of the Arab troops . . . , even if they fired first—a fact which will be difficult to establish without a qualified observer—their fire was not heavy and does not constitute a regular assault."

A typical example of our troubles was recorded by me in a memorandum on the second day of the second truce:

This morning [Sunday, July 18], at about 5:30, very heavy firing began, at first with rifles and machine guns, and then shells began to explode. One of the mortar shells hit my house. Fortunately it hit the building high up, making a hole in the wall and shattering windowpanes. A few minutes after this Mr. Nieuwenhuys telephoned me to ask what was all this firing about. He understood our people were attacking the New Gate. I replied that the only direct information I had up to that moment was that my own home had been hit by a mortar shell and I didn't think it had been fired by Jews. This took him aback and he said he had understood that our people were entering the New Gate. I said that I would make inquiries as to the position but clearly the question was who had fired first. If the Arabs had fired the first shot, then our people had every right to hit back as strongly as they could. He said that he was anxious that firing should be stopped and asked me to do what I could about it. I promised to inquire and let him know.

I got in touch with our Army Headquarters and was informed that firing had been begun by the Arabs from opposite Yemin Moshe and the Jewish Agency buildings (which I was told had been hit) all along the western wall of the Old City to beyond the New Gate. It seemed that the Arabs had fired from machine guns and later from mortars on the city walls. Subsequently, there had

*also been firing at us in the neighborhood of Notre Dame and from
Musrara. I requested that the suggestion that we had attacked and
tried to enter the New Gate be inquired into carefully and that I
should be informed. Some minutes later, I received the reply that
there was no foundation to the allegation that we had tried to force
the New Gate. I telephoned Mr. Nieuwenhuys and conveyed to
him the information I had received, stressing that firing had been
begun by the Arabs and that there was no truth in the report that
we had entered or tried to enter the New Gate. I mentioned that
the Jewish Agency had been hit and requested him to convey this
information to the Security Council. He said he would do so. He
urged that we should stop the firing, which by that time had died
down. I suggested that he should make this request of the Arabs. If
they did not fire we would not fire.*

*On arrival at the Agency building this morning, I found two
mortar shells still unexploded and imbedded in the ground, one in
the courtyard, the other just behind the building. At this time shells
were exploding all around us. I telephoned Mr. Nieuwenhuys and
informed him that shells were again falling in Rehaviah and invited him to come and inspect the two mortar shells in the Jewish
Agency grounds which had fallen there early in the morning.*

Brigadier General Yigael Yadin, Chief of Operations of the Israel
Defense Forces, summed up the results of the ten days of fighting in
a press conference on July 22. He pointed out that the second truce
would not be in our favor, since the Arab position had become desperate when it was imposed. In ten days of fighting the Arabs had
suffered more than 5,000 casualties, some twenty per cent of their effective forces in Palestine. The Egyptian losses were 740 killed,
1,000 wounded, 200 prisoners. The Arab Legion lost 660 killed, 250
wounded and 80 deserters. The Syrians had 215 killed and 400
wounded. The Iraqis lost 300 killed. The casualties inflicted on the
forces of the Syrian freebooter Kawkji accounted for the remainder
of the Arab losses.

During the whole war, of 10,000 Egyptian soldiers who fought,
4,000 had been lost. Kawkji had begun with 3,000 men, including
Pakistani, Yemenite, Saudi, German, Yugoslav, British and Turkish
soldiers. On July 19 he had 800 men left. We had 5,000 prisoners,
General Yadin reported.

The territorial position had changed greatly in our favor in the ten days, during which we had taken all of Lower Galilee and part of western Galilee. Of the area originally allocated to the Arab state in the partition, we held 501 square miles, of which 418 had been captured during the ten days. All the Arab armies together held only 128 square miles which had been destined for the Jewish state.

The Jews had lost fourteen settlements, eleven of them in areas assigned to the Arab state, plus Mishmar Hayarden, Naharayim and the Jewish quarter of the Old City. The second cease-fire had cost us a probable victory at Latrun, which was almost within our grasp when fighting stopped. The Egyptians still held large portions of the Negev, Kawkji had a stretch of western Galilee, and the Arab Legion held the Old City—all prizes we might well have won had the fighting continued a little longer.

The ten days marked the end of organized Arab military efforts to conquer Jerusalem. The jerry-built coalition of Arab states proved to be no more durable in defeat than it had been in war. Abdullah moved quickly into the vacuum created by failure to set up the Arab state called for in the original United Nations resolution on partition. The former Grand Mufti, too, backed by Egypt and Syria, announced an "Arab Government of All Palestine" on September 22, 1948, and convoked a constituent assembly at Gaza on September 30 to set up a government, made up of his supporters but based on the Egyptian troops stationed southward from Bethlehem. Led by Ahmed Pasha Hilmi, one of the Mufti's ablest lieutenants, this government was recognized by all the Arab states except Jordan, but in October the Egyptians had gone home and by the time the Israeli-Egyptian armistice was signed, in February 1949, the Mufti's government in exile had vanished into thin air.

By December 1948, Abdullah had convoked a conference of some two thousand hand-picked Arab mayors, tribal leaders and *mukhtars* at Jericho to invite him to unite Palestine and Jordan in a single monarchy. The Arab Legion had been busy liquidating the Mufti's henchmen from village after village. The British had given up their last hopes of an Arab victory in the field, and they urged the Arab League to accept Abdullah's *de facto* control of the Arab parts of Palestine. The final face-saving formula was a decision by the Arab League "to treat the territories [of Palestine] that Jordan had annexed as a trust in its hands until the Palestine case is finally solved in the interests of its inhabitants."

When the war had ended, a member of the American diplomatic service asked a leading Arab politician in Beirut how it was that the comparatively tiny Jewish community of Palestine had been able to withstand the all-out attack of five Arab states that surrounded them. To this the Arab leader replied that the Arabs had lost the struggle because the Jews outnumbered them ten to one. When the American with amazement asked him to explain, since the Jews were only 650,000 in all and the Arabs numbered some forty millions, the Arab replied, "Yes, but there were ten times more Jews ready to lay down their lives for victory than there were Arabs." And so there were.

XI

THE SECOND TRUCE

ЛЛЛЛЛЛЛЛЛЛЛЛ

THE SECOND TRUCE, which came into force in Jerusalem on July
17 and in the rest of Palestine two days later, had been ordered
by the Security Council as a truce of indefinite duration, to last
"until a peaceful adjustment of the future situation of Palestine is
reached." Unlike the first truce, it had come at a bad time for the
Jews; we were fighting inside the Old City walls, we were tightening our pressure on the Latrun bulge, big victories were just beyond
our grasp. But once the truce was in force, it was to our advantage
to help maintain it. To stop the shooting we would have to contend
with the Arabs' lack of discipline and their continuing hatred for
the new state of Israel. To save Jerusalem, to bring water and supplies to the city and to secure its integrity as the capital of the new
state, we would have to struggle with the Consular Truce Commission and the United Nations Mediator. From the middle of
July these two struggles filled my days and nights. As I look back on
them now, the summer and autumn of 1948 seem in many ways as
ugly and as trying as the earlier months of military fighting, and as
crucial in the final establishment of the new nation.

Our first meeting with the Arabs took place on July 21. The U.N.
was represented by a single officer, Colonel Frank Begley. The
Arabs had no British officers with them, but brought an Iraqi
captain and an Egyptian contingent headed by Lieutenant Colonel
Ahmad Abdul Aziz, who had commanded a battalion organized by
the Moslem Brotherhood. Shaltiel was our chief representative, and
he met Abdullah el Tel and his Arab Legion officers almost as old

friends who had not seen each other for several weeks. The Arab Legion and the Egyptians would not sit down with each other at the same table, and we were obliged to meet with them separately.

Colonel Begley read the terms. The lack of contact between the Egyptian and Arab Legion officers was so complete that neither knew the disposition of his colleague's forces. Shaltiel demanded Arab withdrawal from several buildings near the Mandelbaum house, which they had seized since the truce, and offered to evacuate certain other positions in order to widen the no man's land through the city. The Arab Legion seemed to sense that the lines established were likely to last a long time and argued stubbornly over each house and street corner. In the end, the Arabs refused to withdraw from any position they had captured, but a line was agreed on.

During the numerous meetings that followed there were amusing incidents. An Egyptian captain present on one occasion warmly greeted and embraced an Israeli officer who had been in command of the sector of our line facing his company. He then whispered to him how grateful he was to us that his superior officer had been killed, thus opening the way to his own promotion. On another occasion, Abdullah el Tel advised us in a friendly spirit to stop wasting our six-inch mortar shells on the Moslem school near the Mosque of Omar, since he had moved his headquarters to another place and it would be a pity if we hit the mosque. The Iraqi officer, named Al-Askari, told us that we had shown the East the way to get rid of an imperialist ruler.

If the inhabitants of Jerusalem hoped that the truce would bring them respite from the noise of bursting shells and gunfire and that they would at last enjoy quiet, if not peace, they were doomed to disappointment. For some five months, until the end of December, there were few pitched battles and there were intermittent days of complete quiet. But it was a period of small-scale or static warfare. From the very first day, we received reports of Arab violations of the truce by building fortifications, mining roads and firing at our men. That very night Ramat Rahel was shelled for two hours. The next day Hadassah Hospital reported that "the vicious bombardment of the early afternoon resulted in gruesome casualties," followed the next day by "a number of severe casualties." On July 20 I complained to the Truce Commission that there had been "a mighty explosion in which the Arabs blew up the upper story of the French convent opposite Notre Dame, apparently to create a barricade to facilitate their firing at us."

Somewhere, buried in now-forgotten files, are the chapter-and-verse records of the long series of complaints I delivered over these months to the Truce Commission and the Mediator. Each Arab violation of the truce was carefully reported by us, but it did no good. It was our practice to have our Army liaison officer with the U.N. observers' staff send as frequently as necessary, almost daily, in the name of the commanding officer of the Sixth Brigade (which defended Jerusalem) to the chief U.N. observer in Jerusalem a statement drawing his attention to Arab breaches of the truce agreement, giving the time and particulars of the breach and requesting that the necessary action be taken. Sometimes the observers investigated the complaints; more often they did not; rarely was any effective action taken by them, nor did they make any serious attempt to prevent their recurrence.

On August 19 Count Bernadotte felt compelled to cable the U.N. Secretary General:

I am very concerned about present situation in Jerusalem. Owing to mutual distrust of parties and also lack until now of sufficient number of observers and transportation and despite my constant efforts and the efforts of the United Nations observers not only has firing practically never ceased in Jerusalem but situation is gradually getting out of hand. It is presently reported to me that general tension is mounting locally. Under prevailing conditions it is difficult to assess responsibilities and idle to try to ascertain which of parties is more to blame. They both have come deliberately to ignore the authority of the United Nations. The situation is at present of local character, one party firing against the other without any alteration of positions. Nevertheless it should be borne in mind that further deterioration of the situation in Jerusalem may lead to general resumption of hostilities.

A month later, the Arab attacks were still continuing. One typical entry in our records at this time reads: "The Jewish areas of Jerusalem were again blasted by salvos of shells and mortar guns accompanied by machine gun fire when the Arabs launched a sudden assault all along the battlefront on Thursday night. For over an hour the city was rocked by the explosions and the sky streaked with tracer bullets and the flashes of the heavy guns."

On September 16 Shertok called a press conference in Tel Aviv at which Brigadier General Yadin and Colonel Moshe Dayan put on public record some details of what we had been reporting to the United Nations. The next day the entire Hebrew-language press attacked "the inadequacy of the supervision" and argued that the Jews had reached the end of their patience and that it was high time "Israel's hands were untied."

The month of October witnessed a similar state of affairs, the people trying to go about their daily tasks but harassed by continued explosions of shells, houses being blown up, sniping, persons being killed, attempts by Arabs to penetrate no-man's-land areas and occasionally to attack our troops' positions. This month the Egyptians to the south of the city were particularly active. On October 10 it was reported that all the U.N. observers were alerted for three days because of serious breaches of the truce and the expectation that the Egyptians would launch an assault on Jerusalem.

A few days later, on October 16, coinciding with the flare-up of fighting in the Negev, a pitched battle was fought on Mount Zion. Arab Legion forces opened with a dawn attack against Israeli positions outside Zion Gate, and intensive military action followed on both sides. In the early hours of the next day, the attack was beaten back. In the course of the battle the Arabs lost one of the bases from which they had mounted the attack. Early in the month heavy fighting had broken out in the Negev which resulted in our breaking through to open the road to our settlements. Before the end of the month we had captured Beersheba and thus broken the Egyptian front in Jerusalem. All of the Negev was freed of Egyptian troops before a cease-fire was arranged.

Once again the Truce Commission found it necessary to warn the Security Council, then meeting in Paris. They complained against recurrent attacks of the Arabs on members of the Truce Commission: a white U.N. car with U.S. Consul Burdett in it had been heavily attacked when entering the courtyard of the French consulate. They also warned that battles might be renewed if the Security Council did not take immediate action. The telegram, signed by Neuville as chairman of the commission, stated that "Arabs were firing indiscriminately and often deliberately at Consulates and at U.N. Staff Headquarters, 21 wounded at French Consulate. Three shots fired at U.S. Consular car entering French premises and day after that firing at Consulate continued for 35 minutes. Arabs fired with automatic arms on October 13 for several hours from area under U.N. supervision and without any provocation by Jewish Forces." On October 14 his car was pierced by three bullets. "Continuation of this situation leads Truce Commission to conviction that neither Transjordan Government nor Arab Legion Command are capable of maintaining necessary control of their soldiers."

The last entry in our records on October 31 reads: "Last night the cannons thundered again in most parts of the city. There were 108 instances of Arab firing at Jewish positions in the city during the last week." But all this fighting and shelling did not deter the inhabitants of the city from celebrating their most solemn High Holiday of Yom Kippur, the Day of Atonement, which fell earlier in the month. Soldiers who had to remain in their outposts foregathered there to say their prayers in the traditional *minyan*, or group of at least ten men.

This state of uneasy truce continued through November, with the usual shelling, firing and sniping. The extent of the firing lessened toward the end of the month, but the Prime Minister, speaking to the Provisional Council, still had to report on November 5, "Jerusalem has as yet hardly enjoyed one night of quiet."

The firing during all this period was not one-sided. From the very outset we made it clear to the Security Council and to the Mediator that we would observe the truce and would not open fire upon the Arabs or initiate any form of attack upon them. Our troops had the strictest orders to comply with this undertaking. But we stated in the clearest terms to the Mediator and the Truce Commission that we would fire back if we were fired upon and would beat off any attack upon us. Shelling of our areas compelled us to try to silence the Arab guns, and machine gun and rifle fire was replied to by counterfire. Attacks on our positions were beaten off. But on no occasion did we initiate any action. Any isolated instances of our soldiers sniping were unauthorized and in violation of their orders.

It was Bernadotte who first made the seemingly sound and proper proposal that neither party to the truce should take counteraction in the event of the other side committing an act of aggression. This was a view which the Security Council accepted. Actually the principle was grossly unfair and served only as an encouragement to the aggressor. This should have been obvious to anyone familiar with the situation and with the Arab mentality. For by now there was no doubt that the Jews had accepted the decision of the U.N., while the Arabs had not. The Arabs had tried to reverse this decision by the use of force and proclaimed their determination to continue to do so. It was natural, therefore, to expect that it would be the Arabs and not the Jews who would be the ones to begin attacking. The

Jews wanted the position, as it was, to be recognized and therefore were anxious for peace. To tell the Arabs and the Jews that the aggressor should, in effect, be free to attack his opponent without fear of retaliation meant to the Arabs that they could fire at the Jews with impunity and would be supported by the Mediator and his staff if the Jews, in self-defense, retaliated.

The Mediator, persisting in his view, wrote me on August 11: "No party can expect to profit by the sporadic firing by rifles, automatic weapons, mortars and guns which has been continuing in disregard of the truce . . . I request that both sides should agree to the following order: firing of any kind even in answer to firing by the other party shall be forbidden . . ."

I refused to fall into this dangerous trap and replied on August 13 to his representative, General W. E. Riley of the U.S. Marines, that we could not regard fire from guns or mortars as sniping and refused to be prohibited from reacting to this kind of fire. "We could not forego our right of self-defense in the event of our men or positions being attacked," I wrote.

This illogical and unreasonable policy of Bernadotte's was in no small measure responsible for the continuation of the fighting. The efforts of the Mediator and his staff were not directed to prevailing upon the Arabs—who were in the very nature of the situation the aggressors—to desist from their aggression, but were concentrated in proving that the Jews had disregarded the unacceptable injunction that the Arabs should be free to attack without even the danger of our hitting back.

By the end of November the Truce Commission succeeded in arranging another meeting between Colonel Abdullah el Tel, representing all Arab forces, and the commander of the Israeli forces in the Jerusalem area, Colonel Moshe Dayan. They met at Government House on November 30 in an endeavor to ensure enforcement of the truce. They signed an agreement that from December 1 "there shall be a complete and sincere cease-fire in the Jerusalem area." Freedom of movement was to be permitted "within the present lines of the two forces. No movement shall be permitted in 'no man's land.' " They agreed to meet again to broaden the scope of the agreement and ameliorate conditions generally within the Jerusalem area.

For twenty-six days this "sincere truce" kept Jerusalem quiet. The novelty of fraternization between Arab and Jewish soldiers had worn off after the first few days of the truce; now they could be seen star-

ing quietly at each other across the thin strip of no man's land
running from north to south through the city. Arab public opinion began at last to take the truce seriously; many Arab refugees
started to stream back into the Old City. Dayan and Abdullah el
Tel held another meeting on December 13, at which we tried to
move the discussion forward from truce to an armistice and a
peace treaty. But no Arab politician could yet run the political risk
which this involved and no important efforts were being made by
United Nations representatives to find a formula which might have
reduced this risk.

On December 27 Arab Legion soldiers stationed on the Old City
walls opened fire on a group of Jewish soldiers, killing one and
wounding seven. A few days later, on January 3, an Arab plane
flew over the city and dropped bombs near the Romema reservoir,
hitting the Sephardic Home for the Aged instead of our military
camp at Schneller's, which I think must have been their target. The
truce was still far from a real truce, but time was slowly beginning
to solve the problem with which the Mediator and the Truce Commission had failed to cope.

Even more difficult than to stop the sporadic fighting was the
effort to resume normal life in Jerusalem under the second truce.
Jerusalem needed water, and supplies. It wanted access to the demilitarized area on Mount Scopus and to its Holy Places in the Old
City, including the Wailing Wall. With the rest of Israel it wanted
the release of immigrants detained on Cyprus. To all of these we
were entitled by the terms of the truce, by historical right, by our
new sovereignty which was now being recognized by nation after nation, by everything except the old prejudices compounded of Arab
hostility, British imperialism, foreign anti-Semitism and the 1,900-
year-old habit of treating the Jews of Jerusalem as exiles in their
own city.

One of our mistakes was that we did not spell out these conditions explicitly in our acceptance of the second truce. On July 6
I had wired Shertok, just before he was to meet Bernadotte to discuss the latter's proposal to prolong the first truce: "Would ask you
to inform Bernadotte clearly that there can be no talk of prolonging
truce before water will be flowing into Jerusalem. Otherwise we
shall certainly not receive water. I must warn you of the gravity of
the situation. It also appears to me difficult to pass over in silence

the non-fulfillment of the condition regarding the Wailing Wall."
This must have had some effect, for Bernadotte stressed in his cable
to the Security Council the next day that no truce would be possible
without United Nations guarantee of a flow of water and supplies
into Jerusalem. But to my chagrin, I learned later that our government was not prepared to insist on the flow of water being made a
firm condition of the truce. So on July 14 I wrote Ben Gurion in the
strongest terms:

*I write you as Prime Minister regarding the information Moshe
Shertok sent me a week ago that the Cabinet does not consider that
we may make the continuation of the truce conditional upon renewal of the water supply to Jerusalem. I cannot but express my
amazement at this attitude. Permit me to tell the members of the
government that when I spoke about this to Colonel Begley, the
principal American Observer, he told me he understood very well
that we cannot speak of continuing the truce without giving the
Jews of Jerusalem the water they are entitled to receive. He added
that Count Bernadotte explained this to King Abdullah who also
understood the matter and agreed that water be supplied to Jerusalem if the truce is renewed. I do not know what sin the Jews of Jerusalem committed that their government is prepared to forego their
rights, especially as they will suffer the consequences.*

It did no good. Our government agreed to the truce without our
water supply having first been renewed. So I had no choice but to
bombard the Jerusalem representatives of the United Nations with
protests. We had enough water to maintain minimum rations, but
no more. The ration of nine to ten quarts of water a day was close
to the barest minimum.

On July 21 I informed the Truce Commission that our experts
could repair the Ras el Ein pumping station in ten days but that
they had not yet been given a chance to examine the Latrun station.
The commission in turn urged the Security Council to take some
action. "There is reason for fear," the commission cabled, "that in
utter despair and under pressure from the civil population of Jerusalem, whose water has been strictly rationed since May 10, the Jews
may launch an attack on the Latrun sector." By the end of July,
Jewish engineers were at last taken to the Latrun station by U.N.
observers and began to repair the pumps. But a few days later the
Arab Legion withdrew this permission. I kept up my pressure on

the commission and on Count Bernadotte. By August 12 we had repaired the station and water was ready to flow. The end of this story is best told in Count Bernadotte's own words:

> I myself had to go to Latrun, accompanied by General Lund-strom, partly to settle certain disputes with regard to the front line in that vicinity, partly to inspect the pumping-station there, which had been placed under United Nations protection and was to be set in order now to ensure the water supply for Jerusalem. The ne-gotiations with the Jewish military authorities about the front line were quickly disposed of, and then I went on to look at the pump-ing-station, which was in no man's land. The machinery was obvi-ously in perfect working order and the installation only required general supervision to be fully operative. The Jewish engineers we had engaged were to start work that afternoon . . .
>
> When I left Jerusalem on August 11 to return to Rhodes, the situation was accordingly tense and the atmosphere uneasy. I still felt, however, that there was hope of an improvement setting in, and that I might now be free to travel to Stockholm to take part in the International Red Cross Conference.
>
> Then came news that the pumping-station at Latrun had been blown up and completely destroyed. It was General Lundstrom who gave me this report when I rang him up in Haifa the following day. He said it had not yet been possible to establish who had committed this outrage. But it was believed to have been a patrol belonging to irregular Arab forces.
>
> I readily admit that I felt bitter when I received this news. I had asked time and again for a month that the 40 armed police who were needed to guard Latrun should be sent. They had not yet come. And now the pumping-station had been blown up. The con-sequences of this act were incalculable.

We were in complete accord with the Mediator. We shared his bitterness.

Our efforts to get food were more successful, but no easier. We had our Burma Road but the main road ran past the Arab Legion positions at Latrun. The United Nations people tried at first to es-cort our convoys, but on July 31 two of their officers were wounded when the Legion tried to stop a convoy. It was not until August 23 that General Aage Lundstrom, the Mediator's chief of staff, an-nounced an agreement with the Arabs that we could traverse the road with one convoy a day, and on August 31 the first convoy of passengers arrived in Jerusalem over the main road past Latrun.

Three weeks later the Arabs renewed their attacks. On September 23, a group of trucks under U.N. escort found the road blocked. The passengers in the convoy were told to take cover in the ditch while the U.N. observers walked forward to talk.to the Arab soldiers. Several of the soldiers came down the road and opened fire on the passengers in the ditch. Four of them were killed, including Mrs. Simcha van Vriesland, the widow of the former Dutch Consul General in Jerusalem and a very close friend of my family. Another of the victims was the Jewish liaison officer with the convoy, Lieutenant Balfour Cohen, the son of one of Jerusalem's best-known Sephardic families, who had risked his life day after day in accompanying the convoys unarmed, as the United Nations observers had insisted.

The road was not reopened until October 15. After this day there were no more serious incidents, mainly because by then we had switched nearly all traffic to the Burma Road, which bypassed Latrun. This road and later our new Valor Road were our effective answer to the Mediator's desire to continue treating Jerusalem as a beleaguered city entitled only to restricted quantities of food. He wanted to resume the control he had had over our supplies during the first truce, but this time our possession of our own roads made the argument between us a purely academic one.

I had my troubles with our own people, too. It needed constant pressure on Tel Aviv to make sure that Jerusalem got its share of the nation's short food supply. It took a long time to work out with Kaplan, the Minister of Finance, the equitable adjustment of prices and taxes which would not require Jerusalem to carry the entire cost of handling problems that concerned the whole country. But these obstacles were gradually overcome and rations were slowly increased. We maintained our strict control of prices, strengthening the public tribunals set up to punish profiteers. We were still short of electricity, with no street lighting.

These matters were within our own control. Where we depended on the Truce Commission, we were worse than helpless. In the agreement signed on July 7, which had demilitarized Mount Scopus, it was provided that Jewish convoys should be allowed to move personnel and supplies to the Hebrew University and the Hadassah Hospital. Only one convoy actually went through, a fortnight after the agreement, and then the Arabs refused to pass them. I wrote memoranda to the commission, its members talked to the Arabs, the Jews on Mount Scopus somehow survived without replacements or fresh supplies. It was not until November 30 that Dayan and Abdullah el Tel worked out an agreement which allowed convoys to go up to Mount Scopus regularly twice a month.

We never succeeded in getting the access to the Jewish Holy Places which the truce should have brought us. One of those was the cemetery on the Mount of Olives. Throughout the ages, religious old Jews had made their way to Jerusalem to be buried in this cemetery overlooking the site of the Temple, there to await in their last resting place the coming of the Messiah. The Arabs seized it with the Old City, and for months Jerusalemites could actually watch them taking away the tombstones for building purposes. Neither the number nor the eloquence of the complaints we made to the Consular Truce Commission and the Mediator's office could change this situation, which continues to this day.

So does our exile from the Wailing Wall. In this matter I am still inclined to place a major responsibility on the Truce Commission, and especially on Burdett, the American Consul who often sat on it. This was the man who had worked so hard to cut down the number of calories to be allowed the citizens of Jerusalem during the first truce. In this matter, too, he devoted hours of time and letter after letter to the legal quibble that Jewish access to the Wailing Wall, stipulated expressly in the Security Council decision of May 25 that there should be a truce, was not repeated in the documents actually establishing either the first or the second truce. My position was supported by the French Consul General and by the Mediator himself. But I have never felt that the Truce Commission, engaged in such a quibble over the right of Jews to access to the holiest shrine of their religion, could have been either an honest or an effective broker in negotiations about it with the Arabs. In 1948, for the first time in many centuries, Jews were unable to visit the ruins of their Temple on the sad and solemn day of the year when they had traditionally gone there to bewail its fate. To this day, the United Nations has not honored its own commitment on this matter. If any Jew has worshiped at the Wailing Wall since then he has gone there in disguise and in peril of his life.

Another issue on which the Mediator defaulted was the release of Jewish immigrants who had been intercepted by the British and taken to detention camps on Cyprus. After the end of the mandate and the establishment of Israel there was not the shadow of a legal justification for detaining these people. The British could not even claim to be protecting their neutrality after British officers had appeared openly in command of the Arab Legion and had even been replaced, during the truce periods, by new officers posted to the Old City from British military camps in the Suez Canal zone.

There were twenty-five thousand of these Jewish immigrants, according to Count Bernadotte's figures, including four thousand men of military age. When Abba Eban pressed the Mediator at the United Nations on this point, he finally drew an admission that the wholesale detention of these immigrants on Cyprus had never been recommended or requested by the Mediator as essential for the preservation of the truce. Yet there they stayed. It was not until January 24, 1949, when the Egyptians had already been brought to the armistice table at Rhodes and the other Arab states were at last prepared to talk about a permanent truce, that an Israeli passenger ship, the *Galila,* moved into the port of Famagusta to take the first load of these Jewish exiles from Cyprus to their homeland.

Who were the members of the Consular Truce Commission?

The French Consul General was an old personal friend of mine. He had served in Palestine in a lesser capacity a good many years previously, when it had been my privilege to act as honorary legal counselor to the French Consulate General. I had attended his wedding in Jerusalem. He knew me as a true friend of France, and our relations then and now had been most cordial. But I knew that we were bound to have difficulties with him, for I was well acquainted with his views on Jerusalem. Neuville was a most devout Catholic and held very decided opinions on France's paramount role as defender of the Catholic faith in the Holy Land, and in particular in the Holy City. He was sympathetic to our aspirations to national independence and held a very poor opinion of the Arabs. His contempt for the Arabs was based on his experience with them in North Africa, and his attitude to them was exacerbated by their constant firing at his consulate building.

One reason why he sympathized with us in our effort to throw off the British yoke was his profoundly anti-British sentiment, especially since World War II. *"L'Albion perfide"* was a favorite phrase of his.

When my wife and I attended a reception he gave soon after the Free French became active, the British officials boycotted it, since

Britain had not yet adopted a firm policy regarding them, and he laughingly remarked, in referring to us, that the only Britishers who had accepted his invitation were Canadian Jews.

Yet despite his lack of sympathy for the Arabs and the British and his understanding of our struggle for independence, I knew that on one score he would oppose us bitterly: our claim to include Jerusalem within the Jewish state. He used to argue violently with me about this. His deep Catholic conviction that Jerusalem must be internationalized, with the Christian Holy Places under Christian control, was an abiding passion with him. He saw himself as entrusted by Providence with the task of saving the Holy City for the Holy Church. Nothing on earth, not even the decision of his own government, would deter him from this sacred duty. He once expressed concern over a speech in which De Gaulle, whose fervent disciple he was, said that France should acquiesce in the prospect of the Jews gaining control of the entire country, including Jerusalem.

He was, to boot, a highly nervous and very excitable gentleman, quick to anger. His state of mind changed with the wind, alternating from one extreme view to another. He was too intellectual not to realize how wrong it was for him to be carried away by his feelings. Thus, soon after attacking us in conversation with me for daring to want to include Jerusalem in our state, he would assure me that his views would not influence his friendship for us and for me personally. He would then proceed to try to convince me that it would be for our own good to renounce our claim to Jerusalem and agree to its internationalization, as otherwise the entire Christian world would be against us. His failure to convince me would result in another outburst of anger and threats. This overriding passion colored his official dealings with me and his reports to the U.N. and to his government. It led him to assert authority he did not possess, to be biased against us, openly to attack my conduct of our affairs, and to seek to thwart my efforts to assure the Jewish character of the city.

The following is an extract from a letter I wrote our Foreign Minister about Neuville on October 6:

I rather think that the reason for his attack is the hitch in arranging for his son to cross our lines to proceed to Amman and from there to France. As you know, Neuville has often given vent to his spleen because of some difficulty or delay in arranging to comply

*with his very numerous requests as French Consul. Our trouble has
been, as I often told you, that the members of the Truce Commission have been unable to distinguish between their capacity as members of the Commission and as Consuls General of their respective
countries. You will be interested to know that at Rosh Hashana
Neuville sent Cohen [an official of his consulate] to try to assure me
that we had exaggerated or misunderstood their meaning, that they
had not meant to attack us, so that he was even prepared to call a
press conference to explain this, etc., etc. I told Cohen quite frankly
that we are somewhat tired of Mr. Neuville, as his nerves are getting
worse every day, but, as I have no personal quarrel whatever with
him, but, on the contrary, have always been on the most friendly
terms with him, I shall try to smooth over these painful incidents,
until he comes to realize that we shall not be bullied into abandoning our position by such attacks upon us, however they may be disguised.*

The Belgian Consul General represented a government which
was not then among our supporters, a Catholic power not too well
disposed toward the newly created Jewish state, perhaps because it
too was concerned about the Christian character of the future
Jerusalem. Not that we were without many good friends in the
highest places in Belgium. The Queen Mother herself was a loyal
friend of the Jews. She repeatedly expressed her sympathy with our
effort to rebuild our national life in Palestine, after the Nazi holocaust had overwhelmed our people in Europe. Vandervelde, one of
Belgium's greatest public figures and political leaders, was a devoted
supporter of the Zionist cause. He was, indeed, one of the first European statesmen to visit the new Israel when it was still not entirely safe to be here.

But Nieuwenhuys was a devout Catholic and supported with unusual zeal that part of his government's policy which expressed itself in opposition to Jerusalem becoming a part of the Jewish state.
He was most anxious to make a success of the task entrusted to him
and spared no effort to achieve this end. Unfortunately he was of
the type that is prone to mistake activity for action. Despite his constant running back and forth between Jerusalem and Amman, he
got little done. He was most profuse in his assurances of good will
and understanding, but he dispensed his assurances with such liber-
ality to both sides that they both came to realize that no reliance
could be placed upon his declarations of good intentions. He was a

very cultivated person, pleasant personally, so that it was easy to get along with him, and I felt he wanted to be friendly to us. He sought to show this in his conversations with me, when he lost no opportunity to deprecate the conduct of the Arabs, their disregard for the truth and their complete failure to keep their promises to the Truce Commission. But I happened to know from our intelligence reports that he spoke to the Arabs in somewhat similar terms about us.

I suspect that Nieuwenhuys did not realize how obvious his pro-Arab bias became in the course of that summer. He was highly susceptible to influence, especially by his colleagues on the commission. Unlike Neuville, he was deeply pro-British. As a Western diplomat with long experience in the Middle East, he found it almost impossible to regard our Jewish claims to manage our own city as anything but an impertinence. On August 3 I wrote him a letter about our willingness to discuss the internationalization of Jerusalem. It was an exceedingly delicate question, which I had discussed at length on that same day, in separate conversations, with Bernadotte and with Shertok. Some days later I discovered that a copy of my letter had found its way into Arab hands. I had no choice but to write him about this. I went out of my way to express my confidence in the three members of the commission, but I asked them to investigate possible leakage from their offices, since it was, I wrote, "possible that some member of one of the staffs concerned has been guilty of an indiscretion, if not of a deliberate act of espionage."

This was too much for career consuls who had never, in their professional careers, treated with Jews except as suppliants or humble petitioners. Before they could reply to me, Nieuwenhuys had been succeeded in the chairmanship of the commission by John Macdonald, who signed their answer to me on August 30. It read, in part:

The Truce Commission rejects categorically this calumnious charge, based on pure speculation if not malice, directed against the Commission and personnel associated with its work. You are requested to retract the statement immediately in writing with an appropriate apology. Charges of this nature cannot be bandied about lightly, and if you do not see fit to honor this request the Commission will be obliged to draw the Security Council's attention to the accusation. The Truce Commission's report will necessarily include a request for a public apology by the Representative of the Pro-

visional Government of Israel to the Security Council and will point to the impossibility of the Commission continuing to work with a person who professes to entertain such a suspicion.

This rude and incontinent letter addressed to the Military Governor of Jerusalem, appointed by a properly constituted government, required a sharp reply. I wrote to Mr. Macdonald and told him that my letter had definitely not suggested any implication against the three consuls. I went on to say:

It is, in my humble view, somewhat extraordinary for you to suggest that members of the staffs of consular offices are immune from suspicion of improper conduct. I know of no principle of international law which confers such remarkable immunity on consular employees. I consequently cannot agree that I was not entitled to suggest that one of the members of your staffs might possibly have been guilty of an indiscretion or even an act of espionage. Nor is there the slightest justification for your suggestion that I have "bandied charges about lightly." I am sure that you will appreciate that the fact that a letter addressed to the then Chairman of the Commission could have come to the knowledge of our enemies is a very serious matter indeed and fully warranted my addressing myself to the Truce Commission as I did.

A dozen years later, I can see large elements of what is both stuffy and childish in these records of the Western consular mind resisting a new idea. But these incidents had at the time a life-and-death meaning for us. The American consul could forget more easily than we that a bomb placed in one of his consulate's cars, a car left by an Arab driver in the courtyard of the Jewish Agency and flying an American flag, had a few months before taken a toll of Jewish life.

This was by no means the only unpleasantness we had with Macdonald, a man with whom it was hard to have the friendly personal relations we maintained with his colleagues. When he first arrived in Jerusalem he seemed to be the normal type of foreign-service official, matter-of-fact, rather colorless and taciturn, not normally talkative, seemingly more accustomed to the economic side of consular service than to dealing with complex political problems. We were naturally eager to be on good terms with the representative in Jerusalem of the United States government. Unfortunately it takes two to create a friendship. There is a Hebrew saying that one can tell a man *"bekisso, bekosso, bekaasso,"* three words that sound alike but mean "touching his pocket, when in his cups, when in anger." It did not take us long to discover on the basis of this adage that Macdonald was no friend of ours.

It is my personal view that his conscience was an important factor in his aggressiveness toward us. On August 16 he was being accompanied to the Mandelbaum Gate by Ze'ev Herzog, a Jewish liaison officer with the United Nations. As Herzog stepped out of the United States car he was shot by Arab snipers. Macdonald drove off, leaving Herzog dead in the street; a half hour later he telephoned the Magen David Adom to notify them of the incident.

Whether or not this was the cause, Macdonald quickly became obsessed with bitterness against those of us who were trying to organize and to govern the city. He resented deeply our decision to restrict to the barest minimum the occasions on which we would permit him, or anyone else, to cross our lines into the Arab-occupied areas of Jerusalem. The lethal sniping which often took place on such occasions produced from him invariably protests to the Jews and not to the Arabs. Arab violations of the truce drew from him only the cynical resignation with which all Europeans tended to regard Arab lack of discipline. Violations by us, even when they were clearly perpetrated by dissident terrorists whom we were trying desperately to control, were regarded as willful and official acts.

Toward the end of August, an American member of his staff named George Paro invited a couple whom he had met at a hotel to his home for a drink. The couple turned out to be members of a terrorist group, who kidnaped him and held him for seventeen hours. We caught them and released their victim, unharmed. Macdonald had every right to intervene. But he had no right to use the incident, as he did, to score points against Israel rather than to help George Paro. I had no alternative but to instruct him patiently that kidnaping is a criminal offense under ordinary civil law in all countries and not a problem of international law. I naturally expressed our regrets over the incident and our gratification that it had been ended quickly and without injury to the victim, but I rejected as strongly as I could Macdonald's contention that the kidnaping had anything to do with the legality of my position as Military Governor of Jerusalem.

He went out of his way consistently to picture us as violators of international law, deliberately scornful of the representatives of the

United Nations. We felt compelled in the end to make representations in Washington about his deliberate unfriendliness to Jews. Evidently complaints of a nature even less palatable to those responsible for the high repute of the United States consular service reached the State Department from other sources. In any case, an investigation of his conduct was made by a senior State Department officer, who came to question me about it at my home, and in October Macdonald left Jerusalem, not to return. For this we were not sorry.

It would be impossible and unrewarding to relate here all the countless incidents in which these three men, inheritors of old traditions and prejudices, became embroiled with the new Jewish state and with me, its daily and hourly contact with them. Some of the incidents were important, involving human lives, or water for Jerusalem, or our right of access to the Wailing Wall, or the future of the finest hospital in the Middle East, left derelict and unused on Mount Scopus. Some of them were entirely unimportant, involving dignity or prestige or the niceties of diplomatic protocol. I am certain that we were guilty, on our side, of impatience, of stubbornness, perhaps sometimes of the kind of inefficiency which came from our lack of experience and the Arab determination not even to talk about peace. But I am equally certain that a large part of the blame must be placed on the power politics of the cold war which had led the United Nations to set up this commission of local consuls without any special qualifications to deal with an agonizingly urgent and dangerous situation. They never understood their mandate or the terms of reference given them by the United Nations. They could never distinguish between consular matters and those related to the truce. No effort was made to check the momentum of generations which led them to regard the Jews of Jerusalem as either inferior but aggressive people or religious fanatics. Unfortunately for us, and unhappily for the future of the Middle East, the United Nations assumed its responsibilities—once the partition resolution had been voted—in a spirit of indecision and wishful hoping that events would solve the questions it did not have the courage to face.

And this, of course, is just what happened in the end.

But it was a rough summer. Even before the second truce, the commission showed its unfriendliness when a terrorist unit of the

Etzel kidnaped, on July 6, five British officials of the Jerusalem
Electric Corporation. We were directly in touch with the British
consulate and eventually dealt with the matter to its satisfaction.
But the Truce Commission saw a chance to report to the Security
Council a sinister Jewish plot to seize the power station as part of
a larger plot to prevent the internationalization of the city.

A few days later, when the Mediator had failed to secure a prolongation of the first truce, his staff evacuated the King David Hotel,
a key position within our lines, and we immediately occupied it.
The Truce Commission had wanted the building for themselves for
a variety of reasons: Arab pressure on them, entreaties by the manager of the hotel, a man named Hamburger, and the legitimate interest of the French Consul in the safety of his consulate, which
was adjacent to the hotel. Yet the Truce Commission, which had
lodged no protest when the Arab Legion shelled and destroyed
Jewish synagogues in the Old City, reported to the Security Council
that our occupation of the King David Hotel, during which no shot
was fired, was in disregard of the elementary principles of international law.

We made formal protests ourselves to the Security Council
against the language used by the Truce Commission in reporting on
its troubles with us. On July 14, Eban cited one of the commission's
cables (Security Council document S891) in which the commission
reported that "Jews boast that it would not take more than a fortnight to conquer the whole city." What Jews? he asked. In cafés or
on the streets? Was the boast made by any authorized or responsible
body? He pointed out that the message had been sent when no truce
was in operation in Jerusalem.

I tried, too, to pin the commission down on its charges of breach
of faith. In all sincerity, I wanted to know on what they based their
accusations. But I was refused even copies of the charges; Nieuwenhuys wrote me that "inasmuch as reports of the Commission are
concerned, my colleagues and I agree that they are of a confidential
nature that only the Security Council has a right to alter."

I sent a copy of this correspondence to Shertok and wrote:

*I think in general the time has come to raise the question of their
behavior to us. This is the proper moment, since one of the principal U.N. observers told me that he is taking steps to try to put
an end to their activities. He defined them thus: The Belgian runs
around like a chicken with its head chopped off; the Frenchman*

decides everything on the basis of his personal feelings towards you at the moment; and the American is not in the picture at all. He is of the opinion that they are not serving the interests of the U.N. adequately and sometimes act on the basis of a consular approach. He added that the Belgian was more concerned about what the Jews and the Arabs said about him than to fix a just attitude to the matter itself. The observer is thinking of proposing to Bernadotte to entrust matters in Jerusalem to one person as his representative.

I think that we cannot expect much good to result from their efforts. The Belgian is outwardly friendly but very weak and under the influence of the Americans and, in my opinion, also of the British. The Frenchman is latterly convinced that we have definitely decided to capture the entire city and to bring it within the Jewish state, and since he opposes this, heart and soul, and is most anxious that the city be internationalized, his approach to every matter affecting us is a priori hostile. The American apparently acts on the advice of his assistants, who, I am sorry to say, are entirely under British influence. As that is the case, what can we hope for from them? Therefore, it is perhaps desirable that we also act along the same lines as the U.N. observer. Let me have your opinion on this.

One of the basic reasons for the commission's failure was that it had been set up to arrange and enforce a truce but devoted most of its efforts to trying to secure the internationalization of Jerusalem. This was a problem for the United Nations, which had in no way delegated it to the Truce Commission. This body made no perceptible effort to internationalize those parts of the city held by King Abdullah and his Arab Legion. But at different times they pressed us to surrender to them the city's power station, the Hadassah Hospital on Mount Scopus, and a zone containing the United States and French consulates and the King David Hotel. We had assured them that no Jewish soldiers were stationed in this area and that the sniping at it was entirely Arab.

Neuville has published an account of one of our interviews on this matter at my house, on September 24. "The Military Governor made a visible effort to appear friendly and gracious," he wrote. "We too were delighted to notice, as we thought, a pleasing evolution both in the Israeli policy and the normally unfriendly character of our interlocutor."

He added, "M. Joseph is a brilliant advocate. Without doubt, the most theatrical in the Holy Land, but his pleadings outside the bar indicate a poor estimation of the critical faculties of his fellow citizens." He went on to explain in detail why he considered this should be a neutral zone. He said the main reason in his opinion why the Arabs continued to snipe at it was that they thought Jewish troops were there or that it was in Jewish hands. If it were a neutral zone they would not do so. He claimed that when the commission made simultaneous approaches to both sides on August 30 about the suggestion, the "Arab commander, shortly afterward, indicated his consent in principle, while the Jews remained mute."

At the end of September the Truce Commission apparently decided to hit back at the constant critical comment upon them in the Hebrew press. Since their action took the form of a personal attack upon me as Military Governor, I should include their cable to the President of the Security Council, dated September 30, and signed by Macdonald:

Deliberate Jewish campaign led by Military Governor, Dr. Joseph, to discredit Truce Commission and Acting Mediator, Dr. Bunche, now apparently developing along lines of attack launched against late Count Bernadotte prior to his assassination and marked by such deliberate discourtesies as release to Press of communication sent to United Nations organizations before their receipt by addressees. Obviously undertaken in effort to destroy public confidence in and arouse public animosity towards the two bodies now striving to enforce truce in Jerusalem and bring about demilitarization of Jerusalem in accordance with Security Council resolution of 15 July. Coincides with Jewish effort before General Assembly to obtain incorporation of Jerusalem in the State of Israel and is calculated to prove both Jewish determination to keep Jerusalem and inability of United Nations to internationalize city in accordance with late Mediator's recommendations.

In reply to Dr. Bunche's statement that Israel authorities were lax in providing security for Count Bernadotte, Dr. Joseph in a press release blamed United Nations authorities for negligence in security measures. He claimed United Nations had declined Jewish suggestion that United Nations personnel be accompanied by Israel military personnel. He maintained: "Jewish authorities, had they received slightest intimation that United Nations representatives wished to have special protection accorded to them, would have gladly complied with the request." Truce Commission is writing to Dr. Joseph as follows: "As long as Jewish officials pretend to exer-

cise governmental authority in Jerusalem for safety United Nations
personnel will hold him personally and Israel army Jerusalem Com-
mand responsible for acts by Jewish terrorists; however, restrictions
on freedom of movement of United Nations personnel under pre-
text of 'safety reasons' will not be tolerated; if safe, free movement
throughout Jewish area cannot be guaranteed, Dr. Joseph should
acknowledge inability to maintain law and order."

In a second press release a proposal by the Truce Commission
that a zone comprising the King David Hotel, Y.M.C.A., French
and American Consulates-General be considered a neutral area was
declared unacceptable by the Israel army. Dr. Joseph claimed the
Truce Commission had no authority to designate neutral zones and
reserved freedom of action. He stated no Jewish troops were now
in the area. In accordance with instructions from the late Mediator
to implement the Security Council resolution of 15 July with re-
spect to the demilitarization of Jerusalem and in an effort to assure
the safety of United Nations personnel, the Truce Commission on
30 August proposed to both military commanders the creation of
zone as demilitarized area. The Arab commander accepted in prin-
ciple but the Jewish commander ignored the letter until the press
release of yesterday. Truce Commission and United Nations observ-
ers here consider such a zone not only as logical first step towards
demilitarization but necessary for the safety of United Nations per-
sonnel here. The Truce Commission considers it essential to bring
to the Security Council's attention the actions of the Military
Governor and the local Israel army command in view of the grave
consequences which may result from malicious and distorted at-
tacks on United Nations bodies. The attitude adopted appears to
be expressly designed to hinder the carrying out of the Security
Council resolution of 15 July. The Truce Commission believes
that the non-cooperativeness towards United Nations exhibited by
local Jewish authorities is diametrically opposed to the statements
of responsible spokesmen of the Provisional Government of Israel
pledging utmost cooperation with the efforts of the United Nations.

This document was castigated by Eban, our representative at the
U.N., in his communication to the Security Council. He said that
it presented,

over the signature of Mr. John J. Macdonald, a series of personal
attacks on a distinguished public official, Dr. Dov Joseph, in intem-

perate language seldom seen in public communications. We regret to state that in our view these charges have no substance. There is no Jewish campaign to discredit the Truce Commission or Mr. Bunche. Dr. Joseph has never published or written or spoken a word against the Truce Commission. If he had, the Security Council could have been sure that these words would have been reproduced in Mr. Macdonald's communication. Nor has he uttered a single word of criticism of Mr. Bunche.

Further, if the Government of Israel considers that the Jewish parts of Jerusalem should be incorporated in Israel and makes an effort to persuade the General Assembly to that effect, there is nothing wrong in holding or advocating that view. And it can scarcely be a prerogative of the Truce Commission to censor this forthcoming international discussion. . . .

I cannot conceal that, without being too sensitive to legitimate criticism, we do recognize this as a deplorable letter. You cannot walk in the streets of Jerusalem these days without a sense of tragedy over the place. And with all their imperfections on their heads, Dr. Joseph and his colleagues have made a bigger contribution than anyone else towards restoring the processes of ordinary life which would otherwise have been chaotic.

A spokesman in Jerusalem refuted, on October 1, each of the allegations made by the Truce Commission with such malice. There was no need to stir up Israeli public opinion against the commission. It had created for itself an unpopularity with the Jews that matched its loss of the confidence of the United Nations which had originally set it up. An editorial in *Davar* on October 6 summed up feelings which were by now held in circles far removed from Israel and the Jewish cause, when it pointed out that the commission's first charge "attacked the Military Governor of Jerusalem, Dr. Dov Joseph, for activity designed to destroy the confidence of the Jewish inhabitants in the Committee. This is a strange charge. Dr. Dov Joseph is well known in the country from his legal and political work and no one would think of suspecting him of wasting his time on a deed which would be devoid of any purpose—to destroy something that doesn't exist."

The other newspapers in Israel wrote in even stronger language. The commission's document had been unfortunately worded in that it showed too clearly its bias against Israel and its obvious desire to apply to the Jews standards and restrictions which it had no remote intention of applying to the Arabs. By now, the sands were running out for this strange adventure in consular diplomacy. Macdonald was recalled from his post; I learned privately that his signature of this cable had been looked upon askance by his own superiors. On October 9, Neuville informed me that he had succeeded to the chairmanship of the commission. So eager were the consuls to continue that the commission refused to pass out of existence even after the United Nations had appointed another body as a Palestine Conciliation Commission in December. I find from my records that Nieuwenhuys was still calling on me as late as January 3, 1949, to discuss truce matters. But well before this, its work undone, this body had become a dead letter.

In January 1948 the British officials in charge of Palestine had invited the International Red Cross to help minimize the sufferings caused by the growing conflict between Arabs and Jews. A delegation arrived in March and immediately appealed to both Arabs and Jews to respect the Geneva Convention. They were only a few doctors and nurses, headed by a Swiss Red Cross official, Mr. J. de Reynier. They took over five buildings in Jerusalem, including the government hospital in the Russian Compound. This move was to ensure medical services to both sides impartially, in addition to those provided by Jews and Arabs for themselves.

I soon learned that nowadays even an international organization whose aims and purposes are solely humanitarian, whose very existence depends on its maintaining complete objectivity and dissociating itself from political considerations, does not seem to be free from influence by powerful governments. No one can question the great humanitarian work of the International Red Cross and the invaluable services it has rendered mankind throughout decades. But it is, like all organizations, run by men, and, like all other men, they are not angels. Nor, as I discovered, could this Red Cross team sent to Israel free themselves from their personal predilections, and from a desire to be helpful to the British authorities.

One of the problems the Red Cross had to face in its humanitarian efforts in the Jerusalem zone was uncertainty as to whether the Arabs would respect its flag. As De Reynier himself pointed out, this was the only protection he could afford. Indeed, he insisted that if any attempt were made to add to its purely moral protection, then he could not even extend that much. This was emphasized very early in the career of the Red Cross unit in Jerusalem at a meeting which took place on April 18, to discuss the question of convoys of personnel going up from new Jerusalem to the Hadassah Hospital and the Hebrew University on Mount Scopus. This negotiation took place only a week after the massacre of doctors, nurses, professors and other civilian personnel on the way to Mount Scopus.

Mr. de Reynier opened the meeting by outlining some of the complexities in the international law governing the Red Cross. He stated that his authority in Palestine derived from his invitation by the Palestine government with the agreement of the Arab and Jewish responsible bodies. He said that Hadassah had to choose whether it was going to put its trust in the International Red Cross or in the Hagana. There was no way of mixing the two possibilities. If we chose to put our trust in Hagana, then he had no function. If we chose to trust the International Red Cross, then he would suggest the following program: Hadassah's convoys, in unarmed trucks and ambulances, would leave Jerusalem at fixed times each day. He would meet the convoys and search them, and if the material was clearly hospital material and supplies, and the passengers hospital personnel, he would inform the Arabs that the convoy had the protection of the Red Cross and must be allowed to pass without hindrance. He believed he could get the Arabs to agree to this. This he called a minimum program.

He also put forward a maximum program which involved the complete neutralization of the whole of Mount Scopus. He would also ask for the neutralization of the Augusta Victoria Institute, between Mount Scopus and the Mount of Olives, which was in Arab hands; but this neutralization would not extend as far as the Sheikh Jarrah quarter. In case of the acceptance of this program, the university would have to be closed because, in his opinion, a professor could serve as a military expert or a member of the military forces.

This was, to say the least, a peculiar request. Technically it may have met the requirements of international rules, as far as the Red Cross was concerned. In practice, it meant closing the university, the loss to Israel of an important position on Mount Scopus, leaving the key position of Sheikh Jarrah in Arab hands, and exposing the neutralized Mount Scopus to the doubtful protection of Arab regard for the Red Cross. In the course of questioning, Mr. de Reynier made it clear that the presence of an Army escort car in a hospital convoy would give the other side grounds for attacking. In such a case the International Red Cross could not intervene. He also said that, if we accepted his minimum program, the Red Cross would extend protection to our convoy only as far as the hospital gate. He regarded the hospital at that time as having the "attributes of a fortress." Finally, he was fair enough to point out to us that any arrangement with the Red Cross would be purely a matter of confidence and that there was no absolute security that he could promise.

Both programs were, of course, out of the question for us, since we had already learned to our cost that the Arabs would not make and could not enforce the kind of commitments the Red Cross demanded. Mr. de Reynier was soon to learn this himself when, on May 23, while traveling in Jerusalem, he was hauled out of his car by Arab National Guard men, undressed and beaten. On the same day it was reported that a woman Red Cross worker was shot in the head near Lydda.

Several of the Red Cross doctors served with devotion and helped wholeheartedly and at risk to themselves, as behooved Red Cross men. We could not feel the same about their chief, nor were we alone in considering Mr. de Reynier a very intractable person. Count Bernadotte, himself one of the world leaders of the Red Cross, had as little luck with him as we had. So it was not long before the Red Cross began to show signs of the political appetite and tendency to exceed its terms of reference which in the end vitiated much of what it had tried to do.

One of the functions which the Red Cross was able to perform, with the co-operation of both sides, was supervision of the treatment of prisoners of war under the Geneva Convention rules, which were reasonably well observed. At the time of the first truce there were 100 Arab prisoners in a camp in Jerusalem. These consisted of Iraqi, Syrian and Transjordan soldiers. They were visited by De Reynier. Red Cross representatives stationed in Tel Aviv also supervised the humane treatment of the Arab civilians and refugee population in Jaffa, including especially those who were temporarily interned there. In Arab hands, at this time, were 625 Jewish prisoners in the Mafrak camp in Transjordan, and in another camp outside the Jerusalem area we held some 1,200 Arab prisoners.

The Jewish prisoners of war posed certain problems. In the Old City surrender agreement it had been arranged that noncombatant personnel would not be taken prisoners but would be interned. Nevertheless, among the prisoners were forty-five old people, one of them a man of eighty and ten of them septuagenarians, and thirty-five youngsters, one a boy fourteen years old. In a report on August 16 submitted by our Foreign Ministry to the International Red Cross, it was pointed out that the return of these persons had not yet been achieved.

We also had to complain that the local Red Cross unit made its reports only to Geneva on its visits to the prisoner-of-war camps. It would have been easy for them to have prevented a great deal of inflammatory propaganda if they had made public in Jerusalem the positive results of their visits to camps where Arabs were being held.

On the credit side of the Red Cross account is to be placed the successful return of twenty-four Jewish prisoners of war on November 30 after six months of captivity. They were all aged or ill and were exchanged for Arab prisoners of war. Negotiations for these exchanges began through the intervention of the Red Cross at the end of September. Egyptian agreement in principal was secured, but the big obstacle was Transjordan. Their refusal was clear enough. We held only some twenty Legionaires, while they held 700 of our people. At the end of 1948 there were still 600 Jewish prisoners of war in the Mafrak camp in Transjordan. There was also the question of missing persons. We listed as missing some 600 persons, of whom we believed 400 were dead and 200 held by the Transjordanians as well as by the Iraqis, Syrians and Egyptians, without notification to the Red Cross.

As early as April 22, the Red Cross announced that it would set up security zones for women and children under the Red Cross flag. These would be called Geneva Homes and were to be situated at the King David Hotel, Terra Sancta and Government House. They were to serve as refuges for noncombatants when fighting took place in their vicinity. These three places, however, were remote from any thickly populated Jewish area. What their real purpose was is not quite clear, but one thing is certain: no Jewish women or children found shelter from the bombing in such zones. This led to a suspicion among the Jews that the Red Cross representatives, through their close contact with the British when they arrived in the country, had come completely under their influence and, possibly through failure to realize the political implications of what they were doing, were serving British interests.

There was, in any case, no response to the request of the Jewish authorities to set up such zones in exposed places where Jews dwelt in large numbers. Our impression was that the British were interested in ensuring that these particular buildings should not fall into our hands, and that Mr. de Reynier was prepared to help in this direction. In any case, the Arabs entirely ignored the presence of such zones when they bombed the city. The same was true of hospitals. Hadassah, in the Street of the Prophets, and the Bikur Holim Hospital were heavily shelled and suffered direct hits in which patients were injured.

The King David Hotel episode was a curious one. The Red Cross had declared the hotel part of one of its security zones. When the United Nations moved out of it, just before the end of the truce, we moved in. The Consular Truce Commission wanted it, and so did the Red Cross. On July 18 De Reynier came to see me; he was all honey on the outside. But he told me that our refusal to turn over the hotel to him showed a lack of good will and that he was therefore thinking of discontinuing Red Cross work in Jerusalem. I politely informed him that it seemed to me it was the Red Cross which wished to give up this security zone, as well as the Y.M.C.A. Building across the street, which we suspected to be a center of Arab espionage. There were no residents in the neighborhood anyway, the King David Hotel was empty, and I could see no need for its maintenance as a refuge for nonexistent refugees.

On July 22, to our regret, the flag of the International Red Cross was lowered from its central office in the Y.M.C.A. In the Holy City the flag of international aid had failed to maintain itself. But the fault lay with those to whom the flag had been entrusted. We had welcomed the delegation and contributed willingly from our depleted funds to their activities. The fact is that, from the very outset, the activities of the Red Cross delegation were guided into the wrong channels. Instead of adhering strictly to traditional Red Cross functions they developed a desire to deal with political problems. The duty to help women and children in the city of Jerusalem, subjected to constant shelling, was neglected for weeks on end. Instead efforts were made to place Jerusalem under the Red Cross flag, a matter which was in the exclusive jurisdiction of the United Nations. When this effort failed, Red Cross efforts were directed to setting up security zones. Thus control of these areas was gained, but no help was forthcoming to refugees there. In effect the representatives of the Red Cross in Jerusalem performed a minimum of their traditional functions and even those only after pressure from us. Upon our refusal to return the King David Hotel to them they withdrew into Government House and sulked.

In contrast to the attitude of the Red Cross in Jerusalem, the Red

Cross representative in Tel Aviv, Dr. P. Gaillard, maintained the most harmonious relations with the Jewish authorities and also gave great assistance to the Arabs of Jaffa. He did not sit tight in a safety zone but exposed himself courageously to the same dangers that all those living in the district were obliged to face.

At the end of September 1948, the Red Cross departed suddenly from their zone south of Jerusalem around Government House, and from the city as a whole. They gave no prior notice of their intention, despite the fact that De Reynier had given an assurance that the area would not be evacuated without prior notice to both sides. There had been rumors which reached me of the move, and when I taxed De Reynier with them he had answered, somewhat vaguely, that he had "not received instructions to haul down the Red Cross flag." I asked him for a clearer answer but his second reply did not satisfy me either. I therefore wrote to him and said that I concluded from his letters that the Red Cross did not intend to leave the building. To this I received no reply.

On September 30, nevertheless, they left Government House without notifying us, thus breaking their promise to me that if they decided to evacuate they would let me know in good time beforehand. Without any consultation with the Jewish authorities, they handed Government House over to the United Nations observers, who put up their flag as the Red Cross flag went down. When I met the head of the U.N. observers, Colonel Millett, at 6 P.M. and spoke about the Red Cross zone, he did not mention that the Red Cross would be leaving. There is little doubt that they had a secret arrangement with the U.N. staff which they concealed from us. I radioed Shertok to protest to the Red Cross at Geneva against this conduct, which constituted a deliberate deception.

XII

COUNT BERNADOTTE

ᒐ ᒐ ᒐ ᒐ ᒐ ᒐ ᒐ ᒐ ᒐ ᒐ ᒐ ᒐ

UNLIKE the Consular Truce Commission, the United Nations Mediator and his staff officers and senior observers were outstandingly able men. They had been specially picked for this assignment; many of them had remarkable records in the armies or navies where they had served. Nearly all of them looked with pride on their new assignment as international civil servants. At our specific request, Count Bernadotte agreed on June 14 to appoint no British officers as observers in Jerusalem, and his senior staff brought to their work none of that subtle subconscious bias which infected almost all Westerners who had lived in Jerusalem under the British mandate. Yet in the end these men, too, failed to accomplish their high mission or to fulfill the bright hopes of people all over the world who wanted the United Nations to rise above Big Power politics and function as the representative of mankind.

They were defeated, it seems to me now, by the same forces which had wrecked every attempt to work out a rational solution in Palestine for a generation. To close one's eyes to power politics does not eliminate them; for even the most trivial decisions, as for forty guards to protect the Latrun pumping station, Count Bernadotte was dependent on the Great Powers. To accept the fiction that the Arabs constituted as yet a nation, or several nations, willing and able to make, commitments and then carry them out does not make that fiction a fact. Finally, to revise their mandate as they proceed, to play by ear and to put forward new proposals without authority may be a very human response by men faced with unprecedented assignments, but it wrecks the only process which, slow as it is, may eventually substitute the rule of law for the rule of force.

I am now strongly inclined to think that no mediator and no staff could have overcome these difficulties in 1948. The Jews were right, I believe, in doing everything in our power to try to help the Mediator, but I believe we were also right in our knowledge, acquired through sacrifice and suffering, that in the end we would have what our own strength, moral and physical, could hold—no more and no less. The world seems to be a little richer for what was learned during this experiment in direct United Nations action. But this does not change the fact that the experiment ended in failure. The tragedy that cost Count Bernadotte his life was played out against the somber background of still another demonstration that good will and good intentions are not enough to establish peace and justice among men.

There was plenty of good will among Count Bernadotte's senior advisers and observers. General Aage Lundström, his first chief of staff, was a tall, blond, distinguished-looking Swedish gentleman who could as well have been a university professor as a soldier. His successor in this post, General W. E. Riley, was a stocky, tough-looking Irishman with a winning smile, a fair-minded, sensible officer of the United States Marines who had the courage of his convictions. Our relations with both, as with nearly all the U.N. observers, were steady and good. There were occasional intelligence reports that a few of them had been instructed by their own governments to gather strategic and political information, and we had reason to think that some Belgians were operating in this way for the British. But most of these men behaved with great correctness and with an obvious desire to do a fair and honest job, even at the risk of their lives. We organized a staff of Jewish ex-officers of various Allied armies to maintain constant liaison with them. They were on night-and-day duty and rendered exemplary service, under the leadership of Emil Pikovsky, a local industrialist who had served in the French Army.

There were too few observers. The situation called for several times their number. The record of my correspondence with them during the summer months reads like that of my protests to the Consular Truce Commission: unending lists of Arab violations of the truce which they were powerless either to prevent or to punish. As late as Christmas Day, an American journalist, Freda Kirchwey, watched some of these observers busily taking notes in the huge basement library of Notre Dame, the French hospice just across the street from the New Gate of the Old City. "What, I wondered, came of this daily chronicle of falling shells and mortars?" she reported. "The young Frenchmen conferred and scribbled in the dim light. And out beyond the walls, a few feet away, the Arab invaders held their positions and fired at will—frequently at truce observers. The authority of the United Nations did not seem very impressive in the basement of Notre Dame."

It was Count Bernadotte himself who unwittingly helped to undermine the authority of the United Nations in Palestine, and chiefly by one major mistake: his gradual relinquishment of his task of mediating between the Arabs and the Jews and his preoccupation instead with the self-assigned effort to work out an independent, new solution of the Palestine problem. Although the United Nations had appointed him to work out a peace along the lines it had already set down, in the partition resolution, Count Bernadotte named himself a committee of one to draft a new partition. He thus made himself vulnerable to all the intrigue and pressure of the Arabs and the British. He forfeited the confidence of all those— especially the Jews—who had slowly and reluctantly come to accept the compromises hammered out by the United Nations during 1947. The wisest man in the world and the ablest negotiator might well have hesitated before trying to put forward a solution of his own.

In his posthumously published book, *To Jerusalem,* Count Bernadotte has left an interesting record of how he decided on this course, and it is abundantly evident that he started his mission with serious reservations about the settlement he was supposed to enforce. Even before his first visit to the Middle East, he asked the French Foreign Minister, Georges Bidault, whether France would be "willing to agree to Jerusalem being made an Arab center." Bidault replied that if Jerusalem were made an Arab center the whole Christian world would join in a new Crusade. It is surely remarkable that the United Nations Mediator-elect should already have harbored an idea so glaringly inconsistent with the United Nations decision which had been adopted after exhaustive inquiry and debate as the basis for the Palestine settlement.

Instead of coming straight to Palestine to inspect conditions on the spot, the Mediator's first step was to visit the Arab states which had openly and arrogantly defied the United Nations, to consult with the Arab leaders. The reason he gave for this procedure was that "it was the Arabs, after all, who were adopting the offensive and it was consequently with them that we ought to seek first contact in any question of a Truce or Cease-fire."

He saw the Egyptian Prime Minister, Nokrashy Pasha, on May 29, and Azzam Pasha, the secretary general of the Arab League, a few days later. Both men argued to him that the Security Council, in appointing him as Mediator, had repudiated the General Assembly's resolution on November 29, 1947 There was, of course, neither political nor legal basis for this argument, but Bernadotte from this early date insisted that he had "a free hand as far as putting forward new proposals for the future of Palestine was concerned." This naturally diverted him from his real job, which was to work out a truce and an armistice. Much more disastrously, it was all but decisive in convincing the Arabs that intransigence and violence could wreck the settlement at which the United Nations had arrived. I learned about Arab mentality at first hand many years ago when watching an Arab demonstration; the crowd kept shouting two slogans—"The religion of Mohammed is by the sword" and "The government is with us." The Arabs are past masters at playing one side against another, and at securing gains for themselves from any situation in which those negotiating with them are uncertain or at cross-purposes with each other. This is not a statement made out of any anti-Arab animus; the Western oil companies learned its truth before the Jews did. It was a deep misfortune for everyone, including the Arabs themselves, that Count Bernadotte never learned it.

So on June 27 he submitted to our government, through John Reedman, who was special representative of the United Nations Secretary General, a document called "Suggestions for the Future of Palestine." Although he emphasized that the suggestions were submitted "with no intention of preciseness or finality" and were designed "solely to explore the possible basis for further discussions and mediation," it was obvious that such a plan, emanating from the Mediator, would be understood by the world at large, and by any party benefiting from them, as creating a new starting point and would vitally influence the further course of events. Indeed, Count Bernadotte stated in concluding his introductory statement that "if . . . these or subsequent suggestions, if any should emerge, are rejected as a basis for discussion, . . . I shall promptly report the circumstance fully to the Security Council and shall feel free to submit such conclusions to the Security Council as I may consider appropriate." There was no doubt in our minds as we read this document that if we rejected its proposals we would be placed at a serious disadvantage in the further proceedings at Lake Success.

One further paragraph in the introductory statement of the Mediator's suggestions deserves to be quoted in full. "Despite the present conflict," the Mediator said, "there is a common denominator in Palestine which, happily, is acceptable to and affirmed by both sides. This is the recognition of the necessity for peaceful relations between Arabs and Jews in Palestine and of the principle of economic unity." Since the Arabs had repeatedly declared that they regarded the Jewish community in Palestine as a foreign growth, which they would like to wipe off the map, and had declared their implacable opposition to the United Nations' proposals which were designed to afford the Jews the opportunity to safeguard their future, it is not easy to take this statement seriously. On the assumption that Count Bernadotte really believed that it was true, it is not difficult to understand why his proposals were built on a completely unsound foundation.

The suggestions proposed a union of a Jewish state and an Arab state in all the territory of the original mandate, including Transjordan. Boundaries would be determined by negotiation. Immigration was to be within the control of each state for two years, after which either one could demand restriction with eventual appeal to the Economic and Social Council of the United Nations. This would have amounted, in effect, to the old British policy of giving the Arabs the right to restrict the admission of Jewish refugees. But the sting of the document was in its tail. This was an annex suggesting "certain territorial arrangements," which

might be along the following lines:

1. Inclusion of the whole or part of the Negev in Arab territory.

2. Inclusion of the whole or part of Western Galilee in Jewish territory.

3. Inclusion of the City of Jerusalem in Arab territory with municipal autonomy for the Jewish community and special arrangements for the protection of the Holy Places.

4. Consideration of the status of Jaffa.

5. Establishment of a free port at Haifa, the area of the free port to include the refineries and terminals.

The Soviet delegate to the United Nations, Gromyko, pointed out at once that "in making those proposals the Mediator and those whose interests were served by them absolutely ignored the fact that a resolution on the future of Palestine already exists; in other words, they ignored the General Assembly resolution of November 29, 1947. It may be said that in discussing the comparatively narrow question of the truce that fact can be left aside; but that is not so, because the publication of those new general proposals in connection with the truce added fuel to the flames and went a long way to encourage those who started the fighting in Palestine. Such proposals increase the chaos in Palestine, inflame the struggle taking place there and, by inciting the Arabs still more against the Jews, exasperate nationalist feelings on both sides; and those who may be interested in prolonging the fighting in Palestine, though they may stand aside from the whole matter, are warming their hands at the flame."

It is easy to understand the shock that was felt not only by the members of the Provisional Government but by all Jews, practically without exception, at these suggestions and at the line of thinking which lay behind them. There could be no question of their being accepted as even the most tentative basis for discussion.

The Provisional Government's reply, dated July 5, opened by pointing out that the Mediator appeared to ignore the General Assembly's resolution, which "remains the only internationally valid adjudication on the question of the future government of Palestine." At the same time the Mediator had not fully taken into account the effective establishment of the state of Israel and other territorial changes which had resulted from the repulse of the Arab attack.

The reply then recalled that the Jewish people had accepted the settlement of November 29, 1947, as "a compromise entailing heavy sacrifices on its part, and the territory assigned to the Jewish state as an irreducible minimum," and expressed the conviction that the territorial provisions now stood in need of improvement, in view of the perils revealed by Arab aggression and of Israel's success in repelling this aggression. In addition, the inclusion of the Arab portion of Palestine in the territory of Transjordan would "fundamentally change the context of the boundary problem." This fact would also basically affect the provision for an economic union, which we were now asked to apply to a partner state different from the nation of Palestinian Arabs provided for in the Assembly resolution.

The Provisional Government could not agree to "any encroachment upon or limitation of the free sovereignty of the people of Israel in its independent state." This applied particularly in regard to immigration policy. "Complete and unqualified freedom to determine the size and composition of Jewish immigration was the very essence of the Jewish claim to statehood," the Israel reply declared.

Particularly painful was the suggestion concerning the future of Jerusalem, which the Provisional Government described as "disastrous," a word which I regarded as understatement. The proposal showed an utter disregard of the fundamental facts of the problem: "the historic associations of Judaism with the Holy City; the unique place occupied by Jerusalem in Jewish history and present-day Jewish life; the Jewish inhabitants' two-thirds majority in the city before the commencement of Arab aggression—a majority greatly increased since then as a result of Arab evacuation; the fact that the whole of Jerusalem, with only a few minor exceptions, is now in Jewish hands; and not least, the fact that after an exhaustive study of the problem and as a result of an overwhelming concensus of Christian opinion in its midst, the General Assembly resolved that Jerusalem be placed under an international regime."

The statement emphasized that the Jewish people, the state of Israel and the Jews of Jerusalem would resist the imposition of Arab domination over Jerusalem with all the force at their command.

It will readily be understood what an effect this proposal had on us in Jerusalem itself. After six months of siege, starvation and bombardment, after the entire civilized world had left us to our fate and only the determination and heroism of the soldiers and the people had saved the city, we were now expected to put ourselves and the city, to which the hearts of Jews the world over have turned since the dawn of our history, under the rule of those Arabs who had done their best to starve us into submission and who would have massacred men, women and children if we had not successfully defended ourselves. And this incredible suggestion was put forward as part of "a reasonable framework of reference within which the two parties may find it possible to continue their consultations with me toward the end of a peaceful adjustment"!

Throughout the summer, Count Bernadotte's suggestions were disputed in diplomatic notes, in the newspapers and in general discussion throughout Palestine. As the truce gradually became more stable in the weeks after July 19, both Arabs and Jews turned increasingly to the problem of restoring normal life in their areas, and as they did so the unreality of the Mediator's plan became steadily more marked. It was a fairly spectacular gamble in one-man, personal diplomacy, but the odds against it were compounded by all the earnestness with which men were trying to adjust to the hard reality of things as they were.

On July 1 Bernadotte arrived in Jerusalem, and we met that evening. Despite the fact that we were all deeply distressed at his suggestions, I decided to discuss current matters as if they did not exist. I told him we would be prepared to consent to troops being withdrawn from Mount Scopus and replaced by an agreed number of Jewish policemen in our Hebrew University and Hadassah Hospital area and an agreed number of Arab police in their Augusta Victoria area. He suggested that our police be gradually replaced by U.N. observers. I was reluctant to accede to this proposal without first referring the matter to Ben Gurion, and I told him so. I protested vigorously at the Arab procrastination in implementing their promises to enable the flow of water to Jerusalem to be resumed. He admitted that this conduct of the Arabs was contrary to the truce agreement and promised to try again to put this right the next day when he met the Arabs. I spoke strongly about our right under the truce agreement and the U.N. resolutions to have free access to the Wailing Wall. He admitted the Arabs had agreed to this and promised to see what he could do about this too.

On July 9 the twenty-eight days' truce came to an end. The Arabs refused to renew the truce and reopened hostilities. The Mediator, therefore, decided to go to Lake Success and report to the Security Council on the situation in person.

The Arabs had replied to the Mediator's suggestions by proposing the creation of a unitary state of Palestine, with vague and indefinite safeguards for the Jewish minority. This proposal, of course, had been put forward repeatedly during the lengthy discussions which preceded the adoption of the November 29, 1947, resolution. It had been unanimously rejected by the United Nations Special Committee on Palestine and turned down by a decisive majority of the General Assembly. It might have been expected that the U.N. Mediator would point out this fact. However he might interpret the meaning of the term "mediation," it could hardly be taken to include the right to effect a complete reversal of a United Nations decision, adopted after lengthy inquiry and full deliberation.

In his statement to the Security Council the Israel representative, Eban, laid particular emphasis on the injustice of the Mediator's reference to the problem of "unrestricted immigration into the Jewish area of Palestine." He pointed out that if they were to inquire into the population problems of the Near East they would certainly find that they arose from "the pressure of excessive population in Egypt, and the consequences of an inadequate population throughout the entire area of the Fertile Crescent." It was absurd to portray the small state of Israel, approaching its first million of population, as a potential threat to the far-flung Arab empire with forty millions of population. He declared emphatically that immigration into Israel was the business of Israel alone. And, indeed, any attempt at outside interference with the right of Israel to provide a home for any Jew wishing to settle in it would make nonsense of the very basis of its sovereignty and one of the fundamental purposes for which the state had been created.

It was not surprising that the Jewish press and public opinion, especially in Jerusalem, were shocked by Count Bernadotte's attitude. "Why does the Count not understand the feelings of the Jews, which were deeply hurt by his decisions as regards immigration and the future· of Jerusalem?" a newspaper editorial asked. The writer pointed out that his approach was surprisingly similar to that of the British. "He wants to keep the scales balanced, even if one party is right and the other wrong, and sacrifices the interests of those in the right on the altar of Arab aggression, as the British did . . . There cannot be equal rights for the aggressor and the victim of aggression."

A similar attitude was expressed at a meeting on July 15 of the Municipal Committee, which comprised representatives of the Vaad Hakehilla (Community Council), the Municipal Council, Agudat Israel and the Jewish quarters of the city. Speakers pointed out that 80 per cent of the population of Jerusalem were Jews, and that nearly all of its territory was occupied by Israeli troops. Had it not been for the truce, it was pointed out, the whole of Jerusalem would undoubtedly have been in Jewish hands. It was unanimously decided to ask for an urgent meeting with representatives of the Provisional Government and to place before them the demand of the people of Jerusalem that the city should be declared part of the

state of Israel. Only the Agudat Israel representatives abstained
from voting, as they did not believe that the time was opportune
for demonstrative resolutions.

It was generally believed by our people that the Mediator's surprising proposal in regard to Jerusalem, which flew in the face of
the fact that we had established a broad territorial corridor and
secure lines of communication between Jerusalem and the rest of
the country, originated with the British. It was obviously designed
to increase the prestige and power of King Abdullah of Transjordan, who was an ally of Britain, and thus enable the British to
strengthen their foothold in the Middle East.

Even Count Bernadotte must have been impressed by what he
learned during the summer of the true state of affairs in Jerusalem.
When his last report to the United Nations was submitted on September 18, he had abandoned entirely this notion of turning over
the Holy City to the Arabs. Instead, he recommended that "Jerusalem should be placed under effective United Nations control, with
maximum feasible local autonomy for its Arab and Jewish communities and safeguards for access to the Holy Places."

At a meeting between Count Bernadotte and Shertok on July 26,
one of the main topics of conversation was the question of Jewish
immigration. The first truce had included a provision which the
Mediator interpreted as placing restrictions on the immigration
of men of military age. Since the second truce was of indefinite duration, the Provisional Government could no longer submit to
such restrictions, and indeed it understood the Security Council resolution to mean that there was to be no numerical limitation on
the entry into Israel of men of military age. Shertok added that he
had reason to believe that many members of the Security Council
endorsed this interpretation. Count Bernadotte declined to alter his
interpretation, although, he said, the Israel government was at liberty to take the matter up again with the Council and attempt to
secure a clear ruling.

The Mediator also brought up the question of the Arab refugees
and proposed that they be allowed to return to Israel. In reply,
Shertok pointed out that this would facilitate the renewal of the
war by the Arabs. So long as the threat of the renewal of the war
existed and no peace treaty had been signed, Israel saw no possibility of even considering the return of Arab refugees, as this would
constitute a military, political, economic and social problem of the
first magnitude. The government, therefore, rejected this proposal,

but left the question open to be dealt with in peace negotiations. In spite of this statement, Count Bernadotte repeated, in a note dated July 28, his proposal that "a limited number, to be determined in consultation with the Mediator, and especially those formerly living in Jaffa and Haifa, be permitted to return to their homes as from 15 August."

On August 1 the Provisional Government, while declaring itself not unmindful of the plight of the Arabs who as a result of the present war find themselves uprooted from their homes, reiterated its inability to agree to the proposal. It pointed out that the return of thousands of displaced Arabs during the truce would seriously handicap Israel's war effort by bringing into its territory a politically explosive and economically destitute element at a time when the Arab states had resumed the fighting despite the truce. "In these circumstances," the reply declared, "the mere fact that the Security Council has ordered the truce to be of unlimited duration is not a firm enough foundation on which the Provisional Government could build so far-reaching a measure as the re-admission *en masse* of Arab refugees."

When the Arab states were ready to conclude a peace treaty with Israel, the government said, this problem, which was a direct effect of Arab aggression, would come up for constructive solution as part of a general settlement. Then it would be possible to bring into account such questions as the long-term interests of the Jewish and Arab populations, the stability of the state of Israel and the durability of the basis of peace between it and its neighbors, the actual position and fate of the Jewish communities in the Arab countries, the responsibility of the Arab governments for their war of aggression and their liability for reparations.

When the war had finally petered out, the population structure of the country had completely altered. The great majority of the Arabs who had lived in the area held by the Israel forces were no longer in their homes, but in the part of the country in Arab hands. Tens of thousands of them had gone farther away and were in the Lebanon, Syria and Transjordan. The greater part of these Arabs to this day make up the group known as the Palestine Arab refugees, most of whom live in refugee camps. A large number settled down comfortably in Jordan, where they became an important factor in the life of the country.

I can testify to the fact that we Jews were more than surprised when we learned of the large-scale exodus of Arabs from their towns and villages. We never dreamed they would react in this way in the struggle which followed the November 29 resolution. We realized the advantages this gave us. The great tasks of winning the war, setting up a state and maintaining its integrity would now be easier. We would not be saddled with large and hostile Arab settlements in our rear when we were fighting, and thereafter with a mainly unfriendly population of Arabs living among us. As matters turned out, we were a homogeneous group of people united in the common struggle to build a Jewish nation. Indeed, the expression heard on everybody's lips, when we realized that the Arabs were picking themselves up and clearing out of the country, was "the hand of God." Others, after our victory was clear, were wont to say we won because of two factors, the bravery of our soldiers and the mass exodus of the Arab population.

Although there were instances of Arabs who abandoned their villages only when they were actually attacked, and some where the inhabitants fled before our advancing troops, there is no doubt that the overwhelming majority of the Arabs were not driven out by the Jews, but left their homes of their own accord. Many, particularly the well-to-do, decided that they did not wish to face the dangers to life and limb inherent in the armed struggle that began in December 1947. These left in December and January in their thousands from Jerusalem, Jaffa, Haifa and other towns for the safety of the Lebanon, Syria and Transjordan. Other thousands left when the districts they lived in began to come into the area of fire between Arab and Jewish forces. Many tens of thousands left on the advice of their political leaders, who assured them that the Jews would be crushed in a few days after May 15, when the Arab armies would invade Palestine, and then they would be able to return to their homes and to take over the houses and property of the Jews as well, when we had been destroyed or driven into the sea.

Thus in Haifa the Arabs sought British help to leave the city. On April 29 the Arab National Committee of that city wrote Major General Hugh Stockwell, the officer commanding British forces in northern Palestine:

You will doubtless recollect that at the meeting on the 23rd inst. you promised to provide this committee with the necessary transport to facilitate the evacuation of the Arab inhabitants from Haifa. We were assured that about 80 trucks would be placed at our disposal . . . Hagana people prevented yesterday three trucks

*loaded with evacuees from leaving the town . . . The general con-
dition of the persons awaiting evacuation is distressing, and unless
immediate action be taken to provide the committee with the necessary transport to complete the evacuation of the Arab inhabitants
without delay it will be impossible to describe the consequences.*

Those who remained found in the subsequent decade how sincere
was the Jewish appeal to them. They were accepted as equals in
trade unions. They saw a network of primary and secondary schools
in their towns and villages. Electricity was extended to their homes,
piped water brought into their houses and fields. They shared in
the tractor stations, agricultural expertise and all the advantages
the state afforded its citizens. Several Arabs sit in the Knesset,
Israel's parliament. But all this was in the future.

The problem of these refugees remains to this day, and it is one
about which no Israeli citizen is happy. Our offer to negotiate
their future as soon as the Arabs are prepared to negotiate a peace
remains an open offer. The tragedy is that no Arab leaders have yet
appeared who are prepared to recognize that Israel is on the map
to stay. So the refugee camps have been maintained as breeding
places of enmity against the Jews, and time is more likely than the
United Nations or traditional diplomacy to liquidate one of the
unhappiest consequences of the 1947-48 war.

Conclusive proof of the hypocrisy of the Arab refusal to entertain
the proposals that these refugees be taken out of their camps and
settled in Arab lands was provided by the Prime Minister of Jordan,
Hazza el Mejalle. When in the summer of 1959 there were signs of
the ex-Mufti Haj Amin el Husseini wishing to revive the idea of a
separate state for the Arabs of former Palestine, the Jordan Premier
forgot the protestations of the Arab political leaders that the only
solution of the problem was to return the refugees to Israel. He
now proclaimed that all the occupants of the camps in Jordan were
no longer refugees but citizens of Jordan. His government would
welcome the refugees in other Arab lands who wished to settle in
Jordan.

On August 2, Count Bernadotte was informed by the Israel
government of its intention to proclaim Jerusalem occupied territory. Shertok explained to him the legal and economic reasons
that had prompted the government to take this decision, and the
Count did not object. The same day he visited Jerusalem. The
Arabs marked his visit with a hail of shots fired by their snipers at

the Jewish quarters. A number of mortar shells were also fired. The shooting began shortly after his arrival and continued throughout the night.

The next morning Count Bernadotte called on me at the Jewish Agency offices, accompanied by Colonel Brunsson, Colonel Begley and the three Truce Commission consuls. Among the matters discussed were breaches of the truce, the problem of assuring the city's water supply, and the demilitarization of Jerusalem. We pointed out that though the Provisional Government had not excluded negotiations on this as one possible measure for the protection of Jerusalem, the removal of Jewish forces and arms would be a terribly grave risk, and before discussing that measure other and more urgent steps should be dealt with. The first thing was to stop the shellings and sniping and to make the truce real. I maintained that at the moment, in view of the constant violation of the truce by the Arabs, the atmosphere was not yet ripe for discussing demilitarization.

I reiterated our position on the question of food supplies for Jerusalem. Jerusalem was a city in Jewish occupation, firmly linked up with the rest of Israel, and we had freedom of movement on the Burma Road and hence free access to Jerusalem. There could be no question of our right to bring in food. I insisted that as the period of the truce was not fixed and might last for months there should be no restriction of the quantity brought in. Count Bernadotte would not accept our contention on this point, and we finally agreed to let the question remain open for a few days until we saw whether the Arabs would fulfill their previous undertaking to let water come through to the city, when we would return to the question. Ultimately my approach to the problem was proved right, since the truce went on indefinitely and the U.N. observers, realizing the absurdity of their position, stopped trying to check the quantities of food coming into the city.

Count Bernadotte again came to Jerusalem on August 10 and he continued to discuss these questions with me. We met at the Belgian consulate rather late at night. With me were Ben Zvi and the mayor, Daniel Auster. Once again the Arab Legion signalized the Mediator's visit by a flagrant violation of the truce. Throughout the entire night they staged a heavy attack, of an intensity we had not known since the second truce began. This full-scale military attack was later described by the Arabs as an act of "irregulars."

During this visit some of the Stern Gang staged a demonstration

against the Mediator. As he was entering the Belgian consulate, a
number of young men and women sat in front of the building in
jeeps. They were displaying posters which read: "Stockholm is
yours; Jerusalem is ours"; "Your work is in vain; we are here." The
posters were signed "Israel Freedom Fighters." When I received
word of what was happening I telephoned to Colonel Dayan, who
had been named commander of the Jerusalem area on August 4,
and requested him to have the demonstrators dispersed. In a manner
characteristic of him, Dayan jumped into an armored car, drove to
the consulate and told the demonstrators to go home, and that was
the end of the incident. This theatrical demonstration was distaste-
ful and annoying, as much to us as to Count Bernadotte, but it is
hardly likely that anyone would have remembered it had it not been
for the crime which was committed over a month later. There was,
of course, no reason for us to take it seriously at the time. Bernadotte evidently had a similar view of the matter, for he made no reference whatever about it to me.

On September 12, General Lundstrom told me that the Count
was thinking of moving his headquarters from Rhodes to Government House, so as to be nearer the center of affairs. I pointed out
that the Iraqi Prime Minister had been threatening to renew the
attack on us, and that it might therefore be unwise to expose the
Mediator to the dangers of residing in such a spot. We might be
blamed if anything happened to him, and I was reluctant to take
the responsibility. I suggested that Haifa would be a less dangerous
place for him. General Lundstrom wrote the following note on this
talk in his epilogue to Count Bernadotte's book:

*It had already been decided that Folke Bernadotte was to call on
Dr. Joseph, the Jewish Military Governor of Jerusalem, at 6:30
P.M. It was now settled that before that we should go and see
Government House . . . Government House had been handed over
by the British Government to the Red Cross, which, in turn, with
the permission of the British, offered to hand it on to the United
Nations. We had come to the conclusion that a transfer of headquarters to Government House was not practicable. The supply
question alone, as regards water and food, presented obstacles. It
was also too far from Kalandia airfield, and to reach that meant
passing through both the Jewish and Arab lines with all the complications that might follow. Finally it would be difficult to heat
this enormous building during the winter months.*

In spite of this result of our investigation, I felt that it would be valuable to hear the Jewish view on the matter. I therefore went to see the Military Governor, Dr. Joseph. He received us with unusual graciousness in his beautiful villa. We admired his distinguished picture collection and large library of gramophone records, from which he played us Sibelius' Finlandia—*a most unusual introduction to negotiations in Palestine. The next time I was to hear these strains was at Folke Bernadotte's funeral a few weeks later, when he himself had asked that* Finlandia *should be played.*

Our first step if war should break out again would be to occupy the Red Cross Zone, said Dr. Joseph. Count Bernadotte would then be in the very center of the fighting. Besides that, I should like to point out that in Government House he would be completely at the mercy of the irregular bands all about him. I cannot imagine anything worse than that anything should happen to the Count. My political and personal views coincide here. I don't like it at all! he ended. Little did he know then how prophetic his words were to prove. It was on the return from the visit to Government House that the murder took place.

The records of the Hadassah Medical Organization for Friday, September 17, show that "at approximately 5:15 P.M., Count Folke Bernadotte and Colonel André Pierre Serot were brought in dead to the casualty clearing station of Hadassah Hospital A." A few minutes later the terrible news was telephoned to me at home, where I was expecting Count Bernadotte for tea. Here is the memorandum I dictated on the following day, setting out the facts as I knew them at the time:

Yesterday we were informed that Count Bernadotte and his party would be coming into the city across the Mandelbaum line at 2 P.M. The information was given to the Liaison Office, who were to look after the necessary arrangements. In the afternoon from four to five, I was at the office of the southern-area military administration, where I had a conference on current problems with Major Maurice Bassan, Joshua Simon, Ivri of the Field Security Service, Arnold Spaer [my legal assistant] and Zvi Wachs [my military secretary]. We concluded our conference shortly after five o'clock. As we were standing outside, several United Nations cars passed us. I did not notice Count Bernadotte, but as it later transpired these were three cars of his party returning from a visit to Government House.

From Major Bassan's office I proceeded to the German Colony,
where I visited some of the newly arrived immigrants we are hous-
ing there. I returned home about 5:30 P.M.

Shortly afterward Major Adler [one of our liaison officers with
the U.N. observers] telephoned and informed me that Count Berna-
dotte and his chief of staff had been assassinated by some men who
had blocked the road with a jeep. I requested him to come to my
home immediately and with him I proceeded to the Hadassah
Hospital, where, I had in the meantime been informed by Dr.
Davis, the bodies of Count Bernadotte and Colonel Serot had been
brought. Before leaving home I had communicated with the Super-
intendent of Police, Yeshurun Schiff, and requested him to meet
me at the hospital. I ordered a strict check to be imposed at once by
the police of all persons seeking to leave the city.

At the Hadassah Hospital, the former English Mission Hospital,
I found Colonel Begley and the Swedish observer, Colonel Frackt.
Moshe Dayan arrived soon afterward. I discussed with Dayan the
action we should take. We agreed there was little doubt that one or
the other of the dissident groups was responsible for the outrage,
and in all likelihood it was the Stern Gang. We agreed that the only
practicable way of dealing with the situation was by a large-scale
military operation to round up the whole Stern Gang. Dayan in-
formed me that he would require the assistance of a special mili-
tary force to carry out such an action. I decided in the circum-
stances to proceed at once to Tel Aviv and suggested that he send
his deputy with me. He proposed instead one of the officers of his
operations staff.

I then spoke to Colonel Begley, who gave me the details of the
occurrence. He said that when the three cars in which they were
driving approached the turn in the road leading up from Katamon
to Rehaviah, near the Silberstein house, a jeep drew up into the
road, blocking their advance. In it were a driver and three other
men dressed as soldiers, wearing Afrika Korps caps. The men
jumped from the jeep and fired from automatic weapons at the
three cars. One of the men approached Bernadotte's car, which was
driven by Begley. The other occupants were Commander Cox, sit-
ting next to Begley, and in the rear of the car General Lundstrom,
sitting nearest to the assailant, Colonel Serot in the center, and
Count Bernadotte. The assailant stuck his weapon into the car;
Begley tried unsuccessfully to seize it. The shots fired hit Serot, who
was killed instantaneously, and Count Bernadotte, who was shot

*in the forehead and face and died a few minutes after he reached
the hospital. I saw all the cars, which were riddled with bullets.
I suggested to Colonel Begley that we would arrange for a guard
of honor to be mounted in the hospital. He said that he thought
they should remove the bodies and the whole affair from the Jewish area and proposed that they should take the bodies to the
Y.M.C.A. He thought of flying the bodies to Haifa with the entire
Swedish party. He asked whether I would wish to come to the
Y.M.C.A. I at once agreed. I also received a report of the occurrence
which corresponded to Begley's report, from Hillman, our liaison
officer, who was escorting Bernadotte's party. He said he recognized
the jeep as one that had been stolen from the United Nations some
time previously by the Lehi.*

*I then proceeded to the Y.M.C.A. with Dayan, Schiff, Alexander
Brodie [Dayan's assistant] and John Adler. At the Y.M.C.A. I found
General Lundstrom. I expressed to him my profound regret at the
terrible outrage. I told him that I proposed to proceed to Tel Aviv
to consult with the head of our government and assured him that
we would do everything in our power to discover and punish the
perpetrators of the crime. He thanked me warmly and said that he
understood how I must feel that this should have happened in
Jerusalem. He told me that he would have to withdraw all the observers at once from Jerusalem. He did not feel he could accept
responsibility for their safety here. I said that the decision would
have to rest with him and I would be unable to accept responsibility,
but from what I knew of the mentality of the dissident groups I
doubted very much whether, after committing an act of such
magnitude, they would carry out attack on ordinary observers on
the same day. General Lundstrom asked the opinion of Dayan, who
expressed views similar to mine. He then asked Colonel Begley's
opinion. The latter was definitely of the opinion that Bernadotte
would not have wanted them to take such a hasty step. He thought
they should remain until they got instructions from headquarters in
Haifa. I offered General Lundstrom a guard to protect the observers
in the Y.M.C.A. He gratefully accepted the offer, and Dayan agreed
to make the necessary arrangements. General Lundstrom told me
that he thought the Swedish government would probably withdraw
all their observers and possibly the French would do the same, as
four of their observers had now been killed. Mr. Macdonald, the
American Consul, who arrived and sat down with us, barely greeted
me. As I was leaving, General Riley arrived from Kalandia Air-*

field; he learned from us that Count Bernadotte had been killed. I also informed him that I should be going to Tel Aviv to consult with the government, as this was not a case for ordinary police action. An American Army major commented to Schiff, "This means the end of your state."

I returned home and Ginsberg of the Public Information Office requested my instructions as to what statement to make to the press. I told him to stick to the bare facts. I also informed him that I had visited the hospital and had expressed our sincere regrets to General Lundstrom. I added a condemnation of the crime and a statement that I would do everything in my power to discover the culprits and bring them to justice. The censor telephoned me to say that he had been allowing correspondents to telegraph the bare facts without any indication as to the nationality of the assailants.

I then left for Tel Aviv at 7:30 P.M. without Dayan's operations officer, as Dayan had in the meantime decided that he could not spare the officer and he would be able to get his instructions directly from headquarters.

In Tel Aviv I met at 10 P.M. with Ben Gurion, Felix Rosenblueth [later Rosen, Minister of Justice in the Provisional Government], Kaplan and the senior members of the General Staff. It was decided that action should be taken at once to arrest and disarm all members of the Stern Gang and to fire at any persons resisting arrest. A considerable number of special troops were to be sent to Jerusalem for the purpose. Instructions to Dayan were formulated in writing and I brought them with me to Jerusalem, where I returned and met with Dayan and Brodie at 1:30 A.M. Dayan informed me that the troops that we had agreed in Tel Aviv would leave for Jerusalem at midnight would not be arriving till 8 A.M. He opposed the application of a curfew before he was ready to commence the operation. I agreed to place at his disposal such police as were available for the purpose, as well as half of my Military Administration Unit to enforce the curfew.

At 8 A.M. I sent for Schiff and Elstein, the officer in charge of the Military Administration Unit, and gave them the necessary instructions in this respect. I also instructed Schiff to telephone the American, French and Belgian consuls general to inform them that I had instructed him to place a police guard around their respective consulates. At 8:45 A.M. I went with Wachs to the Y.M.C.A., where the bodies of Bernadotte and Serot were lying. I paid my respects at the bier and then spoke briefly to General Lundstrom, who informed me of the arrangements for transferring the bodies to Haifa. I also spoke to the French Consul General, to whom I expressed our deep regret at the murder of Colonel Serot. I told him of the action we proposed taking. He was friendly and appreciative. I added that I had given instructions for police guards to be placed at the disposal of the consulate. He thanked me but said that so far as he was concerned this was not necessary, as he had his own guards. He urged me to make such arrangements, in particular, at the Belgian consulate, since the Stern Gang had been threatening the Belgian Consul General for some time.

The cortege left the Y.M.C.A. at about 9:15 A.M., after military honors were accorded by French gendarmes, American guards and Israeli soldiers.

Wachs reported on his conversations of the night before with Etzel and Lehi representatives. Boaz and Shaul of Etzel categorically denied that they had any connection whatsoever with, or any prior knowledge of, the incident. The Stern Gang man said he knew nothing about the matter, declined to say whether any of his men were responsible, and ended up by declaring he was not authorized to speak on behalf of the Stern group.

Police Officer Rabinovitch telephoned me that he was conducting the investigation into the crime. I telephoned several times during the morning to Dayan and Brodie, as I could not understand the delay in starting the operation and putting the curfew into effect. They told me there had been technical hitches in getting the special force up to Jerusalem. Curfew was eventually imposed, and the operation began at 2 P.M. The Lehi camp was surrounded; forty youngsters who were found in the camp offered no resistance. Some arms were found and the troops then proceeded to search other specified localities where it was believed Lehi men were in hiding.

I received a copy of a typewritten note which had been left at various consulates in which a group describing itself as the Fatherland Front declared that they had killed Bernadotte because he was a British agent carrying out British orders. This group is said to be a dissident section of the Stern Gang which has gone underground. At 4 P.M. Brodie came to report on the progress of the operation.

This account varies in only one particular from the account published later by General Lundstrom, who was sitting in the same seat with Count Bernadotte, in his epilogue to *To Jerusalem*. General Lundstrom reported that they had passed me, riding in an armored car, shortly before the shooting. I had no armored car, and when the party passed me I was standing next to the Chrysler I always used. Only on one occasion did I ever use an armored car in Jerusalem. This was when, during the first truce, I had to attend a meeting of the Truce Commission at the French consulate to arrange for the food convoys into Jerusalem. The French Consul General telephoned me not to come, as there was heavy firing at the consulate. I replied that I would get there somehow and, remembering an old armored Ford car Dr. Weizmann sometimes had used in the days of Arab rioting, I telephoned the Jewish Agency, who got it out of the garage and sent it to me. Our liaison officer, Captain Hillman, who was the source of this information, mistook someone else for me.

I cabled at once to Countess Bernadotte: "Deeply grieved at tragic death of your revered husband in our midst. During months it was my privilege to meet with him in fulfillment of his duties as Mediator, he commanded our utmost respect and admiration for his tireless efforts in cause of peace. Pray accept sincerest condolences personally and on behalf Jerusalem Jewry." She replied, "Sincere thanks your message, Estelle Bernadotte."

The first reaction to the murder among the United Nations observers was as serious as might have been expected. Colonel Begley gave the impression that all the observers would be withdrawn from Jerusalem immediately. The Americans were particularly agitated, and one of their men lost control of himself to such an extent that it was necessary to send him to Haifa. There were demands for protection by an international force, and some even went so far as to advocate retaliation. Many of them demanded that the Jews be "taught a lesson" by applying economic sanctions and withdrawing all the observers. General Riley, however, took matters into his own hands and calmed them; otherwise they might have left the city. The French observers controlled their feelings to a much greater extent, which is all the more remarkable since the murder affected them more than it did the Americans.

So ended in tragedy the last mission of Count Bernadotte—a tragedy which cast its shadow over our effort to defend ourselves against the Arab onslaught and consolidate our infant state. The senseless crime of a handful of irresponsible gunmen, who had never even dared to come out into the open as an organized group, who knew that their methods would have been repudiated by the entire Jewish community, had stained our record and inflicted

grievous harm on our cause. The world looked on the murder of
the representative of the United Nations, who had been sent to
bring peace to the Holy Land, as little short of sacrilege, and we
felt that it was a flagrant violation of the ideals of our national
movement, and of everything the Jewish people had stood for
throughout the centuries.

The Fatherland Front, which had signed the note left at various
consulates accepting responsibility for the crime, proved hard to
find. All travel from Jerusalem was prohibited for several days. We
arrested 170 dissident terrorists in Jerusalem and fifty more in Tel
Aviv and other localities. Their leaders appeared nervous and
shocked and denied responsibility for the assassination. On September 21, the Etzel dissidents accepted an ultimatum from the
government and formally disbanded; a delegation of the Herut
movement, which was its political arm, called on me to announce
that they now wished to abandon terrorism and take part in the
political life of the community. The Stern Gang could be broken
up only by police action. Two of its leaders, Nathan Friedman-Yel-
lin and M. Shmuelevitz, were apprehended by us on September 29
and subsequently tried by a military court. But we never succeeded in pinning responsibility on them for the crime, or discover-
ing who had organized and carried it out.

Dr. Ralph Bunche, who was immediately appointed Acting Mediator in place of Count Bernadotte, made two charges which deserved
and received answers from us. His first was an intimation that attacks on the Mediator and his staff in the Israeli press, based partly
on a press conference held by Shertok on September 16, had forced
on the Israel government a measure of responsibility for the climate
of hostility in which the assassination had taken place. Shertok
publicly rejected the implication, pointing out that the crime had
obviously been prepared days in advance and that at his press conference he had gone out of his way to state his conviction that
Bernadotte and his staff were "trying hard to discharge faithfully
their difficult and often dangerous duties." A long and careful report made for the government of Sweden by its Chief Prosecutor,
after a thorough investigation, made it clear that the strongly critical attitude toward Count Bernadotte in Israel, insofar as this was
relevant to a terrorist act, was no product of any press campaign
but an inevitable consequence of his proposals to the parties and
his recommendations to the United Nations, especially his suggestion that Jerusalem be included in the Arab area.

Dr. Bunche's second charge was directed primarily against me as Military Governor of Jerusalem. In a report to the Secretary General of the United Nations on September 27, he claimed that Bernadotte never asked for protection but accepted it readily when offered, and that when we offered protection it was primarily in order to restrict the movements of United Nations personnel. This accusation of negligence on our part was no part of the report on the murder by Bernadotte's closest friend, General Lundstrom, who was a trained soldier experienced in security problems. Nor could the charge stand up against any fair-minded study of the evidence available.

I answered him at once in a press conference I called on September 29. I pointed out that one of the first differences between the Jewish authorities and U.N. observers in Jerusalem had been about our proposal that on all their trips U.N. observers should be accompanied by Jewish soldiers while the U.N. representatives insisted they be free in their movements without any escort whatever. One of the reasons given at the time by the Jewish authorities was that it was inadvisable from the point of view of security to allow United Nations observers to move without escort because of the presence of irresponsible dissident groups within our lines.

I added that this was not Bernadotte's first visit to Jerusalem and his associates knew very well from previous visits what the security arrangements were. If they considered these arrangements inadequate for the safety of Bernadotte and his men, the responsibility rested on them for not drawing the attention of the Jewish authorities to the matter. Had the Jewish authorities received the slightest intimation that the U.N. authorities wished to have special protection they would have gladly fulfilled such request.

As early as June 23 Colonel Nils Brunsson discussed with me arrangements as to the freedom of movement of the U.N. observers. I proposed that they be accompanied by our armed liaison officers. He claimed they must be free to go about unaccompanied when and where they wished. On June 26 I radioed Shertok: "Brunsson insists categorically upon right of all his men go where they wished on basis of his credentials and without any escort of arms." Two days later Brunsson wrote me requesting a reply as to "free movement of U.N. observers." On June 30 he also wrote Colonel Shaltiel in the same terms. It was obviously impossible for us to be responsible for their safety if they insisted on the right to go about unescorted without even telling us beforehand when or where they were going.

The U.N. observers objected consistently even to Jews carrying arms for their own protection when accompanying them. One day Colonel Begley called for me at home to take me to the Latrun pumping station, just before our engineers were to put it back into operation. Before we left he asked me whether I had any small arms on me. I replied that I had a revolver. He said he was sorry but he must ask me to leave it at home, since he could not agree to arms being carried in a car flying the U.N. flag. I said that as we would be meeting with Arabs I could not be sure what might happen and thought it wiser that I have a revolver in self-protection. To this he replied that I would have the protection of the U.N. flag on his car. I said that was all very well, but the Arabs would be able to tell by looking at me that I was a Jew and might ask me to step out of the car. "Then I will step out with you," he said. In view of this chivalrous attitude, I yielded to his wishes, put my revolver back in my desk and went with him unarmed.

It is necessary to assess objectively the role which Count Bernadotte played in the efforts of the United Nations to deal with the solution of the Palestine problem, and it may be easier to do so now that more than a decade has elapsed and the shock of the assassination has been numbed by the passage of time.

His major mistake still seems to me to have been his arrogation to himself of a role which no single man was entitled to assume or able to fulfill. His effort to rewrite the November 29, 1947, resolution on partition was certainly wrong. It encouraged the Arabs to continue their violent attack on the whole concept of partition. It produced no single idea or suggestion which outlived him. Even he recognized this. In his last report to the United Nations, submitted the day after his death, he wrote: "I do not consider it to be within my province to recommend to the Members of the United Nations a proposed course of action on the Palestine question. That is a responsibility of the Members acting through the appropriate organs." Finally, it prevented him from concentrating on the more specific tasks where mediation might have been successful.

One point which has never been thoroughly cleared up, and probably will not be finally established until secret government documents are available, is the Mediator's relations with the British. There is some reason for the conclusion that these were closer than would be expected of a Mediator representing the United Nations, who should have been guided solely by the expressed policy of the international organization and the welfare of the peoples of Palestine. Bernadotte always turned first to the British.

His first meeting, according to his own account, was with the British chargé d'affaires in Paris, Ashley Clarke,

who came to call on me. He emphasized that the British Government was not prepared for the time being to take any steps against the Arabs. In fact, he added, the British were still continuing to supply arms to the Arabs, and the British officers who had joined the Arab forces as instructors were also taking an active part in the war. Nor were official British circles anxious to accept the American proposal that the Arab action should be regarded as provocation and a flagrant breach of the United Nations Charter.

When he came to Cairo he first met the British Ambassador, Sir Ronald Campbell. The same happened in Transjordan: "So at last we reached Amman, where I immediately called on the British Minister, Sir Alexander Kirkbride. When I entered his office he was in the thick of a conversation with the British General Glubb Pasha, the Commander-in-Chief of the Arab Legion." And later he wrote of the British Minister: "I began to entertain hopes that he might be a very great help to me in the future."

It may be, of course, entirely coincidental that the revisions of the United Nations resolution proposed by the Mediator were entirely in line with British interests. The annexation of Jerusalem by Transjordan would have meant a tremendous reinforcement of King Abdullah's prestige among the Arabs. By strengthening his position, it would at the same time have bound him more closely in gratitude to the British and enhanced the significance of this last British stronghold in the Middle East. The same applies with equal force to the proposal to give the Negev to the Arabs. Drew Pearson, the American columnist, has stated that Bernadotte's last plan "came directly from Bevin as the price of accepting any solution of the Palestine problem." Pearson reported that Sir John Troutbeck, head of the British Middle East Office in Cairo, had frankly admitted that he had instructions from Bevin not to support any plan unless it included the handing over of the Negev, which contained great possibilities, to the Arabs. The U.S. representative in Cairo, Robert McClinton, had telegraphed Washington about the British proposal.

It was only much later that the truth became known about Count Bernadotte's connection with the tragedy of European Jewry. The world had believed that it was Bernadotte who was responsible for the negotiations with the Nazi S.S. chief, Heinrich Himmler, which saved thousands of Jewish and other prisoners from extermination during the last months of World War II. Later investigation by H. R. Trevor-Roper, British historian and author of *The Last Days of Hitler*, showed that the credit should have gone to Felix Kirsten, a strange figure of German origin but born in Estonia, who was Himmler's personal physician and achieved a remarkable influence over that sinister man.

Unfortunately, Bernadotte became the subject of a grandiose publicity campaign—in which, according to Trevor-Roper, he played no small part—which built him up as the sole hero of these negotiations. It is hard to know how much this reputation was responsible for his Palestine appointment, or how justified was Trevor-Roper's grim conclusion: "At all events, whatever the motives which led him afterwards to make his improper claims, Count Bernadotte paid dearly for them. But for the self-glorifying myth which he manufactured, it is unlikely that he would ever have been chosen as U.N. Mediator in the Arab-Jewish war of 1948, or fallen in Palestine, a premature victim of the assassin's bullet."

Looking backward, it is hard to put into words the impression which Count Bernadotte made on me. The circumstances were so unusual that each step one took was a first step. In his book, he shows that he was attracted to the special type of human being produced by Arab life; he found something appealing in every Arab leader he met in all the Arab countries.

In his book as in conversation, he showed this admiration for the Arabs. Thus he wrote: "The last item on the day's program was the meeting with Azzam Pasha. It was a most interesting experience. The Secretary of the Arab League attracted me strangely. I felt an instinctive liking for him . . . I left this interesting man, firstly hoping that I should soon see him again, secondly with a feeling that I had in him a friend who would help me in every way in my difficult task." He was similarly impressed when he met King Abdullah, who "gave me the impression of being a decidedly fascinating personality," and he described the Regent of Iraq as "an elegant and attractive young Prince."

For Jews he did not feel this attraction. I was, in all probability, quite a new type of human being for the Count, and he must have sensed that, in spite of my background and education, I was different from the kind of Jew he had known in the past. This alone, no doubt, worked against an immediately friendly contact. It must have seemed strange to him to be forced to discuss matters of international import with the representative of a state which was still in its swaddling clothes. He probably knew nothing of the many years of political activities of the Jewish Agency, although even British officials understood this very well before they left the country. I remember, at a time when the Jewish Agency was in difficulties with the British, asking the then High Commissioner, Sir Harold Mac-Michael, to make a statement to the Jews of Palestine. He lost his temper and said, "Who am I to make statements to the Jewish people? To them I am only a Colonial Office official and you are the government. They will never listen to me." More than once they referred to the Jewish Agency as a government within a government. Count Bernadotte had had no similar experience with Jews, and it probably irked him no little to have to deal with such newcomers to the world of governmental authority and status in which he felt at home.

And yet, in all our meetings, he was invariably the diplomat and perfect gentleman, and negotiations were always on a high level. Neither of us ever lost his temper. I sometimes have the feeling that if his first contact with Israel had not ended in the catastrophe which shocked the entire world, he would have learned to understand us better. In spite of the suavity of his Arab contacts and their pleasant manners, he would have come in the end to realize that with us, after all the arguments and discussions, an agreement could have been reached and that an agreement once reached would have been kept.

He was originally to have come to us for tea at four-thirty on the afternoon he was assassinated. A women's meeting in our house in connection with the distribution of food and supplies had been postponed several times and could not be postponed again, since there was still plenty of sniping, and no transport, and the women had to come in from outlying districts at no little risk. My wife had asked me to put off the meeting with Bernadotte until later in the afternoon. Actually, the meeting of the women was still in progress when the dreadful news was received. My wife told them what had happened. The news stunned everyone in the house.

The assassination of Count Bernadotte was a rude awakening from the expectation that with victory all would be well in the state of Israel. We felt there was urgent need to ensure that assassination would have no place in our public life. The first months of statehood were marred by Bernadotte's death and the universal regret was most sincerely and deeply felt.

A conversation my wife had with Count Bernadotte may throw some light on his character. At a dinner party at the home of the Belgian Consul General, Nieuwenhuys, in an after-dinner conversation Count Bernadotte went to a great deal of trouble to explain what was waiting for the Jewish leaders now that they had a state. He described the loneliness, the heartache, the tremendous disappointments which would be the lot of people like myself, and he suggested that one must find some form of relaxation, or "padding," as he described it, to ward off the blows. Speaking of the criticism to which public leaders are exposed, he quoted an old saying, "The winds blow cold on the high mountains," and he added that worse than the cold was the feeling of being all alone.

XIII

JERUSALEM

⊓⎍⊓⎍⊓⎍⊓⎍⊓⎍⊓⎍⊓⎍⊓⎍

THIS STORY must end where it began, with the city of Jerusalem. More than ever before, it had become, for me as for all the Jews of Israel, the living memorial of our history. We knew that what we were living through was no more than a page in that long history, but it was a new page, filled with words of new hope. So Jerusalem in the summer of 1948 was more than the citadel of our ancient glories; it had become the symbol of our future.

During the second truce, I found myself once in a curious but revealing argument, late at night in my home, with one of the United Nations observers. He was a good friend of mine, a man of great ability and courage, a good Catholic. When I pressed him for a straight answer as to what he would be prepared to sacrifice for Jerusalem—the city itself and not the idea—he admitted that it was not worth the little finger of one of his children's hands. I could not help thinking of the words of the mother of a Jewish soldier who had been killed in the fight for Mount Zion, a devout Jewess who said, "I shall go down to my grave mourning my son, but if his death helped in a small way to save the city the sacrifice is not too great."

So even if my appointment on August 2 as Military Governor of Jerusalem did little more than legalize an authority I had held and exercised for many months, it filled me with pride and humility at the same time. The last Governor of Jerusalem we had known as a people was Pontius Pilate. For the first time in over two thousand years, Jerusalem once again had a Jewish Governor. One of the members of our Provisional Government said to me, "Many Zionist leaders would have given their right hand to have this privilege for only a day."

It came as no surprise, since I had been urging for weeks that Jerusalem be declared occupied territory in order to give our administration of the city legitimacy in international law. No sovereign rights over Jerusalem had remained in any nation when the British mandate was terminated. Formal proclamation that Israel troops were occupying the city was an important step toward the full integration of Jerusalem into the nation. On the evening of August 1, my wife and I, listening to the radio at the home of the late Gershon Agron, heard the news I had been expecting, and the next day Ben Gurion, as Minister of Defense, signed my appointment as Military Governor of the Occupied Area of Jerusalem. The responsibility I had been exercising, in effect, for a considerable time had been shared by the other members of the Jerusalem Emergency Committee. Now I would have to stand alone and be answerable to the Jewish people for what happened in the future in Jerusalem.

I was greatly relieved when some days later I received letters from the American Consul General and from the Italian Consul General addressed to me as "Military Governor, Israel Occupied Jerusalem." Evidently the foreign powers had decided to recognize the status we had given Jerusalem according to the rules of international law.

The people of Jerusalem welcomed the move as a step in the right direction, but did not hesitate to express the view that they would have been happier had the city been completely annexed to the Jewish state and administered by the Israel authorities like every other city in the state. They shared my hope that this arrangement was only temporary. They were pleased at the government's statement that the city's administration would be adapted to "the complexion and needs of Jerusalem as a Jewish city." They now knew that our government did not regard us as any longer morally bound by the United Nations resolution regarding the internationalization of Jerusalem and that the way was open for a renewed struggle for a Jewish Jerusalem.

Ben Gurion, in his capacity as chairman of the Jewish Agency Executive, wrote handsome letters of thanks to all the members of the Jerusalem Emergency Committee: David Aboulafia, Daniel Auster, Charles Passman, Hayim Salomon, Reuven Shreibman, Yitzhak Werfel (later Raphael) and myself. A long, hard day of negotiating was required before I could get the local Etzel to agree to accept my authority while maintaining their opposition, in principle, to declaring the city an occupied area. The other dissident organization, the Stern Gang, went completely underground rather than compromise in any way their belief that Jerusalem should have been bluntly annexed to Israel.

The second truce was then only a fortnight old. Firing was still going on nearly every day. No armistice was even in sight, and the all-out war could be started again by the Arabs at literally any moment. No more than fifteen countries had recognized Israel by the beginning of August. I knew that I faced three major problems. First, I would have to protect our military control of the city, which would mean resolute resistance to any plan for demilitarization which might rob us of what we had won and held in bitter fighting. Second, I would have to administer the city, against formidable obstacles, in such a way as to keep up the fighting spirit of its citizens while convincing the outside world that we were able to manage our own affairs. Finally and most important of all, I would have to thread my way through the long and dangerous period needed before the United Nations and world public opinion would finally realize that the Arab attack on us had made impossible for all time the internationalization of Jerusalem.

Talk about demilitarizing the city had gone on since the first Arab riots in December 1947. Before giving up their mandate, the British had approached the Jewish Agency and the Chief Rabbi with a proposal to place the city under the protection of the Red Cross, with all fighting forces to be withdrawn and administrative functions given to local bodies in Jewish and Arab zones. We had expressed readiness to agree to such a plan, but the Arabs were in a fighting mood and nothing came of it. Another proposal, advanced by the International Red Cross a few days before the mandate ended, was doomed by the fact that fighting had already started.

On July 7, Bernadotte discussed with our Foreign Minister the possibility of demilitarizing Jerusalem. Shertok radioed me he had told Bernadotte that "Government decided we are prepared to discuss demilitarization of Jerusalem provided it will not affect the administrative status quo. Government wants more information about military aspects." I radioed Ben Gurion on the same day, stressing "the importance of fixing the character and legal basis of the administration of Jerusalem before commencement of discussions on its demilitarization."

Subsequently a set of "draft suggestions" as to demilitarization, intended to serve as a basis for a detailed discussion of the problem, was submitted to Shertok by the Mediator's representative in Tel Aviv, John Reedman, on July 22. They provided for the withdrawal of Jewish and Arab forces from Jerusalem and its surrounding localities, under the supervision of the U.N. Truce Commission. Police forces organized by local committees were to operate under the control of the Truce Commission, with armaments authorized by it. All military operations would be prohibited within the area or against it. Severe restrictions were to be placed not only on the maintenance of fighting personnel and the entry of fighting personnel into the area, but also on the admission of civilians. Men of military age not normally residing in the area, or who had at any time been enrolled in the military or defense forces of either party (even if normally residing in the area) were to be admitted only with the special permission of the Truce Commission. The same applied to the admission of men of nonmilitary age, women and children not normally residing in the area. No arms or other military supplies could be stored in the area. The commission was also to control the import and storage of food and other civilian supplies. These proposals would have given the Truce Commission ample opportunities for constant interference in the life of the population and given rise to constant friction and bickering.

Another scheme, emanating from Arab quarters, was put to us through the United Nations on August 20. This was even more far-reaching. Nonmilitary supplies for Jewish requirements were to be subject to joint U.N., Arab and Jewish control. While Arabs and Jews were to run their respective areas, central services, such as electricity, sewage, water supply and telephones, were to be administered by the United Nations. Arabs and Jews were to return to their former homes, and former government buildings were to be placed under U.N. auspices. Jewish visits to the Holy Places were to be permitted on dates and in numbers to be fixed under U.N. supervision. A final version of the proposals, based mainly on the first draft but containing one or two features of the August plan, was worked out in October.

A significant feature of Count Bernadotte's plan for "demilitarization" was the provision of about six thousand well-armed and fully trained soldiers to defend the city against trouble from either side. Ordinary police forces armed with revolvers would be quite inadequate, he was convinced. What was contemplated, therefore, was not really demilitarization, but placing the city under the rule of a foreign army, and its citizens under the administration of an international commission.

The Arabs, whose defiance of the United Nations and assault on Jerusalem had created the problem, showed signs of being willing to agree to demilitarization when that assault had failed to attain its objective. The Egyptian and Transjordan prime ministers gave the Mediator to understand that they were willing to accept his point of view in this respect, and Azzam Pasha agreed to the proposal in principle on behalf of the Arab League, serving the League's attitude toward "certain details" in connection with the implementation of the scheme. What these "details" were can be gathered from the conditions announced by Azzam Pasha at the end of July. They were:

1. Cessation of Jewish immigration during the truce.
2. The return of the Arab refugees to their homes in the Jewish area.
3. An embargo on the import of arms to the state of Israel.

If the Jews objected to these conditions, he threatened, the Arabs would renew the war. It was obvious that there was a long way between the agreement "in principle" and a practical arrangement such as would be acceptable to the government of Israel.

My own attitude was from the outset that we must make certain that our rights to govern the area of the city which we controlled were not affected. Demilitarization must not be exploited to introduce internationalization by the back door. "Today we rule by virtue of the rights in international law of our army," I told Shertok on July 11. "We must make certain that this right does not disappear because of the withdrawal of our army or arms from the city." Shertok replied that the government had said in an official statement that the demilitarization of Jerusalem must be based on the status quo in regard to the actual administration of the different parts of the city.

At a meeting between Shertok and Count Bernadotte at the Ministry of Foreign Affairs on July 26, the Israel Foreign Minister told the Mediator that the government's reaction to the draft suggestions submitted a few days before was definitely negative. If these proposals, or anything like them, were ever to be carried into effect,

Shertok said, the Truce Commission would in many respects become the supreme arbiter of the daily lives of the people. It was essential for the orderly life of the city that it be controlled by a legal Jewish authority and be subject to the laws of Israel. While he did not reject the idea of demilitarization, he could not say, in view of the trend of the Mediator's proposals, that Israel was in favor of it in principle.

The future of Jerusalem was an open question. There was strong and increasing public feeling that Jerusalem should be included in the state of Israel, and our government hoped that it might yet persuade the world to accept its point of view on this question. The demilitarization project was liable to prejudge the issue and make the transition to an Israeli Jerusalem much more difficult.

When I met Bernadotte in the first days of August, I explained why we could not agree to demilitarization according to this plan, though I stressed that we had no objection in principle to the demilitarization of the Jerusalem area if that could be assured without prejudicing our position. I agreed that the idea was important, since none of us wished the inhabitants of Jerusalem to suffer from war and shelling. In general, it was not we who had wanted war or begun it.

We all realized that once Jerusalem was "demilitarized" in the spirit of the Mediator's plan—i.e., placed under the effective rule of the Truce Commission—we might find ourselves helpless to resist a settlement which would be fatal to the Jewish community of the city. If, for instance, the Mediator attempted to implement his own outrageous suggestion of handing the city over to the Arabs, he would be in a position to threaten that he would simply open the gates and admit an Arab occupying force, and it would be almost impossible for us to do anything about it.

Besides, we had had experience with a kind of pilot plant of demilitarization. In July we had agreed to the demilitarization of Mount Scopus, and the area had been placed under United Nations control, with Jewish and Arab police forces in their respective sections, separated by a no man's land about two hundred yards wide. In spite of all the security measures, the Jews on Mount Scopus did not feel at all like residents in a peaceful city but, rather, like helpless, unarmed persons surrounded on all sides by well-armed gangs who might attack them at any moment. The Arabs had contact with all the Arab villages around the Scopus enclave, but a Jew who wanted to enter or leave the area could not do so except at long intervals and only in a United Nations convoy dependent on Arab good will. The fate of our people on Scopus depended entirely on the U.N. guarantees and the readiness of the Arabs to honor their pledges, and our experience had shown us that neither could be relied upon.

The Scopus experiment was an example of another and more immediate consequence of demilitarization. A few months before, the classrooms, wards and corridors of the Hebrew University and the Hadassah Hospital had echoed with the voices and footsteps of thousands of students, teachers and doctors. The fighting had silenced all this, but demilitarization had simply perpetuated the silence. There was no teaching at the university, and the Hadassah Hospital was closed to all patients. There was peace on Mount Scopus, but it was the peace that comes with death. A demilitarized Jerusalem, controlled by an alien body, might well be transformed from a center of communal life and economic activity into a conglomeration of people unable to support themselves, in a moribund town. Demilitarization was a negative and barren solution to the problem, if it was a solution at all. We were certain that there was no future for the city except as an integral part of the Jewish state, and no guarantee for the lives of its citizens except protection by Jewish forces.

Ultimately both the Truce Commission and the Mediator appreciated that there was little chance—if any—of the demilitarization proposal being put into practice. Count Bernadotte reported to the Security Council that our attitude was "due more to political reasons relating to the future status of Jerusalem than to mere military considerations regarding present conflict." This was a strange description of our concern for the life of the city and its inhabitants. At the same time, his message continued: "Besides, even if both parties were to agree on the issue, demilitarization could not be put into effect without strong and adequately armed United Nations forces to be provided immediately." And it was evident from the way the U.N. had handled the entire problem that there was not the slightest hope of such a force.

All these efforts amounted to no more than flogging a dead horse. There was no attempt to meet our objections by drafting a plan which would include a true safeguard against an Arab breach of the settlement, or provide for the restoration of normal life in the city. The latest draft of the demilitarization plan, proposed by the Truce Commission on October 12, was almost identical with the "draft suggestions" submitted to us two and a half months previously.

It should be added that even if both the Arabs and the Jews had agreed to the demilitarization plan, nothing would have come of it in view of the opposition of the U.S.S.R. in the Security Council. Its representative declared in July 1948, "The Mediator told us that he envisaged, in connection with the implementation of the demilitarization proposal, the creation of some kind of military force for the city of Jerusalem, either a United Nations force or a force placed at the Security Council's disposal. Probably both my assumptions are correct, and what is contemplated is a force created within the framework of the United Nations and placed at the Mediator's disposal. But the General Assembly resolution does not provide for anything of that kind for the city of Jerusalem. It is clear that if such a proposal were put forward at any time it would have to be emphatically rejected. Proposals regarding the creation of any military force for Jerusalem are in practice directed against the United Nations decisions on the future status of Jerusalem."

Eventually the attempts to secure demilitarization petered out. There was no sign of any readiness on the part of the Arabs to agree to peace, which would have made demilitarization unnecessary. In the end it was left to us, as it had been all along, to protect the lives of Jerusalem's citizens and the future of that part of the city which we held.

The day after my appointment as Military Governor, six ministers of the Provisional Government came to Jerusalem empowered to help me set up a council representing the inhabitants of the city. It was hoped to keep the council down to thirteen members, the same number as in the Cabinet, but this would not have allowed each of the city's religious elements the representation required by its traditions and dignity. We summoned a meeting of representatives of all the parties, including Mapam (the left-wing labor party) and the Communists, and all the religious groups, including the ultraorthodox Agudat Israel. I explained how I saw my assignment, stressing that I could not regard myself as a party man in this post. It was not hard to get general agreement on an outline of my powers and functions, but it took eight long sessions before we admitted defeat in the effort to keep the Governor's Council down to a reasonable size. Old traditions die hard, and over generations the

Jews of Jerusalem, denied real power over their own destinies, had developed countless fractional vested interests in the trappings of power. So we set up a council of twenty-five members, plus two Agudat Israel representatives who finally agreed to serve on the council's committees but not on the council itself.

At the time I became Military Governor, Colonel David Shaltiel left Jerusalem and was replaced by Colonel Moshe Dayan as commander of the area. The groups of Hagana men who had fought Jerusalem's battles a few months before had now become a somewhat more conventional military force. I set to work, also, to reorganize the setup of ninety officials who, together with countless volunteers, had helped me keep Jerusalem running. My new post required me to take over all the usual civilian functions of an army of occupation, including internal security, plus heavily increased duties in external affairs. It still included the older economic and governmental functions of the Jerusalem Emergency Committee and a great many new ones which had not been possible during the full-scale fighting and the siege. The administrative machinery I devised was still based solidly on the experienced officials who had been running the city, like my principal assistant, Dr. Avraham Bergman (later Biran, Israel's Consul General in Los Angeles). We were now able to call on the Provisional Government and the Army for special services, and to use the Governor's Council and an extensive system of advisory public committees to strengthen our links with the population.

One of our new problems was the custody of enemy property. It was not easy to stop the looting of abandoned property which had started, especially since much of it was done by men in uniform. During the late summer of 1948, at a Red Cross party, my wife discussed the whole ugly question of looting with a Quaker who happened to be in Jerusalem. She apologized for the behavior of some of our people, particularly in the homes of Arabs with whom we had been on friendly terms. Whereupon the Quaker said to her that there was no reason for her to give it a second thought—he had seen the senseless destruction in the Gush Etzion and in the Old City of Jerusalem, compared to which the looting of furniture and even doors and plumbing installation was child's play.

We managed to collect much of the property for later allocation to war victims, and to protect abandoned houses until these could be assigned to refugees and other persons who had lost their own homes. From September 1948 to the end of August 1949, our Housing Department found housing for 3,906 families, consisting of 15,800 persons, placed in 5,655 rooms. This total did not include accommodation made available to public bodies, hospitals, clubs, workshops, warehouses and shops.

After the truce had been in effect for about a month we were pressed to abolish the requirement of permits for persons wishing to travel from and to Jerusalem. I had to explain to the public that this matter depended on the military high command, who insisted that for security reasons the Military Governor's office exercise strict control of all persons entering and leaving the area. This applied to all persons without exception, including the consular corps —who came to us for travel permits when wishing to cross into the Old City or to proceed to any part of Israel outside Jerusalem.

Despite the existence of the truce, military problems continued to be our primary concern. As late as the middle of October my records show that in view of the urgency of certain essential defense works in and around Jerusalem, our Manpower Office ordered all men in Jerusalem between the ages of eighteen and forty-eight, not on active military service to leave their work and report for defense labor for fourteen consecutive days. The Chief Rabbinate gave approval for work to be done on Sabbaths and holidays. These works were urgently necessary, as the rainy season was approaching and ditches, lookout posts and soldiers' quarters had to be repaired.

Food rationing and control had, of course, to be continued throughout the second truce period. Our food control department revised the rationing system, improved it and issued new ration cards to the entire population. I entered into an agreement with a large professional warehousing company to hold and manage our stocks of food for us. We put an end to the practice that had again crept in of wholesalers compelling retailers to buy commodities they did not want as a condition of selling them what they did want.

As I told the Advisory Council, our objective food situation had improved. But the editorial writer of *Davar Yerushalayim*, on September 6, seven weeks after the truce began, was still able to comment:

It is true the food situation has improved greatly in Jerusalem and the Governor was right in pointing out in his report to the Council that the position as regards food supplies is now better than it has ever been since the beginning of the year. But none the less

*there is still discrimination against Jerusalem. Surely the state
should have worried about Jerusalem being treated with equality.
Jerusalem went through a difficult siege which has not yet ended.
For months it endured privation bordering on hunger. For example,
throughout the country Tnuva supplies milk and even distributes it
to homes; only Jerusalem has forgotten the taste of this luxury.
For a considerable time no milk whatever was brought to the city
and to this day it is supplied only to children and only one glass per
day. As for meat—since the war began Jerusalem in all has had only
a few rations in very small quantities. Fuel can be purchased readily
in Haifa or Tel Aviv, but not in Jerusalem.*

I encouraged the Jewish Agency to set up a Jerusalem Development Corporation, which began at once to build premises for small
industries and crafts that might be attracted to Jerusalem by favorable terms the corporation would offer them. It also began building
a central wholesale market for agricultural produce to help rehabilitate the agricultural settlements around Jerusalem and improve our regular supplies of these commodities.

As a result of representations I made to Tel Aviv, industrialists
and artisans in Jerusalem began to receive governmental orders. We
set up a special department to deal with these matters. A delegation
of industrialists and bankers was invited by me to spend a week in
Jerusalem visiting plants with a view to helping local industry.
They agreed to arrange a bank consortium which would furnish
loans to Jerusalem businessmen, and their representatives remained
some time in Jerusalem in this connection. Electric power was now
available for industrial purposes and this encouraged many industrialists to reopen their plants.

Soon after my appointment, the Jerusalem Lawyers' Association,
of which I had been a member for some twenty-seven years, made
representations urging that the Israel Supreme Court be transferred from Tel Aviv to Jerusalem, where the Supreme Court had
sat during the British regime. Jerusalemites were overjoyed when,
on September 14 in an imposing ceremony, the Supreme Court was
opened in Jerusalem. The five judges of the Supreme Court took
the oath "to be faithful to the state of Israel and its laws, not to de-
viate from justice, not to favor anyone in trial and to judge the
people in just trial."

This followed the opening of the Land Registry offices a fortnight earlier, when, for the first time since the Palestine Land Regis-

try services broke down, it was possible for the inhabitants of Jerusalem to execute land transactions, since according to existing law these could be validly consummated only in the Land Registry. The registers had been placed in the Y.M.C.A. for safekeeping by the Acting Director of Land Registries when he left the country on May 13, since the British, in keeping with their policy, were unwilling to hand Palestine property over to us. I now requested the Y.M.C.A. to give the registers to us and they did. At the same time the government opened a district immigration office for use by Jerusalem inhabitants. This too was another step in the direction in which we were aiming.

At the end of September I returned from Tel Aviv by the Valor Road. Remarkable progress had been made in laying down this new highway. It was deeply moving to pass through territory which was in the heart of ancient Judaea, the birthplace of Samson. It had been practically closed to us in the time of the mandate as a purely Arab area without decent roads. Now we would be able to travel through the area in safety, since it was all in Jewish hands.

On December 12, before a gathering of thousands of people from all parts of Israel, this road was formally opened by the Prime Minister. Some fifteen miles long, connecting Jerusalem with the coastal plain, it was built in only eight weeks although it runs through difficult mountainous terrain; in part it passed over what had been used as a camel track for thousands of years. The workers who had built the road paraded before us. They were Jerusalemites, above military age, many of them with gray beards.

Although there was always so much to be done I now had to find time to receive visitors from abroad. When it was reasonably safe to venture into Jerusalem, important men and women in public life, American Congressmen, and trade-union leaders, writers, Jewish leaders and newspapermen from many countries came to see for themselves what had happened in the new Israel and particularly in Jerusalem. Henry Morgenthau, Jr., former Secretary of the U.S. Treasury, who then headed the effort to raise funds for Israel in the United States, spoke glowingly of our efforts at a reception tendered him. "The Jewish state without Jerusalem would be like the Jewish people without its history," he said. "The Burma Road was carved out of the rock and hills of Judaea because the Jews of Israel had to link up with the heart and core of their nation and with their traditions. The Burma Road is an unbelievable achievement in human stamina. It could not have been possible if the men and women who built it were not motivated by an unquenchable search for freedom and peace in their own land."

The office of Military Governor also entailed formal duties which consumed a frightening amount of time. These included calling on all the chief rabbis to preserve unity among religious groups, inviting U.N. and consular officers to our home, visiting schools, children's camps, rehabilitation centers, food and handicraft exhibitions, going to various quarters of the city to talk to their leading citizens, to military hospitals to talk to the wounded, to nurses' graduation exercises, to Mishmar Ha'am functions, to consulate receptions.

Between August 31 and December 15, there were seven full-dress meetings of the Governor's Council, to each of which I made a full report. We also considered problems dealt with by a number of subcommittees in respect of food supplies, economic development, housing, internal security, price control, health and social services, transport and Old City matters. The discussions which followed served as an outlet for pent-up grievances and as training for the difficult business of responsible government. I was able to inform the council that the first group of 220 immigrants had been brought to Jerusalem. I had also been promised by the Jewish Agency that they would within the next few days bring 1,000 immigrants to Jerusalem direct from the ship. I was deeply aware during these troubled months of the danger presented by Jerusalem's lack of experience in running its own affairs, the separateness and backwardness of its ultraorthodox communities, their fanaticism and poverty. Indeed, these factors brought about a complete collapse of local government in Jerusalem a few years later, in 1955, when the government was forced to dismiss the mayor and the council of the city. But at least this did not happen while we were still fighting for our existence and trying to prove to the world our right to learn and grow in our own way.

On December 1, Dr. Chaim Weizmann paid his first visit to Jerusalem since the War of Liberation began. He had been the president of the World Zionist Organization for most of three decades. In that capacity, he had been at the helm of our political struggle designed to achieve independence for our people in Palestine. Now, in his old age, he had been chosen to be the President of Israel's Provisional Government and later to be the first President of the state. This was a moving day for him and for those who welcomed him to the city. He was received at the entrance to the city and con-

ducted with an escort of mounted police to the courtyard of the
Jewish Agency buildings. Here he inspected a guard of honor of
Jerusalem veteran fighters and I was privileged to welcome him to
Jerusalem. We proceeded to the conference room, where the two
chief rabbis, the members of the Military Governor's Council, the
Jewish Agency Executive, and the Municipal Council, as well as
the president of the Supreme Court and other notables, awaited
him.

After speeches of welcome by the chief rabbis, myself and others,
Dr. Weizmann answered with a speech of unusual eloquence even
for him. "I have come to Jerusalem many times in different periods," he told us. "The first time was forty years ago. . . . More
than once I was criticized for my patience. I do not wish to boast. I
am a Jew from Motele [a small village in Lithuania] and there I
learned all my higher politics. At any rate I believe that only with
unusual patience, and by work such as you here have experienced,
shall we reach our goal. We shall do what we can and then will
come others to continue and finish the work. Do not worry because
part of Jerusalem is not now within the state. All will come to pass
in peace. Again I counsel patience. Now I have had my reward."

He spoke of the special place Jerusalem holds in the hearts of
all Jews and of the old history which binds this people to this city.
He quoted the Archbishop of Canterbury, who, ten years before,
had backed the Zionist vision because he had realized what lay behind the Hebrew words "If I forget thee, O Jerusalem, may my
right hand forget its cunning." Then Dr. Weizmann went on:

"The Archbishop spoke true words. It is not possible for us to
forget Jerusalem. And if this was true then, how much truer is it
now; for this last year we have made our covenant anew with our
ancient maternal city, with the blood of our sons and daughters.

"In addition to the historical connection between us and Jerusalem, in addition to the unbroken chain of Jewish settlement in this
city, in addition to the fact of our being a majority in it, your supreme bravery in defending the city gives us the right to proclaim
that Jerusalem is ours and shall remain ours. Where are all those
who spoke high-sounding phrases about the spiritual significance of
Jerusalem to the entire civilized world? Did they raise a finger to
protect Jerusalem, its men, women and children, its buildings and
houses of prayer, against the shells of the Arabs who for months,
day and night, rained death upon your homes? Did they do anything when the Jewish quarters of the Old City with their revered

synagogues were turned into rubble heaps by Arab cannon and were desecrated after the surrender? Did they protest by one word that for over a year Jews have been prevented from approaching the Wailing Wall which is the holiest of our Holy Places?

"Fear not, my friends—the old synagogues will be rebuilt anew and the way to the Wailing Wall will be opened again. With your blood and sacrifices you have renewed the covenant of old. Jerusalem is ours by virtue of the blood which your sons shed defending it. You suffered hunger and thirst in the burning heat of the summer and you defended Jerusalem against murder and destruction, and not only the soldiers among you. Every man and woman, indeed even the small children—you all carried on your work, when the bullets were flying around you and many of your dear ones fell, victims of the enemy's marksmen. All of you, every one of you, has a share in the defense of Jerusalem."

My hardest task as Military Governor was also the longest and slowest: helping to secure the recognition by the world that Jerusalem had become irrevocably a part of Israel. The fact was relatively easy to establish, but Jews know better than most people how long and how stubbornly an idea can resist facts. The original United Nations resolution on partition was the basis in international law on which we had founded a state. Yet that resolution had called for the internationalization of Jerusalem.

A great deal of water had flowed under the bridges of the world since then. The Arabs had tried to block partition by violence and had laid siege to Jerusalem; they had shelled it for months on end and had captured and held the Old City, with most of Jerusalem's Holy Places. The United Nations had defaulted on its own proposal to set up a trusteeship for the city, and the shabby exigencies of the cold war and big-power politics had led its Mediator to the fantastic proposal that the whole city be given to an Arab king who had no legal claim to any part of it. It was our task to work and to wait until time and our own efforts could convince the world that there was no alternative to Jewish rule over Jerusalem.

The local consuls proved to be less difficult than I expected. Even before we saw the last of the Consular Truce Commission most of the consuls recognized the Military Governor de facto, sometimes before their countries had recognized Israel. Some of them had never been friendly to the Jews, and most of them resented the restrictions involved in living under a military regime. But they paid courtesy calls on me, asked for our help in getting food and travel permits, and did their grumbling to each other.

The friendliest of all the consuls was the Netherlands Consul General, Dr. Johan A. Nederbragt. He was a fine old gentleman and a genuinely devout Christian. He knew and loved the Bible, and he had no innate dislike for the People of the Book. He made no secret of his admiration for the achievements of the Jews. He had stayed on in Jerusalem, which he loved, and he expressed the view that the Jews had fought valiantly. When he was accredited later to the government of Israel, he saw no reason, as he told me, why he should advise his government to move their offices from the city. The Netherlands Embassy has remained in Jerusalem.

The U.S.S.R. Ambassador called on me early in September and thanked me for the way we had taken care of Russian property in the city, including a great deal of church property. The British at first kept their only consular office on the Arab side of the line in Jerusalem, but at last on December 17 Mr. Beaumont, the deputy to Sir Hugh Daw, the British Consul General, paid a courtesy call on our side of the line. I had a friendly talk with him. In the course of conversation he asked whether the Jews had any expansionist ambitions. I explained that Jews were interested in coming to Zion and not to Babylon.

Our personal relations with the American consulate were friendly, as they were with the French and the Belgian, and when the Consular Truce Commission had finally folded up we found we could co-operate effectively on a wide range of problems. One of the most important of these, naturally, had to do with the various church buildings and religious monasteries in the New City or its surroundings, and I am quietly proud of the respect and gratitude which were expressed to me for Israel's constant efforts to keep religious properties, including mosques, unviolated and intact. Msgr. Testa, the Apostolic Delegate, who visited the churches on Mount Zion, was among those who expressed satisfaction with the way in which our responsible officers were protecting church property.

I saw relatively little of the United Nations Conciliation Commission for Palestine, a three-man body set up on December 11 to wrestle with the tired old problem of Palestine. Dr. Pablo de Azcarate, its chief secretary, arrived in Jerusalem on January 23, 1949, and its members, Huseyin Yaltchin of Turkey, Mark Ethridge of the U.S., and Claude de Boisanger of France, came a few days later.

I had talks with them all but none that convinced me of any new realism in the United Nations approach to the Arabs. The commission moved off soon to Lausanne in Switzerland and a series of furtive interviews with Arab leaders who professed to be unable even to talk in public about Israel, and no good came of it that I ever heard of.

The internationalization problem was worried about during the second half of 1948 only inside the Israel government and in its relations with the United Nations. The Zionists were, after all, on the record as having accepted some kind of trusteeship, even if with a heavy heart. The ultraorthodox Jews in Jerusalem were actually in favor of it, deeply distrusting all temporal power, including Jewish power. I had served on a committee with Ben Zvi and six others appointed by the Jewish Agency and the Jewish community of Palestine to prepare to co-operate with the United Nations in setting up a trusteeship. Daniel Auster and Mordechai Eliash, speaking on behalf of the Jewish Agency, pressed the United Nations as early as January 1948 to appoint a governor for the city and get on with it. Many of us whose hearts were heaviest over the compromise we had been forced to accept thought Auster and Eliash were far too energetic and zealous in trying to get the international regime set up.

There was no need to worry. The United Nations dragged its heels for months and months. Its Trusteeship Council had drawn up a detailed constitution for an international city, but on March 11 it postponed voting on it for six weeks. On April 21 it referred the plan back to the General Assembly for further instructions. On May 14 Harold Evans, of the Society of Friends, agreed to act as head of the Jerusalem Municipal Council on behalf of the United Nations, but time had run out on him, the war had started, and he never took up the post.

So by midsummer the whole idea had been overtaken by the march of events. Since the Arab states had refused to allow the formation of a provisional Arab government in Palestine, both the economic union and the internationalization of Jerusalem envisaged in the original partition resolution had become impossible. All that was really needed by then was a face-saving formula for the United Nations, and it is an unhappy fact that its paralysis in the grip of power politics has kept the search going now for a dozen years.

The British abandoned all support for the internationalization proposal as soon as their ally, King Abdullah, was securely in control of the Old City. The Americans lost interest in the plan in measure as they saw that any international regime in Jerusalem would give the Soviet Union a new foothold in the Middle East. Catholic countries continued to support it, especially in Latin America, but there were well-founded reports that the Vatican would be content with the internationalization of the Old City.

In effect, it was the Arabs as much as the Jews who finally killed the plan in the United Nations. Once their attempt to capture the city had failed, they came out in favor of internationalization with one notable exception. This was, of course, Abdullah. He held the great majority of the Holy Places, with a consequent enhancement of his prestige and his power. By the autumn of 1948 he was busily engaged in liquidating his old quarrel with the former Grand Mufti of Jerusalem by doing away with the latter's henchmen and his "Arab Government of All Palestine" which had been set up at Gaza under Egyptian protection. Without the Old City, an internationalized Jerusalem would have been a caricature of the original plan, and Abdullah had no intention of even talking about the surrender of what his Arab Legion had seized for him.

Meanwhile I was busy trying to forge a common front on the issue. I carefully read and passed on to Ben Gurion representations in favor of internationalization which were made to me by the ultra-orthodox Agudat Israel. But their proposals were not strengthened by their insistence on a 25 per cent representation on the public committee which they wanted to set up to conduct negotiations with international bodies on the future of the city. On the other extreme of the political spectrum, I had to cope with the Revisionists, an extremist Zionist faction which wanted to launch a massive public petition in favor of immediate annexation of Jerusalem to Israel. Their campaign was a total failure, thanks partly to the late Professor Joseph Klausner, a revered mentor of the Revisionists whom I persuaded to oppose it on the radio, and to the commander of the Israel Defense Forces, who called on all soldiers not to sign the petition. But both groups hurt us because they raised unnecessary doubts and dissension.

On September 26, a special and fully representative delegation of the people of Jerusalem appeared before the Provisional Government in Tel Aviv and voiced our unanimous demand that the city be included in the state of Israel. The delegation was headed by myself and included Daniel Auster, the acting mayor; Hayim Solomon, chairman of the Jewish Community Council; N. A.

Elmaleh, representative of the Sephardic community; Reuven Shreibman, representing local labor; and Dr. Feivel Meltzer, of the Mizrahi, or liberal religious element. It was on the eve of the United Nations Assembly at which the future of Jerusalem was to be one of the subjects discussed.

Speaking on behalf of the delegation, I told the government that the problem could not be approached in the abstract on the basis of considerations unconnected with the actual life of 100,000 Jewish inhabitants of the city. The Jews of Jerusalem would not feel that they were dwelling in safety unless the city formed part of the state of Israel. "It is difficult to portray in words the depth of this feeling among the Jerusalem public," I said. "If the government agreed to the internationalization of Jerusalem, the Jews in the city would feel that they were being utterly and unjustifiably abandoned." This was the deep-felt and firm conviction of the inhabitants of the state, young and old. There was no hope for the city, or its sons, outside the confines of the state of Israel. They had fought the War of Independence and played their part in the task of building the land like their brethren in other parts of the country, and they felt that they were entitled, no less than Jews elsewhere, to be citizens of the state of Israel. They had endured foreign rule long enough.

The original proposal to internationalize Jerusalem, I continued, had been part of the plan for establishing a Jewish state by peaceful means with the co-operation of the Arabs. This had failed. We had been obliged to set up the state by our own military efforts. The U.N. did nothing to take over the city from the British when they withdrew. They had left the Arabs and the Jews to fight for control of Jerusalem. We had won the area we held by our own struggle. That being the case, we had every right, apart from the Jewish historic claim to Jerusalem, to insist on our part of Jerusalem—which was in fact entirely Jewish—forming part of Israel.

The views expressed by our delegation made a profound impression on the Cabinet. We were told later that some of the ministers, who, in view of the tremendous international pressure that was being brought to bear, had been inclined to agree to discuss internationalization, had changed their views after hearing our arguments. The government decided that it would insist at all costs on the inclusion of Jerusalem in the Jewish state and its connection with the coast by a continuous Jewish corridor, and I was able three days later to bring the good news of the decision to the Military

Governor's Council, which represented the Jews of Jerusalem. Our speedy and resolute action had borne fruit.

I was able to make the same report to the whole city over the radio a few days later at the onset of the Jewish New Year. I spelled it out in great detail directly to Dr. Paul Mohn, the acting Mediator's political representative, when he asked me for my opinion in an interview on October 18. Shertok gave a masterly exposition of our position directly to the United Nations General Assembly in December. The United Nations failed then, as it has since 1949, to find the diplomatic formula which will put on its own records the end of its plan to internationalize Jerusalem. But life has killed it.

In the truce as in the war, and as in all the bitter days since the British launched their drive to break the spirit of the Jews in 1946, the ultimate decision proved to be in the hands of the people of Jerusalem. They had reluctantly accepted partition, and then war, and then siege. They had had to fight for their lives and for their future. They had won. Jerusalem was the historic capital of their land and its only true capital. They were not prepared to hand it over to an Arab king or to an international commission, and this is the basic reason why they hold it now.

There was, of course, no alternative solution. The Arabs were paralyzed by defeat and by their suspicions of Abdullah. The United Nations' plans all foundered on the hostility between the Soviet Union and the West. Our dream of nationhood, meanwhile, had become a reality, and it is hard for any people to turn backward when it has started on its road to freedom.

The last milestones along that long road which are big in my memory now are all dates when this quiet determination of the Jews to incorporate Jerusalem as the capital of their nation took voice on some public occasion. One was November 2, the day when Jews celebrated the Balfour Declaration. We called off the blackout for the one night, the city blazed with lights, and its citizens crowded the streets and cafés to taste the future they had fought for. Another was the day in December when I was handed the first identity card to be issued in Jerusalem—the same identity card used in the rest of Israel. Many Jerusalem families who had left before the siege returned to the city. We were making arrangements for a series of conventions which would bring archaeologists, architects, journalists and the B'nai B'rith to Jerusalem. I managed to persuade the government that a few departments, such as the statisticians working on the census, could operate as well in Jerusalem as in Tel Aviv.

Then on January 25, 1949, came the historic day when the people of Jerusalem voted in the first elections in the history of Israel, the election of the Knesset, or Constituent Assembly. The Governor's Council held its final meeting, proving to me, at any rate, as Governor, that Jews had won the greatest freedom of all: the right to legislate for themselves, to control and criticize the authorities. On February 2 came the official declaration that Jerusalem was no longer to be considered occupied territory. This ended my short career as Military Governor. It had been a short-lived job, which I gave up without a pang of regret but with a lifetime's worth of memories of the soldiers and truck drivers, the bakery workers and plumbers and civil servants, members of the Governor's Council and housewives, all the citizens of a great city who had worked and fought with zeal, with loyalty and with love.

It had taken time to translate these human assets into physical possession of our city. It took a little longer for them to be recognized by the world's public opinion as the basis of our right to be there. It will take still more time before they are spelled out in fairly negotiated treaties and friendly agreements with our neighbors. This comes as no surprise to us. Most foreign governments decided not to accept our invitation to the first session of the Knesset, which was held in Jerusalem on February 14, and at which Dr. Weizmann was elected President of Israel.

By the end of that year, in December 1949, the decision was taken to move the Knesset and the government permanently to Jerusalem. I was put in charge of finding quarters for them. Ben Gurion came to Jerusalem and invited a group of us to lunch with him, to discuss the implications of the move. My wife, who was the only woman present, asked him how he saw the future, and to our surprise he answered in English. "We have embarked on a daring adventure," he said.

He went on in Hebrew to explain the maximum and minimum dangers of formally moving our entire capital to a city which the world still did not recognize as ours. I spoke only at the end of the discussion. Then I said, "From years of experience in this city, and especially after the last thirty months, I think nothing is going to happen. There will be a lot of talk. But only what we do right here will count. It may be unpleasant for a while, but that's the only price we'll pay. The few people who dislike us anyway will dislike us a little more. The good people, who are usually in the majority, will admire us a little more for our courage. What we have done is good and just and will be recognized as such by all men of good will."

And so it has worked out. Since December 26, 1949, the Knesset has met in Jerusalem. The ministries have been moved there, the Ministry of Supply and Rationing, which I headed, being the first important one to move. The world has accepted us. Jerusalem has become in fact what it has always been in our hearts: the capital of Israel.

GLOSSARY

ARAB HIGHER COMMITTEE. A committee of Arab leaders representative of outstanding Arab families or political groups in Palestine, more or less self-appointed. They represented the Arabs of Palestine in negotiations with the British authorities.

ARAB NATIONAL GUARD. Groups of Arabs organized in various parts of the country to fight the Jews in their respective areas in their effort to prevent the implementation of the U. N. resolution to set up a Jewish state.

BAR MITZVAH. The occasion when, on reaching the age of thirteen, Jewish boys are for the first time permitted publicly to read a portion of the Law in synagogue and assume religious responsibility for their future conduct.

BATEI MACHSE. A block of tenements within the Old City built with donations a hundred years ago for housing poor Jewish families; literally, "houses of refuge."

EFFENDI. A title of respect applied by Arabs to a man who can read and write. An Arab of this standing is addressed with the word *effendi* after his name.

ETZEL. An abbreviation comprising the Hebrew initials of the words Irgun Zvai (Tzvai) Leumi—"National Military Organization"—the name of the larger of the two terrorist paramilitary organizations set up by dissident elements of the Hagana.

FELLAH (plural, *fellaheen*). An Arab peasant or cultivator of the soil.

HAGANA. The underground Palestine Jewish defense organization set up to protect Jewish life and property against attack by Arabs; literally, "defense."

HALAMITH, or *khubeiza*. A weed (malva), the fresh leaves of which are edible and can be used liked spinach.

HAMEKASHER. The Jewish transport co-operative operating the principal bus service in Jerusalem.

HISTADRUT. Literally, "Federation"—an abbreviation of the Hebrew name of the General Federation of Jewish Labor in Palestine, the trade union comprising the overwhelming majority of all the workers in the country.

IRGUN ZVAI LEUMI. See *Etzel*.

JEWISH AGENCY FOR PALESTINE. The public body set up in 1929 by the World Zionist Organization and non-Zionists to serve as the agency representing the Jewish people vis-à-vis the mandatory power under the terms of the British mandate for Palestine. It conducted the political, economic and cultural affairs of the Jews in their efforts to bring large numbers of Jews to Palestine and to settle them there in the effort to establish the Jewish national home.

JEWISH SUPERNUMERARY POLICE. A force of Jewish special constables, sworn in by the Palestine government as policemen in times of emergency. Jews volunteered into this force to protect Jewish settlements from attacks by Arabs and to patrol the settlement perimeters and the roads between them.

KEREN HAYESOD. An incorporated body set up by the World Zionist Organization in 1920 to collect funds by voluntary contribution to establish the Jewish national home in Palestine.

KIBBUTZ. A Jewish communal co-operative agricultural settlement in Palestine.

KOL HAMAGEN. "The Voice of the Defender," Hagana's illegal radio broadcasting station.

KUPAT HOLIM. The Workers' Sick Benefit Fund, established by the General Federation of Jewish Workers (Histadrut) for its members to furnish them with free medical treatment and medicines at its clinics and dispensaries, as well as hospitalization and surgery at reduced rates.

LEHI. An abbreviation comprising the Hebrew initials of the words Lohmei Herut Yisrael—"Fighters for the Freedom of Israel"—the name of a small terrorist group of fanatical young Jewish nationalists. The group was also known as the Stern Gang.

MATZO (plural, matzoth). The unleavened bread which is eaten during the seven days of the Jewish Passover festival, when ordinary bread is forbidden.

MISGAV LEDAH. The name of a Jewish public hospital in the Old City.

MISHMAR HA'AM. The "people's guard," or Home Guard, was set up to perform civilian defense and emergency duties for the Jewish community of Palestine. It was similar in some respects to the Home Guard in Britain during World War II.

MUFTI. An official whose duty it was to give canonical rulings on Moslem religious law. There was a Mufti in every large town in Palestine. The Mufti of Jerusalem was termed the Grand Mufti and was popularly regarded as the outstanding Moslem religious dignitary in the country.

MUKHTAR. An Arab headman, a villager selected by the authorities as spokesman for his village and as its representative in official matters.

NETUREI KARTA. The Hebrew name of a group of fanatically religious Jews of Jerusalem; literally, "guardians of the city."

PALMACH. An abbreviation of the Hebrew words *plugat machatz*, "a striking force," the designation of a section of the Hagana specially trained for commando fighting.

ROSH HASHANA. The Jewish New Year's festival; literally, "the beginning of the year."

SHOFAR. The ram's horn used as a trumpet at religious services on the Jewish New Year and the Day of Atonement and, in ancient Israel, on other solemn occasions.

SOLEL BONEH. The name of the contracting and building co-operative established by the Histadrut to carry out public works and set up industries.

SUCCOTH. The Jewish harvest Feast of Tabernacles, commemorative of the Israelites dwelling in tents during their wandering in the desert on their way from Egypt to the Promised Land.

TALMUD TORAH. A Jewish religious boys' school; literally, "the study of the Law."

TNUVA. The name of a co-operative organization which markets the dairy and agricultural produce of Jewish settlements.

TISHA BE'AV. The ninth day of the Hebrew month of Ab (which corresponds roughly to August); a day of mourning and fasting, commemorative of the destruction of the Temple in Jerusalem.

VAAD HAKEHILLA. The Hebrew name of the Jewish Community Council of Jerusalem.

VAAD LEUMI. The National Council of the Jews of Palestine, an elected body dealing with the general communal problems of the Jews of Palestine and representing them in their relations with the British Administration of the country.

YESHIVA (plural, *Yeshivoth*). A seminary for the study of Jewish learning, where religious Jews spend all their time in study of the Jewish Law pursuant to the religious injunction so to do.

YISHUV. The Hebrew collective name of the Jewish community of Palestine prior to the establishment of Israel.

INDEX

ABOUT THE AUTHOR

by DAVID BEN GURION

DOV JOSEPH, *like the President of the State, the Mayor of Jerusalem and thousands of volunteers from the U.S. and from Palestine, enlisted in the Jewish Legion during the First World War. He was one of the few volunteers who came from Canada, and I believe he was the only Canadian who settled in this country after his release from the Army.*

Dov Joseph secured his place in the contemporary history of our people in the days of the siege of Jerusalem, when the capital was cut off from the rest of the population, shelled and starved. Dov Joseph was appointed by the Provisional Government as Military Governor of Jerusalem, and by his organizing skill, his energy and his devotion he saved the city from the danger of starvation and the peril of destruction.

He subsequently served the Government of Israel in many difficult and diverse capacities and was charged with many an unpopular task, which he always performed with great courage, diligence and loyalty. As Minister for Development he displayed considerable initiative in many directions and was rewarded during his term of office with the discovery of the first oil well.

Dov Joseph's activity has not ended even though he will this time remain outside the Government, and he will continue to serve the state as a representative of the people, who will continue to enjoy the benefit of his wide experience, his extensive knowledge and his wise counsel.

> —*Extract from an announcement by Mr. David Ben Gurion—then Minister of Defense—on the composition of the new government at the 19th session of the Third Knesset, November 2, 1955*

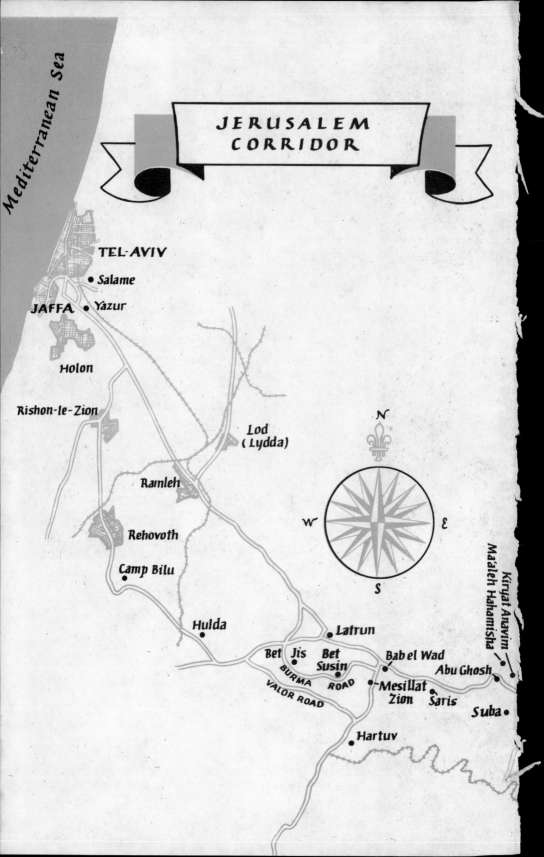